TEX!
The Man Who Built
The Dallas Cowboys

Bob St. John

PRENTICE HALL
Englewood Cliffs, New Jersey 07632

PRENTICE-HALL INTERNATIONAL (UK) LIMITED, *London*
PRENTICE-HALL OF AUSTRALIA PTY. LIMITED, *Sydney*
PRENTICE-HALL CANADA, INC., *Toronto*
PRENTICE-HALL HISPANOAMERICANA, S.A., *Mexico*
PRENTICE-HALL OF INDIA PRIVATE LIMITED, *New Delhi*
PRENTICE-HALL OF JAPAN, INC., *Tokyo*
SIMON & SCHUSTER ASIA PTE. LTD., *Singapore*
EDITORA PRENTICE-HALL DO BRASIL, LTDA., *Rio de Janeiro*

© 1988 *by*

PRENTICE-HALL, Inc.

Englewood Cliffs, NJ

10 9 8 7 6 5 4 3 2 1

ISBN 0-13-911975-2

PRENTICE HALL
BUSINESS & PROFESSIONAL DIVISION
A division of Simon & Schuster
Englewood Cliffs, New Jersey 07632

To the guys at the old Five-Thirty Club, where life was not always as it was but as we would have it be.

CONTENTS

	Introduction 1
chapter one	The Next Voice You Hear 3
chapter two	The Way They Are 11
chapter three	America's Team and Perspective 31
chapter four	Growing Up Laid-Back 53
chapter five	Friends and Foes 71
chapter six	USLF Falls, Walker Rises 85
chapter seven	Here Today, Gone Tomorrow 101
chapter eight	Players, Different and Alike 113
chapter nine	Drugs Too Real 133
chapter ten	Schramm versus NFLPA and Agents 139
chapter eleven	Reeves and the West Coast 161
chapter twelve	The Bomb and the NFL 175
chapter thirteen	Bringing in Rozelle 199
chapter fourteen	Learning, Doing at CBS 213
chapter fifteen	Original Move to Texas 221
chapter sixteen	War II and Peace 229
chapter seventeen	Lamar and the AFL 245
chapter eighteen	Getting Computerized 261
chapter nineteen	Middleman in Merger 273
chapter twenty	Fighting the Color Line 281
chapter twenty-one	Schramm and Landry 301

chapter twenty-two   A Change of Owners   319
chapter twenty-three Waves in Fishing   327
chapter twenty-four   Most Powerful Committee   333
chapter twenty-five   Looking for the Big One   347

INTRODUCTION

Things Texan are bigger than life for many of us in our dreams and fantasies, if not in the world as it really is. There was the Western hero, the cowboy, the legendary Texas Ranger, the outlaws, Indians and the Alamo. There is a vast expanse of space, of desert and pine forests and beaches, and the faraway hills and mountains that stir the wanderlust that is somewhere in us all. And there are the sprawling metropolitan areas of Houston, San Antonio and Dallas-Fort Worth, which not only seem forever to climb upward but also outward as the small surrounding towns of a decade or so ago have now become little more than suburbs, retaining only individuality in their names. Sure, the oil industry was severely shaken in 1986 but is expected to recover, if not this year, then the next or the next. Texans will tell you that it always has, so there is no reason to think it won't do so again. Anyway, the dry holes and gushers, the overnight riches and losses are just another part of the mystique. So the current economy notwithstanding, Texas remains, with perhaps one foot in legend and the other in reality, oil and cattle and pretty girls and Cadillacs and limousines. The Lone Star State is a place from which *Forbes* magazine in recent years has listed H. Ross Perot and Caroline Hunt Schoellkopf, both of whom live in Dallas, as two of the five richest people in America. It is a continually popular, overblown soap opera called *Dallas*; and a place where James Michener would come to write an immense volume on the state at the bequest of the governor and a setting in which books concerning money, sex and mayhem appear to have a better chance of success than if those staples of publishing were dealt with elsewhere. Texas is Willie Nelson and the armadillo, overindulgence and where Prince Charles came to cut "The World's Largest Birthday Cake" in celebration of the sesquicentennial.

As John Bainbridge wrote in *Super-Americans,* "Texas is a mirror in which Americans see themselves reflected, not lifesized but, as in a distorted mirror, bigger than life."

Perhaps the greatest personification of the state's popularity has been the Dallas Cowboys. The team put together an unprecedented string of 20 winning seasons (1966-85), which did not end until 1986, and Texas E. Schramm likes to point out that the current closest challenger is Washington with six straight winning years (through 1987).

And Dallas has remained, even after suffering through lean times recently, among the most popular teams with the networks and fans. Only the Chicago Bears have supplanted the Cowboys in recent years in some popularity categories. A key example was the 1986—Dallas' first losing season in 22 years—Neilsen ratings for primary games on CBS, the network that carries the most popular NFL contests each week. Dallas was involved in eight primary games, those sent to the majority of the country, which was more than any other team. Dallas drew a 16.7 rating, followed by the Bears with 16.3, Washington with 15.6, San Francisco with 14.6, and the NFL champion Giants with 14.4. The admitted policy of CBS has been, when in doubt televise the Cowboys.

"The won-lost record might not justify it, but the Cowboys always seem to ride the wave of popularity," said Doug Richardson of CBS sports. "They have remained a big ticket."

Most Texans believe there is a correlation between the oil economy and the Cowboys; that they will be fighting for the championship once again, if not this season then the next . . . or the next.

The organization has enjoyed tremendous success on the field, but its popularity and, if you will, folklore, have outdistanced any won-loss record.

"Traveling around the world, there are always things people ask you," said former Dallas mayor Starke Taylor. "One is about the TV show *Dallas,* and another is about the Dallas Cowboys."

"I think Clint Murchison and his Dallas Cowboys did more to make a glowing, shining metropolis out of the name Dallas than anything else," noted Washington Redskin owner Jack Kent Cooke.

And in an editorial the *Dallas Morning News* stated what many city leaders had been saying for years—that the Cowboys should get a great deal of credit for changing the city's image after the assassination of President John F. Kennedy in 1963. ". . . there was little the Dallas leadership could do to change the media-fueled opinion that this was a 'city of hate,' " the editorial said. "The emergence of the Dallas Cowboys as one of the most successful franchises in professional football history provided a welcome boost of positive publicity for the city. . . ."

Stars such as Meredith and Lilly and Hayes and Staubach and Dorsett and Walker have become household names. And there is nothing in sports quite like the new home to which Schramm has now taken his team. It, too, seems bigger than life.

Actually the massive, sprawling 200-acre Dallas Cowboy Ranch is a city within a city, just north of LBJ Freeway in far North Dallas, the direction in which the Metroplex is most expanding. It is a monumental testimonial that sports and the local football team are indeed big business. The Cowboy Center is the focal point of the 2,500-acre Valley Ranch development, an upper-middle-class, commercial-residential community that seems so clean, well planned, orderly and modern that you feel somewhat surprised, for instance, that people there actually have trash to discard. The Cowboys originally joined Triland International in the venture but now are majority owners of the Ranch.

When the $70 million Cowboys Center, called by *Newsweek* the "Emerald City for the Cowboys," is completed, the projection for which is 1990, it will include a conference center and hotel, a golf course, a sports medicine clinic, a retail-restaurant pavilion, a $3.1 million ice-skating arena and Schramm's special project, the Cowboys ShowPlace, a high-tech, multimedia building which not only will honor the club's history but also allow fans, through modern technology, to experience how it feels to be in the Cowboy huddle, with the coaches on the sidelines and in the press box at Texas Stadium. Through simulation, fans will see what a Tony Dorsett or Herschel Walker see as they follow blockers downfield, trying to avoid tacklers. The ShowPlace will offer fans experiences of sight, sound and touch—of football as played by the Dallas Cowboys, past and present.

Schramm has always been very history conscious and has also wanted the fans to get as close to the team as possible, creating a feeling of "we" rather than "they." And with the popularity of the Cowboys, plus the proximity of the Dallas-Fort Worth Airport, some 650,000 visitors are expected to come to the ShowPlace in its first full year of operation.

The Cowboys Center is located on 200 acres in Valley Ranch, a 2,500-acre community, and includes three football fields, an 80,000-square-foot, single-level sandstone-colored building that houses club officials, scouts, coaches, a Cowboy Cheerleader dance studio, a Cowboy travel agency, the *Dallas Cowboys Weekly* publication and a retail store selling Cowboy apparel and memorabilia. In the dressing room each player has a separate area, complete with desk for use in answering correspondence, and there also is a fully equipped television studio and media room complete with terminals. And there is, of course, much more. It is more than state of art; it is Circa 2001.

"Tex built one of the best organizations in the history of the National Football League, and now he has put together that complex at Valley Ranch which, in this day and time, is unequalled in sports," said Pete Rozelle, who smiled and added, "but that's just like him. He always wants the best."

The Dallas Cowboys Ranch, with its complex, seems too big— too much really. It is a place that even Schramm could not have envisioned when he first set up headquarters in 1960 for his organization in a single rented room in the Automobile Club Building on Central Expressway and arranged for the use of practice facilities at a rat-infested, old minor league baseball park. The team's record in those days seemed to justify the facilities. But those days seem so long ago, so far away . . . mostly forgotten in the great push to make the organization what it became.

And the Dallas Cowboys are the house that Tex Schramm built, literally from scratch. He accomplished this by conjuring, outsmarting, manipulating, wheeling-dealing, charming, intimidating and, certainly, pushing and shoving when it came down to that. It is no matter that he is not a native Texan, his given name notwithstanding, because he can be as political as former Texas and U.S. Secretary of the Navy John Connally was when he stood at the crest of his political career, playing time and place to his greatest advantage, and he also can work both behind the scenes and in the foreground like a Lyndon Baines Johnson.

Tex Schramm heads but one of 28 NFL franchises, and yet he is one of the most widely quoted and recognizable executives in sports, his only rivals in pro football being Commissioner Pete Rozelle and, perhaps, Al Davis. This was never more in evidence than during the 1987 National Football League Players' Association strike and negotiations. Schramm was a member of the five-man Management Council, whose chairman was Hugh Culverhouse of Tampa Bay. Yet it was Schramm who became spokesman for the NFL and was personally blamed by key union members for the players' failure.

Schramm has been sarcastically called "The assistant Commissioner of the NFL" by his detractors, and certainly few would argue that he long ago established himself as the second most powerful man in the league. More than anybody, Schramm can be blamed or credited with the major changes that have taken place on the field of professional football in the last two decades. He heads the Competition Committee, the most powerful group in the NFL, and has ramrodded the new rules which have put more offense, more scoring into the game which has become a Sunday afternoon tradition. He has built the prototype of a successful sports organization, one that has stood the test of time and is studied by business establishments and corporations both in and out of sports. And during a self-imposed three-year exile from the NFL while with CBS, he came up with the ideas and innovations that are still with us in television, and he put into motion the wheels which would bring the computer into scouting.

Schramm inaugurated discussions and then worked behind the scenes with Lamar Hunt to lay the foundation for the AFL-NFL merger, one of the most significant events in league history and, because of his reputation for toughness and insight, was chosen by his peers to head the owner's negotiation committee during the first confrontation in 1970 with the NFLPA. John Mackey, NFLPA president at that time, called Schramm the toughest man with whom the players ever had to negotiate. As is usually the case, Schramm was diplomatic at times but hardly straddled the line of diplomacy.

About 5 A.M. during a marathon negotiating session in 1970 over individual travel expenses, Ken Bowman, the Green Bay center who was a key member of the union, tired of arguments and doubletalk and snapped, "I don't give a damn about all this crap! What I want to know is how much money I'll get if I'm traded from Green Bay to Dallas! Understand!"

Schramm, almost coming across the negotiating table, yelled, "That's one goddamn thing you don't have to worry about!"

During the 1987 confrontation, union executives and players called Schramm much worse things than the toughest man with whom they had to deal. He had not taken such a key role since 1970, but when the union said it was going to strike down free agency, Schramm snatched the NFL flame from some of his more conservative and softer-spoken peers and led the charge. When Schramm threw himself into the fray, he told union leaders right away, "The owners are the stewards of the game and the players are the transients!" He was just trying to define each side's role.

Schramm put sex, if you will, into football with the Dallas Cowboy Cheerleaders, who have become unbelievably popular and an entity in themselves, and he is easily the most outspoken of sports executives. He probably is "on the record" as far as his opinion on controversial subjects more than anybody, although in retrospect he sometimes wishes he'd been more . . . well, diplomatic.

When Tom Dempsey, part of whose foot was missing, kicked a record 63-yard field goal to give New Orleans a 19–17 victory over Detroit in 1970, it was an inspiration to all handicapped people and the world applauded. Schramm said Dempsey was using an illegal shoe. Privately, a number of NFL coaches and officials agreed, although they certainly appreciated how Dempsey had overcome his handicap. But they, too, believed his special shoe, the toes and front part reinforced with steel, was not legal and that it gave him an unfair advantage. However, they weren't about to say anything about it.

Schramm had been thinking about the shoe for some time and, after the record kick, said it was like taking a mallet and striking a football. He said it gave Dempsey an unfair advantage over other kickers and that his shoe should be made illegal. Mail flooded the Cowboy offices from handicapped people and Schramm, feeling bad he had hurt their feelings, apologized. But he maintained he was right.

So he does not always completely consider the effect of what he has to say or, if he does, prefers to say it anyway. When recalling his dealings with Lamar Hunt, the widely respected AFL founder and owner of the Kansas City Chiefs, Schramm said he was tired of hearing about the clean-cut boyish image the man had and of how he was so philanthropic as far as sports were concerned. He added, to the contrary, that Hunt was "selfish, devious, and, as far as accomplishment, is the most overrated man in all of sports." He launched into a tirade about the new breed of NFL owners and said, because they lacked understanding, they were dangerous to the very structure of the NFL. He indicated what baseball's hierarchy has let happen should live "in sports infamy" and called the NFLPA, whose leaders are obviously one of his more frequent adversaries, "unrealistic and childish" in its approach to controlling drugs.

Schramm branded many sports agents as little more than "thieves" and added that professional sports would be better off without them. He discussed "cheap tricks" journalists use and how they sometimes employ selective quotes and words out of context to express what they want to write at the expense of accuracy. He has been simmering for years over Al Davis taking credit for causing the NFL-AFL merger and explained that the man behind the Raiders had again let his ego get in the way of the facts. "That isn't," he said, "unusual for Al."

Regarding his own club, he indicated that Tom Landry was one of the best coaches the game has ever known but that he developed some "blind spots" in recent years, as had other people in the organization, including himself. He said so many players had problems dealing with the real world, because they expected everything to be handed to them, and he questioned what he termed their "misplaced priorities."

Schramm, to put it in the Lone Star State's vernacular, shoots from the hip with opinions and statements that need no interpretation and, yet, can become poignant when reflecting on his relationship with Dan Reeves, the great innovator and the man who pioneered major league sports on the West Coast before the baseball Giants and Dodgers even thought about moving and who broke the NFL color line in 1946.

Schramm learned about the NFL and operation of a team with the Rams and Reeves, who was ahead of his time but also a flawed genius, who barely could function in Schramm's final years with the Rams, because of his drinking problems. Tex opened the doors of the NFL to Pete Rozelle, watching and supporting him as Commissioner, and then brought him word that he would be fired if he didn't change his mind and support the NFL-AFL merger.

Schramm is a man who likes attention, the cameras, the microphones in his face, and to be on the podium in Canton, Ohio, inducting Rozelle into the NFL Hall of Fame. He certainly is a man of reasonable wealth and moves comfortably and easily among the affluent, but he also seems just as much at home with those of more modest means. He is good copy and enjoys being with the media, sometimes furnishing them with insights and background material and at other times trying to tell them how to do their jobs.

Perhaps 85 percent of his heart and soul, his being are devoted to football in some form or fashion, but he will launch into a discussion and be very opinionated on most any subject, including his philosophy of life or even, for instance, books. He has read only two books in his life but will tell you how they should be written. Well, actually, the statement about his reading isn't entirely accurate. He read this book three times before publication.

However, do not read into any of this that he lacks feeling or is not sensitive to a degree. His is just an uncommon mind, one which if channeled in a certain direction or into a particular area can be extraordinary. His is also a mind which might fumble for hours trying to fix a simple gadget.

And this is the same Tex Schramm who tearfully embraced Don Meredith on the sidelines after a devastating loss and the person who gave moving eulogies when his friends, broadcaster Frank Glieber and journalist Steve Perkins, died. Schramm had become so angry with Perkins in 1968 that he didn't speak to him for over a year. Perkins, then a "beat" writer for the *Dallas Times-Herald*, had written a book about the Cowboys' 1967 season. Schramm said Steve had violated a number of confidences and that he didn't want to have anything to with him. Yet, when Schramm wanted to get the club's *Cowboy Weekly* in shape, he hired Perkins, because he believed he was the best man he could get for the job. Subsequently, Perkins built the *Weekly* circulation to some 100,000, proving Schramm right.

Director of publicity Doug Todd recalled the team's twenty-fifth anniversary party in which Schramm was passing out Christmas gifts and giving silver anniversary books to everybody, including the women who worked in the lobby.

"He was mentioning everybody and telling them how much he appreciated what they'd done, and then he got all teary-eyed, his voice cracked and he was barely able to finish his speech."

"The thing most people will never know about Tex is how compassionate he can be," said Suzanne Mitchell, a former Schramm secretary who became director of the Cheerleaders.

And Kay Lang, Schramm's longtime friend and ticket manager,

who retired a few years ago, recalled something Tex said when they attended the funeral of Jim Berling, a Texas Stadium Corporation executive. The church had been packed and, as they were leaving, Schramm said, " I wonder how many people will come to my funeral if I ever die."

Once when Schramm was asked to characterize himself, he thought for a while, sipped on his J&B Scotch and finally said, and he was very serious, "I'm just an ordinary person trying to do a job." No matter what you know or think about Texas E. Schramm, be assured he is not an ordinary person.

In the archipelago of the Bahamas lies the small island of Spanish Cay, which was owned by Clint Murchison, Jr., until he became ill and his financial empire crumbled around him. There was a landing strip lined with palm trees, a large open house connected to quarters for visitors by covered walkways and a smaller house nearby for house servants and people who worked the fishing boats. It was a beautiful place with white sand stretching from the shoreline to a myriad of palms, which swayed softly in the ocean breeze. The Atlantic around the island was clear and blue and green, and the fishing usually was good with the possibility of landing a marlin and the chance, if you so chose, of catching a wahoo, tuna, grouper or various other species.

But sharks and barracudas also lurked in the waters. Dallas Cowboy patriarch Texas E. Schramm, who was raised near the ocean and had been an avid fisherman since early childhood, mentioned to a small group, with whom he stood on the beach down from Murchison's house, that sharks probably were as afraid of men as men were of them. A fin had just been spotted about fifteen to twenty yards offshore, and Schramm had been trying to put the predator in perspective for those not familiar with the ways of the ocean. However, someone said the shark probably did not know he was supposed to be afraid of man. Schramm considered this, then found a sharp tree branch on the beach and went into the water, where he proceeded to try to harpoon the shark. Shortly thereafter Schramm began swimming madly in one direction while the shark took off the opposite way. No doubt the story of the day Tex Schramm confronted the shark has grown over the years with the retelling, but it remains the only report in which a man has attacked a shark in the Bahamas off Spanish Cay.

chapter one

THE NEXT VOICE
YOU HEAR

The long and many and sometimes seemingly blind halls connecting the various offices in the sprawling, massive, single-story sandstone building in which the brain trusts are situated at the Cowboys Center are confusing to the infrequent visitor, and you half expect to see road signs, such as "Tex Schramm's Office, two miles," or "You are now leaving Tom Landry's Area." But you could hear Schramm's voice booming through the open door of his office and into the adjoining area where his secretary Connie Medina was working. She is the seventh secretary he's had and does not seem as fidgety as some of her predecessors. One former secretary went to a nunnery and another had to be treated for mental disorders. Schramm does not mistreat his secretaries and women, as a rule, love him because, perhaps, they can see through the sometimes gruff surface to the little boy inside. But they must deal with his moods, which often are hair-triggered, and become accustomed to his voice that seems it might shatter glass at times and to his outbursts of profanity, usually more indigenous to waterfront bars. He also can appear to be very calm and settled and then, all at once in a burst of energy, throw fifteen ideas at you all at once.

Connie is a mature, attractive woman, as Schramm would have his secretaries be, as he would have women in general be. Schramm does not try to temper nor, certainly, hide his affection for attractive women. This is personified in many ways, such as his interest in Cowboy Cheerleaders and his friendship with former Miss America, Phyllis George. He can be very egotistical and, certainly, is vain. He enjoys his drinking but has also been known when his weight has gotten out of hand to go on the wagon or, as you might put it in his case, throw himself under the wheels of the vehicle. He does not do things halfway. And he consistently exercises to some degree or other, keeping a particular fitness program going, no matter whether he has had a good night's rest or little sleep at all.

And his telephone never seems to stop ringing when he's in his office. He gets calls from Cowboy officials, NFL people, other owners and general managers, the press, his family and the general public. The public can also call him at home because he has a listed telephone number, but he often chides newspaper friends because they do not. But Schramm is very real, sometimes almost too real.

He was yelling into the telephone at Commissioner Pete Rozelle. "Lookit," said Schramm, "it can't be done that way. What! That's bullshit! Goddammit, you know what will happen next!"

Shortly thereafter Schramm cheerfully and calmly asked Rozelle how his wife was doing and added, "Okay, I'll call you back."

There is an aura in his presence that causes him to seem larger than he is. Perhaps it is his booming voice and the fact that he certainly can be overpowering at times. Yet he is a man of 5-11, claiming he has spent his adult life trying to get that extra inch, and 190, give or take a few pounds, and one who is balding with gray in his sideburns and in the hair on back of his head. He has that somewhat flushed face of a person who spends a lot of time outdoors, which he does, and has been known to, in fact, take a drink or four. And his outbursts are spontaneous.

During an NFL playoff game Rozelle was sitting in an adjoining booth from Schramm, who was in the press section. They were separated by glass, preferably bullet proof. When an official made a very controversial call, Schramm, as is his nature, shouted a few profanities. Then he looked through the glass at Rozelle, who was looking at him, and raised the middle finger of his right hand at the Commissioner, who looked down and put his hands over his face.

Don Meredith, the former Cowboy quarterback who was one of Schramm's favorite players, was "doing color" on an ABC Monday night game when, while scanning the crowd, a camera focused in on a fan who immediately raised his finger in the universal sign. Meredith, without missing a beat, said, "And lookee there. Well, that's just his way of saying we're Number One." Schramm, of course, was saying that and more to the Commissioner.

Schramm grinned, somewhat sheepishly, when I walked into his office. He appeared bright and was clear-eyed. We had had drinks the previous night, and this writer had that awful feeling in the head and stomach that is called a hangover and whose cure has not been found since time immemorial. But Schramm, a man who was 66 at the time, seemed to feel fine. It is generally conceded by those who know Schramm that you do not seriously drink with him or you'll be hurt.

He turned in his chair behind the desk and stared out the large picture window through decorative patios to the landscape of carefully placed trees, plants and walkways. Schramm retained the habit of turning in his chair and staring out the window from the team's previous headquarters on the eleventh floor of Expressway Towers. It was there, in his previous office suite, that Schramm received one of the most shocking and unexpected thrills of his life.

Tex was subconsciously looking out the window toward the freeway traffic far below, as he talked long distance to an NFL official, when his thought pattern was rudely interrupted. Right before his very eyes, standing on the narrow ledge outside his window was none other than Roger Staubach, making a face at him. Schramm almost flipped over backwards in his chair, fumbling to keep from dropping the receiver of the telephone. He gasped, then sighed, and when the party on the other end of the line asked him if he were all right, if something had happened, Schramm, calm again, said, "Oh, nothing really. I just looked out the window, and my quarterback is standing on the ledge of the eleventh floor, making faces at me."

Staubach, somewhat given to mischief in spite of his public image of being straight and square, had wanted to see Schramm but was told he'd have to wait. When Roger tired of the delay, he found a side door, used only by the maintenance men, which opened out onto the ledge. The door had been left unlocked so Roger walked onto the ledge and carefully made his way around the building to Schramm's window.

When Schramm confronted him about behavior hardly befitting a player who was the closest of any to being The Franchise, Roger explained, "It wasn't nearly as dangerous as you might think. The ledge was at least three feet, and the wind wasn't even blowing very hard so I wasn't likely to fall.''

Schramm turned away from the window of his office at the new one-story complex and the telephone rang again. Connie told him it was his wife Marty, who wanted to make sure he remembered the time they were supposed to be at a particular function that night.

"Tell her I'll call her back," he said. "I didn't even remember the function. Don't tell her that!"

Gil Brandt came into Schramm's office. He had talked to John Mackovic and was filling Tex in on the details regarding the former Cowboy assistant's firing by Lamar Hunt. Mackovic had been in the process of negotiating a two-year extension of his contract after coaching the Kansas City Chiefs to a 10-6 record and their first trip to the playoffs in fifteen years.

Schramm pieced together the scenario in which the players got the head coach fired. The situation reminded him of his days with the Los Angeles Rams and the late Dan Reeves, who more than once fired coaches after first listening to complaints of players. This was something of which Schramm totally disapproved and almost quit the Rams prematurely because of it. Mackovic had two assistants who were very popular with the players, special teams coach Frank Gansz and defensive coordinator Walt Corey. The special teams and defense had been keys to the team's success.

"I contacted Gansz to see if he might be interested in coming to the Cowboys and coach the specialty teams," said Schramm. "He told me he wasn't, because he wanted to be a head coach and didn't believe he could get there from coaching the specialty teams. My understanding is that he went to Mackovic after the season and told him he wanted to be the offensive coordinator. Mackovic told him he couldn't promise him that job so Gansz resigned. There also were rumors that Corey was going to Buffalo. So the players called a meeting at kicker Nick Lowery's house and invited Lamar and Jack Steadman (Chiefs' General Manager). Hunt listened to the players, which doesn't surprise me, and fired Mackovic the next day. Now I'll tell you what will happen. Lamar will name Gansz head coach."

Two days later Hunt named Gansz head coach. "The chemistry of an organization is an intangible that is critical of its success," said Hunt after firing Mackovic. "My evaluation is that our football team is lacking that ingredient."

"Chemistry my ass," said Schramm. "It's just typical of Lamar and Jack Steadman. The consistent thing about them is that they keep having losing seasons. They get a guy who finally wins for them, and they fire him because some players are upset. There are always some players upset about something, but you can't have a situation in which they go over the head of their coach to the owner. There have been players griping about Landry and his system, especially in the early years."

Schramm was very proud that four former Landry assistants, including John Mackovic, Ray Berry at New England, Mike Ditka at Chicago and Danny Reeves at Denver, had had teams in the 1986 playoffs and that in 1987 Gene Stallings seemed to have taken a big step in turning around the Cardinals program. Reeves had taken his team to two straight Super Bowls and lost, and Ditka had gone there and won. But, in spite of his outstanding record, all wasn't at peace with Ditka in Chicago, where president Mike McCaskey had been known to take a personal hand in matters, such as firing Ditka's friend, general manager Jerry Vainisi.

McCaskey became head of the Bears because he was the grandson of the late George Halas. He is a Harvard Business School graduate who knows little about football or the operation of a team. When Schramm talks about the new breed of owners, whom he fears might diminish or even destroy the league because of their naiveté in dealing with the National Football League Players' Association and long-range planning, he often cites McCaskey as a prime example. McCaskey did not want Vainisi and Ditka to sign Doug Flutie. He also basically had been ignored by the media, as the Bears climbed to power, and some believe this has grated on him. He cited "philosophical differences" in firing Vainisi. "It's not all that difficult to have philosophical differences with Mike McCaskey," said Schramm. His telephone rang again. It was his private line.

"Great," he said. "Tell them to come on in."

Schramm got up and walked to the entrance of his office to greet Tom Landry, who was on crutches after having off-season knee surgery, and Jim Erkenbeck, the New Orleans offensive line coach the Cowboys were trying to hire. Landry's face looked drawn and he appeared tired. For so many years he never seemed to age that much. He stayed in good condition, working out and not drinking or smoking or, as some said, even having evil thoughts. While others in his profession were becoming alcoholics, fighting nervous breakdowns and ulcers, Landry was able to put football into perspective, and his actual age totally belied his appearance. He remains a good, Christian gentleman who nearly always seems to remain calm and collected while those about him, such as Schramm, erupt. In recent years Landry has begun to show his age, whereas Schramm, four years his senior, does not appear to have added any more years. Schramm is hyper, worries and paces, drinks, doesn't get enough sleep. There is no justice.

However, Schramm does recall a time in the early years with the Cowboys that Landry was known to partake of a martini, which is one of the most potent of civilized drinks and one of which James Thurber wrote, "One martini is just right, two's too many and three's not enough."

"When Tom was with the Giants, they had what they called a 5:30 Club during training camp," said Schramm. "The coaches, club officials and writers would all gather in a room, set aside for such things, after practice and have a beer or whatever they wanted to drink and relax and talk. Tom brought that tradition to the Cowboys."

Jimmy Parker, a teetotaler, was the Cowboys' business manager then and, although he abstained, often went to the 5:30 Club. One day he asked Landry what he wanted to drink and Tom replied, a martini. "How do you like it?" asked Parker, somewhat puzzled. "Oh, five to one," replied Landry. Parker then proceeded to mix the drink and gave it to Tom, who thanked him and took a big sip.

"If you think Tom doesn't show much expression, you should have seen him then," recalled Schramm. "Parker had mixed FIVE parts vermouth and ONE part gin. Maybe that's why Tom stopped drinking."

When Landry brought Erkenbeck to see Schramm that afternoon, the line coach was in the process of agreeing to replace assistant Jim Myers, who was retiring after 25 years as offensive line coach of the Cowboys. Myers had had a tremendous success over the years and has developed All-Pros and Pro-Bowlers such as Ralph Neely, John Niland, Rayfield Wright, Blaine Nye, Herb Scott and Pat Donovan. But the talent has waned in recent years, and times have changed. After the 1985 season when Schramm initiated the hiring of Paul Hackett to bring in fresh ideas to the passing game, he also had tried to hire a line coach to assist and work with Myers and explore new techniques. He thought he had Los Angeles Rams line coach Hudson Houck hired. "I believed we had a commitment from him," said Schramm, "but right before he was going to get on a plane and come here, he backed out. So we didn't fill the position. Oh, I don't know if it would have made a difference or not.''

Erkenbeck was given a great deal of credit for the tremendous improvement of the Saints' offensive line in 1986, something which apparently carried over into 1987 when the Saints had their first winning season in history. When Erkenbeck was with New Orleans, the Saints had lowered their sack total from 58 to 27, and rookie Rueben Mayes had rushed for 1,353 yards, fourth highest in the NFL. That same year Cowboy quarterbacks had been sacked 59 times; Danny White had suffered a career-threatening broken right wrist; and Steve Pelluer was battered and beaten up so much that he seemed to be looking to escape the rush more than finding a receiver. Dallas also had lost a dependable running game, something upon which the best Dallas teams were based.

Blocking techniques have changed in the NFL. Whereas in the past, concepts were predicated on use of shoulder blocks, now they are based on the use of hands and leverage.

''You see so many successful running plays on film, and not one blocker or defender is on the ground,'' explained Schramm. ''It's now all a matter of getting position and leverage and shielding off tacklers and using your hands. This creates a little gap for the ball carrier to go through. Erkenbeck is an outstanding practitioner of this philosophy.''

There also is a fine line between holding and legally blocking, or being caught holding and not being caught holding, on pass protection. Insiders have said the Saints were the best holding team in the NFL when Erkenbeck was there.

When the meeting was over that day and Jim Erkenbeck had agreed to come to the Cowboys, Schramm figured that another elusive piece of the puzzle to get the Cowboys back on top was in place. After Landry and Erkenbeck left, Schramm began staring out the window again. Football is life, not a game for him, and so recent times had left scars. He still laments the 1986 season because, after the 6-2 start, he believed his club would continue its winning streak while making a transition. This, of course, didn't happen. It was as if another piece of the puzzle, another answer was out there somewhere, outside his window.

Connie came back into his office at 6:30 P.M. that Friday and said, if it were all right, she would go home. He smiled and, without a word being spoken, she brought him popcorn, which had just come alive in the microwave and fixed him a J&B Scotch and then left. Finally, he said he was excited, because another training camp was starting. There have been so many . . . but each camp is both different and alike.

chapter two

THE WAY THEY ARE

Tex Schramm gradually approached the narrow walk separating the shallow from the deep end of the swimming pool. It was near noon and the sun was high, and the day seemed hotter than usual for Southern California but certainly not as hot as it would have been in July in Dallas. He had his shirt off to soak up the sun's rays and wore Bermuda shorts, tennis shoes and a white coach's hat, which had "Cowboys" written in blue script across the front. The bill of the hat was crooked, almost sideways on his head, and suddenly he started walking across the divider, perhaps a foot and a half wide, as if he were a high-wire artist. There was little chance he would lose his balance and tumble into the water, but he stuck out his arms for balance and then when he made it across the pool, tipped his hat as if hearing applause from an audience that only he saw or heard. He then smiled and sat down on a lounge chair by the pool. This was another attestation of a theory I have that grown people still have a child inside them who sometimes takes control. But a person who knows only the public figure of Tex Schramm would not expect such an act from him.

We sat for a while in the chairs by the pool on the large patio, shaded by giant oaks, of the spacious ranch-style home owned by friends of Schramm and the Cowboys in Thousand Oaks, California. The patio overlooked a well-groomed golf course, and Schramm got up and walked to the edge of the pool to look out and see if anybody was playing. When he was growing up, his family's home had been across from a golf course in San Gabriel, California and, perhaps, for ever so brief a time, he remembered this but although he feels it, Schramm isn't one to linger on sentimentality. Two women moved into view, looking for their golf balls. One came to a tree below and within calling distance of the patio and seemed a little disgusted with her lie. But she got out her iron and struck the ball, somewhat awkwardly. She swung the club in the unorthodox way young women used to try to hit a softball in the days when they really weren't into sports, because it wasn't the ladylike thing to do. She still was able to lift the ball, and it hit, bounced and rolled to the edge of the green.

"Great!" yelled Schramm, clapping. He looked back at those of us on the patio and we started clapping, too. The woman appeared to be a little embarrassed by the attention at first but soon was waving and smiling.

A bird had made a nest at the top of a light on the outside of the house, overlooking the patio and pool. The owners apparently had been away for a while and had only recently returned. It was like so many homes in California which seem to have been built with the pool and patio in mind, rather than they for it.

"Look at that bird," said Schramm. "See its tail sticking out, just above the light. He has a nest there. He'll look down every once in a while and say, 'What the hell you doing here at my house?'"

"What kind of bird is it?" I asked, not having seen it.

"Wha' . . . well, it's a California bird," said Schramm.

"Oh."

Schramm, as he sometimes will do during training camp, was having a noon Bullshot, vodka and beef bouillon. He was relaxing with friends before going back to California Lutheran College, where the Cowboys have training quarters and he has a suite in a dormitory which houses club officials and coaches. Players stay in another group of dorms, and visiting media are placed in still another place, which is called "The Third World Dorm."

The telephone on the patio rang, rang again, loud and piercing, and the bird flew from above the light, across the patio, flapping its wings wildly and then gliding over the golf course, almost as if it were suspended in air. The call was for Schramm, who'd left a number at training camp so he could be found if needed.

"Hello," said Schramm. "Howard? Have you heard anything?"

"What the fuck do you mean, Howard? . . . Then he told you a goddamn lie! Lookit, I explained the situation to you. Witt Stewart got him into it. We tried to help him. What? . . . Listen, I told you what we did. That's a lie.

" . . . No, I'm not mad at you, Howard. I'm just trying to explain. Wha'? Lookit, I'll be back in camp in an hour. I'm surprised Tony said he was so goddamn unhappy, because we've been his savior. Call me at camp if you hear anything. Okay, Howard. Nice to talk to you."

Schramm had been talking to Howard Slusher, the Los Angeles agent-lawyer who had been brought into the unbelievably odd but, if you will, not surprising Tony Dorsett Saga of training camp, 1985. But it could have been another player in so many other training camps. Tony had come to Schramm six months earlier to explain his disastrous financial condition. He was broke, mostly due to astonishingly bad investments recommended by Don Cronson, a New York agent who represented Tony as a business manager and tax consultant from 1978 through 1981, and Witt Stewart, who had not only talked Tony into getting the deferred payments on his contract—this would have paid him $100,000 a year for 15 years— for the face value of the time, $700,000, but also advised him to invest some $600,000 in oil stock, whose value was almost immediately worthless. The IRS disallowed other investments as tax writeoffs and had liens on both of Tony's houses, his car and was picking up his check each month from the Cowboys for back payments. Furthermore, Dorsett had borrowed $500,000 from the Cowboys to give his wife a $250,000 divorce settlement and to try to settle other debts. He had three years to run on his contract, which was for $450,000 in 1985, $500,000 in 1986, and $550,000 in 1987, excluding, of course, the deferred payments he'd already taken. The contract also stated Tony would not try to renegotiate a new deal until it was concluded. In all Tony owed the IRS $414,247.91 and, considering the government agency compounds interest and penalties daily, it appeared he might break even about the year 2500.

Dorsett had asked Tom Landry if he could report to camp 24 hours late to try to find a solution to his problems and was given permission. Stewart and Dorsett had contacted Slusher, who had previous represented Randy White and talked the All-Pro defensive tackle into missing an entire training camp. They figured Slusher with his financial and legal background might make some sense out of the mess Tony was in.

"Slusher's all right," said Schramm. He'd used other words to describe him when he represented Randy White. The plot would thicken considerably, placing Schramm again in a familiar, though unwelcome position. Few things irritate Schramm more than strong media coverage of contract and financial problems of the players and union and management hassles. He believes fans are tired of hearing and reading about such things and want only to know about the aspects of the game that pertain to competition on the field. But once again a season had started with off-the-field sound and fury for Schramm and the Dallas Cowboys.

Thousand Oaks is one of the seemingly endless number of communities just off any freeway from Los Angeles that appear to spring up overnight and then, just as quickly, turn into budding cities. The city is situated in the Conejo Valley and surrounded on three sides by bluffs and mesas and has its own picturesque beauty just before dusk when the fading sunlight casts a pinkish glow over the mountains and shadows and outlines the rocks and brush and trees and wild flowers. Conejo means rabbit in Spanish and the cottontails often can be seen scampering across roads and trails and highways on the outskirts of the city.

Thousand Oaks once was part of a vast ranching area, where cattle and horses were raised. It once was a popular place for studios and production companies to shoot movies and television shows. The countryside lent itself to Westerns and also had the vastness and space for other film projects. Part of *Gone with the Wind* was filmed in the area as were segments of the *Lassie* series and various Westerns, including *The Rifleman*. A number of Hollywood celebrities have lived in the city and nearby Westlake, including Ben Johnson, Strother Martin, Dub Taylor, Virginia Mayo, Joel McCrea, and Alan Ladd.

The city is 40 commuting miles on the Ventura Freeway from Los Angeles and a 35- 40-minute drive through Malibu or Decker Canyon to the Pacific coast. Temperatures are usually in the high 70's during the day, the low 60's on summer nights, and the atmosphere is very laid back, very Californian.

This was the place Tex Schramm was looking for to establish the

Dallas Cowboy training camp, but he didn't know it for three years, previously making Pacific University in Oregon, St. Olaf College in Minnesota and Northern Michigan University the spots where the Cowboys prepared during midsummer for the long season. But he wasn't satisfied with the locales nor facilities of these places, although he knew it would be impractical for his team to train in Dallas during July and early August, because temperatures would be in the mid-90's and sometimes even reach 100.

Glenn Davis, the former West Point All-America, had played for the Los Angeles Rams while Schramm was with the team. Davis, who had become director of special events for the annual Los Angeles Times-Charity game, was looking for an opponent for the Rams in the annual preseason game and contacted Schramm. Tex was aware that the vast publicity given the Times-Charity game certainly would benefit the fledgling Cowboys but he wanted more.

"I'd been thinking about the area," said Schramm, "because I was raised there and knew we could locate good facilities somewhere in the area. So I told Davis that if he would find us a place to train out there, we'd play in the game."

Davis checked around and one day phoned the fire department at a small hamlet of 2,000 people called Thousand Oaks. He was told that a new college, California Lutheran, was opening that fall of 1960 and that school officials would be glad to have the Cowboys and their money and would allow them to use the dorms and athletic facilities. He also learned that temperatures were ten degrees cooler than most places in Southern California. So by 1963 the Cowboys established a permanent training camp in Thousand Oaks and played in the Times-Charity game for fourteen straight years, the string being broken when Ram owner Carroll Rosenbloom became angry with Schramm over a league matter.

The Cowboys have continued to train in Thousand Oaks because Schramm likes the town and the people and because Landry feels the weather is conducive to grueling two-a-days and that the players are far enough from family and friends that he can get their undivided attention. The facilities at Cal Lutheran were more than adequate but have been improved over the years, with Schramm's approval at the Cowboys expense. Tex believes this not only benefits his team but also gains more goodwill from the school, which has awarded both Schramm and Landry honorary doctorate degrees. The Cowboys have built the school a new practice field, a free weight and exercise area and improved the equipment, dressing, and training rooms. However, Schramm does not like the scales in the dressing room, feeling they are not accurate and that sometimes they just downright lie. After a recent camp opened, Schramm, who had been trying to lose weight, walked over from the practice field to weigh, inviting me to join him.

"Training camp is the time to lose weight," he said, proudly. "I weighed the other day and was down to 190. I'm on a strict program. I have cut out Scotch, been skipping breakfast and have had only a salad for lunch for over a week. Okay, now I'll see how much weight I've lost."

He carefully took off his hat and laid it aside and stepped on the scales. "Why you sonuvabitch," he said to the scales. "This can't be right. I've gained two pounds . . . 192."

He stepped back and insisted I get on the scales to check them, because they must be wrong. I weighed 174, the same thing I'd weighed in Dallas, and told him so.

"To hell you say," he said and got back on the scales. I edged behind him and pressed my foot on the edge of the scales. They registered him at 197. His eyes opened wider . . . Then he realized what I had done.

"That's a chickenshit thing to do," he said, but he was smiling. He tried again and still weighed 192. "What the hell!" he bellowed. "Throw the scales away! They're no good!"

A young helper in the equipment room, who had been working nearby, quickly slipped away through a door, and a player, who was injured and unable to work out, got up from a bench by the scales and went into another room.

Schramm remained upset for a few more minutes but was reminded that, perhaps, Willie Townes was right. Willie was a good defensive end for Dallas in 1966 but his career ended in 1968 after a knee injury. Another big problem was his eating. Willie had a recurring dream he was a grocery store. He'd report to camp 18 to 20 pounds overweight and be fined accordingly. He was fined so much so often that a "Willie Townes Memorial Fund" was established. At the end of the year the money Willie had to pay for being overweight went into the fund and was used for a team party. One year Willie kept claiming that he was going to make the weight, that he'd been working extra hard during the off-season. He reported to camp 21 pounds too heavy. Willie complained to anybody who would listen that he was being treated unfairly, that he had weighed the prescribed amount in Dallas before boarding a plane to get to camp. He thought for a while and said the conclusion was obvious.

"Sea level is different here than in Dallas," explained Willie. "It's lower so my weight goes up. So I shouldn't be fined."

"But," said Schramm, "I weighed 190 three days ago here."

Schramm drank Scotch that night after the scales betrayed him and, as far as I know, continued to do so the remaining nights in camp.

There are a number of fine restaurants in Thousand Oaks, and residents not only welcome the players, club officials, and members of the media, who cover the team, with open arms but also embrace them, both literally and figuratively.

Some of the more revealing times have taken place in the Westlake area. There was a popular hangout right on the lake called "The Levee." One night a group of reporters and club officials were there, sitting outside on the patio. Sometimes you could hear muttered sounds of voices from outside the condos just across the lake. That night we suddenly heard a man yelling, "Nelva! Nelva!"

There followed the sound of splashing in the dark water. A woman had jumped in and was swimming across the lake toward us. She reached shore and got up out of the water near where Schramm was sitting. She didn't have a stitch of clothes on.

"I just walked over to her because she was, uh, apparently having trouble," said Schramm. "I was, well, a little shocked to discover she didn't have on any clothes. No, the fact that she didn't have any clothes on had nothing to do with my helping her."

Schramm grabbed a tablecloth from a nearby table and handed it to the woman. He seemed a little stunned and she smiled and put the tablecloth around herself.

Schramm was kidded because, for once, he was at a loss for words. "Well, hell," he said, "just what am I supposed to say to a naked woman who suddenly comes out of the water near my table?"

At least he saw her coming. Another time Schramm and club officials had been invited to a poolside party in the area. They mingled and mixed with various citizens, all of whom were naturally Dallas Cowboy fans. One particular lady asked the hostess if that were

Tex Schramm standing over there, talking to a group of people. Told that indeed it was, she asked to meet him. Schramm was obliging as usual and sat down to chat briefly with the lady. In this particular case timing was not one of his attributes. He suddenly felt something hit him on the back of the head, and was knocked out of the chair. He turned to see a man with a crazed look on his face holding the chair with which Schramm had been struck. Alert Cowboy personnel pulled off the accoster and suggested Schramm leave. They had to do little urging to get him to do so, posthaste.

There was a great deal of puzzlement and confusion as to just what had happened and its cause. It was later determined that the lady in question was estranged from her husband, a hot tempered, jealous man who did not want her to leave him. The husband, who had been drinking, had followed the lady and her escort to the party. He sat outside the house, fuming. Finally, he stood it all he could and charged inside and saw his wife at poolside, talking to a man he presumed to be the one with whom she had been. He did not know Tex Schramm, so he clobbered him with a chair.

Schramm, his head sore, was back on the job, the next morning. He admitted having a headache but remarked in the great tradition of the NFL, "Well, you've got to learn to play hurt."

He did not see the lovely couple again, although he admitted he jumped for a while whenever somebody would come up behind him. And sometimes, for a while, he jumped when they didn't.

Over 2,000 residents of Thousand Oaks will attend a simple rookie scrimmage, and some 500 will come to see an early-week morning practice. Residents think of the Cowboys as their team, and they will travel all the way to Dallas to see the club play in Texas Stadium. Residents walk with players to and from practice, and it is a tradition for children to adopt players and carry their helmets and shoulder pads to the dressing room after practice.

At a typical practice Schramm will stand on the sidelines, watching players and talking to fans who say they always wanted to meet him. In recent years actor Gary Busey, who became well known when he portrayed Buddy Holly in a movie, has been a frequent visitor to camp. He became acquainted with Schramm, the coaches and some of the players while preparing for his film role as Paul (Bear) Bryant. He also attends games in Dallas. Over the years Burt Reynolds, Glenn Campbell, Kenny Rogers, Joey Heatherton and

David Keith have come to practice. Visitors in show business draw a great deal of attention, as do local female fans who come to practice and seem to be wearing less and less each year. Most are what is thought of as the typical California girl. She is tanned, blond, well endowed, and she is many. It must be something in the water.

Schramm, preparing to jog along a trail that leads to and up the hill behind the practice field—he didn't jog up the hill but to its base—stopped to talk to a couple on horseback. Riders often can be seen on trails around the field. You might say Schramm has gone from a sprint to a jog to a walk. He now walks up to the mountain, along its base and then back down. During a camp in the early 1960s he attempted to regain his old sprinting form. Larry Karl, PR man for the club at the time, had been bragging about what a good sprinter he'd been in college. Schramm tired of hearing this and challenged him to a 50-yard sprint. Players, officials, the press and fans all showed up to watch. Tex, in his early forties, won in a diving finish.

There is just a great closeness between the people of Thousand Oaks and the Cowboys. The Cowboys are real, more real for instance than the Raiders. Cowboy players, officials and coaches are reachable, touchable. Schramm likes that. It means more fans. As a great contrast the Raiders, who train in nearby Oxnard, practice behind fences, guarded gates and do not willingly allow the public to watch. Al Davis likes that. He wouldn't have it any other way.

During a National Football League meeting in Palm Springs in the mid-1970s, a group of men were sitting on the terrace of a villa where they were staying. These men constituted most of the power structure of the league. They had had their meetings that day and were relaxing as the sun began its descent behind the nearby mountains. It was a somewhat mellow time.

"You know," said Al Davis, "I'm a great fan of Hemingway's. Somehow, looking out there at the mountains, it reminds me of Mount Kilimanjaro."

There was a long pause. The other men were quiet, listening, whether they liked Hemingway or were even aware of his famous short story, "The Snows of Kilimanjaro," about a dying man who looks back on his life while waiting for a rescue plane to pick him up at the base of Africa's highest mountain.

"Someday," continued Davis, whose team had lost Super Bowl

II and had not been back to the championship game since that time, "after we win the Super Bowl, I'm going to take off, just say to hell with football, and go see Mount Kilimanjaro."

"Are you sure it'll still be there?" cracked Tex Schramm, his team having already been to three Super Bowls and having won SB VI in January, 1972.

"Tex and Al used to have some classic exchanges like that," said Pete Rozelle.

Schramm and Davis actually once were friends and worked together on the Competition Committee, the group which devises policy and rule changes, but any camaraderie haulted ever so abruptly when Davis bucked the league by moving his Raiders from Oakland to Los Angeles without permission and then sued the NFL for trying to stop him. Schramm, always a league man first, became the epitome of the NFL establishment, whereas Davis, as has been his nature, played the role of the maverick, the rebel to its fullest. Simply put, Schramm strongly believes those in the league must adhere to its policies if the NFL is to remain strong and not stumble over the pitfalls that have befallen other professional sports. He believes that all arguments must be hashed out within the league, that it must be the all-powerful ruling body in order for all its franchises to remain viable and successful.

"I've strongly believed in the league for all these thirty-six years," said Schramm. "To be continually successful at a league level, we must pull together. Listen, when we play somebody on Sunday I hate the hell out of our opponent, but when the game is over, it's over, and we're all a part of the league again."

Although Schramm, more than anybody outside of Rozelle, guides league policy he also has vehemently disagreed at times with the majority. Yet he knows the majority must rule. Davis sees no other god before himself and the Raiders. The Raiders are considered first and last, and he doesn't try to disguise his dislike for Rozelle that goes back over twenty years.

The twist, the irony is that Schramm understood and might well have supported Davis in his move to LA had Al gone through the NFL's proper channels. Davis had talked about taking his team out of Oakland, because he felt the city fathers were not treating him fairly as far as leasing Oakland Coliseum. Before any move was made, before his animosity toward the league turned to war, Davis flew to Dallas to confer with Schramm. They discussed his problems, and Davis asked to see the circle suites at Texas Stadium. He wanted to build some similar ones in LA Coliseum if he moved this team there.

"Al never liked Oakland," said Schramm. "He thought it was a hick place, a small town. He was a big city guy, a person who liked glamour places like Hollywood, Vegas and New York but never Oakland.

"He told me he was looking for some way to get out of Oakland. But he said the city had changed its stance and offered him such a good deal on the lease to try to keep him there that he'd have to stay.

"I told him I understood how he felt. I said I was sorry things had worked out that way, because I knew how much he wanted to move. Furthermore, I said I thought he would have a good chance of getting permission from the league to move. He seemed to have a good basis for wanting to move.

"Well, Al went back to Oakland, and that's when the city made a big mistake. It changed some part of the deal it had offered him, and he didn't give the city a second chance. He took off with his team like a freight train for Los Angeles. Therein lies the difference in the way I felt and reacted. If he had submitted the move to the proper league channels, I might have felt different. But he said to hell with the league, and he lost me there.

"I know some people in the league got mad at me, because I'd made the statement that, if Al had brought the situation up at a meeting, he might have gotten approval. The thing they missed was that I also said, and made it clear, that if he didn't, he was on his own as far as I was concerned. I would in no way support him and would do everything in my power to try to stop his moving."

"Tex and I were tremendous friends," Davis said. "I've always responded to him. But I thought he could have been more of a neutralizing factor in this thing against the NFL. He didn't have to take a side. I still feel he could have been a factor and got this situation straightened out. He knows I'm right. He didn't, and I just said to hell with it. I got screwed. He knows I showed them. I moved. Tex stood with Rozelle. I felt like I did, but he still goes along with Rozelle."

"I'm the type person that if I have a friend and he does something against me I don't particularly like, I can accept that and still be friends," said Schramm. "But as close as I am to the league and what it means to me, it's just difficult for me to accept as a friend anybody who is so detrimental to it."

When Davis challenged the NFL, Schramm worked to try to hinder his move to LA. "I went to Los Angeles to try to make a deal with the Coliseum people," admitted Schramm. "We talked and my idea was that if they dumped Al, then in X-number of years we'd put an expansion team in LA to play in the Coliseum. I think that might have worked, but Rozelle killed the idea."

Davis' battle with the NFL continues in the courts in California at this writing. The Ninth U.S. Circuit Court of Appeals ruled the NFL had violated antitrust laws by trying to stop Davis' move. When $34.6 million in damages was awarded Davis, the NFL appealed. In mid-June of 1986, the Ninth Circuit Court decided that the amount must be reduced, and even possibly eliminated, because by moving to LA the Raiders had deprived the league of a valuable site for possible expansion, which was Schramm's original idea.

The NFL has spent from $6 to $10 million in Congress lobbying for antitrust exemption. Currently, there are nine bills before Congress which would grant the league limited antitrust exemption for establishing its own guidelines for franchise relocation and the right to share TV revenue.

Schramm took the time and spent the money to be in court during the Davis trials. Al Ward, an assistant to the commissioner, said NFL lawyers were amazed at Schramm's grasp of the legal aspects of the situation, considering he had no formal training in law. But Davis obviously also was impressive.

"Al can be a charmer," said Schramm. "Give him time to study a situation and think about it, and he's outstanding. About the only way you can get him is to pull out something he's not expecting or something new, and he'll back off."

Aspects of the case remain under appeal, but whatever monetary values or penalties are or are not established, it's unlikely the Raiders ever will be told to move back to Oakland. Furthermore, after Davis moved his franchise and was supported by circuit court decisions, other owners have threatened to move, a situation Schramm said would happen if Davis had his way. Robert Irsay did pack up the Baltimore franchise and move it to Indianapolis in the dark of night. John Mecom, before selling the Saints, had flirted with a move of his franchise, and Cardinal owner Billy Bidwell moved his St. Louis Cardinals to Phoenix before the 1988 season. And Leonard Tose had also mentioned moving to Phoenix before selling the Philadelphia Eagles.

Davis has suggested the league could save itself further aggravation by adopting clear guidelines for franchise relocation and using an independent panel, rather than one made up of league people, to review an owner's motives for wanting to move. The panel, not the league representatives, then would allow or turn down the request. Schramm insists such a process would still leave the NFL exposed to lawsuits and that it no longer would be its own boss.

"Al Davis has done some good things for the league, such as his input on the Competition Committee," said Schramm. "But the negative things he's done far outshadow the positive ones."

"Oh, even when he was on the committee, he was doing some things that didn't help the league's image, but he still made a lot of contributions. He was the guy behind the suit against the Pittsburgh Steelers and Chuck Noll, which didn't help our image."

Noll, angered at what he felt to be dirty play in the NFL, stated that the league had what he termed a "criminal element." He cited Oakland's Jack Tatum as being a part of that element and was taken to court.

"So Pete took him off the committee," said Schramm. "That angered me, and Pete and I clashed over the decision. I told him Al did a good job and that I needed him. At that time, at least, I didn't feel some of the negative things he did overweighed his input on the committee. Maybe in the league as a whole but not the committee. I told Pete it was a disservice to the league to take Al off. But Pete did it anyway. That was a mistake on his part."

Davis' hatred for Rozelle apparently began when Schramm and Lamar Hunt worked out terms for the AFL-NFL merger in 1963. Davis was Commissioner of the AFL and wanted no merger. So, whereas Rozelle was kept informed of what was happening, Davis didn't even know meetings were taking place because the parties involved believed he would take steps to try to prevent what was happening. One of the details agreed upon by Hunt and Schramm was that Rozelle would be commissioner of the combined leagues.

"Al was very bitter about being an outsider as far as the merger and also that Rozelle was named commissioner," said Schramm. "He couldn't fault me because I was an NFL man, but the whole situation really upset him."

Davis has stated bluntly, "Rozelle will destroy the whole league if we're not careful. Rome burned. He is a phony and a fraud and he is scurrilous. The dirty tricks he's pulled to try to defeat our organization are just unbelievable, and he's still trying."

"I respect Pete and resent Al, because he's so unrelenting in his relationship with the Commissioner," added Schramm. "I don't think this will change until one of them quits or dies."

So it was somewhat unusual to see Schramm and Davis chatting peacefully at a rookie scrimmage between their two teams during training camp in a late July. From a distance they might have been friends.

But that day they were together in the Dallas Cowboy training camp in Thousand Oaks, Al Davis and Tex Schramm were not talking as friends or about their situations and feelings in regard to the NFL but only about the scrimmage they were watching. They looked and acted very differently. Schramm seemed very calm and in control next to Davis. Davis, lean and slightly shorter than Schramm, appeared ill at ease in the open surroundings of the Cowboy training camp. The reporters, cameramen and radio and television broadcasters were close to them, and the scrimmage was open to the public.

In a scrimmage the previous week at the Raiders' training quarters in nearby Oxnard, a white line had been drawn to form a box in which Davis, some of his assistants and Schramm were to stand. The media was told it could not enter the box, and guards patrolled the field. Fans were not invited, although some watched from a second-story apartment, which gave them a view over the fence. The atmosphere was as guarded as the situation at the Cowboy training camp was open.

Schramm wore his usual attire of shorts, tennis shoes and Cowboy knit shirt of the year. This one was white with blue stripes and with the team insignia on the pocket. The Cowboys have a different-type shirt each year. Gil Brandt gives them to visiting college coaches and members of the media. Schramm likes to talk about the mystique of the New York Yankee baseball team in its heyday, the power of the Yankee pinstripes. The new Cowboy knit shirts with stripes on them made you think of that. Schramm probably already had.

Davis wore a white jump suit, with long sleeves and the Raider insignia on the pocket. It is said that most everything he wears will have the logo or some reference to the Raiders on it. Al has a sharp face, a crooked smile, and his hair, combed straight back, has a kind of greasy look of the 1950s. He just looks fifties in a way, somewhat like an aging street gang leader from Brooklyn, where he was raised. Both men had sun glasses on but, watching them, you got the feeling that Schramm not only could see out of his but that you could see inside. Davis gave no impression whatsoever that you could see inside.

"No," Schramm explained to the media gathered around him, "we haven't become friends again and, no, I don't think you make too much of our rivalry. We're both interested in winning. I saw Al at the league meetings, and he mentioned that he was moving his camp to Oxnard, near us. So we agreed it would be beneficial to both teams to hold scrimmages. We don't kid each other about the NFL suit. We just don't talk about that."

The Cowboys and Raiders are alike only in winning. Schramm wants as many people as possible to think of the Cowboys as their team, as "we," and tries to perpetuate that feeling in his actions and the actions of those who work for him. Dallas wears white helmets with stars, and the Cowboys have been, mostly, Tom Landry and Roger Staubach and, to a degree, apple pie. The team certainly has had its share of rebels and troublemakers, but the Cowboys seem to be able to sweep them under the rug, as it were, whereas the Raiders emphasize them.

The Raiders are as Davis wants them to be, in the image he likes to convey. Their colors are black and silver, hardly appealing to the naked eye, and their emblem is a man in a helmet, wearing an eye patch with crossed swords behind him. They are an isolated island in the NFL, operating independently from the other twenty-seven clubs, challenging the league, belonging to no scouting combine. They do not reach out to the general public but close ranks. The Raiders are against the world.

Dallas has built its teams over the years almost solely through the draft and free-agent market. In recent years only Mike Renfro, swapped from Houston for Butch Johnson, and John Dutton, who came from the Colts in 1979 for a first- and second-round draft choice when Ed (Too Tall) Jones temporarily quit to try his hand at boxing, were acquired in trades. And Dutton was cut in 1987. Davis, as much if not more so than through the draft, goes after free agents and trades for older players. To a great degree many of his employees have been known as renegades or oddballs, such as Jack Tatum, Ted Hendricks, Malcolm Barnhill and the inimitable John Matusak, whose antics and night life almost outshone his ability as a football player. Hendricks, a fine linebacker, once came to practice wearing a knight's suit of armor and riding a horse. Barnhill was arrested for carrying a concealed weapon, which was loaded. Dallas, of course, suffered through its notorious incidents. Lance Rentzel was charged with indecent exposure, and Rafael Septien with sexual conduct involving a minor. But Rentzel was suspended and traded and Septien cut. The Raider players generally stay around. Unlike Tom Landry, Davis and his coaches do not have strict rules. Players are not fined for being a few minutes late to a meeting, and the team slogan is, "Do what you want as long as you win." And the Raiders win.

"Al gets a kick out of his image and that of his team," said Schramm.

"Once Al and I were discussing the word, devious," Miami's Don Shula remarked. "He thought it was a compliment."

Davis got a great deal of satisfaction when he picked up Todd Christensen, a running back from Brigham Young that the Cowboys had drafted in the second round in 1978 and then cut. Christensen was moved to tight end for the Raiders and became a Pro-Bowl selection. Members of the media, especially television commentators, kept saying the Cowboys had given up on Christensen and let him go. This made Schramm burn. Nobody mentioned that the New York Giants also had cut him. And the truth was that Landry believed Christensen could not make it as a running back and asked him to move to tight end. Christensen refused to change positions and Dallas cut him. He obviously thought better of making the move with the Raiders. Christensen also didn't talk much about the Giants but said he liked the Raiders better than the Cowboys, because he was treated like a man.

Davis was a former coach and retains input into what is happening on the field. He watches films, will point out a player's mistakes at practice and consults with Mike Shanahan, as he did Tom Flores, John Madden and John Rauch before him. Tom Landry had been totally in charge of everything that relates to the field, although Schramm did seem in 1986 to cross previously drawn lines of authority when he took the initiative in the hiring of new offensive coordinator Paul Hackett from San Francisco.

Rozelle tells a story about the time Schramm, then general manager of the Los Angeles Rams, hired him as a publicity man and also assigned him the job of keeping track of prospects playing on armed service teams. Rozelle would check with coaches at various army bases, asking them not only about their own players but also prospects on other teams they regarded as possibilities for professional football.

"The army coaches were very cooperative," recalled Rozelle. "They seemed glad to help and wanted to see any top prospects they had get a chance. I called this one coach at Fort Belvoir, and he said he had a lot of information on army players. Then he stammered a little and asked. 'Well, how much do you pay for my information?'

"I told him we didn't really have a budget for it and that all I did was just telephone around the bases, and the coaches made recommendations.

"So the guy said, 'Well, you ought to be paying for something like that.' That guy was Al Davis. He was the only one I ran into who wanted money."

Davis also coached at Adelphia College, The Citadel, Southern California and with the old Los Angeles and San Diego Chargers of the AFL before coming to the Oakland Raiders in 1963. He has served the team as coach, general manager and managing partner. When the Raiders began to publicize that they had the NFL's winningest team and then went to Dallas and beat the Cowboys, 40–38, in 1983 Schramm took a Raider release and began picking it apart with members of the press watching. He was typically angry after the loss, but at that particular time the Cowboys actually had the winningest record since turning the corner from their expansion years in 1966. Schramm just wanted to make that perfectly clear.

But through 1987 the Oakland-Los Angeles team has an overall mark of 251–142–11 to 246–148–6 for the Cowboys. Oakland once had 16 straight winning seasons but Dallas had 20, a mark that stands as the third longest in the history of professional sports. Only hockey's Montreal Canadiens with 32 consecutive winning years and the New York Yankees with 39 from 1926–1964 have done better. Dallas also holds the record for nine straight playoff appearances, a streak which was broken in 1984. Only three times since 1966 have the Cowboys missed the playoffs, once by a single game, and in 1984 by a tie-breaker. The Raiders have been to four Super Bowls, winning three, and Dallas has been to five, winning two. So the argument goes on and on as to which team, depending on which year you begin, has been the most successful. As far as popularity there is no contest.

Of the five sporting events through the Super Bowl of 1987, which attracted more viewers than any other in television history, Dallas has been a part of two. In 1980 the Cowboys had been involved in three of the top four viewed sports events. In the early 1980s Dallas held the highest ranking for Sunday, Thursday, Saturday day and night games, and for divisional, wildcard and conference playoff games. Until the Chicago-Miami game in 1986, Dallas and Washington had the highest ranked Monday night game. The

Cowboys to date have been involved in four of the ten Monday night games which drew the largest percentage of the audience. Sunday games that begin at 3 P.M. draw a much higher audience than the ones which start at noon. However, in 1985 when Dallas played Cleveland at noon in a home game that was blacked out within a 100-mile radius of the Metroplex, it ranked a full point ahead of the Raider-49ers game, which began at 3 P.M. This means it was watched by 850,000 more homes in spite of the fact that the Raider game was not blacked out in Los Angeles, a massive television market. Dallas also has the highest ranking of any NFL team in England and is easily the favorite in Mexico.

Until the mid-1980s Cowboy-related products sold by NFL Properties accounted for 20 to 30 percent of all sales. The only change in the pattern has been that the Super Bowl champion in the 1980's usually places first with Dallas second. Currently, the Chicago Bears, with Refrigerator Perry becoming a national institution for fat men the world over, surpass Dallas in sales. In a late 1986 *CBS-New York Times* poll, Dallas and Chicago tied at 12 percent for the most popular team. Considering Dallas has not been to the Super Bowl since January, 1979, and has not advanced past the first round of the playoffs since 1982, the continuing popularity is amazing.

These points are only in conjunction with other sporting events and against all other NFL teams. But there are many other illustrations of the Cowboys' popularity, which is both planned and unplanned, with Texas E. Schramm smiling in the background. . .

When the scrimmage against the Raiders ended at Thousand Oaks that afternoon, Schramm and Davis spoke briefly and parted. Tex, as he walked off the sidelines to his car, stopped to talk to reporters, then did a brief radio spot and a television interview. Fans stood a few feet away, watching and then approached him when he was finished. A couple explained they were from Dallas and had come to Thousand Oaks on vacation in order to see the Cowboys in training camp. Schramm talked to them for about ten minutes, told them how happy he was to have them, and then went over and shook hands with a gentleman from the Southern Baptist Convention, hardly his kind of group. When he finally got to his car he stopped, before getting inside to drive back to the dormitory, and looked around. You got the impression that he was still looking to see if there was anybody else who wanted to talk to him.

Davis lingered, talking to some of his people about the scrimmage. Again, he seemed uncomfortable in the open atmosphere. He told a television crew that he didn't want to do an on-camera interview, but was very polite in his refusal. Then he carefully explained to a radio sportscaster that, under the circumstances, he didn't want to be interviewed regarding his situation with the NFL. A woman approached him, holding a small boy by the hand. Al smiled and was cordial with them, shaking hands with the youngster.

"Mr. Davis," asked the woman, "could I get his picture with you?"

Al appeared a little embarrassed, then he politely refused, mentioning how awful he looked after the long afternoon scrimmage. "It's been so windy . . . my hair is going in all directions. Some other time. I'm sorry."

I had tried to reach him for six months in regard to the Schramm book, carefully explaining each time I telephoned, or wrote a letter, that I wanted to get the best contrast with Schramm, because he, Al Davis, stood on the opposite side of the NFL and also ran his organization differently but, certainly, just as successfully. I had no luck with the public relations department, where some nice people work when you confront them directly, but, as most NFL "beat men" know, are of little help. This might or might not be because Davis wants it that way. I talked to his secretary on three different occasions, and each time she said she'd call me back but didn't. Schramm always returns calls, sometimes almost immediately and at other times within the hour. Once he carried on a telephone relationship with a 12-year old superfan named Reggie. Reggie would call Tex at home to discuss the Cowboys and offer his impressions. This went on for an entire season.

Finally, Schramm introduced me again to Davis—I'd met him in the 1970s when I was a sportswriter-columnist—and explained that I was working on a book and that he'd appreciate Al's input. Davis was nice, almost charming, and not only said he'd be glad to talk to me but added, "Why don't you come on back to our camp, and we can go out to lunch. That might be better for talking, getting away from camp. Call me or I'll get in touch with you this week."

He did not call. I did, three more times. I never got through to him, and once when I asked a man who answered the phone for Al, introducing myself and explaining the circumstances, we were disconnected, perhaps by him.

I had had no problems over the years talking to Rozelle, George Halas, Don Shula, Chuck Noll or anybody in the NFL but began to resent Davis. Schramm said I was just getting to know Al like many people did. So I waited until he had talked to the woman and small boy and then moved toward him. He met me, smiling and shaking hands. He apologized for what had happened and said he didn't know I'd called. Then he explained that he'd decided not to be interviewed for a book on Schramm. I told him that was fine, but it would have been nice to have known this six months earlier.

"I hope you understand," he said, "but the book will be done one way and would do me no good."

I told him, to the contrary, that I'd planned to state his views and feelings as objectively as I could, and also his ideas on his relationship with Schramm, but just could not fully do so without his cooperation. I explained Schramm had wanted it this way, too.

We talked informally. He said it was off the record as he tried to explain why he didn't want to talk but didn't really say anything that he hadn't at the scrimmage. He also said he'd had an offer to do a book himself and was saving his thoughts for that. We then discussed books, Hemingway and F. Scott Fitzgerald, both of whom I admired too, and then he said, "Okay, just to help you, I'll send you a transcript of some of the testimony during the suit against the NFL and that way you'll better understand my feelings." I thanked him and said I'd send him a copy of my last book. Something Schramm had said came back . . . "Al can be very impressive and charming when he wants to be." In spite of everything, the runarounds and wasted time, I liked Al Davis. Oh yes, he never sent me the trial transcripts, but I never sent him my last book either.

And in 1987 Davis was offered a better deal for his team in Irwindale, California and wanted to move his Raiders there as soon as a proposed stadium was finished.

chapter three

AMERICA'S TEAM AND PERSPECTIVE

If you are around Tex Schramm on a day when the madness is all about him it will tire you quickly, but he seems to thrive on it. He is too accessible, if anything, but appears to gain energy and momentum the more he has to do. During training camp reporters and columnists continually knock on his door or phone from Dallas, Fort Worth, Los Angeles and New York. And Gil Brandt, as he does in Dallas, keeps popping in and out of Schramm's suite with the latest developments on this or that, or to bring him up on some rumor which probably involves the Cowboys or NFL but also might relate to anything from the NCAA to major league baseball.

In early afternoon of a day during the Tony Dorsett Saga in training camp it was not untypical. . . .

Tony Dorsett had said he only wanted some time off to think, but Ron Springs had told media representatives that Tony *had* contacted him and indicated he wanted a new contract. Ron couldn't seem to stop talking to journalists about his friend Tony.

"Why the fuck doesn't Springs join the agents' union or whatever the hell it is?" said Schramm. "I'd say if he is serving as Tony Dorsett's spokesman, that Tony has problems."

Ron Springs will never make the Cowboys' "Ring of Honor" nor Schramm's favorite player list. Schramm had become extremely angry with Springs and cornerback Everson Walls before the 1984 season started, because they kept saying the team would be better off if Gary Hogeboom, not Danny White, was the starting quarterback. White, since replacing Roger Staubach, had twice quarterbacked Dallas to the NFC title game and in 1983 to the divisional playoffs. Dallas had lost each time. Some players felt Hogeboom, who had a much stronger arm, might be the answer. Most players did not think they were the problem. A big controversy began with many prominent members of the media suggesting that Landry start Hogeboom. Some think Landry finally succumbed, and that's why he started Hogeboom when the season began. Some believe Landry made the move to show what might happen. Others feel that Landry believed he had to take a chance with Hogeboom in order to improve the team. Schramm said all the publicity and controversy got to White, making him a lesser quarterback, and that thus, early in the year, Landry had no choice but to start Hogebooom. The way it turned out White might not have been able to win the Big One, but Hogeboom could not win the Little One, being unable to take his team to a touchdown against a team such as Buffalo, as the Cowboy string of nine straight playoff appearances was broken—by a single game. Landry did insert White, and Dallas made a strong run but finished 9-7, losing a playoff tie-breaker with the New York Giants.

The team was obviously on the decline and, as the 1984 season ended, many of the coaches and players were talking about the troublemakers on the team but doing so quietly. Schramm said, frankly, he was sick of the "finger-pointers and those who had negative attitudes on the team" and that, if he had his way—this is Landry's domain—he would ship them off somewhere else, the implication being to Russia. Landry must have cringed but said nothing other than that Tex was entitled to his opinion. Schramm obviously included Springs and Walls among the finger-pointers. Walls continues to annoy Schramm. He staged a three-day walkout before the 1986 opener with the Giants and threatened to skip the game completely if the Cowboys didn't increase their offer in renegotiating the final two years of his contract. He had earned the right to renegotiate by reaching certain performance levels that are specified in a special clause in his contract. Schramm accused him of deserting the team and said he would not respond to blackmail, no doubt being reminded of what Lee Roy Jordan had once done to him. Walls relented and eventually agreed to terms. Schramm, as he has with others in the past, must put down his sword in the case of Walls because of Everson's ability and the team's need for him. This was not true of Ron Springs.

His feelings about Springs put him into a comic situation when the team went to Philadelphia in 1984, attempting to clinch its nineteenth straight winning season, something Schramm was well aware of but which Landry seemed to ignore. Tom worries about winning and then, if he loses, is able to put it into perspective, that it is over and done, and nothing can be changed. Tex worries about winning a game and has a terrible time forgetting the ones which Dallas loses, especially if they are of historical significance.

In the Eagle game Springs took a short pass from White and ran 56 yards for a touchdown to give Dallas impetus for a 26-10 victory. Tex leaped to his feet in the press box and yelled, "Way to go, Ron baby!" Reminded shortly thereafter that he often has referred to Springs in anything but endearing terms, Schramm grinned innocently and said, "Why, I don't know what you mean."

Springs had further alienated Schramm and other Cowboy officials when he was charged with being drunk, disorderly, resisting arrest and assaulting a Dallas woman police officer at the Million Dollar Saloon, a Dallas striptease club. He was cleared of the particular charge of assaulting the officer just before Dallas played Detroit in 1985. The team had opened the season by upsetting the Redskins and seemed to have gained an unexpected momentum. But a number of players, whether called or not, skipped team meetings to go to Springs' trial. Dallas played a terrible game and lost to Detroit. Schramm blasted the players who attended the trial without being asked, stating they "couldn't get their priorities straight, which was trying to get ready to play Detroit." He couldn't understand why Landry would tolerate them missing meetings. Tex drew criticism in many quarters, people claiming that a man's trial was more important than a football game and that Springs' friends should have been there to lend moral support. Schramm did not back down from his statements, and two weeks later Springs was placed on waivers and eventually signed by Tampa Bay, where he sat on the bench and then was placed on waivers.

"It's just not Landry's nature to be critical of players in a situation like that," explained Schramm, recalling the incident. "He's got to get the best out of them and deal with them on a daily basis. They don't see me at practice once we leave training camp, so let them get mad at me. I was just completely angry about the situation and also wanted to shake them up. If Tom thought it was all right for them to go to the trial during practice or meetings, then he should have changed the times for those things. The coaches were as much at fault as the players. The coaches might have gotten their attention if they'd said something like, 'You aren't going to miss your work if you go to the courthouse. You're still going to put in your eight hours of practice and meetings. We'll work around it, but you can't miss the work.' The way we played against Detroit, a team we should have beaten, it looked like the players had missed too much of something.''

So Tex Schramm wasn't particularly happy when Ron Springs and Everson Walls indicated Dorsett wanted a new contract similar to the one All-Pro defensive tackle Randy White, the team's best player at that time, had gotten the previous year.

White had been handled in negotiations by Slusher who, as is his habit with exceptional players, had talked Randy into hiding out during training camp. White missed five weeks but eventually signed a contract which would pay him $2.25 million over five years and a $6.4 million in deferred payments over twenty years.

Tex kept telling Slusher, who at that time was known by the media only as the mysterious third party, that he was willing to restructure Tony's contract so that it would allow him to walk away from football with money and also had offered to help him with a real estate investment which would pay him $500,000 after five years.

Brandt, shaking his head slowly and somewhat in disgust, said, "Tony is under contract. He should be in camp. I wouldn't give him a penny more. But Tex likes him. He's been good and thoughtful to Tony. He's tried to help him. When Tony's father died, Tex flew all the way to Pittsburgh for the funeral."

Dorsett had seen Schramm on the flight to Pittsburgh, and later said he had just assumed Tex had business there and never realized he was going to attend the funeral.

"I believe," said new Cowboy owner Bum Bright, "Mr. Dorsett already has a contract. But that's Schramm's department."

When the media had cleared out of his room, Schramm talked to Brandt, and then got in touch with Slusher over the telephone again. "That's a lie!" Schramm said. "I did not tell him we would give him a new contract . . . No, Gil Brandt didn't either! He wouldn't lie to me!

"What? What the hell are you saying! Are you telling me you'd believe a Witt Stewart over a Gil Brandt! That's the most fuckin' stupid, ridiculous thing I've ever heard!''

An episode of *General Hospital*, an afternoon soap? When Slusher had told White to hide out so the Cowboys couldn't try to convince him to sign a contract, Brandt had contacted Stewart, who knew White. He tried to get Stewart to help the club find Randy. Stewart said that Brandt told him at that time, if he helped them, he'd give Tony a contract like the one Randy was trying to get. Brandt said he didn't. Stewart said he did. Dorsett, who wasn't even around at the time, said Brandt did. Schramm was caught in the middle.

So many members of the media wanted to talk to Schramm that his publicity department set up a press conference in the foyer and lounge of the dorm. There were nineteen media members there; they all were staying at the college to cover the Cowboys and, in this case, the story of Tony Dorsett facing life.

Schramm walked in, sat down at the table. Reporters had notepads at the ready, tape recorders were turned on, and there were lights, cameras, action. Schramm held up a page of the *Dallas Morning News* from the day before. There were pictures and a full-page story on how Schramm had caught a 537-pound blue marlin off San Salvador the previous month to win his own fishing tournament.

"Here's a copy of the story," said Schramm. "I'm sure that's why all of you wanted to talk to me."

Some laughed. Some booed. Then Schramm held his press conference, answering questions and telling the media what he wanted them to know about the Dorsett situation. He'd told Slusher he wouldn't bring his name into it, so he just mentioned that a third party was trying to straighten out the financial mess Tony had gotten into and that he would restructure the contract but not renegotiate it.

Schramm is good in interviews and at press conferences. This probably has something to do with his background in journalism— he has a journalism degree from the University of Texas and worked for the *Austin American-Statesman*—but also because he is a ham. He might be feeling terrible, in a bad mood, but when it's show time he's ready, even under the most adverse of circumstances.

Due to bad weather in Dallas prior to the Cowboys playoff game with Los Angeles in Texas Stadium in 1983, Schramm decided to take his team to Houston so it could work out in the Astrodome.

At that time Schramm was having slight stomach problems and had been given medicine by doctors to help prevent ulcers. Before leaving for Houston he had the prescription refilled and took a pill before going to bed. He immediately zonked out and didn't remember a thing until the next morning. The next morning he took another pill before he was supposed to do a press conference and began feeling very strange.

"I had noticed the pills looked a little different than the ones I'd been taking but I just figured they'd, you know, changed the looks or something," he said.

"But when I took another one that morning, I suddenly was in a haze, like I was sleep walking. Then I couldn't even stand up. I was staggering around like a drunk, and I hadn't even had a drink."

"I went up to his room to get him for the interview and, my god, he couldn't stand up," said Vice President Joe Bailey. "He was slurring his words, stumbling around. I couldn't figure out how or why he'd get so drunk so early. But we had an interview scheduled, and I knew we were in trouble."

It was later discovered that the pharmacy had made a mistake and given Schramm a bottle of pills used to calm down mental patients. It was a very heavy dosage of Thorazine.

"The really unusual thing about it," said Bailey, "was that I almost had to carry him downstairs, but when we got there he actually sat down and did the interview. He looked awfully sluggish and lethargic but answered all the questions and sounded like he knew what he was talking about. I think the media people just thought he was very tired. I was worried. I thought he was having a heart attack or something."

Bailey got Schramm back to the hotel room, and Tex immediately fell on the couch. They had to catch the team charter flight back to Dallas, so Bailey packed Schramm's clothes and, with help, got him into a taxi to go to the airport.

Schramm was swaying in the backseat and when the driver took a turn, Tex bounced against the door, which opened. He was about half way out of the cab when Bailey grabbed his arm and pulled him back inside.

"Buddy," said the cabbie, "it's none of my business, but that guy must be on something. You sure you can handle him?"

Schramm just sat there, a silly grin on his face. They got him on the plane and to his seat. After he was strapped in, he opened his eyes and ordered two J&B Scotch and waters. When they got him home, a doctor was immediately called. He was puzzled and then almost panicked when he was shown the pills Schramm had been taking. He said they were strong enough to knock out a horse and, along with the J&B, might have killed him. Schramm slept well that night and didn't go to work the next day. He did forgive the people at the pharmacy, who lost a few years off their lives when they found out what they had done. Incidentally, at his age, Schramm is eligible to get a senior discount on prescription drugs. He adamently refuses to take it.

Schramm talked on the telephone after the press conference on Tony Dorsett's situation and was late leaving for a scrimmage with the Los Angeles Rams at their training base in Fullerton. Schramm didn't want to cope with the freeway traffic so was given a driver. He'd planned to talk to Carlton Stowers en route, so they could do his "Ask Tex Schramm" column for the *Dallas Cowboy Weekly* and also be interviewed by me regarding the book.

Tex had been carrying on a dialogue with the computer voice in his rent car, a red Riviera. After we'd gotten into the car, the computer voice said, "You have forgotten to buckle your seat belt."

"Oh, is that right," answered Schramm.

"Your door is not shut," said the computer voice.

"Fuck you," said Schramm.

We drove through the campus and Thousand Oaks and entered the Ventura Freeway, Highway 101, going south toward Los Angeles, and Schramm said, "I've got this great idea for a short story. It's about a woman who falls in love with the computer voice in her car."

"Send it to Stephen King."

"I've always had good ideas but just never was much of a writer."

Traffic was reasonable on 101 and Schramm, in the passenger's seat in front, looked west toward the range of the sierra which separated the freeway from the Pacific Ocean. Lines of restaurants and endless car dealerships and short order spots which seemed more neon than building hid the base of the sierras and smog, a leading import from Los Angeles, hazed its peaks. The mountains were pretty and there were pinkish-red California poppies along the road and also eucalyptus and avacado trees and yellow tule grass on the mountains. The scenery was nice but polluted and you wondered the way it once might have been before man came west in such an abundance or even during the time Schramm was growing up in Southern California in the 1920s and 1930s.

Pines and firs and live oaks and cactus would have grown unhindered by prograss at the base of the mountains and the pines also would have been spread along the inclines and peaks. The eucalyptus would have spread free, sometimes spouting their white flowers, and endless beaches along the coastlines would not have been cluttered by generations of footprints nor littered by yesterday's empty drink cans. If you could not have seen for a great distance, forever, it would have been because the fog had come in and. . . .

Remnants of the wildfires that had rampaged through some 310,000 acres of bone-dry chapparrel in California during the mid-summer of 1985 could not be seen from the freeway but the charred ruins they left were very evident in the nearby canyons. The runaway fires had severely damaged Ojai in Ventura County, near Thousand Oaks. And in many places in Decker Canyon the dense brush and small trees had disappeared along the mountain sides, leaving a black carpet that had crept very close to many of the homes.

The traffic grew heavier just after noon but nothing like during the rush hours when cars going and coming and passing through Los Angeles freeways are bumper-to-bumper, edging along like locusts in endless but confined space. A young woman passed us in a yellow sports car. It was a nice, new car and her hair was blond so the assumption was that she had gotten the car to match her hair. She was attractive and moved past the traffic with her hair blowing free.

"That might be your next secretary," I said.

"But," said Schramm, "can she type?"

We passed a pickup, dented and repainted red and sagging in the back on worn shocks. It was full of Mexicans, with three in front and four in the back. All but one were wearing a straw hats, and those in the back did not seem to be talking but just staring blankly at the traffic. They might have been illegal aliens going from one harvesting job to another and had not noticed the girl in the yellow sportscar.

A couple in a nondescript middle-sized car pulled up beside us and the man, driving, waved and yelled, "Yeah, Cowboys!" What? I couldn't believe it. Here we were in summer in the middle of a California freeway and not only had found Cowboy fans but they had recognized Schramm. Actually, Tex was wearing his hat with a Cowboy logo.

He was accused of planting the fans in the middle-sized car. "I'm never surprised," he said, "to find our fans anywhere."

I remembered taking a trip to Philadelphia with Schramm for the Eagle game. From the press box at Franklin Field somebody had noticed a young man in the stands with an unusual haircut. He'd had the hair on top of his head shaved in a Cowboy star. The national television cameras found him, and he said, "Go Cowboys!"

After the game Schramm had gone to the Cowboy dressing room, which was below the stadium. As he walked back up the ramp, there must have been 75 to 100 people waiting for the players.

"There's Tex!" yelled a fan.

"All right!" yelled another. "He's the one who built the Cowboys."

Schramm was accused of importing fans to Philadelphia.

Schramm smiled and started shaking hands with people in the crowd and began signing autographs. It was amazing that this man who did not play quarterback nor even wear a helmet was so recognizable, surrounded by admirers in Philadelphia, a rival city in the Cowboys' division. You find yourself wondering what other official from another club would they have known.

The popularity of the Cowboys is phenomenal. It is not happenstance. Schramm, with his public relations background and tenure in highly profiled Southern California, laid much of the groundwork for this and has sat back and watched the returns come in. The players and coaches cringe when the Cowboys are called "America's Team," because it gives opponents just one more reason to resent Dallas. Schramm, however, loves the tag put on his team and accepts the ribbing from his friends and enemies around the league. One of his ideas when the team was in its formative stages was that if you do not find the Cowboys, they will find you.

Since the 1970's the Cowboys not only have an unmatched record for ratings over national television as aforementioned but obviously have also made a strong impression on the regional market and, for that matter, even in Mexico. During one period, Tex Schramm's television show, *The Dallas Cowboys Weekly* had higher ratings in the Metroplex than *Miami Vice, Dynasty, Dallas,* and other popular night entertainment. In its time slot, from 6:30 to 7:00 P.M. on Saturday, it consistently has the best Neilsen rating. For instance, during one period Schramm's show showed a 13 point rating and

25 share, meaning 13 percent of the 1.5 million sets in the Metroplex were tuned in, and 25 percent of all sets turned on were watching him. In actual numbers 195,000 sets were turned on to the Schramm show, which has a network of 28 stations. Furthermore, the team easily has the largest radio network in the NFL, with its games in 1987 carried on 156 stations in 13 states and in Spanish on 12 stations.

It's obvious that Schramm's three-year experience at CBS in the late 1950s helped him with his locally produced show. Dallas television critics credit Schramm with knowing more about packaging a show in the electronic media than anybody in town.

"When they first contacted me to do the show, I told them I didn't want to do the stereotype sit-down bit," said Schramm. The show is produced by Lee Martin Productions, a local sports firm. As host Schramm takes viewers to training camp in Thousand Oaks, the press box at Texas Stadium to watch the media work, the coaches' offices, the training room and other places they might never see. He has featured Danny White, an accomplished pianist, performing, visited team physician Dr. Marvin Knight at his ranch north of Dallas and shown players at home trying to bake a cake.

"We try to make the viewers feel a part of the organization," said Schramm. "We want them to have a closer relationship with our coaches and players instead of seeing them only as athletes who perform on Sundays. There is very little football in the show."

Schramm also does one weekly call-in radio show over KRLD in Dallas and another which goes out over the 100-station Texas State Network. He has a completely different show over WOAI in San Antonio, a station which reaches all over the Midwest. Not many NFL officials would take the time to do a show in a city such as San Antonio, almost 300 miles from Dallas.

Sounding like an evangelist, Schramm said, "The radio shows give us a great exposure and a chance to get our message out to the public. Sometimes things come out different through the printed media than we think they should. Plus people call in and give us some feedback. We can find out what they're thinking about us. I hear their opinions, and they hear mine. It's a good exchange.

"Sure, I'm a ham, always have been. I like to get up in front of people on television or do radio shows. The time I spend doing all those shows is invaluable, because it brings people closer to the Cowboys. They feel personally involved and know that we're very approachable."

Schramm models his television show after the *Dallas Cowboys*

Weekly, unsurpassed as far as a team publication. Its circulation has reached near 100,000, making it the second largest tabloid publication behind only *The Sporting News*. That puts it ahead of *Pro Football Weekly*. A Spanish version has been inserted in newspapers in Mexico City and Monterrey, giving it a 300,000 circulation in Mexico. In his weekly column Schramm answers questions from the readers. However, the questions very often seem to concern something he wants to express his opinion about, causing some skeptics to believe a few of the letters might be ghost-written by his staff.

And then there are the Cowboy Cheerleaders, another Schramm innovation introduced in 1972, but one that didn't come into national prominence and attention until Super Bowl X, which matched the Steelers against the Cowboys in Miami in January 1976. The national television cameras zoomed in on the Cheerleaders, as the naked eye of men of all ages had been doing at Texas Stadium, and they became a phenomenon in themselves. These were not the typical high school or college cheerleaders that most other teams used but a—uh—mature, sexy yet tasteful group of young ladies who went through dance and various other routines that might have made the Solid Gold Dancers proud.

A movie about the Cheerleaders in 1979 ranked, at that time, second to only the final episode of *Roots* as the top-rated made-for-television movie. So a second movie about the young ladies was filmed. Since their rise in popularity, the Cheerleaders have made 15 tours overseas to entertain our Armed Forces, hosted a one-hour special on ABC, made guest appearances on two major network specials, appeared on "Miss Teenage America," a two-hour *Loveboat* special, and joined a group of Cowboy players on a segment of *Family Feud*, which turned out to be that particular show's highest rated program. They have appeared at children's and veteran's hospitals around the country. The Cheerleaders are directed by Suzanne Mitchell, a former Schramm secretary who survived with her psyche intact.

"When I came to Dallas, we had contests to pick our group from the cheerleaders of the local high schools," said Schramm. "That was all right, but they didn't seem to be getting a good reaction from the crowd. They were just there. At that time the Baltimore Colts were the only team which really seemed to cause the fans to respond to their cheerleaders, and their cheerleaders were always holding up signs like 'Go Colts' and trying to get the crowd to yell with them.

"We tried that, too, and I still wasn't satisfied with the response. We'd tried a lot of the same things when I was with the Rams. It finally occurred to me that you're just not going to get a professional crowd to react to cheerleaders like the fans do in college. So I just said to hell with that stuff.

"We wanted our cheerleaders to be pretty, sexy in a clean sort of way, and have talented young women do their thing and just leave the crowd alone to do whatever it wanted. The Cheerleaders would be there to entertain them."

At first the selections were friends of friends picked from girls gathered in a small room. Now tryouts draw 1,000-1,500 young ladies from all over the country. They dance, high-step, kick, wave pom-poms and are dressed in very short shorts and halter tops with Cowboy stars and colors, and they have no problem drawing attention on the sidelines. Once a pro football reporter from New York said the only reason he really wanted to come to Texas Stadium to cover a Cowboy game was to watch the Cheerleaders with his binoculars.

"That doesn't make him a bad person," said Schramm.

Tom Landry was not particularly happy with the way the Cheerleaders dressed and some of their sexy routines. He did not volunteer his feelings but did mention them when interviewed by a national magazine. He visualized cheerleaders as they had been in his time, before the advent of Schramm. They did not wear such revealing outfits and were usually not as endowed, as far as you could tell.

The magazine quoted Landry as saying he didn't think the Dallas Cheerleaders were particularly "wholesome" looking on the sidelines and that they distracted from the game. Tom did not mean to raise a fuss, but about that time the organization was mounting litigation to stop the pornographic movie *Debbie Does Dallas* from being shown in the city, because the star of the show was supposed to be a Cowboy Cheerleader. Schramm worried that Landry's statement might be misconstrued and used by the opposition.

"What the other side will say," Schramm told him, "is that even you admit our Cheerleaders aren't wholesome, that they are pornographic looking."

Landry explained he only meant wholesome in the context of the way cheerleaders used to look. Schramm obtained a copy of the pornographic movie and asked Landry to please step into his office. He started showing the film, and Landry watched for all of three seconds and walked out of the room. "That's not wholesome," said Schramm.

Actually, the term "America's Team" did not originate with the Cowboy organization. From the outset Schramm had visualized an organization that did not just attract fans in the Dallas-Fort Worth area but from throughout the state and the region. Even Schramm was surprised when it went beyond that.

The people who do NFL Films had observed as they visited the various cities around the NFL that they'd continually see Cowboy pennants, banners and hats in the crowds. It didn't matter whether the Cowboys were playing in New Orleans' SuperDome or Giants Stadium in East Rutherford or wherever, there always seemed to be an abundance of Dallas fans. So they titled the 1978 Dallas Cowboy highlight film (they do highlight films for all NFL teams), *America's Team*. The term caught on and Schramm, never one to miss an opportunity, certainly encouraged its use. Realizing the position the term put on the team, he eased back on promoting it, although he certainly didn't discourage its usage.

"The facts speak for themselves, whether football zealots from Pittsburgh to Washington to Houston like it or lump it," wrote Tom Boswell, the *Washington Post* columnist. "The Dallas Cowboys really are America's team."

"Deep in the heart of Texas is the most popular franchise in the National Football League, and undoubtedly one of the most successful," said *San Francisco Examiner* columnist Art Spangler. "They have the best looking uniforms . . . and the best-looking cheerleaders and one of the best-looking records."

And the Boston Globe's Leigh Montville wrote, "The Dallas Cowboys are the team I would put in the time capsule. If the dominant sport of our generation has been pro football—and it has been—then the Cowboys are the logical choice. No team better describes pro football and stay-at-home Sundays of the past decade. . . . They are a team of efficiency and controversy and rhinestone glitter. They have been the best characterization of the pro football team imaginable."

Schramm certainly got more than he ever bargained for but even after what has happened, when he talks about success, he reminds me of something Edward G. Robinson said when he played Johnny Rico in *Key Largo*. Rico seemed to have it all, money and women and wine, but when asked what more he possibly could want, he said, "More. I want more."

We'd turned off Highway 101 when it began to disappear into the complex, many-directional freeway system in Los Angeles, and headed southeast toward Fullerton, where the Cowboy-Ram scrimmage would be held. We'd also cross Highway 10, the San Bernardino Freeway, which passes over San Gabriel, the small town where Tex Schramm had been raised and a place which, perhaps, he displayed some of the traits that allowed him to open the doors to success.

Schramm kept watching traffic, as if he expected to see more Cowboy fans. And then he said, "The first reason we became so popular was that we were winning. It all starts with winning. Without that, nothing else would have been possible.

"Then you have to remember we've had a number of very colorful players, the kind who have captured the public's imagination."

There was Don Meredith, with his laid-back, easy-going exterior, who sometimes would sing "I'm So Lonesome I Could Cry" in the huddle. And Bobby Hayes, the Olympic hero and, in the heyday of his career, "The World's Fastest Man"; and Walt Garrison, a real live Cowboy who had rodeoed. When asked what kind of money he was talking about for a signing bonus, Garrison remarked, "Just buy me a new Inline horse trailer." And there were Bob Lilly, the good ol' countryboy from Throckmorton, and Randy White and Tony Dorsett and, of course, Roger Staubach, whom Schramm calls "the greatest sports hero of his time." Then there were the storybook success stories of free agents such as Cliff Harris and Drew Pearson, who personified the Great American Dream, and now there's Herschel Walker, a man so modest he sometimes doesn't seem real.

"Then," continued Schramm, "look at Tom Landry. He's steady, cool, calculating, a man who never seems to get rattled. He exudes confidence and coolness under fire, the way we'd like our leaders to do. He's God-fearing, moral and all those things that made up the heroes of our youth and, yet, he has a flair, coming up with the multiple formations in 1960 and putting the spread formation back into pro football in 1975 and just playing an exciting brand of football all those years. He's the constant in so many people's life."

And then there is Schramm, who watches, calculates, oversees and whose surface, sometimes comical reactions belie a mind which put the organization together and who now, in the twilight of his career, is trying to make sure it's reestablished as the best. And, unlike Landry, he is one who will not turn the other cheek when the organization's reputation is questioned.

"It shocks me sometimes when members of the media, such as Skip Bayless *(Dallas Times-Herald)*, portray us as being arrogant," explained Schramm. "Maybe that's because our people act with self-confidence. If they confuse self-confidence with arrogance, then that's their fault. We're confident throughout the organization, because we've been winners. And we certainly have pride. From the beginning I determined everything should be first class. Everybody in our organization stays at the best hotels and flies first class. I think this helps the pride association. I also think, as many members of the media have told me, that they get a good reception with the Cowboys. They can talk to the players, coaches, me, or anybody, and they're treated with respect when they visit us, even if we don't particularly like some of them. And there's usually good copy, not always the kind we want, but good copy for them."

Not always the kind they want . . . the enigmatic Duane Thomas, who became known as "The Spinx"; the well-publicized marriage of Lance Rentzel and actress-entertainer Joey Heatherton, and then Rentzel being charged with indecent exposure; and Craig Morton's shenanigans and night life; and Pete Gent and his book *North Dallas Forty*; and Bobby Hayes caught trying to sell cocaine to federal officers after his retirement; and rumors that players such as Harvey Martin were involved in drugs; and Thomas Henderson, going from loveable to likeable to prison on charges of selling drugs and of rape; and Tony Dorsett exploding when he thought Herschel Walker made a lot more money than he did; and Rafael Septien pleading guilty to charges of sexual abuse of a ten year old.

"We always seem to be in the news," said Schramm.

Schramm enjoys being around members of the media. This was especially true in the early years through the 1970s. In recent times he's remained tireless in his dealings with the press but doesn't spend the leisure time with them that he once did. He says the time just isn't there anymore, that he's busier, but some believe he doesn't feel as secure talking off-the-record.

"I enjoy being around members of the media, because most of them are pretty well versed in what's going on," he said. "I understand they have a job to do, because I was in journalism, too. So was Pete Rozelle, which certainly has helped him with the press. We're both aware of the influence the press has.

"I have to admit my, uh, accessibility also has a selfish aspect. The press does give you an opportunity to get your message across if you are intelligent and ingenious enough to do it. It's a 50–50 exchange. They get a story, and we get over our point. You can either just answer questions or try to help create a story. Even if I'm asked the wrong question regarding a situation, I'll try to help sometimes by giving a pertinent answer. I study what makes a good quote and usually try to say something with substance, rather than just giving a bland answer. I wasn't a natural writer and had to work too hard at it, but I think I have a knack for knowing what's interesting.

"You spend a helluva lot of time giving people something to write about when it doesn't necessarily benefit you for the few times that it does. You have to be available to talk and help the press and create a rapport so that when there is something you believe is important to convey, you'll have a better opportunity to do so.

"I tell you as far as the "beat" writers or people who cover us a lot are concerned, well, they'll do better over the long run to have a relationship of trust. If they have their facts right, I'm not going to tell them a story isn't true, even if it's detrimental to us. If they have something that just isn't correct or they didn't interpret it right I might help them off the record on the background. But if I can't trust them, sometimes I'll just sit back and let them screw themselves.

"One thing that bothers me is when a guy has a story that concerns us and won't check with me, because I might tell him something that would ruin it for him. Some don't want to get your side, because it might mess up the angle they've already decided to take."

Schramm said Blackie Sherrod, the noted *Dallas Morning News* columnist, used to call him a lot regarding situations in the NFL or with the Cowboys. "He'd phone and say, 'Hey, I've got this. Is this correct?' I'd tell him the truth. Sometimes he'd say, 'Well, you just blew my story.' "

He added that Skip Bayless of the *Dallas Times-Herald*, at times, already had his mind made up about an approach he was going to take to a story and would do so regardless of what he found out to the contrary.

"Bayless has what he thinks is this trick, where he'll call you about something and pretend he agrees with your side," said Schramm. "Oh, he'll say something like, 'Hey, what do you think of those damn players making all that money? That situation is really getting out of hand.' I'll say, 'Well, the salaries are escalating.' Then

I know damn well what he's going to write. He'll pull a couple of quotes out of his hat and have me complaining about escalating salaries and write something like, by god, 'The players are the game and should be making more money.'

"There are some who'll sacrifice accuracy just to try to be clever and impress their contemporaries. That's a poor motivation at the expense of what's correct.

"I don't like it either when they use an 'unnamed source.' Now that's a helluva note. Somebody supposedly says something about you, and you're not allowed to confront your accuser. When we had all the Danny White-Gary Hogeboom trouble, they kept quoting unnamed sources as saying this or that about Danny. That's just a bunch of . . . "

Schramm paused, then grinned. He repeated that, as a group, he liked journalists and that the subject was closed. Then he thought for a while and opened it back up again.

In October of 1985 the *Miami News* printed a gigantic headline that usually is seen only if a war starts or, in the case of the Washington Post, if the Cowboys are coming to town to play the Redskins. The headline said: NFL, FBI Probing Allegations Cowboys Fixed Games for Coke.

The story was based on statements made by a former FBI agent who pleaded guilty to charges of bribery, conspiracy and possession of cocaine with the intent to distribute. The agent said a convicted drug smuggler told him five Cowboys fixed games in the early 1980's in exchange for three kilos of cocaine.

Teammates got a laugh when one of the players named was Danny White, who doesn't smoke and seldom drinks. But Schramm knew the damage had been done once again.

"When all the inquiries are made and when it has been found out there is no basis for any of this, you won't find a headline that big in any newspaper. It will be reported in a small story, buried somewhere, with a small headline."

By the end of the month FBI officials said there wasn't even any basis to investigate the allegations in the first place, that it was a nonissue. Schramm was correct about the stories which followed.

"Of course, I wasn't satisfied, but what can you do," he said. "It's like somebody who's convicted and goes to jail. Ten years later they find out he wasn't guilty, but he still spent those ten years in jail. It's a prime example of exploiting a story which has no basis. The unfortunate thing is that well-meaning members of the media and fans will continue to carry the impression with them that something like that happened in Dallas.

"Don't tell me the press isn't a lot like the courts, because you can be convicted, sentenced, and hung in the newspapers, too. If there's going to be that First Amendment, then a way ought to be found for a greater responsibility to go with it. Libel laws are sometimes ridiculous. You have to go so far to prove malice . . . Well, it's almost impossible.

"Some writers don't recognize the strength and impact they have on the public. They don't realize how many people think everything they read in the newspaper is totally accurate."

Schramm is also angered at times by what he calls "selective journalism." He questioned the integrity of reporters who secured a confidential file on drug tests the NFL had run on prospective draft choices in 1986 and printed the names of some who tested positive.

NFL scouting combines test college prospects on basic skills before the draft and also give them physicals, including drug tests. The players are told the results of the drug tests will be held in the strictest of confidence. But a reporter was able to get a list and printed some of the names of those who tested positive.

"I think something like that comes under the category of ethics," said Schramm. "They take the tests, because the results will remain secret. What we ought to do is go through all the newspapers around the country and give the reporters drug tests. Do you imagine some of them might test positive?"

Told that there probably would be a mass suicide of his public relations staff when some of his feelings about the newspaper business became known, Schramm smiled again and added, "They are allowed to criticize us."

The Cowboys' national popularity began in the late 1960's, which were the years when the younger generation began to revolt against The Establishment, the established way of doing things. In those years the Cowboys, in a way, were good for the times. There was the excitement of Hayes and Meredith, and no less than eight free agents, underdogs and people who were overlooked were in the starting lineup when Dallas played Green Bay for the NFL title in 1966. Two starters, Pete Gent and Cornell Green, had been basketball players in college, and Mike Gaechter and Hayes were more noted for track than football. Yet the Packers barely won the game, 34–27, after a great Dallas comeback fell short when Meredith was hurried into throwing an interception from the Packer two-yard-line in the final minute. The following year Green Bay once again beat Dallas in the final seconds for the NFL title, winning 21–17, in a game that became known as the Ice Bowl, because it was played in 16 below zero temperatures. Green Bay, The Establishment, had won the games but it was the Cowboys, the team from Texas, that would begin to capture the imagination of pro football fans throughout the country.

"Our popularity got started, and we wanted to keep it going," said Schramm. "And, frankly, I think we're probably just more image conscious than many other professional organizations."

There's a story about Gil Brandt that illustrates the lengths to which the Cowboys will go to gain fans. Years ago Brandt was sitting in his office when Penn State coach Joe Paterno called. "Brandt," he said, "you don't miss a bet. My kid's a big Cowboy fan, and I couldn't figure out why. Then I saw him wearing a Cowboy T-shirt and knew you'd sent it to him."

Brandt, with Schramm's carte blanche, sends fountain pens, brochures, T-shirts, etc., to college coaches and players all over the country. He also sends them to children of coaches. Schramm hopes they'll grow up to be Cowboy fans.

The Cowboys are everywhere. They set up a hospitality room for visitors and the press at the hotel in which they stay on the road and even have one at the NCAA basketball tournament. When the tournament was held in Dallas, Brandt sent Indiana coach Bobby Knight a basket of strawberries. Knight loves strawberries.

"Again," said Schramm, "none of these things would have worked if we hadn't been winning.

"I'm also very history conscious and admit it. I know Tom says he doesn't worry about how he'll be remembered, but I certainly care how this organization is remembered. We were a dominant team for 20 years. Our reputation has suffered, and now I want to build it back and see it extended. We've turned the team over and won Super Bowls with different casts of players. (Only Staubach, Harris, and Jethro Pugh were starters for the championship teams in 1971 and 1978.) We just missed making the Super Bowl a couple of other times in the early 1980s with still a different team.

"We had our first losing season since 1964 in 1986, but if we can get back on track and keep winning when the rules in the league and even the scheduling format are designed to preclude dominance by one team . . . If we can do it when every team we play counts it as an outstanding achievement to knock us off, then I think history will recognize us as one of the great teams, the great organizations, much as it did the New York Yankees in baseball during their heyday from the 1920's to the early 1960's. Now that was an organization! The players would come and go, and so would the coaches and club officials, but the organization maintained its excellence.

"There was so much pride. Everybody said when a player put on Yankee pinstripes that he automatically performed better. I'd like to think the same thing happens when a player puts on a Cowboy uniform.

"Hell no, I don't hide the fact I'm history conscious. I want the organization to be remembered in such a way that everybody who was a part of it—the players, coaches and people working in the front office—will look back and know they were a part of something special, something great.''

There was a slight traffic jam on Highway 5. We crept along slowly . . . slower.

"We'll be late for the Ram scrimmage now," said Schramm. "That's the thing about the freeways out here. You never know when something like this is going to happen."

He was silent for a while and then said, "Why the hell didn't the computer tell us there was a traffic jam! Now it'll probably tell us we're going to be late. Computers have no loyalty."

Schramm put loyalty right after winning. It made him think of a story. "When we first built our house in Dallas in 1961, I contacted a company called Superior and talked to their people about putting in a sprinkler system. Well, I checked around and decided the Hall Sprinkler Company would be better for what I wanted.

"The Superior people were mad as hell, but I wanted to keep goodwill with them, so I gave the company some season tickets and other favors."

About three years ago—some twenty-three years later—Schramm was going out of town on a holiday weekend, when the sprinkler system came on and would not shut off.

"We were in a panic," he said. "It was the weekend, and I couldn't get the people from Hall or anywhere to come out and turn it off or fix the damn thing. I couldn't leave, because our whole house would have sunk. So I finally called Superior."

"Listen," Schramm told the guy who answered, "I'm Tex Schramm, and I have problems with my sprinkler system. Have you got anybody who can come out and fix it, or at least find a way to turn it off? I don't care what it costs. We're leaving town, and I just need it turned off."

There was a long pause on the other end of the line, and then the guy said, "Fuck you! Call Hall!"

"Then," said Schramm, "he slammed down the telephone. Over twenty years and he still remembered. I bet that made his day. I can see it now. Everytime he saw my name in the newspaper all those years he got mad. Then he finally got his chance and jammed it to me." Schramm stared ahead at the stalled traffic. "But I really kinda like that. Now there's a company man for you."

chapter four

GROWING UP
LAID-BACK

The massive, complex, never-ending Los Angeles freeway system was begun in 1940 with the completion of the Pasadena Freeway. Further construction of freeways was put on hold during World War II, but throughout the 1950s and 1960s they were built to go in every direction as they passed over and around the large and small cities that have branched out from Los Angeles. We drove the San Bernardino Freeway en route to the Ram-Dallas scrimmage and then, to avoid traffic, Schramm's driver (a student at Cal Lutheran) moved onto the San Bernardino Freeway near Alhambra and San Gabriel.

"See all those buildings and things down there," said Schramm. "That's where I grew up. When I lived there, the freeways didn't exist. The whole countryside, as far as the eye could see, was covered with orange groves."

We were quiet. Schramm thought, remembered.

The orange groves are gone now, crowded out and then replaced by houses and parking lots and business establishments, and a mix of cultures that did not exist when Tex Schramm was growing up in San Gabriel, which is 35 miles from Los Angeles. There now is a very large Asian element which has taken its place amidst the Anglo and Mexican cultures in the 30,000 some odd population. The streets of San Gabriel and the adjoining city of Alhambra still have the old Spanish names and architecture that was influenced by their heritage. But there also is a Han Wan Supermarket, *The Chinese News* and, perhaps significant of the times, a small building shared by a dentist named Charles Cheng and Dr. A. J. Dega. Most stores have signs written in both English and Chinese.

The old San Gabriel Mission, from which the community got its name, still stands as a kind of punctuation mark, a pause to progress, with its capped buttresses and long narrow windows and coats of stone and brick and mortar. Its fountain and bell remain intact, and plaques tell of its history. On the side of the building someone has carved the initials HLS and MID, which do not belong to history but, perhaps, to a local high school student or an insensitive tourist.

Lt. Col. Juan Bautista de Anza, by degree of Carlos III of Spain, led an expedition to the site of the mission, which was founded by Father Junipero Serra in 1771 and is said to be the oldest building in Southern California and the first of 21 missions the Spanairds built in what is now California. It was from San Gabriel that a company of Spanish soldiers accompanied 11 families who crossed the Los Angeles River and founded the Pueblo de Nuestra la Reina de Los Angeles de Porciuncula, which became Los Angeles, the City of Angels.

San Gabriel is still a pretty city, its streets lined with palms, jacaranda trees, bottle bush and California poppies. But it isn't nearly as pretty as it must have been.

The two acres surrounding the two-story frame house in which Tex Schramm was raised is now mostly occupied by Safe Buy Used Cars, a Saab and Lincoln-Mercury dealer, and a Kentucky Fried Chicken. More than anything else, there are car lots on Las Tunas Drive instead of orange groves. The country club, which his father was instrumental in building and where he often played golf, remains across the street but seems somewhat like a mansion inhabited by a formerly wealthy family that is trying to keep up appearances after all the money is gone. Its beige brick walls are covered with ivy and there are some orange trees left on the course. In the parking lot older luxury cars are parked next to compact imports, both new and used.

At first the old Schramm residence wasn't there at 416 E. Las

Tunas Drive, but you could see the roof of a two-story frame house over the fence behind the car lots. It was the Schramm house, having been moved to the very back of the property to make room for more cars. Nobody answered the door nor did anybody seem to be living there, although there were remnants of people . . . a tricycle, toys, empty boxes. It was still a good, solid looking house with a chimney and a fine entrance, built with benches on both sides of the porch. But nobody was trying to keep up appearances as far as the house was concerned. It was different from the country club.

"I haven't been back to see the place since my mother died in the early 1960s," said Schramm. "I just drove by to look then. When my father had died in 1955, we moved my mother out of the house into an apartment.

"It was an odd feeling when I went back. Everything had changed so much. It just wasn't the place where I grew up. Time had passed and the way things were had gone. But, you know, you live in a place a long time as I did, and you still can imagine how it was in detail . . . the orange groves all over our property, the rose bushes around the house. I can imagine it so clearly that if you could just put me back into my room at that particular time when I was young, I could go through all the steps I once took, catching the red street car which went by our house, or getting a ride with my father to school, or driving the 1932 Ford I had my junior year in high school. When I think about it, everything comes back so clear."

Tex Schramm was born in 1920 when the 19th Amendment gave women the right to vote, Warren G. Harding was president, and mail was flown by air for the first time, although people were skeptical of sending letters that way. A left-handed pitcher named Babe Ruth was traded from Boston to the New York Yankees. They said he could hit fairly well, too, but you never knew about those things. And before Schramm started high school, there were flappers, the Charleston, gin in a tub, prohibition, speakeasies and Henry Ford's Model T. Women wore short dresses with waistlines below their middles, and in general, people had such optimism the great economic prosperity would never end that psychotherapist and philosopher Emile Coue seemed to sum up the general feeling very simply when he said, "Every day, in every way, I'm getting better and better."

Only a small minority of people knew about professional football, unless they were directly involved, but a group of men formed an organization in 1920 that was to become the National Football League. Professional football prior to the turn of that decade had been played on a kind of makeshift basis by company teams, athletic clubs and by rival cities such as Canton and Massillon, Ohio. They played the games on minor league baseball fields, using circus bleachers, and few of the game's stars got notice, except a fellow named Jim Thorpe. But the American Football Association was formed in 1920, and two years later, the 25-year-old player-coach of the Decatur, Illinois, Staleys moved his team to Chicago, renamed it the Bears and suggested the association change its name to the National Football League. The young man was George Halas, who later would play a key role in not only getting Tex Schramm the job as general manager of the Dallas Cowboys but also in gaining for the city a team in the first place. Halas also installed in Chicago a strange offensive alignment in those days, called the T-formation.

A lot of young men were taking Horace Greeley's advice and going West, escalating the population of California from two million at the beginning of the century to over five million by 1928. California had come into prominence during the Gold Rush and was a land of plenty. It had the ocean, the mountains and mild temperatures. Hollywood had replaced New York as the nation's movie capital. Oddly enough, as of 1910 no moving pictures had even been shown in Hollywood, because the city fathers felt that particular recreation was of dubious morality. But then men such as Mack Sennett, Cecil B. DeMille and Charlie Chaplin went to California, and the new industry began to boom.

Texas E. Schramm Sr., the youngest of a dozen children, and his bride, the former Elsa Steinwender, left San Antonio and joined the migration to California, settling in San Gabriel, a small, sleepy town through which a two-lane road led to Los Angeles. Mr. Schramm worked in Los Angeles but had decided the daily drive to and from the city wouldn't be that bad. A lot of other people already had begun to think like that in those days, and they were pioneers of the age of commuting. The senior Mr. Schramm, who was in the brokerage business, was of German descent, his parents having come from Germany and settled in New Braunfels, later moving to San Antonio. He had gone to the University of Texas and became an outstanding basketball player in the early 1900s. Elsa's first husband was an army man, stationed in San Antonio.

Her father was Julius Steinwender, one of the most prominent coffee brokers in New York. When he died, he left Elsa and her four sisters a large trust.

"I can remember when I was very small, my father took us back to Texas to visit my grandparents," recalls Tex. "They lived in a big house and had a pecan orchard. My grandmother was very sick, and they wouldn't let me see her. They called my grandfather, "Captain," because he had been in the army. There was a main, large staircase in the living room and another one in the kitchen. Their house looked like something out of one of those horror movies I'd seen. It used to scare me.

"Half of my father's family were boys. But, would you believe, when I die there will be no more Schramms? I was the only male child in the family, and I have three girls."

The Schramms were affluent, well adjusted and a leading family in San Gabriel. The senior Mr. Schramm was so respected that his advice often was sought in the community.

"He was a tremendous person," said Alan Cameron, a classmate of Mr. Schramm's son, Tex. "He was one of the reasons I stayed at the Naval Academy. At the end of the war I went to talk to Mr. Schramm about my options. He advised me to stay in the Navy.

"My gosh," he said, "you can retire with $500 a month. You'd have it made. You came this far. Stay in."

Cameron, now a retired navy man living near San Diego, took Mr. Schramm's advice. He later became athletic director at the Naval Academy and advised a young man named Roger Staubach that he might be better off signing with the Dallas Cowboys than the Kansas City Chiefs. Both teams wanted to sign Staubach after he graduated and gamble he'd be able to play professional football after finishing his four-year obligation to the navy.

Elsa Schramm is said by those who remember her to have been a very motherly woman, who often doted over her son, spoiling him to a degree.

When Tex started school something went wrong, and his father and mother became very concerned and puzzled. Tex kept flunking. He failed the first, second and third grades, and they not only had to hire a tutor to help him but had to send him to summer school each year. Nobody could understand what the problem was. He seemed very bright, alert and had a sharp mind but tended to be impatient in class and often would cut up. His attention span was very short. At first they thought he was just lazy, a term used in those days to describe someone who had problems in school. Teachers finally told the Schramms that, perhaps, their son simply had a learning disability.''

"If they hadn't kept hiring tutors, I'd have been so far behind I'd never have finished," recalls Tex. "But, finally, I just became so disruptive in class that they sent me to military school."

The Schramms believed their son didn't have enough discipline at home and that life in a military school might straighten him out. They didn't want him to go, and Elsa barely could stand the thought of him leaving, but they wanted to do what was best for him.

"In order to get a weekend pass to go home from military school, a student had to avoid a certain amount of demerits," said Tex. "So for eleven straight weekends, I had to stay at school, because I had too many demerits.

"Oh, I liked some of the things about the school—the drills, for instance. Somebody took a snapshot of me in uniform, sitting on top of a tank. I once showed it to a girl to try to impress her. She said I looked like a general. Naturally, I let her think whatever she wanted.

"Then I got sick with measles and almost died. That, along with the fact I never got to come home, caused my parents to change their minds. They just finally said to heck with it—we want our son home. So they put me back into public school for my sixth-grade year. Right. I promptly failed the first semester."

The teachers didn't know at the time that Schramm was a hyperactive child. He had problems staying put. He had to be challenged mentally, or he'd lose interest. More and more these days, teachers understand hyperactive students and are able to motivate and deal with them.

"My grandson, Shane, is the same way," said Tex. "I can see so much of my youth and problems I had in him. I think what I went through helped me better understand and help him."

"Two of my step children have learning disabilities," Pete Rozelle said. "My wife, Carrie, has a big fund-raising dinner each year to help children who have the problem. They were putting out this magazine for the fund raiser, and Tex wrote this nice column for it, explaining what he had gone through. There were 75,000 copies sent out. But because of what Tex has done and made of himself, it has to be very encouraging for parents of children with the problem and also for the children. A lot of people stay in the closet on something like that. Tex didn't. And he doesn't even like to write letters.''

Eventually, Tex was able to blend in and graduate from Alhambra High School, where students from San Gabriel also attended. He would not be a leader in scholastics but in just about everything else he tried.

To this day Schramm isn't able to sit down and read a book or play card games. He's just too hyper, too restless. The only two books he's read in his life are Mario Puzo's *The Godfather* and a long forgotten biography of Wyatt Earp. The only consistent reading he does are newspaper stories. He scans all stories on the Cowboys to see if anything controversial has been written. Anybody who has ever covered the team and been what Schramm considered unfairly critical will attest to this.

In the mid-1930s when Tex Schramm was in Alhambra High School, freeways did not rush traffic past or over nameless towns, so motorists had to drive through communities such as San Gabriel and Alhambra. Automobiles had become prevalent, especially in California with its vast space and affluence. By 1938, 35,000 Americans would die from accidents involving the contraptions that, contrary to the beliefs of many, replaced the horse and buggy. But the primary transportation for the people of San Gabriel was the streetcar, painted red and holding magnetically to the tracks, as it slowly but surely dropped them off near their destinations. They called it simply, the Red Car. Small bungalows and some large homes, such as the one occupied by the Schramms, dotted the area but were not squeezed in, and there was space for orange groves and palm trees and vacant fields and lots in which to play. You did not have to go to the park to play. Most of the city was a park.

San Gabriel was touched, as was everywhere, but not devastated by that Black Thursday in October of 1929 and its aftermath, which sent the country reeling as it never had before and probably will never do so again. The high-rolling Roaring Twenties crashed with the stock market, and at the peak of the Depression in 1932-33, 12 to 15 million Americans were unemployed and 25 to 30 million people stood in bread lines and ate in makeshift soup kitchens, set up to try to keep them from starving. The situation began to improve steadily after New York Governor Franklin Delano Roosevelt easily won the presidency over Republican incumbent Herbert Hoover, a man blamed by most for the country's downfall. Millions huddled around their radios and found hope when Roosevelt delivered his inaugural address in March, 1933.

" . . . This great nation will endure as it has endured, will revive and prosper . . . So first let me assert my firm belief that the only thing we have to fear is fear itself . . . nameless, unjustified terror which paralyzes needed effort to convert retreat into advance. . . . "

Roosevelt's National Recovery Act created fair competition among businessmen and set maximum hours of labor and new minimum-wage levels, and the Work Progress programs put hundreds of jobless to work on state and government projects, such as bridges and parks. The Federal Emergency Relief Administration furnished $20 million in wages and relief payments.

"My father was in stocks but didn't go down the drain like so many others when the market crashed," recalls Schramm. "The only real exposure I had was my half brother (his mother's son by her first marriage), who was twelve years older than I was. His name was Fitzgerald B. Alderdice, and he apparently lost heavily. He had gone to Stanford but then quit so that he could make a bundle in the stock market.

"We lived in a kind of neighborhood which, I suppose, was just not subject to the Depression that much. I was shielded to a great extent, although I was aware that there were such things as bread lines, stuff like that."

Schramm was fortunate in that his parents took him with them to so many places, such as football games, movies, shows and to Ocean Park where they played bingo, while he tried his hand at various carnival games.

"You couldn't play bingo for money," recalls Schramm. "So, if you won, they'd pay in cartons of cigarettes. That's how they got around the gambling laws. But I also remember going with my parents to gambling ships that were anchored outside the three-mile (gambling) area."

He became an expert in the games at Ocean Park, such as knocking over bottles with a softball, and had shelves at home full of dolls, caricatures of Olive Oil, Popeye, Mickey Mouse and the cartoon characters of the time. In fact he became so adept that he was barred from playing some of the games.

"As I look back, I know how fortunate I was that my parents exposed me to so many things," he said.

The Thirties were a time when people had a great fascination with airplanes and the men and women who flew them. They followed the exploits of Charles Lindbergh, Admiral Richard Byrd and Amelia Earhart. Air circuses, featuring stunt pilots and barnstorming daredevils and wingwalkers, were popular, and traffic and work would literally stop when a light plane flew overhead. *Wings*, a silent World War I film about men and their flying machines, won the first Academy Award. Schramm said the movie left a big impression on him. It starred Buddy Rogers and Richard Arlen, flyers who both loved the same woman, played by Clara Bow. In the final reel Rogers unknowingly shoots down Arlen and escapes through enemy lines in a stolen plane. A tall, lanky newcomer, Gary Cooper, had a small role in the film.

"Well, you fantasized about being a pilot like those in the movie," said Schramm. "Of course, when I fantasized I always got the girl."

Shirley Temple charmed movie audiences, and Boris Karloff and Bela Lugosi scared them, and Charlie Chaplin made them laugh. And people sang "April in Paris," "Stormy Weather," and Hoagy Carmichael's "Georgia on my Mind," a song that would become a hit again in the 1980s.

They watched William Powell and Myrna Loy in *The Great Ziegfeld* and might not have noticed Lana Turner, Judy Garland and Hedy Lamarr among the Ziegfeld beauties. They tried to emulate Fred Astaire, danced to the big band sounds of Glenn Miller, Fred Waring, Benny Goodman and Kay Kayser with his Kollege of Musical Knowledge and listened to the vocals of Rudy Vallee, the first of the popular crooners, and a young man named Bing Crosby. Women's hemlines dropped with fashions, and ladies wanted the Garbo-look, with pronounced cheekbones, a fuller, painted mouth and pencil-thin arched eyebrows and feathery eyelashes.

Gas sold for anywhere from 10 to 25 cents per gallon, magazines were 10 to 25 cents, and automobiles had begun to change to the rounded more bulky look with headlights sticking out of fenders like eyes bulging from a monster. A new herringbone sports suit sold for $18.50 and a 1936 Dodge for $640. You could buy a hot-dog for a nickle and a hamburger for a dime. Cathedral shaped radios sold for $9.95 to $50, and you had to pay the unheard price of $575 for a four-legged RCA Radiola with six to eight tubes and a 78 RPM phonograph.

When Tex Schramm was growing up the radio was the focal point of family entertainment. Gabriel Heatter, Drew Pearson, H. V. Kaltenborn and Lowell Thomas gave the news, and people were glued to their favorite drama, adventure or musical show. The most popular program was Amos and Andy, the adventures of two black characters from Harlem, played by two white, former vaudevillians, Freeman Gosden and Charles Correll. The 15-minute show, Monday through Friday night, had a listening audience of 30 million. People also liked the Jack Benny show and Fibber McGee and Molly. That program always started with Fibber opening the hall closet and the subsequent crash. "I've got to straighten out that closet one of these days," said Fibber. But he never did.

Mothers relaxed in the afternoons with shows such as *Mary Noble, Backstage Wife:* "The story of Mary Noble, an Iowa girl who marries Larry Noble, handsome matinee idol, dream sweetheart of a million other women, and her struggles to keep his love in the complicated atmosphere of backstage life. Brought to you by Dr. Lyons' tooth powder."

Schramm was like most of the other kids his age in that he was lured by many popular serials on radio, such as *The Lone Ranger,* whose adventures were brought to you by "Wheaties, the Breakfast of Champions," and *Tom Mix,* who told his listeners, "I'll send you my mystery ring *"freee"* for two Ralston boxtops, or one Ralston box top and ten cents in coin." Or you could get badges, watches and be a member of the Dick Tracy Secret Service Patrol.

Dashiell Hammett became popular with *The Thin Man,* and people read Raymond Chandler and listened to the radio shows which said crime did not pay. Some real-life dramas seemed to back this up during the 1930s when crime didn't pay for Al Capone, who ended up in prison and, after his release, died a broken, diseased man, and when noted gangsters John Dillinger, Pretty Boy Floyd, Baby Face Nelson, and Bonnie Parker and Clyde Barrow, all were gunned down by authorities.

One of Schramm's favorite shows was *The Witch's Tale,* which advertised chilling stories told by Nancy, a 117-year-old witch and her yowling black cat, Satan. You listened if you had "the fascination for the eerie, weird, blood-chilling tales . . . They're waiting for you NOWWWW!"

People got into their jalopies and flocked from the Dust Bowls of Oklahoma to California, attracted by adventure and mildness of climate which was better to endure privation even if they found their dreams unfulfilled. The KKK ran rampant in the South, although, ironically, two of the most famous athletes of the 1930s were black men such as Joe Louis, who lost to and then beat the German Max Schmeling for the heavyweight championship, and Jesse Owens, who in 1936 went to the Olympics in Berlin and embarrassed Hitler and his so-called Super Race by winning four gold medals. Schramm had listened to the radio and read about sports since his early memories.

And the National Football League, of which he one day would became an integral part, had become an established commodity, with stars like Bronco Nagurski, Sammy Baugh, Don Hutson, Davey O'Brien, Ernie Nevers, Johnny Blood and a naging Red Grange. Top executives were Art Rooney, Bert Bell, George Preston Marshall, Tim Mara, Earl (Curly) Lambeau and, of course, George Halas. One day Schramm would meet and be influenced by some of these men.

Tex Schramm, the new sports editor of the *Alhambra High School Moor*, was not particularly enamored by professional sports. He had cheered for Southern California's Trojans against Notre Dame and been taken by his father to the 1932 Olympics in the new Los Angeles Coliseum, which would remain a bastion of amateur sports until Dan Reeves moved his professional team there from Cleveland.

In his first sports column in the fall of 1936, Schramm told his readers that he was always open to suggestions from them and ended by telling of an incident that had come to his attention which involved a high school football player, who might have gone on to become an All-American at UCLA. Schramm wrote that the young man had left his high school to go to a smaller college to try to get his grades up to the necessary level to enter USC.

"But this summer," wrote Schramm, "baseball moguls took an interest in him and before long he had signed in the money racket. He is no longer with the club that signed him but was farmed out to a smaller team. Nobody knows how he will do from now on, but if he doesn't make the grade a potential great college career will have been sacrificed for a small salary. We hope luck for his sake but would like to see something done to curb this signing of young stars before they have a chance to complete their high school and college careers."

In those days Schramm often thought how the professionals were contaminating amateurs and expressed his opinion. Reminded how he felt at the time, Schramm said, "Well, I wasn't enlightened then."

Besides his early interest in journalism, the root of which was his interest in sports, Schramm also developed a passion for fishing. His parents had a second home at Manhattan Beach, south of Los Angeles, and he was strongly attracted to the ocean and fishing.

"Back then you could fish right off the pier and catch halibut, barracuda, bonita and all kinds of fish," he said. "They're gone now. You can't do that anymore. You have to go out into the ocean to get them. But we'd go to the beach in the summers, and I'd go fishing every morning. I'd go home for lunch and then down to the beach and swim or body surf. Hey, I'd make money, too, although I guess my family might have had enough, because I wasn't required to work. But I'd sell bait to people around the area who wanted to go fishing and would get a nice, tidy little sum."

Martha Anne Snowden, who also attended Alhambra High and would become Mrs. Tex Schramm, has a pet name for Tex. She calls him "Tec." That's what his mother had called his father. She recalled, "Tec might have been a little better off than most of the kids he ran around with, but you'd never know it. He'd dress like the other kids. I remember sometimes he'd show up for our dates in a suit, but he'd have on an old sweat shirt under it.

"His father was an avid golfer and spent a lot of time at the country club. Tec caddied some but didn't play much or spend a lot of time there. I think it was because so many of his friends weren't members."

There was a time, however, that Schramm did take what some might consider undue advantage of his affluence. "I tried out and got the lead in the school play," he said. "I played the part of a gangster. I suppose the fact that I got the part might have had something to do with the fact that I had access to my father's big overcoat. The part I played called for me to wear a big, expensive overcoat. My father might have been the only dad in town to have one of them. I wasn't about to let somebody else wear it."

When Tex was a junior in high school, his parents bought him a 1932 Ford coupe which, he admitted, "was a helluva deal at that time." Few students had their own cars. The coupe gave Tex and his friends the freedom of not having to depend on their parents or the streetcar to get them places. They could drive to the beach on weekends or to the Civic Auditorium in Pasadena or to the Palomar or Paladium and dance to the music of the big bands or go over to catch a steamboat to Catalina, the small island some twenty-five miles off the coast of California. He'd also drag race on the streets, a practice that became so dangerous that participants were told to move to a nearby salt flat. Eventually, this would become a popular sport in this country. The car also gave them easier access to the movies, where they could not only see the feature but also a vaudeville-type act for a quarter.

Schramm's classmates remember him as a friendly, nice looking guy with blond hair but also one who was figuring all the angles. The fact that he was sports editor of the school paper and the annual, and also was a pretty good athlete didn't hurt him with the young ladies.

"I thought he was cute, but he didn't ask me out, so I made the first move to get a date with him," said Marty. "I just arranged a situation. . . I can't remember exactly what it was . . . for us to meet. I was a sophomore, and he was a senior.

"We danced, went to movies, things like that. I remember that when we were dating our favorite movie was *Dark Victory* with Betty Davis. Our song was, "Once in a While.""

"Once in a while, won't you try to give one little thought to me. . . . "

Marty thought for a while and said, "We'd go roller-skating. I kid him about that even now, because he told Joe Bailey and his wife that he once roller-skated from San Gabriel to Long Beach. Why, that would take an hour in a car right now. What he actually did was ride his bicycle there. Sometimes he just gets confused.

"We argued quite a bit, and my mother never thought we'd make it. But we've been married over forty years, so I guess there was something to it."

Pete Rozelle and Don Shula both said Marty Schramm was such a nice person. "She's unusual, just super," said Shula. Rozelle said it was amazing how cool she stayed during Schramm's outbursts. Once during a Schramm tirade in a hotel room in Philadelphia the night before a game, she sat quietly working a crossword puzzle.

Marty continued, "Even in high school Tec wanted things, more or less, his way," Marty continued. "So we'd break up, get back together and break up again. Still, we had a lot of fun. The thing I liked best was when we'd go dancing. Tec was a good dancer. He won't dance now. I guess I danced him all out in those days."

Schramm had some problems concentrating in class, but outside of school he was forever the organizer. In grammar school he sold more tickets to a school play than anybody else and set an all-time record, at that time, for selling tickets in high school to a puppet show. He also played football in grammar school and talked to coaches, civic leaders and organized an all-star elementary school football game between grammar schools from San Gabriel and Alhambra.

When he started to go to Alhambra High, the school had only

varsity and B-teams in football. Whether a student was placed on
the varsity or B-team depended on how much he weighed. Schramm
weighed only 96 pounds and that was too small even for the B-team.
No matter. He got all the other kids together in his weight group
and organized a C-team.

"We didn't have a coach or uniforms," he said. "I was manager
of the track team, which was coached by a guy I really liked, Ken
Grumbles. He'd been a trackman at Southern Cal, so that always
impressed me. I talked him into being the coach of the new C-team
in football.

"Coach Grumbles had this theory that you could tell if a guy
was fast or not by looking at his knees. So when all the little guys
came out for the C-team, he looked at our knees. He picked out
eleven guys he figured were the fastest. He put me at center. He
figured I was a 95-pounder with fast knees. He had me out of position. I was a running back, but I forgave him for making that
mistake."

The C-teamers had to furnish their own uniforms. Some had
helmets, and others had pads, so they were a rag-tag looking bunch.
Schramm got another brainstorm. He started goading some of the
B-teamers who had uniforms. He informed them that they probably
couldn't even make the C-team and were only where they were
because they were bigger. His tactics were so effective that the B-
teamers challenged the C-team to a game, the winner getting the
uniforms.

"It was a helluva game," said Schramm. "We lost so they got
to keep their uniforms and we had the same old bits and pieces.
But, as you might have noticed, we had nothing to lose and the
uniforms to gain.

"We also scheduled some games with other B-teams in the area,
so we had plenty of competition. I did have some problems
remembering plays. Maybe I was just too busy scheming. But I wrote
the plays down on the thigh pads of my football pants. When I'd
bend over to center the ball, I'd look at the pants to see what I was
supposed to do."

His junior year Schramm was big enough to make the B-team.
He played fullback, and teammate Johnny Seixas remembered Tex
once breaking 70 yards for a touchdown against heated rival Long
Beach Poly.

"Tex didn't have a temper then like I hear he does now," said
Seixas, now retired from teaching and coaching. "But he was a very

aggressive player. He was a good team player. Football and sports were such a big thing to him.

"In those days we just played sports, and nobody seemed to get into much trouble. Oh, we'd sometimes have fights, using oranges from the groves. We'd pick them up and throw them at rival players."

"We were," said Dave Haskell, another former teammate of Schramm's and a retired teacher, "very square back then. Hey, I remember getting balled out for chewing gum in class. One time I also got caught by the teacher for wiggling my ears. She sent me to the office." He laughed. "I can still wiggle my ears."

"Tex was in my civics and history classes at Alhambra," said Charles Scanlon. "He wasn't a bad student when he concentrated. He was always just so interested in sports and girls that it took up his study time.

"No. No, I never dreamed he'd make a profession out of sports nor become what he is today. He was a go-getter, but I just couldn't see him in a role like being president of the Dallas Cowboys.

"I will say this. He hasn't forgotten his old teacher. I was in Dallas during the mid-1970s and decided I'd just go by and see him. He invited me right in. We talked and he was very nice. That made me feel good, you know."

Alhambra had a good B-team. "We played Long Beach Poly for the B-team championship," said Schramm. "They just beat the shit out of us. They had a lot of guys playing for them who were older. They'd been in the service and come back to finish school. Some of them must have been in their 20s. They just clobbered us. Then somebody found out Long Beach Poly had some guys on the B-team who were ineligible. They had to forfeit, and we got the title. No, I can't remember how they were found out."

Letter sweaters were only awarded to varsity players. But Schramm figured the B-team had won a championship and should be thusly honored. So he went around and talked to various merchants in town and convinced them they should chip in and buy sweaters for the B-team champions. That was another first. But Schramm always has been a good salesman.

"He was that," said Haskell, who was captain of the Alhambra varsity and received a football scholarship to Southern Cal. "And the thing you have to remember about Tex in those days was that he was sports editor of the student publications and, well, was doing his own publicity."

Schramm seemed pleased with the recollection. "I was a fullback on the varsity my senior year," he explained. "We had this one guy, George Leyrer, who was our best ball carrier, our star. He carried the ball almost all the time and I'd just block, running just a few times. But when I listed the final statistics in our annual, I put my name first, ahead of his, because I had the best average per carry."

The list is as follows: 1. Tex Schramm, an 8.1 average on nine carries; 2. George Leyrer, a 5.7 average on 63 carries.

Tex also went out for track because of his friendship for Coach Grumbles. He ended up being the team manager. "I just wasn't what you'd call a great one for training," he said. "I remember going out and running around the track and thinking how ridiculous that was. Coach Grumbles thought I might be able to run the 880, so I tried. I looked around me and figured I was the fastest one in the race. I thought I'd just jog along, toying with them, and then turn on my speed and run off and leave everybody in the stretch. My god, they took off right at the beginning. After about 100 yards, I was 50 behind and tired as hell. That first race ended my track career in high school. I became the team manager."

Schramm had become intrigued with journalism and decided his final year in high school that it would be his profession. "They had this seminar in journalism at the University of California in Berkeley, and I walked around the campus and went to Phi Kappa Psi fraternity house. That had been my father's fraternity at the University of Texas. I had gotten much bigger at the time, and apparently some of the football recruits were on campus at the same time. So some guys in the fraternity thought I was a football player visiting their campus. No, I didn't say anything to the contrary. I kind of liked the way they were treating me.

"Then they called the head coach and one of them said, 'Coach, great news. We've got Tex Schramm visiting here.' So the coach just said, 'Who the hell is he?' Well, that blew my cover."

Schramm had to attend Pasadena Junior College to get his grades in order to be accepted at the University of Texas. "We had a great junior college team," he said. "Jackie Robinson was a running back, but wasn't that big a deal because there were so many stars there then. I never met him. I just know he lettered in four sports, but nobody dreamed of him becoming such a baseball star."

In order to avoid taking a physical education course, Schramm found out he could get the same credit by running intramural track.

For some reason he did very well. He ran a 10.2 and a 10.1 in the 100-yard dash.

He went back to visit his friend at Alhambra, Ken Grumbles. Tex told him during the course of their conversation that he had done very well in junior college as a sprinter. Coach Grumbles was, needless to say, somewhat reluctant to believe this about his former team manager who almost got lapped running the 880. But in the spirit of competition, he set up a race between Tex and his top sprinters. Schramm won.

"What the hell were you doing pissing around as a manager all those years?" asked Grumbles. "Why didn't you tell me you could sprint like that?"

"You never asked me."

It also was while attending junior college that Schramm went to work at the Santa Anita race track. He'd go to class in the mornings and work as an usher at the track in the afternoons.

"That was kind of a glamour job," he said. "I loved it and learned a helluva lot about betting on horses. I learned that you're a damned fool if you think you're going to beat them on any regular basis and that people who are never going to win are the ones who go out every weekend and bet all the races.

"Sure, I won some money. You learn how the horses work and know a little more about how they might do on a particular day. I also read all the racing and breeding magazines. I can remember winning several hundred dollars one day, a lot of money in those times.

"Each usher had a section of people in boxes to take care of. I got to know these people really well, and sometimes they'd even buy me tickets on a race. I listened, learned. If they hit one they might tip you fifty bucks. I got a big kick out of the whole experience. We had baseball games between the ushers and jockeys right on the infield of the track when the races weren't going on.

"The people in my box knew my father, too. I remember after I came back from the war as a captain in the Air Force. I went immediately to the track in my uniform. I felt very proud, dressed like that, when I saw the people I had taken care of five, six years earlier. They seemed proud of me, too. I never lost my love for horse racing."

He got his credits straightened out—at least he thought he had—and enrolled at the University of Texas, following the footsteps of his father who believed the school and the experience of living in the state would benefit his son. But when he tried to take a required journalism lab his second year, it was discovered that he had no high school credit in typing, a prerequisite. He had taken typing only long enough to learn the keys and then dropped the course. But there he was at Texas, ready to take an important course. Something had to be done.

"I had this friend working at Alhambra High and called him," said Schramm. "He changed my transcript so that it showed I had a credit in typing.

"So the rules were bent a little for me, as you read they sometimes are nowadays for superstars and All-America football players to be. I was off to Austin to seek stardom in football. In fact I hadn't even tried to play at Pasadena, because I was saving myself for the Longhorns."

In his quest for stardom on the gridiron, Schramm was to have a very vivid but enlightening experience.

chapter five

FRIENDS AND FOES

Schramm and his entourage in the Riviera with the computer voice arrived late for the Cowboys and Rams scrimmage in Fullerton but missed only some of the warmup exercises and part of the pass skeleton drills and none of the actual scrimmage. Just as Tex walked onto the field, he saw Georgia Frontiere, the former Mrs. Carroll Rosenbloom, riding around the field in a golf cart. She saw Schramm, waved and smiled, and then motored over to where he was standing. She was having problems signing star running back Eric Dickerson so, with Schramm's Dorsett trouble, they had something in common.

Carroll Rosenbloom had been one of the five men who had bought the original Dallas Texans, who had been turned back to the league, and relocated them in Baltimore. He spent $200,000 for 51 percent and was overseer as the Colts climbed to the NFL title.

After Robert Irsay bought the Rams from the estate of the late Dan Reeves, he began talking to Rosenbloom regarding a most unusual proposal. Irsay wanted to somehow get back East and take his football team with him. So they explored the possibilities of swapping franchises. Rosenbloom could hardly hold back his enthusiasm. In Southern California his team not only would have a much larger area from which to attract fans, but also a vast television market, things that were lacking in Baltimore. When the deal was finalized, Schramm said it should rank right up there with the Great Train Robbery.

"That has to go down as one of the most ridiculous transactions in the history of professional sports," said Schramm. "Carroll knew it but you couldn't blame him for doing it. Imagine trading Los Angeles for Baltimore."

Schramm and Rosenbloom had sometimes clashed, yet remained friends. But in the mid-1970s, they had a falling out that caused a number of ramifications. Rosenbloom not only withdrew from the scouting combine with the Cowboys but also stopped using the Cowboys as the Rams' opponent in the annual Times-Charity preseason game.

"He took a stand at the NFL meeting that involved the commissioner," said Schramm. "I can't even remember the specifics. I didn't even realize it was all that important. Anyway, to prove a point he said something that had been told him in confidence, which didn't have any bearing on the situation. But he had broken a confidence and asked me to verify it, because I'd heard the same thing. I wouldn't. He was more angry with me than I realized. I didn't even know he wasn't speaking to me anymore until a year later."

This bothered Schramm, because he thought the whole thing was unnecessary. They had been so close at one time that Rosenbloom, informally, had asked Schramm if he might be interested in returning to Los Angeles to run the Rams. Schramm admitted the subject had come up, but that it was just conversation and he never took it seriously.

Around noon on April 2, 1979, Carroll Rosenbloom, vacationing with his wife Georgia in the south Florida resort town of Golden Beach, was taking his daily swim in the ocean. He swam out farther and farther, and then witnesses said he began to yell and flail his arms.

A French-Canadian, Raymond Tanguay, watching from the beach, grabbed a board and swam out to try to help him. He reached Rosenbloom, but each time he'd get him on the board, a wave would wash him off. The police had been summoned, and two officers went into the water and helped Tanguay get Rosenbloom to shore. He was dead at age 72.

Rosenbloom jogged, swam and worked out with weights, but had had a heart bypass operation a few years earlier. His son, Steve, took over operation of the club and said, frankly, he did not believe his father's death was accidental. Before a Public Broadcasting Service questioned the accidental death and hinted Rosenbloom might have had links with organized gambling, Steve accidentally fell out of a car and fractured his skull. For 20 years Rosenbloom had groomed his son to take over the club but after his death, Georgia, who inherited 70 percent of the team, fired Steve, who apparently did not get along with general manager Don Klosterman. The PBS show quoted Tanguay as saying he'd seen a dark figure in the water swimming away from Rosenbloom, the implication being it might have been a man dressed in a frogman's suit. Rosenbloom's death was ruled accidental, but the controversy continues. Schramm said he had no doubts the drowning was accidental.

"I've been swimming in the ocean enough to know what can happen," he said. "At that particular place, there will be a sequence of four, five, six big waves coming in and then the waters will roll back out to sea. They're strong going back out, and there's an undertow and a riptide effect. If you're out there swimming at a certain time, it's very difficult to swim and fight those elements. I've been caught many times and have had problems getting back. After his heart operation, I believe Carroll just didn't have the stamina and couldn't make it.

"Only weeks before his death, we'd had dinner at his home and seemed to be friends again. I was glad we did that."

As he walked around the field and talked to various Ram officials, Schramm had an unusual feeling. "It's just that a big part of my life was spent with the Rams, and I come out here now and nobody I knew is still around the team. They're all gone."

His thoughts were, perhaps, some concession to the changes that come when you get older. But he lingered on them only briefly. Schramm moves on and, unlike most men in their mid-60s, he doesn't become overly absorbed with the aging process, nor preoccupy himself with the past. He remembers the past, thinks about it, and then goes forward. Literally speaking, Marty might be right when she says Tex doesn't dance much anymore because he's all danced out. But figuratively speaking, if you will, Tex Schramm is still a man who dances every dance.

The scrimmage was like other scrimmages but was well attended. The Rams were more open, like the Cowboys, rather than closed, like the Raiders. One guy watching was Mel Renfro, the former

All-Pro defensive back during the Cowboys' heyday. He was living in the Los Angeles area and had come to visit some of his old coaches. Mel said he was having some physical problems, due to old football injuries, and was looking for a line of work. He was one of the many players who got out of football practically broke, due to bad advice, bad investments, etc. He'd worked for a while in the Cowboys' scouting department and then became a beer distributor. Then he'd been an assistant coach with the Los Angeles team in the USFL. The team didn't make it.

When the Cowboys had their twenty-fifth anniversary reunion in Dallas, Mel was short of money. He once had made Schramm terribly angry over a contract dispute when he said he was going to start playing like he was paid, hinting he might be giving a lesser effort if he didn't get more money. But he eventually had signed and, as usual, had an outstanding season. Schramm paid Mel's way to the reunion and also rented a tux for him. After Cowboy assistant Gene Stallings became head coach at St. Louis, he hired Mel as an assistant.

But that summer Stallings had been an assistant with the Cowboys and lauded defensive lineman David Ponder. He had told Schramm to keep his eye on Ponder during the scrimmage. Ponder had been the final cut of 1984 but was making a strong bid to make the club in the summer of 1985. Schramm had watched him but said he could see nothing special. He mentioned this to Stallings after the scrimmage and, suddenly, they got into a brief yelling match.

"That's bullshit!" said Schramm, and you could hear his voice for 25 yards. "I watched him and saw nothing. He's just like some of those other greats who turn out to be nothings."

"That's because you don't look for the things coaches look for," said Stallings, who was talking loud but, like most people, is no match for Schramm's booming voice. "You just don't know what to look for."

"Bullshit! You guys always think you have some great secrets. But you see what you see!"

They were right in each other's face for a few minutes, and then each walked away, Stallings going toward the team bus and Schramm coming back to the Riviera that talked.

"My god," Schramm was asked. "What was that all about?"

"What? Oh that. Nothing. We just have this friendly, ongoing discussion about certain players."

"Well, you seemed very angry."

"What? Mad? No. I'm not mad. Gene's a friend of mine."

David Ponder tried very hard but did not make the team in 1985. Schramm and Stallings were joking and laughing at practice the next afternoon.

Late July into early August that year had been a frustrating time for Schramm. Marty and others in his family were in Newport Beach when they received a call from a neighbor in Dallas that Schramm's son-in-law, Jim Bob Smith, had suffered a heart attack and was in intensive care.

"I can't believe that," said Schramm. "He's 42 years old, thin, plays sports and is in great shape. He'd just had a physical in May and was okay. It's just not fair. Look at me. That should have been me instead of him."

Jim Bob Smith recovered. Headlines in the *Los Angeles Times* both shocked and depressed everybody. A Delta airline jet, carrying 160 people, crashed on its final approach to Dallas-Fort Worth Airport, killing 122 of the 160 people aboard and a motorist. The plane had tried to land in a thunderstorm, and its crash was the worst air disaster in Texas history. That motorist was almost Tom Landry's wife, Alicia. She was going to D-FW to pick up Landry, who had flown in from Thousand Oaks. They had planned to go together to the Hall of Fame in Canton, Ohio, where Tom would induct Roger Staubach. As she drove to the toll station at the entrance of the airport, she looked back and saw an enormous burst of smoke. She had missed by perhaps a minute or less driving the car the plane hit.

"Something like that happens, and you realize what a fine line there is," said Schramm. "Any of us could have been on that plane."

Stories about the crash dominated the news for days. There also was an article and pictures of Rock Hudson, looking gaunt and thin. Hudson, the heart throb and film idol of millions of women, had admitted to having Aids. There was a killer bee scare in California. The most deadly of the species had apparently migrated over the years from South America and was discovered to exist in small numbers among beehives of California. There was talk about having to kill all bees in the area just to eliminate the killer species. The Tony Dorsett issue was becoming nasty, and baseball commissioner Ueberroth, trying to avoid a strike, sided with players on the salary cap issue in somewhat of a landmark stand by a commissioner of any sport, because players are hired and fired by the owners. Ueberroth, a popular figure in the Los Angeles area because he had planned and merchandised the Olympics in the Coliseum, said he simply could not enter talks as a spokesman for the owners, as the players' union wanted him to do, because he was not in favor of the owners' proposals.

Baseball owners had gotten themselves up the proverbial creek and have been trying to regain some of the concessions that they already had given up in previous negotiations with the players. Baseball had been the only sport with an antitrust exemption, which in effect bound a player to a team for life. Curt Flood first challenged the exemption, the so-called reserve clause, and failed. However, his case did bring a great deal of attention to the fact a player had no recourse but to remain with the same team. The owners refused to give any concessions and, finally, Andy Messersmith and then Catfish Hunter went to court to challenge the reserve clause. The court brought in an arbitrator, Peter Seitz, a nonsports man. He ruled in favor of the players. Then in later negotiations, Marvin Miller fleeced the owners by threatening them with various situations and a strike and getting them to agree to bring in an arbitrator in salary negotiations. Owners such as Gene Autry and, especially, George Steinbrenner, both of whom had money to burn, began signing free agents to outrageous salaries. Since 1981 the average salary for a major leaguer has gone from $51,051 in 1976 to $412,520 ten years later. Because of arbitration a player such as former Texas Ranger Gary Ward, no superstar by any means, had his salary raised $200,000 in his final two years with the team. When he left the Rangers for the Yankees in 1986, he was the highest paid athlete in the Metroplex, drawing a yearly base salary of $800,000 and surpassing, at that time, athletes such as Mark Aquire, Randy White and Tony Dorsett.

Ueberroth said the owners shouldn't ask the players to help them solve financial problems and that a salary cap, such as the one used by the National Basketball Association, was against his belief in the free enterprise system.

"Uerberroth hurt the owners when he said he was against a salary cap," said Schramm. "It seems to me that's the one thing baseball needs to survive after the mess it's gotten itself into. If I were a baseball owner, I'd have tried to get Ueberroth fired the day after he said what he did about a salary cap. And, my god, he's for free enterprise. Well, hell, I bet he's for motherhood and the Boy Scouts. Give me a break!

"Hey, nobody is more for private enterprise than me. Everybody in the NFL knows that. I believe in the individual. Sports are different, unique, unlike any other business, and so the same rules can't be applied. You're partners on one hand and competing on the other. You can't run around signing free agents and upping salaries like baseball, because you'll run your competition out of business. The only way you're successful over the long haul is if the league is strong from top to bottom.

"I just can't believe how stupid the baseball people were. Here they were sitting on an exemption from antitrust, which is the thing that gives us so much trouble. They lose free agency and then salary arbitration by somebody who knows nothing about the game. Peter Seitz's name and that day should go down in infamy, along with the people who let it happen. I think it was the most serious mistake made thus far in professional sports.

"Some form of salary cap might be baseball's only solution. It's a way in which you can operate with the same funds as the other teams and still use ingenuity.

"It might eventually help the NBA. Right now what do you have—three, four outstanding teams with most of the others just furnishing the competition. It's almost like what the Globetrotters used to have when they went around playing the Washington Generals.

"I'd be interested in discussing a salary cap for our league. It would have to be different, more sophisticated, but we might come to that. It's a way you can keep lesser clubs functioning equally with the ones with more money. No sport can exist for long if the weaker clubs don't have a chance competing with the stronger ones."

In the summer of 1987 before it had become clear that the NFLPA would strike, the Management Council's executive director Jack Donlan had phoned Schramm and told him he was having problems knowing what the owners wanted from a structural standpoint in the coming negotiations with the union. They started trying to think of the owners who would understand the issues and be able to see what they might mean down the line. The names they came up with were Schramm, Art Modell, Dan Rooney, Mike or Paul Brown, Wellington Mara and Billy Bidwell. This frightened Schramm.

"That's the old guard," he said. "They won't be around that much longer. Some of these new people coming in scare me to death. It's different in that they're not directly involved with operating the club or what goes on in the league, and yet they'll be making decisions. Who knows what they might eventually give away innocently, and then the league will suffer on down the line. Look at baseball. Those guys didn't dream it would get so bad when they made some of those stupid concessions.

"I've already seen some of this going on at league meetings. When Eagle owner Norman Braman first came into the league he made a statement that we should go ahead and give the players full free agency. They give something away like that, and someday they'll look down and their pants will be gone.

"In my opinion some of us made a big mistake, too. After the decision that Davis could move, there were strong indications in Congress that we could get legislation which would give the league the right to apply our rule in which a team has to get permission from the league to move and also to make sure television revenue is shared equally.

"Early on Pete wanted any legislation to be retroactive so it would apply to Davis. But in the slow. highly political process of attempting to get any legislation in Congress it became evident that any possible action would, in all probability, not be retroactive. So the question became moot because we were unable to get any legislation at all.

"If the Davis decision does hold up through all the appeals, that could mean we aren't a single entity and therefore we can't inforce our rules, because it would be conspiracy. That would open the door for anybody to put together their own television package, and we couldn't stop them.

"If sharing of income is taken away that would break the NFL quicker than anything. We all share the television package equally. If we didn't, what would happen to a place like Green Bay, without the huge television market? Why, one of these new guys coming in would just say, 'Hey, I'll just go my own way on the television and don't want to be part of the league's network.'

"You have to have tremendous amounts of money tied up to get a franchise now. You think if somebody gets in trouble that they're not going to come along and do something like that rather than go down the drain."

Schramm added that it was important for the NFL to be solid in New York. "That city has the largest media concentration, the largest television market, and you need a good team in New York. It hurts our league when the Giants or Jets aren't strong.

"If you look back in history, the NFL had its largest escalation and biggest television growth period in the late 1950s and the early 1960s and that was because the Giants had great teams then. That's when you began to hear about the first umpteenth million dollar television contract.

"You couldn't get tickets to the Giants games. I don't care what anybody says, it all happens in New York. That's where the market is—the largest concentration of advertising agencies and sponsors. If the Giants hadn't been great, the NFL would not have had such an amazing period of growth and become so popular."

Just because Schramm appreciates the importance of New York in the league doesn't, of course, mean that in recent years he has enjoyed the success of the Giants on the field—discounting 1987 when their replacement team was 0-3 and helped bury them for the year. When the Giants didn't have a very good football team, the Cowboys were their most hated rival. It was almost as if New York could have a bad season, but if it beat Dallas everything was tolerable. Now the Cowboys, rebuilding, think of the Giants as one of a small group of teams they most want to beat. Through 1987, Dallas beat the Giants five of the last six times they played, but this was lost in the disappointments of the seasons.

Of the "old guard" of whom Schramm speaks so fondly, Wellington Mara joins Paul Brown as one of the two people with whom he has the most trouble. "Sometimes Wellington Mara's philosophies have not coincided with mine," said Schramm. "He's a much more conservative-type person, and he has difficulty with some of my more progressive ideas. It's nothing personal, but, regarding league matters, we often have what you might call a tempestuous relationship. For many years I got along with him. But for some reason, the Giants now seem to have a fixation about the Cowboys or, perhaps, me. It's just their attitude towards us."

There seems to be some animosity about the reputation the Cowboys have built, and certainly talked about, over the years. *Dallas News* pro-football writer Gary Myers quoted Giants' General Manager George Young as saying, sarcastically, "When the Cowboys do is simply bigger and better than anybody else." But Young went on to add, "Tex has been an outstanding executive in this league. But I don't necessary agree with him."

Mara, especially, fought Schramm over the use of instant replay, and Tex became very upset with the Giants in the 1987 draft when Young snatched Stephen Baker, the Fresno State wide receiver, out from under the Cowboys' nose. Dallas had traded its fourth and fifth picks to Denver for its third choice, planning to take Baker. The trade wasn't reported to the league in time, and Denver was forced to pass when its choice came up. If a team passes, it can make the choice whenever it's ready, but before the Broncos could do anything, the Giants jumped in and took Baker. Schramm charged the Giants with having inside information on the Cowboys' plans. But then he later added that he would have done the same thing.

Schramm also explained that other things have happened off the field of play to strain the relationship. He recalled when the Giants seated the families of visiting officials directly behind their own people in Yankee Stadium. Once Cowboy owner Clint Murchison was, of course, cheering for the Cowboys. Ann, Mrs. Wellington Mara, had enough of this and stood up and tried to club Murchison with her purse. When this failed, she tried to have him thrown out of the stadium.

"The next time we went to New York," said Schramm, laughing, "our owner and families of club officials were seated nowhere near the Giants' people."

Schramm has had problems finding any humor regarding Paul Brown, who also is a member of his Competition Committee. He said Brown always wanted to adopt rules and regulations which would cut costs, but also discourage individual teams from being progressive.

"My philosophical differences with Paul Brown have gotten stronger in recent years," said Schramm. "Speaking candidly, Brown was a great innovator when he was coaching and also an individualist. He was a person who would do things his way and not worry about what others did or thought. Now he's profit motivated and advocates programs and policies to keep other teams from doing things that he doesn't want to have to pay to do in order to keep up.

"For instance, he advocated a league-wide scouting system in which all teams would receive the same information. There would, in effect, not only be a single combine, but also we would do away with individual-team scouting. He'll often propose something and say, 'Look at all the money you'll save.'"

One of the men among the old guard Schramm most likes is Cleveland owner Art Modell who, as Schramm, can appreciate a good joke, even if it's on him.

When Cleveland was in Dallas for the playoffs in 1969, Schramm recalled that Modell went over to Murchison's house to watch a college all-star game on television. When Modell got there, he joined Clint and Bedford Wynne. The game was on, and Clint and Bedford were intensely going over pages of lists and making notes. Modell was very impressed with the seriousness of their demeanor, as they watched the game and checked their lists.

"Art said he was very taken that the Cowboy owner and one of his right-hand men would be so interested that they were watching a game on television and going over the lists of college players they might draft," said Schramm.

Modell's curiosity got the best of him, so he walked over and looked at the lists over which they'd been so engrossed. The names on the list seemed odd. They weren't Randy or Jim or George but rather Jan and Pam and Kathy.

"What they were doing," continued Schramm, "was going over lists of prospective stewardesses to be used for the Cowboy charter flights." Each year certain stewardesses got to work the charter flights and Bedford, especially, took his job of finding them and— uh—getting to know them very seriously.

"He was so thorough," said Schramm, "that he even attended stewardess graduation exercises at the school, checking out the rookies to see if any of them might qualify as replacements. Art was flabbergasted. He said no wonder everybody thought the Cowboys were so thorough."

Modell, as Schramm, was a person who especially appreciated the attributes of the opposite sex. Years ago Schramm and Marty took three other couples to Spanish Cay for a holiday. Well, actually there were four couples in all and two stags, Modell, who was between marriages, and an unidentified lady.

"Things weren't like they are now," said Schramm. "Everybody played it straight or was very careful. Art and the lady went to great lengths, so nobody would think they were together. He wanted everything to be, or look to be in good taste. So whenever anybody would ask Art would say he was staying in Cabin Six, and the lady would tell everybody she was in Cabin Seven."

On Murchinson's island there was a main house and attached rooms, or cabins, for his guests. But there were only six cabins, although none of the other women noticed. The other couples there were Mr. and Mrs. Pete Rozelle, Mr. and Mrs. Jack Landry, and Mr. and Mrs. Bill Mackey.

"Oh, which cabin are you in?" asked Lois Mackey.

"Why, Cabin Seven," said the lady. "It's so lovely."

Modell decided it might be best if he departed early with his friend. They each, in turn, said they had to be leaving early. The Schramms and some of the other people were sitting in the living room of the main house when Lois Mackey walked in, looking all puzzled. "I just went to tell her goodbye and what a fine time we'd had," said Lois. "But, uh, there's no Cabin Seven." Schramm and the other men quickly looked down at the cards they were playing.

"A number of league officials use to go to Bimini a lot," said Schramm. "Rankin Smith (Falcon owner) liked it so much he built a house there. Rankin, the leader of our Bottle Brigade, prided himself on his bone fishing excursions, among other things. A group of us were there one time, including Art Modell and Pete Rozelle who, like Rankin, were not married then. As fate, or should I say fortune, had it they all had an interest in the same lady. They seemed to be offsetting each other, so Rankin cleverly plotted to get rid of his rivals, Art and Pete. He set up a bone fishing trip, which was to begin at 6 A.M., and insisted that everybody be there and ready to go on time. He figured everybody would already be out on the water before they discovered that he wasn't there.

"But Art, the cagey, battle-scared veteran that he was in such matters, diagnosed the evil plot and doubled back, just in time to break up Rankin's tryst."

Asked if that were the end of the story, Schramm said, "That's the end of the story. But, for the record, Gary Hart didn't discover Bimini, and I imagine some telling snapshots were made during those days. But I guess pictures then were not worth what they are today."

For a change Schramm seemed to have all the media on his side regarding the Tony Dorsett situation. Schramm actually believed, if ever so briefly, that after what the Cowboys had done for Tony that he would come to camp without all the usual mud-slinging. Not so. As the Cowboys were returning to Dallas for their first preseason game against Green Bay, after which they'd go back to training camp in Thousand Oaks, Witt Stewart and Dorsett started firing the first salvos. Stewart told the media the Cowboys were lying when they stated they had not said they would give Tony a new contract, like the one Randy White had, and added that the club cheated his client out of his original $662,000 signing bonus from 1977. Tony agreed and said it might be best if he were traded.

Most found it amazing that a running back, 31 that year, who not only was broke but owed the IRS a lot of money, would make any demands. But they also kept hearing that Schramm liked Tony.

Schramm originally had mentioned on his radio show on KRLD that Dorsett had "financial problems." Reporters kept phoning Schramm and coming to see him with information they said they had gotten from sources regarding Tony's IRS problems. Tex would only say whether their figures were in the ballpark. Tony apparently was originally angered, because he believed Schramm had leaked all his financial problems to the press.

Schramm finally had enough. He denied all charges and noted he didn't even answer a letter from Stewart asking to renegotiate Tony's contract. He then released to the press details of Dorsett's original contract, because he said it was the only way to prove the club had not "cheated" him out of the $662,000.

Just before meeting the press to show details of the contract, Schramm lamented, "This whole thing . . . this is just what happens when I fuck around and try to help somebody. I know better. They turn on you everytime." He recalled another top player, who agreed to a contract while he was in the process of getting a divorce. He wanted the contract held until the divorce was final. Schramm respected that request. When the divorce was final, the player reneged on the agreement and would not sign.

Tex told the press, "As far as my integrity of doing things, I believe I can stand on my record of 36 years in the NFL. Tony says he felt doublecrossed. There is no earthly reason to do that because he was, is and remains an important part of our team."

What happened to the $662,000 was documented. The first $62,000 was paid to two agents and a lawyer Dorsett had hired. Dorsett then took out a $100,000 loan from the Park Cities Bank, which the Cowboys agreed to pay off in $20,000 payments for five years with Dorsett responsible for the interest. That left $500,000 that Dorsett was supposed to get, in $20,000 payments over 25 years, beginning in 1983. Dorsett asked for and received $75,000 in 1978. Shortly thereafter, the Cowboys agreed to pay off $83,000 in debts Dorsett had accumulated. These two concessions reduced the annual payment due him to $13,012.31 yearly. On August 24, 1980, Dorsett and the Cowboys agreed to a new seven-year contract, which had a clause stating the remainder of the deferred money was voided. Schramm said a new deferral plan was set up. As mentioned earlier, Dorsett took $700,000, the up-front cash value of the deferment, on Stewart's advice. Witt said he had agreed all along to pay Tony the money back if the oil investment went wrong, and that Tony had reached a livable agreement with the IRS in which he'd pay $200,000 up front and the remainder in the next year. Stewart also accused Schramm of trying to come between him and Tony. But Witt did want Tony to reach an agreement, whereas Slusher thought the best approach would be for him to hide, as Randy White had done, and miss the entire training camp and preseason.

The name calling had begun in the press on August 7. Seven days later Dorsett had agreed on a contract, and Tony's holdout ended after 20 days. Stewart and Dorsett smiled and Schramm said the club did nothing in restructuring Tony's contract that it would not have done in the first place. Nobody would say anything about the contract, but indications were Schramm funded an annuity for Dorsett that stipulated Tony agree not to cash any of it in advance. Schramm was supposed to have included Dorsett in a team sup-ported investment that should net him $500,000 in the next five years.

These things were worked out after Schramm invited Dorsett to come see him after reading various charges and quotes in the newspapers. Schramm went over with Tony what he had tried to do, what he could do and how he felt about the situation that had developed. Some office employees said his voice could be heard for a mile.

"I guess we should have talked in a soundproof room," said Schramm. "But it's over. When you're upset, you say things you don't mean. I feel very good about the whole situation now."

So did Tony Dorsett. He went on to make his ninth season another outstanding one, rushing for 1,307 yards and climbing to sixth place on the NFL's all-time rushing list. In 1986 he missed several games and parts of games due to a knee injury but still moved into third place, behind only Walter Payton and Jimmy Brown. Under the circumstances of suffering his first serious injury and playing hurt, Dorsett had an amazing season. But that season, too, began with Tony in an uproar during training camp. And it had to do with the contract that Schramm had tailored to get him out of debt and secure his future only a year before.

chapter six

USFL FALLS,
WALKER RISES

In mid-August of 1986 Tex Schramm emerged from his room in the official's dormitory at Cal Lutheran College after an all-night session with Herschel Walker's agent, Peter Johnson. Schramm appeared a little tired, but Johnson looked awful, his face puffy and one eye swollen with infection. They had begun negotiations at noon the previous day and ended them just before 10 the following morning. But they had finally agreed on a contract that would pay Walker $5 million over five years. He would receive yearly salaries of $450,000, $450,000, $800,000, $900,000, and $1 million and an additional $1.4 million in provisions which would serve as a bonus over the course of the contract. He would become the highest paid player in Cowboy history.

After Schramm had met with the media and word had begun to circulate about how much Walker was making, reporters approached Dorsett and asked him how it felt to make less money than a man who had never carried the ball in the NFL.

For a man of his age and experience, Dorsett showed immaturity, lack of judgment and let his pride momentarily blind him. It did not matter what had been done for him the previous year. The only thing that mattered was now.

"When they pay this man that kind of money, they're telling me they don't have a need for me," said Tony. "Evidently. I guess I'm on the trading block. I'd better be. It's not going to be in the best interest of all parties involved if I'm not traded or paid accordingly. If I'm unhappy here, I can be a very disruptive force. You have Tony Hill, Doug Cosbie, Danny White and Mike Hegman trying to negotiate here for the longest time, and this guy comes in one day, and they negotiate all night and give him this contract. It shows what they think of us. I will not play second fiddle to any running back on this football team.

"What's Walker ever done? He won the Heisman Trophy. Well, I've got one of those, too. He rushed 24,000 yards (actually 5,562) in the USFL. Well, I guess he's got me there."

Schramm was almost too weary to get upset when he heard Dorsett's comments. He'd spent two months as a key witness in the USFL's antitrust suit against the NFL. Then he'd rushed off to London for the Cowboys preseason game against the Bears. He'd worked tirelessly on bringing Walker into the fold. And he called Tony Dorsett to come see him again.

After United States Football League chief legal counselor Harvey Myerson, an aggressive man sometimes given to theatrics and rudeness to witnesses for the defense, had presented the struggling league's side in the $1.69 billion antitrust suit against the NFL, there was a mounting feeling among the established league's attorneys and some of its officials that a settlement should be reached out of court. Federal Judge Peter Leisure seemed more and more to be leaning toward the USFL and gave indications in discussions with lawyers in his chambers that he believed the suit had merit. The NFL had not yet presented its side of the case, but the prospect of possibly losing was overriding.

"You have no idea how it is to sit in a federal courtroom and look at a jury of six people who admittedly have no experience in football or law and who are going to make a judgment that affects not only the NFL but all established and successful professional sports leagues," explained Tex Schramm. "If they ruled in favor of the $1.6 billion judgment, it could possibly bankrupt the league."

Schramm and other members of the NFL heirarchy believed, however, that the NFL had to take a stand and, once its side was heard, they felt that the jury of one man and five women would reach a fair and just verdict. And furthermore, if the USFL did win the suit and the NFL survived, what was to keep others from forming a makeshift league, knowing they probably would find favor in the courts.

"The sentiments for reaching a settlement out of court were being fanned, as you might have expected, by Al Davis," said Schramm. "He was a proponent of a settlement to accommodate the USFL. He wanted to make a deal in which some of the USFL franchises were taken into the NFL, which was what Donald Trump and the USFL leaders were after all along, and for our league to fund and operate a spring league. Of course, Davis wanted the Oakland Invaders of the USFL to succeed, so the City of Oakland would drop its eminent domain suit against him to return the Raiders to Oakland.

"We met and discussed the situation over a weekend about the midway point in the trial and, fortunately, we were able to convince most of the people that we had to go on with the case."

The antitrust suit was a last ditch effort by the USFL for some form of survival. The 12-team league had been founded in 1982 by a group of football fanatics, most of whom were in real estate. The format called for spring football, a dead time for the sport and one in which the avid fan might be lured into watching his favorite sport, even if the standard of play was a great deal less than he had been accustomed to watching. By 1983, Donald Trump, who had yearned for an NFL franchise, purchased the New Jersey Generals for some $5 million, and the league grew to 18 teams. He signed Herschel Walker to a $5 million contract after his junior year at Georgia and brought Doug Flutie into the ranks with an $8 million contract. Trump apparently believed he could turn his original investment into a $70 million NFL team, because the established league eventually would have to absorb some of the USFL franchises.

ABC had taken a chance on spring football when the USFL was formed and given it an $18 million three-year television contract. ESPN had chipped in an additional $8 million. Average attendance was 27,000, but the television rating quickly tumbled. At the end of the third year the league had dwindled to eight teams, and losses were estimated to be near $200 million. Trump, the most powerful of the USFL owners, led a movement to start playing in the fall for what was to be the league's fourth season. This meant going head-to-head with the NFL. ABC had a five year contract, which ended in 1986, to rotate NFL games with NBC and CBS and could not justify continuing to televise USFL games.

Without a major television contract, needed for survival, USFL commissioner Harry Usher and league owners had filed the antitrust suit, alleging the NFL had willingly attempted to maintain a monopoly to try to drive the USFL out of business by leaning on the networks to withhold television contracts. From the outset, it appeared leaders of the USFL believed the NFL would absorb its top teams rather than go through an all-out fight or face possible litigation. This was not without precedent. In 1950 the NFL took in top teams from the All-American Football Conference (Cleveland, San Francisco and Baltimore), and it had merged with the American Football League in 1966. They were wrong, although they would not have been had Davis and some NFL officials had their way.

USFL attorney Harvey Myerson had believed when he unveiled the so-called "smoking gun," that it would prove that the NFL had been attempting to drive the fledgling league out of business. The "smoking gun" was a transcript of Harvard Business School professor Michael Porter's seminar on, "How to Conquer the USFL." The court heard Howard Cosell testify that ABC executive Roone Arledge confided to him that Pete Rozelle "was all over me" to drop coverage of the USFL. Arledge said no such conversation took place. "Cosell is still talking but now there is nobody listening," remarked Schramm. Trump stated to the court that Rozelle had promised him an NFL franchise if he agreed not to sue the league. Rozelle vehemently denied any such conversation had ever taken place, and it was his word against Trump's. Davis, whose Los Angeles Raiders were the only NFL team not included in the suit, told the court that the NFL and City of Oakland had conspired to put the Invaders out of business.

"A lot of us were concerned about the reason the USFL dropped Al Davis as a defendant," said Schramm. "We wondered what the payoff might have been for his testimony in the case.

"Anyway, when we started putting our case before the judge and jury, calling our witnesses, the tide started turning in our favor."

Rozelle had asked Schramm to come to New York for the trial and testify because he was more versed in all aspects of the NFL and its competitive viewpoints than the other executives. For two months, when he wasn't in the courtroom, Tex conferred with NFL officials and attorneys during lunch breaks and each day after the court had recessed. He was on the witness stand for two and a half days, and NFL officials and lawyers believed the fact that he was able to dispute USFL claims about the Porter report had a great deal to do with the final result of the trial. Perhaps, the worst moment came for Schramm due to an apparent error in briefing by NFL attorney Frank Rothman and his aides. Schramm was led to believe that Myerson, who was trying to prove the NFL had gone after USFL players who were under contract in order to damage the new league's product, was expected to ask him how many players taken in the NFL supplemental draft would play before their USFL contracts were up. He was to answer, "Zero."

However, Myerson asked him, "How many of the 84 players selected in the supplemental draft of the USFL in 1984 were signed to NFL contracts before their playing services in the USFL were over?"

"Zero," answered Schramm.

"Are you asking the jury and court to believe that you didn't know that one of your own players that you signed from the USFL had a year to go on his contract? And for us to believe that, from your personal knowledge, you know no other NFL teams signed USFL players under contract?"

"My answer," said Schramm, quickly recovering," should have been, one . . . my own player. He signed for a period when he was not under any obligation to the USFL. We signed Todd Fowler with full blessing of the Houston Gamblers."

Fowler played out his option and joined the Cowboys. Schramm had changed his perspective about one league signing players to future agreements, while still under contract in another league. He was livid in 1974 when the World Football League signed eight Dallas Cowboys, still under obligation to the team, to future contracts. They were Calvin Hill, D. D. Lewis, Jethro Pugh, Rayfield Wright, Pat Toomay, Craig Morton, Otta Stowe, and Mike Montgomery. Toomay actually agreed to a WFL contract while he was in training camp with the Cowboys. At that time Schramm did not believe the practice was ethical and questioned the devotion of players such as Hill, whose future was in the WFL. However, only Hill actually played for the new league, which folded in the twelfth week of its second season. Dallas, however, with its lame duck players, finished 8-6 and failed to make the playoffs for the first time since 1965. Schramm believed the distractions helped cause this. The WFL, which had come on the scene with a great deal of sound and fury when the Toronto Northmen signed Larry Csonka, Jim Kiick and Paul Warfield of the Miami Dolphins to future contracts, disappeared quietly. The USFL would not.

Myerson asked Schramm if a representative of the Dallas Cowboys had not made the statement that he would like to see Herschel Walker and Tony Dorsett in the same backfield. Schramm acknowledged Tom Landry had said this and that he also would like to see such a backfield.

"But, Mr. Myerson, we had no desire to talk contract with Walker while he was under contract with the New Jersey Generals," said Schramm. "We respect his contract and expect him to fulfill it. We've had great success taking players for the future. Roger Staubach had a four-year commitment with the Navy. He said he was going to complete his commitment, just as Herschel Walker says. We are willing to wait. That makes your point look silly, Mr. Myerson."

Schramm refuted step-by-step the Porter presentation, defusing the USFL's "smoking gun." He explained the Harvard meeting had been for middle management people who work on contract negotiations and that it was merely going to be a seminar on new strategies on how to deal with agents. Gil Brandt, Joe Bailey and Marshall Simmons, a Dallas attorney Schramm was using, attended. Schramm went on to explain that, in the first seminar, Porter deviated from the program and outlined ways to put the USFL out of business.

"I paid no attention to the Porter report," Schramm explained. "It made no indelible impression. I didn't even know who he was. My only recollection was when Joe Bailey came back and said Porter had a lot of ideas. The problem was we couldn't use any of them."

Porter had suggested the NFL move its draft to one week after the USFL held its draft, but this was never done. Myerson also questioned Schramm regarding a Porter suggestion that CBS schedule shows involving popular analysis John Madden opposite USFL games on June 30 and July 8. He handed Schramm two copies of *TV Guide*, showing that the program, *John Madden's Journeys*, was playing opposite USFL playoff games.

When Myerson asked him about the June 30th date, Schramm replied, "I was 400 miles out in the ocean fishing. I don't watch *John Madden's Journeys*. I don't know what *John Madden's Journeys* are. Is that where he gets on a bus and rides around?"

His response drew laughter around the court. When Myerson asked him about July 8, Schramm said, "John is still journeying."

The courtroom then erupted in laughter, and Judge Leisure recessed for the day.

Once after a recess in the trial, Myerson came up to the witness stand and told Schramm, "Look, don't take this personally. I have the greatest admiration and respect for you and the Cowboys. You're doing a helluva job."

When Schramm finished testifying, Myerson got up and shook his hand, which angered some of Schramm's NFL cohorts. Schramm also received very favorable press regarding his testimony. Gary Myers of the *Dallas Morning News* had continually written complimentary reports on Schramm at the trial. Then after the trial had ended, Myers talked again with Myerson and quoted him as saying he believed Schramm hurt the NFL by his testimony.

"That really pissed me off," said Schramm.

Tex Schramm had to leave for London to join his team for a preseason game against the Chicago Bears before the final arguments were heard and a verdict was returned in the USFL's $1.6 billion antitrust suit against the NFL. Near midnight in London on July 29, Tex and Marty were coming back to their suite on the top floor of the London Hilton, which overlooks Buckingham Palace. A member of the crew of Lee Martin Productions, which handles Schramm's television show, told Tex that he'd heard the verdict had come in and the NFL had lost.

Schramm said he had this awful sinking feeling as he went into his suite. The telephone was ringing. An NFL official was calling to inform him the NFL had won the case. The man who had told Schramm the league had lost had heard only part of the verdict. The NFL had been found nominally guilty of antitrust violations against the USFL but had to pay only $1 (tripled to $3 under laws governing antitrust litigation) in token damages, all but signaling the demise of the new league.

Jim Dent of the *Dallas Times-Herald* was in Schramm's room a little later when Pete Rozelle called.

"Hello, commissioner," said Schramm. "Oh, yes, the rockets are bursting all over London! How great could this possibly be! They're bursting just outside my window!"

"I want to tell everybody!"

"You're talking so loud . . . if you open the window, the queen can hear you," said Marty.

"Pete, I love you! We have survived. Can you believe it? We made it. Tell Harvey Myerson that he can spend the $1 on taxi fare back to New Jersey.

"Do you know what this means? It means a successful league has been told it can go on being successful. It means there's nothing wrong with success. For once something finally worked for us. The jury showed we are as clean as little Pilgrims. Right now, I couldn't be happier!"

He heard the rockets that weren't going off all over London and was so excited he couldn't get to sleep until late that morning.

When Tex Schramm got back to Thousand Oaks, he was interviewed on a segment of *Nightline*, along with USFL commissioner Harry Usher. The show was moderated by Charles Gibson, subbing for Ted Koppel, and Schramm successfully refuted statements by Usher. Gibson asked Usher how he thought the NFL had tried to kill the USFL. He replied:

"Well, in a number of ways. This even goes back to 1961 when they got Congress to give them a limited exemption to get all the teams pooled together on one network. Then they swallowed the AFL in 1966 and added NBC to it, and then finally, in 1970, added ABC. So from 1970 on, the NFL has had all three networks completely locked up."

"I think, if Mr. Usher had been in football for the years he's talking about, he would know the background on how we came to be on all three networks," answered Schramm. "Back in those days of the 1960s, it was a tough situation, because the stadiums weren't full and the networks weren't clamoring for professional football. The NFL was first on ABC, and then CBS. NBC took over the AFL and when the merger came it televised the AFL, and CBS kept the NFL games.

"It remained this way until 1970. That year, we were aware that it would be beneficial if we could expand our horizons, as far as television was concerned, because we had agreed to legislation in Congress, which prohibited the NFL from playing on Friday nights and Saturdays to protect high schools and colleges. We decided to try Monday nights. We first offered this package to CBS. It did not want the games in prime time. We then went to NBC, and it did not want us in prime time, either. We tried ABC, which took the package, and it became a great success.

"The USFL was not prohibited from being on the networks, either in the spring or fall. That league's first concept, which I thought was a good one, was to play in the spring. They were trying to capitalize on the popularity of pro football. It was a success. ABC made a good profit for the first two years, even though the ratings dropped. Some people in the USFL were satisfied with the league's progress in the spring. But others listened primarily to Trump and also to Jimmy (The Greek) Snyder and Howard Cosell, who told them the big money was in the fall, and so they went that direction. ABC did not continue televising USFL games, because it did not fulfill its contract to play in the spring."

Schramm felt once again he'd scored points against the USFL by debating Usher on *Nightline*. He later added, "The decision is very significant. It affects all sports—baseball, the NBA, hockey, everything. The decision said 'No' to the USFL's attempt to use the NFL's established success and popularity as a means to show the court that it was discouraging competition. In this case you had the challenge to the right to compete for popular programming. Antitrust laws were designed to protect competition and not to penalize success and popularity."

In spite of the exhibition loss to the Bears, Schramm had returned to Thousand Oaks in a very good mood. He loves training camp and was glad to be back there with his team. The league he loves had won an important case and, without the competition, the Number One draft choice, Mike Sherrard, probably would be ready to sign, and he also would be able to bring Herschel Walker, a franchise player, into the fold. He signed Walker and Dorsett exploded. No matter how well things were going, he always has to deal with something unpleasant.

When the trial had ended and, for all practical purposes, the USFL had become history, Harry Usher negotiated a deal with the players' association that all USFL players under guaranteed contracts or with contractual obligations for future years would have until August 13 at 10 A.M. Eastern time to make a declaration that they desired to be relieved of their obligations. The employer thus also would be relieved of his obligations to the player.

Before the trial Trump had signed Walker to a $5.5 million, four-year contract extension, beginning in 1985. Walker's personal services contract with Trump was guaranteed, meaning he'd get his money whether the USFL ever played another game or not. When the USFL failed to play in the spring of that year and moved its proposed schedule to the fall of 1986, Walker was paid his first year's salary. Trump, obviously, was trying to protect himself when the agreement was reached with the USFL Players Association but if, say Walker and the Cowboys couldn't agree before the deadline, he again would be in control of Walker's contract and could possibly sell him to the Cowboys.

Schramm felt the pressure of the deadline, because he didn't want Trump, with his personal services contract with Walker, to become a player in the Walker situation.

"If we beat the deadline, Trump would be out," said Schramm. "I saw a story which said Trump was playing a game and that he didn't want to get involved but was trying to get us to play our hand. That's bullshit. Trump not only wanted off the hook for the salaries to Walker and Jim Kelly but also hoped to make some money off them, as he had boasted he would do. He had bragged at the league meeting that he was going to sell Walker and make millions. I felt I had to eliminate Trump from the picture."

When Peter Johnson, Walker's agent, came to Thousand Oaks to negotiate with Schramm, he was suffering from an eye infection. Schramm had the Cowboy trainers get him medicine, but he still was very uncomfortable. He had agreed with Schramm to negotiate all night, if necessary, to try to reach an agreement.

"When you start negotiating all night, going through one of those marathon sessions, you're playing right into Schramm's hands," said Joe Bailey. "He's like a bull. He gets his adrenalin pumping, and you can't wear him out."

About 2 A.M. Peter Johnson, exhausted, asked if they could have a break so he could go back to his hotel, take a shower and nap and talk to Herschel Walker. Schramm agreed. He, too, showered and changed clothes but, instead of taking a nap, poured himself a trusty J&B and waited for Johnson to return.

"When Johnson got back, he didn't look much better than he had when he left," said Bailey. "But there was Tex, sitting and sipping his drink and looking as fresh as ever. That had to be disconcerting for him."

They resumed negotiations at 4 A.M. and reached a contractural agreement 15 minutes before the deadline. A franchise player, one who had at best only an even chance of ever joining the Cowboys when Schramm decided to take him as a future in the fifth round of the 1985 draft, would not only play in 1986 but make an immediate impact.

When Dallas traded malcontent Butch Johnson for Mike Renfro in the spring of 1984, Houston threw in what appeared to be a meaningless fifth-round pick for 1985. Fifth-round choices seldom make it in the NFL, so when it became time for Dallas to make the first of its picks in that round, Schramm decided it was time to go for Herschel Walker.

"We had our choice plus the one we got from Houston, so there was nothing to lose," said Schramm. "The odds were as good that he would become available to us as they were for anybody in that round making our team. Everybody concerned agreed it was a good time to take a flier."

Walker was one of three players Schramm personally picked to draft who would more than make his presence known in the NFL. In 1964 after both Tom Landry and Gil Brandt had left the draft room, Schramm chose Bobby Hayes, an Olympic sprinter, in the seventh round, and took a long shot in the tenth round on Roger Staubach, who had a four-year obligation to the Navy and probably wouldn't try to bridge the gap in his career and play professional football.

"Coach Landry and Gil and our other people are so engrossed with working ahead on the college players who are available the coming season that I try to keep my mind on special situations. I'm also more prone to look down the stream into the future than they are."

Al Davis has become aware of the benefits of this. In 1986 he took Navy's Napoleon McCallum in the fourth round, telling Schramm shortly thereafter that he did so because he was afraid Tex would pick him in the fifth round, as he had Walker. McCallum immediately contributed to the Raiders' success, fulfilling his obligation to the Navy and playing for the Raiders during his time off. In 1987 Davis signed Bo Jackson, a full-time baseball player for Kansas City, agreeing to let him join the Raiders after the Major League season ended. It's not clear if Schramm prompted this or not.

But neither Davis nor anybody else took a chance on Walker. Some feared his contract with Trump, even if the USFL did fold, but Johnson said, "Not one team called to ask me about Herschel's contract. They just didn't do their homework like the Cowboys.

All of them seemed to be very afraid of the personal services contract, but all it was was a guaranteed contract.''

New York Giants general manager George Young said, "We never made any future picks. We're not in the future business, and I don't think a lot of people are. It was a 50-50 proposition with Walker, and we wondered at what age we might get him.''

San Francisco's director of college scouting, Tony Razzano, said, "We didn't want to give up money for a position where we felt we were solid.''

"I admire the Cowboys for their courage," said Chicago Bears' director of player personnel, Bill Tobin.

"You have to give the Cowboys credit," said Atlanta owner Rankin Smith. "They beat everybody to the punch.''

New York Giants' owner Wellington Mara said, jokingly, "I told Lamar Leachman (the Giants defensive linecoach) to get the troops ready, because we might be meeting Herschel Walker in Dallas on Monday night." Mara was talking about the 1986 season opener and proved prophetic. Walker furnished the spark for Dallas to upset the Giants.

"I had strong feelings that the USFL would not make it on a long-range basis when we took Herschel," said Schramm. "Some of the negative signs that had caused other leagues to fail were there. The league was killing itself by trying to pay the high salaries and not limiting itself on expenses to what it could afford. The signs just indicated the league was going in the wrong direction, and I believed we'd eventually get Walker, although not as soon as we did.''

Gil Brandt had met Walker when Herschel was in high school and stayed in touch with him through Georgia and while he was in the USFL. Walker and Brandt both indicated they were friends and did not talk contract until Trump freed Walker from his obligation. Brandt did, however, send Walker a Dallas Cowboy jersey.

"The USFL had Herschel hold up the Cowboy jersey during the USFL trial to try to show we tampered with him," said Schramm. "He also displayed the jersey to the media on the courthouse steps. I had no idea he'd actually be wearing it in such a short time.''

"I had watched him a great deal while he was in the USFL. But at first it was from a negative standpoint. The USFL was making such a big deal out of him that it wouldn't have made me angry if he'd turned out to be a bust.

"I kept hearing that he was just a straight-ahead runner who was fast. But he kept making those long runs, and it became obvious that one of his great strengths was that he was so difficult to tackle. He had the ability to break tackles and to accelerate and run away from everybody. You'd watch him and he would not seem to be doing that much, but at the end of the game he'd have 150-200 yards. And, frankly, nobody had any idea he was such a tremendous receiver."

Schramm said he didn't think there was any doubt that Walker brought a new enthusiasm to the Cowboys, and his presence would have been felt even more had he not been hobbled by injuries.

"When you have the success like we've had, it's difficult to get the really outstanding players. But, somehow, you have to do it. I mean we need those who make contributions above and beyond the norm. We were able to make trades to be in position to draft that type of player in Ed (To Tall) Jones, Randy White and Tony Dorsett. Now we've been fortunate enough to get Herschel Walker, who's only 24 years old. He's the type player we can build around for the next eight or nine years, as the Rams planned with Eric Dickerson. In regard to strength and speed, he reminds me of Jimmy Brown, but Herschel can also catch like hell, too.

"One of the things Tony Dorsett didn't understand was that we were not just bringing in somebody for last season but for the future."

Nobody for the Cowboys had ever blown up publicly over the contract of another player as Tony Dorsett did when he heard Herschel Walker was going to receive $5 million over five years.

"I put Herschel in a totally different category in terms of negotiations," said Schramm. "We were taking over a situation we didn't create. He was an established player who had proven himself and already had a guaranteed contract. We had a deadline to beat. If we hadn't beaten that deadline, he'd have cost us a lot more. So I felt comfortable with the contract in regard to the other people on our team. I knew once he started producing the talk about his contract would stop."

There had, in fact, been some complaining among the players when Dorsett as a rookie signed a million dollar contract. But the players weren't as vocal publicly with their feelings. When Dorsett started speaking out, Schramm called him in for a conference.

"I explained Herschel's contract to Tony and went over his again with both him and his advisors," said Schramm." His concerns seemed to disappear. I thought his initial reaction was . . . understandable. He felt bad about his reaction, so I also talked to members of the media and said, 'Lookit, give Tony an opportunity to square things. He wants to.'"

The following day Dorsett said, "I didn't mean to put my business in the street like that. I should have gone behind closed doors. I was overreacting. The only thing I'd want to take back from yesterday is yesterday. I apologize for the way I handled the situation. But I can't say it was uncharacteristic, because I've been known to go off like that before and probably will do so again."

"Dorsett," continued Schramm, "has the faculty of saying things that are not beneficial to him. He recognizes this. I believe some of his reactions have not only hurt his popularity but also his earning power off the field. He just reacts. I don't think he means to be mean when he says things like he does. He just has trouble keeping things in perspective and ends up saying what reporters want to hear. It's just his makeup."

Reminded that he, too, had a knack for sometimes popping off, Schramm paused and said, "Sure, I get angry. But I'm a little older and might be more, uh, calculating in what I say.

"I have talked strongly to Tony about this, because I have concern for him. That's why we restructured his contract in 1985. I just explained to him what we could and could not do regarding money. But I have compassion for Tony. The guy received lousy advice that got him in trouble in the first place with his finances and the IRS."

For a brief time Schramm seemed to become angry all over again about the situation Dorsett was in during the summer of 1985. Certainly, the Witt Stewart and Dorsett attack on the club, and the question of Schramm's integrity, was the worst public confrontation with a player since the enigmatic Duane Thomas in 1971 told the press that Schramm was "sick, demented, and dishonest." When Schramm heard what Duane had said, he shook his head slowly and remarked, "That's not bad. He got two out of three."

Certainly, others have challenged him, but not so much publicly. Lee Roy Jordan made little secret of the fact he did not like Schramm but didn't come out and say so while he was a player.

But there was nothing in Schramm's background or experience, nor of others in the organization for that matter, to prepare them for Thomas, a person who literally followed a "different drummer," one that nobody else heard.

chapter seven

HERE TODAY, GONE TOMORROW

Duane Thomas grew up in the black ghetto of Dallas, being shuffled from relative to relative, never knowing where he might be living next. He was a product of the streets, inhabited by those on the dark side of the moon of society, the pimps and prostitutes and thieves, and at night he was not awakened by a strong wind or storms but by screams in the darkness. Yet, Duane had somehow managed to survive and seemed to have a good mind, although at times he would lapse into a kind of mental never-never land after he'd joined the Cowboys. The one thing that got him out of the ghetto was a unique football talent. That's where he'd take out his anger, his bitterness, on the football field. He'd received a football scholarship to West Texas State, where he played in the same backfield for a couple of years with Mercury Morris and under the iron hand of the late Joe Kerbel, a huge, overweight volatile man, who not only coached with knowledge but by intimidation. Duane was 6-2, 220 and could run the 40 in 4.6. Because he'd played for a small school and had some problems with discipline, he was overlooked by many of the pro scouts, but the Cowboys were right on him. They had him ranked in the top three college football players in the country.

They didn't need a running back. They had Calvin Hill, who had come out of Yale, of all places, and attained instant stardom. It was Schramm, in fact, who had predicted this stardom when others, including the coaches, were more reserved in their judgment. As usual, they took a wait-and-see approach but Schramm, as usual, said what he thought without waiting for the results to come in.

Prior to the second preseason game of 1969 in San Francisco starting halfback Danny Reeves reinjured a knee and Tom Landry decided to start rookie Calvin Hill, who was 6-4, 220 and had tremendous athletic ability but no solid football background in the Ivy League. Before the game Schramm stood on the sidelines of Kezar Stadium with a group of writers. He looked around the stands as the crowd began to file in and then glanced over at Hill, going through warmup motions.

"I have a feeling," said Schramm, "that today a star will be born."

That day Hill rushed for 106 yards, caught three passes and became the Dallas Cowboy halfback. He'd go on to finish second in the NFL rushing with 942 yards and would have become the second rookie since Jimmy Brown to rush for 1,000 yards in a 14 game schedule if a toe injury hadn't slowed him down the final three games.

"Tex had invited me to his office to talk about a job," recalled vice president Joe Bailey. "His secretary told me to go right on in and I did. He'd just gotten a report that Calvin Hill had been seen out dancing up a storm, while he was at the Pro Bowl, bad toe and all. Tex was livid. Then he turned and saw me and very calmly said, 'Oh, hi Joe. Sit down.' Hill was a franchise player, and Tex was understandably upset."

"If there was something we didn't need in the 1970 draft," recalled Schramm, "it was a halfback. We had Hill and Walt Garrison had done an outstanding job taking over for Don Perkins at fullback. But our scouts, especially Red Hickey, kept touting Duane Thomas. I remember a scene in the draft room that year. . . ."

Dallas would pick twenty-third and, as the time approached to make the selection, Hickey kept telling Landry about Thomas. He said Duane had had some problems at West Texas State. Once when he had been taken out of a game, Duane had gone to the sidelines, slammed down his helmet and cussed out an assistant coach.

"But when he went back into the game," said Hickey," he just kept on ripping off the yardage."

"Red told Tom that Duane was a hard worker in practice, but that he'd also had trouble with a trainer at West Texas," said Schramm. "Duane disagreed with the trainer over treatment of his injuries. This went on and on. Red would talk about Duane, and Tom would sit there, thinking. And then Tom would ask Red, 'Tell me about him again.' He must have done this two or three times."

Finally, Hickey said, "Thomas is the best running back in the country, bar none."

"Does that mean he's better than Calvin Hill?" asked Landry.

"If he comes here, Tom," said Hickey, "he'll be your starting halfback."

"Hummmm."

"Tom, I'll tell you what," said Hickey. "If Thomas is still there when the pick comes, take him, if you think you can handle him."

"You say he's better than Calvin."

"He'll be your halfback."

"Landry paused, thought a little," said Schramm, "and then just said, 'Then I think I'll try to handle him.'

"Duane worked hard and was pleasant when we got him. It was obvious he was a super talent."

Hill was slowed by injuries, and Thomas was inserted at halfback early in the regular season. Roger Staubach, in his second season, wasn't ready to play, and so Landry used Craig Morton, in spite of the fact he was playing with a slightly separated right shoulder. The Cowboys went to a running game, because of Morton's shoulder problems, and Thomas was the crux. He rushed for 830 yards and a 5.3 average per carry, leading Dallas to Super Bowl V, which it lost to Baltimore, 16-13, on a field goal of 32 yards by Jim O'Brien with five seconds left.

Schramm has forgiven but not forgotten game official Jack Fette for a call he made in that particular game. Dallas had led 13-6 at halftime and, when the Colts fumbled away the second half kickoff, the Cowboys moved to a second down at the Baltimore one, ready to put the game away for all practical purposes, because the Colts weren't playing well at the time. They'd scored on a tipped pass, and the Cowboys had literally rushed Johnny Unitas off his feet, sending him to the bench in favor of Earl Morrall. Thomas tried to score the touchdown from the one but fumbled as linebacker Mike Curtis hooked the ball out of his hands. Fette's view of the play was obstructed. Films and still pictures in the *Dallas Morning News* showed the ball bouncing right into the arms of Dallas center

Dave Manders, who recovered. But Colt tackle Billy Ray Smith began shouting, "Our ball! Our ball!" and pointing downfield. Fette, under pressure, pointed upfield, too, giving Baltimore the ball. The recovery was officially given to defensive back Jim Duncan. Films showed he was not close to the ball.

Later defensive end Bubba Smith said, "We ought to give the ball to Billy Ray. He conned that official right out of the Super Bowl. Billy Ray Smith, living in Richardson, a suburb of Dallas, said there was no way the Colts recovered the ball. Instead of being ahead 20-6 or 16-6, Dallas had nothing.

"Fette was out of position and had no business making a call on something he couldn't see," recalled Schramm. "No, I won't forget that. I've noticed in recent years Jack is getting fat. Fat Jack Fette!"

Something happened to Duane Thomas during the off-season, or perhaps the thin thread that had held him together broke. Perhaps, the underlying bitterness and resentment, which had been dormant, erupted. Certainly, it would have been indicative of the times. There was talk and continuous rumors that he was on drugs, although Schramm always felt Duane's irrational behavior went far beyond any drug or cultural problem. Duane Thomas became, in a way, symbolic of the effect of the 1960s and early 1970s.

They were tragic, awful times. The 1960s began with the killing of a president, John Kennedy. And within a 68-day period in 1968, Martin Luther King, Jr., the Nobel Prize winner, the symbol of the peaceful civil rights demonstrations, the man who said "We shall overcome, we shall overcome," was killed in a Memphis hotel. Robert Kennedy, the man who would be president and, ironically, the person with whom the younger generation seemed most to identify, was shot down by Jordanian Sirhan Sirhan in Los Angeles. The *New York Times* published the Pentagon Papers. Lt. William Calley was found guilty of his part in the My Lai massacre. Texan Lyndon Johnson would finally give up trying to get through the endless tunnel that was Vietnam and we would see live on television the rise and fall of President Richard Nixon, who had been elected over ultra-liberal George McGovern and left office prematurely after the coverup of the Watergate disclosures.

Those were times that the so-called Establishment was hardly something to look up to. Young people dropped out, became hippies with their capital in Height-Asbury's district of San Francisco. And they spoke out, too, and not only seemed intent on disclaiming authority but destroying it. They ramshackled and took over offices of college presidents, protested Vietnam all over the country, with upwards of 50,000 demonstrators gathering at Lincoln Memorial. A march on poverty delegation broke windows in the Justice Department, and four students were killed by National Guardsmen at Kent State. Young people grew long hair and a musical with nudity called *Hair* and a sex comedy review *Oh, Calcutta*, became popular on Broadway. They sang "King of the Road" and "Born Free" and seemed to emphasize a line from a popular novel called the Comedians by Graham Green: "We cannot always play the parts you write for us." There was change, revolt, disillusionment . . . and there was Duane Thomas.

Duane had finally realized that he hadn't been treated fairly by two different agents. They had taken more than the usual fee from him, and it had cost him $7,500 to buy out of one contract. Salaries were not that high then, and he had signed a three-year contract calling for base salaries of $18,000, $20,000 and $22,000 with Dallas. He had received a $25,000 bonus and had incentives. His total salary for his rookie year was $75,000 but he was broke. He went to Schramm and mentioned he'd like to renegotiate. The club had a policy at that time of not renegotiating contracts until an option year—the last year of a contract. Schramm had refused to renegotiate Calvin Hill's contract after his rookie year. And Duane said, "But I'm not Calvin Hill."

Duane brooded, became angry and went to Los Angeles and into a culture which was hardly conducive to improving his mental state at that time. Some of the people with whom he associated there had dropped out of society and urged him to do the same. They would talk, they would smoke, they would think. They also had no money.

He was late for training camp, but one night he showed up in the coaches' and officials' dorm with a man wearing a dashiki, who said his name was Ali ha ka Kabir. Duane announced he wanted Kabir to get a tryout with the club and stay with him in his dormitory room. This request broke the club record for refusals.

"That was one of the most unusual things I've ever experienced," said Schramm. "Nobody had any idea where Duane was and, suddenly, he's there with this guy in a long robe. The two just stared at me. I wasn't sure whether to bow or run. We refused the tryout, and they left again.

"Duane just had a lot of emotional problems. A lot of people insinuated drugs were involved, but there was nothing requiring testing in those days. So nobody ever knew for sure, but let me say that Duane's emotional problems had gone far beyond drugs. He was just out of control. Writers in those days were saying a contract dispute had a lot to do with Duane's problems. I actually think the media was on his side in that regard, which didn't bother me. I just don't recall that being the main issue. I don't remember ever sitting down with Duane and talking about a contract. We didn't negotiate. His problems were deeper than any contract.''

Gil Brandt found out Ali ha ka Kabir's real name was Mansfeld Collins and that there wasn't a lot of logic to giving him a tryout. Mansfeld later tried to sue the *Dallas Times-Herald* for what it had written about him, but the case was dropped.

Duane next surfaced in Dallas, calling a press conference. Schramm, who was in Thousand Oaks at training camp, got a tape of the conference. Duane rambled endlessly, sometimes almost incoherently. But when you could follow him, and after listening to the tape over and over, some things were clarified. He demanded an $80,000 base salary, plus incentives. He also said Dallas had never made the Super Bowl before he came and would never do it again without him. He said he was treated badly, because he was black. Besides what he said about Schramm, he called Landry "a plastic man, actually no man at all," and said Gil Brandt was "a liar." What he said didn't anger anybody, because they knew he was out of control.

"There was nothing you could do with him, and you usually couldn't even find him," said Schramm. "It became obvious that he wasn't going to report, so we started working on a trade. The chain of events after that were about as bizarre as anything I've experienced in my career."

Schramm worked a deal with New England in which the Cowboys would swap Thomas, lineman Halvor Hagen, and wide receiver Honor Jackson to the Patriots for running back Carl Garrett and a number one draft choice. Garrett reported to the Cowboys in Thousand Oaks, all smiles.

"Garrett told the press and everybody how happy he was to get away from the Patriot offensive line and get some good blockers in front of him," said Schramm. "Everybody wrote stories about that, but the next thing Garrett knew the trade had been nullified by Rozelle and he was back with New England and the same linemen."

Thomas totally disrupted the Patriots. He did report, but refused to take a physical, fanning the fires that he might be on drugs. Then during the first practice he refused to get into a three-point stance, as was suggested by head coach John Mazur. Duane said the Cowboys lined up in a stance with their hands placed just above their knees, and that's the way he would do it. He was ordered off the field. Again, he disappeared, and over Schramm's strong objections, Rozelle reversed the trade.

"I thought a deal was a deal," said Schramm. "The Patriots knew about him and should have accepted the consequences. Calvin Hill was looking good and we didn't really miss Duane. Then he popped up again."

Duane had quietly reported to the team three games into the regular season. Ironically, it was about that time that Hill was injured again, straining a knee. Thomas had worked out a week and, don't forget, had missed all of training camp and preseason and early regular season. Yet, he stepped onto the field in the fourth game, and it was as if he hadn't missed a thing. He would score the first touchdown in Texas Stadium, which opened in midseason, on a fine 57-yard run against none other than the New England Patriots and rush for 793 yards in 11 games to help the Cowboys to a Super Bowl championship. But he took his own peculiar route that season and was a disruption to the team.

Landry had a rule that players wear a coat and tie on the charter flights to road games. Thomas would show up with his shirt unbuttoned and a tie thrown over his shoulder. His only constant companion was a toboggan cap, which he kept pulled down over his ears. He sometimes refused to answer roll call in meetings and when Dan Reeves, who had become an assistant coach, questioned him about this Duane said, "He (Landry) sees me. He knows I'm here." Landry continually tried to talk to Duane, because his teammates were complaining about the way he was acting, but never could reach him. Duane also refused to talk to the media, which dubbed him, "The Sphinx." Hill returned by the eleventh game of the season, and Reeves told Thomas, "We want you to work some at fullback."

"No," said Duane.

Roger Staubach, who had beaten out Craig Morton for the starting quarterback job, said, "Come on, Duane, go ahead."

"You shut up," said Duane.

"Tom knew he had a team that could go all the way," said Schramm. "And nobody realized what a great balancing act he was going through in regard to Duane. He did treat him differently from the other players, because Duane was performing, helping us win, and Tom was trying to help him, to keep him together. He cares about people and will go as far as he can with them if they're having trouble or are mixed up. I don't think there's another coach in the NFL who would have gotten Duane through that season."

Hill and Thomas performed in the same backfield for the final three games. The results were devastating to the opposition, as each ran wild. Dallas demolished the New York Jets, 52-10, the Giants, 42-14, and the Cardinals, 31-12.

"Walt Garrison was the odd man out," said Schramm." He'd done a fine job but was injured and then couldn't seem to break back in the way those two were going. He watched what was happening and, when they asked him how he felt, he said, 'Like the bastard son at a family picnic.' "

Thomas went to the Super Bowl press interviews and, while his teammates were surrounded by the media, sat alone in the bleachers by the practice field. To my knowledge, the only thing he said to any member of the press was to ask, "What time is it?" He also caused a stir when he failed to show up at a Super Bowl practice. Duane by that time had taken up with Jim Brown, the former Cleveland great who also was a rebel or, if you will, a little different. Schramm feared that Brown might have advised Thomas to boycott the Super Bowl. But, it turned out, Duane actually had missed the workout because he was sick.

Duane starred along with the defense and MVP Roger Staubach, as Dallas defeated Miami, 24-3, to win Super Bowl IV. Brown had talked Duane into giving Tom Brookshire an interview after the game. It was his first and only one of the year, and one of the more ridiculous interviews ever done anywhere, much less over national television. An example:

Brookshire: "Duane, uh, are you as quick and elusive as you look?"

Thomas: "Evidently."

Brookshire: "You, uh, your weight seems to fluctuate. You weigh 205 for some games, less for others."

Thomas: "I weigh what I need to weigh."

"Those questions and answers were the highlight of the interview," said Schramm. After the game Schramm, caught up in the moment, made a remark that was widely quoted. "This," he said, "could be the start of a dynasty."

It was, in a way, as Dallas would play for three NFC titles and one Super Bowl in the next four years. But it also was the last hurrah for Duane Thomas.

Thomas came to training camp in 1972, looking thinner than usual. He had become a vegetarian and refused to eat meals with the team, although he skirted Landry's rules by checking in at meals and then grabbing a handful of fruit and going back to his room.

"Tom had tried and knew he couldn't go through another year like he had in 1971," said Schramm. "He talked to Duane, told him what he must do to become a part of society, of our team. He took him each step of the way and, as I recall, thought he was making progress."

Duane looked sluggish in the Cowboys' 20-7 victory over the College All-Stars and then failed to show up for a morning meeting and afternoon practice after the Cowboys returned to training camp. Assistant coach Ray Renfro went to Duane's room to find out what the problem was. Thomas refused to talk to him. Landry went to see Duane, knocking on the door. "Duane, this is Coach Landry. Are you in there?"

"Yeah, can I help you?"

"Well, yes, you weren't at practice."

"I didn't feel like it."

They talked. Landry told him he had to come to meetings and to practice. Duane said he wasn't paid to do those things—only to perform on Sundays. He refused to obey the rules of the team. Landry left Duane's room and went to find Schramm.

"Tom just said, 'That's it, trade him,'" said Schramm. "Tom will go along with somebody, as he also later would do with Thomas Henderson, until the player just becomes too disruptive for the team, until the negative effect outweighs his contribution or the positive effect. When he reaches that point where he's given somebody a good chance, where the minuses outweigh the pluses, then he does something.

"Charger owner Gene Klein's son Michael was enamored with Duane. He thought Duane might be the savior of his team. So it was easy to make a deal with him. In fact, he even drove to our training camp and picked up Duane."

Dallas received running back Mike Montgomery, who became a receiver, and wide receiver Billy Parks for Thomas. They both contributed the next season, but Montgomery was injured and Parks also was somewhat disruptive. Billy was traded along with Tody Smith to Houston for the Oilers Number One draft choice, which turned out to be Ed (To Tall) Jones. Montgomery moved in as the starting flanker in 1973 when Otto Stowe was injured. Then he got hurt again, opening a door for a third string flanker, free agent Drew Pearson, to get a chance to play.

Thomas was active for one game with the Chargers, which was a preseason game against Dallas. In pregame warmups Duane went to the end zone, put his hands on his knees and just stood there for 15 minutes, looking at the ground. He wandered around the stadium and walked away when the National Anthem was being played. But this time the trade stood. Duane was quickly shipped off by the Chargers and for 1973-74 was a backup to Larry Brown in Washington and then signed with the World Football League in 1975. In 1976 he seemed to have things in order mentally and asked for a tryout with the Cowboys. Landry gave him a tryout, but Duane had lost quickness, speed and whatever else it was that made him one of the best running backs in football for two years, 1970-71. In one preseason game when Duane made a simple four yard gain, Schramm almost stood up in the press box, yelling for him. Duane was cut in preseason. He tried out for the Packers in 1979, at the age of 32, and again was cut. For all practical purposes, his career had ended with the Cowboys in the Super Bowl of January 1972. He was 24.

"I'll always have a lot of regrets about Duane," said Schramm. "He obviously had a lot of ability and proved it. But just for two years. That's tragic. I have this sad feeling for people who have problems that keep them from reaching their potential in whatever they try to do. I mean the people who, for some reason or another, just don't seem to have control over what they're doing.

"I don't think I've ever pulled harder for anybody to make our team than I did for Duane in that summer of 1976. The writers covering us and everybody was pulling for him. But his talent was gone. He'd just lost it somewhere along the way.

"In a way, however, I think what happened in the 1960s and Duane helped Landry become more tolerant. The things that happened, the breakdown of discipline in our country, went against everything Tom believed in. Yet, he was able to adjust and get through the period. When he did I think it helped him deal more with people on an individual basis, rather than as a group. His dealings with Duane helped him get a broader perspective for his relationships with players in later years.''

Duane Thomas came back to training camp in 1987 in conjunction with working on a book with Paul Zimmerman about the decline of the Cowboys. He was extremely friendly and talked everybody's ear off, especially Schramm. Times change . . . people sometimes do, too.

Schramm, Landry and the Cowboys came in contact and had to deal with a number of unusual players in the ensuing years. Players became more outspoken, more individualistic and, certainly, many were far more money than team oriented. But they have never had to deal with anybody quite like Duane Thomas.

chapter eight

PLAYERS, DIFFERENT AND ALIKE

Tex Schramm learned a valuable lesson from his mentor Dan Reeves that you can't get too close to players, because it might influence your decisions and could cloud our objectivity. Reeves befriended some of the Ram players, listened to them, and they even influenced him in the firing of coaches.

"It's difficult not to get close to your players, especially when you're younger," said Schramm. "I try not to do it, but sometimes it just happens. But it not only can be counterproductive from a business stand point but also can bother you personally. Hey, we're all human. I explode when something makes me angry, but as you get older, you're more able to put these things aside or forget them and go on. Well, in most cases.

"You might think you have an understanding or a good relationship with a player, but when it comes to personal finances or problems, most of them will turn on you. They'll think of themselves—not the team—first, and any relationship you've developed will become distant very quickly."

He did not say he was thinking of Tony Dorsett, but it was the most recent incident on his mind. He was torn between liking Tony and becoming infuriated with some of the things he said and what Schramm perceived as a type of disloyalty to the organization.

Tony's only perspective was that he had to cope with his financial problems and he also wanted the same kind of deal as Randy White, a man with whom he shared superstardom.

Practically all people want to get what they can, to make as much money as possible, but Schramm is such a strong organization man that he has a problem accepting this after he explains to a player that he must realize his value within the team concept, in proportion to the value placed on the contributions of other players.

Schramm certainly has let his personal feelings get in the way regarding some players and has a special liking for those who pioneered the team's success and helped it bridge the gaps from bad to average to outstanding. They were the Don Meredith's, Don Perkin's, Bob Lilly's, Chuck Howley's and Cornell Green's. If he had to pick a player he most admired and one who understood the system as Schramm saw it, the player would be Roger Staubach. If he had to pick a person he felt was most selfish regarding the system and one against whom he comes the closest to holding a grudge, it would be Lee Roy Jordan. But therein lies another paradox, because in the locker room or on the field, there have been few players more team-oriented than Lee Roy Jordan.

Bob Lilly had been the first draft choice of Dallas and a special player. So, when he bolted training camp and went back to Dallas in 1972, Schramm went after him. Lilly actually had flown from Dallas to Los Angeles and was to be picked up at the airport and taken to Thousand Oaks by a driver. Bob had a few drinks with Jethro Pugh en route, and they began talking about how unfairly they believed they were being paid. This might not have been Lilly's major concern when he got off the plane in LA and caught the next flight to Dallas, but it appeared to be the catalyst for his action. He had gone through a painful divorce involving children, and then met and married an Oklahoma schoolteacher. His wife didn't particularly like football. When Lilly didn't show up and Schramm heard what had happened, he rushed back to his room in the dorm, threw some things in a bag and went back to Dallas after Lilly. It was the fastest he'd moved since his days at Alhambra High. He went to Lilly's home and talked Bob into coming back.

"His new wife, Ann, just didn't think he should play football anymore," recalled Schramm. "I reasoned with them both and finally convinced them he should be playing. So he signed a new contract. A Bob Lilly is like a Roger Staubach. He's a once-in-a-lifetime player. You make exceptions in your ideals for people like that, the very special people.

"The most unusual thing now is that Ann's a great Cowboy fan. She loves football. She's very active in our reunions and has since said the greatest thing that ever happened was when Bob came back that time and played again."

But maybe wives were just more assertive in those days. Lilly's best friend and fellow defensive lineman, George Andrie, would come in to negotiate a contract and always say, "Well, I've got to go home and discuss this offer with my wife."

Schramm, once becoming irritated, snapped, "George, let's just save both of us a lot of time. Why don't you just send in your wife, and I'll negotiate with her."

Remembering Lilly, Schramm continued, "Bob was just a big, good natured guy who wasn't mean. He was just so quick. I think it's documented that most linemen who blocked him rate him the toughest. They'll always be comparing Lilly and Randy White. Randy had more of a mean streak but wasn't any better, if as good as Lilly."

Schramm's voice takes on a different tone, becoming softer and showing a deeper feeling when he speaks of Roger Staubach.

"He was the greatest sports hero of his time," said Schramm. "I can't think of another athlete in any sport in the 70s who could compare. I'm certainly not going to overlook his great contribution to this football team. That's well documented. But the very unique popularity of the Cowboys is based a heckuva lot on Roger Staubach. He was the hero of a nation, not just of the Cowboys or even the league. You see, I'm still very convinced that people want their heroes to be the All-American-boy types. He was a family man, had upstanding ideals and morals like Tom Landry, and yet had that great, gambling flair. He epitomized the adage that the game is never over.

"We've gone through stages in this country when people such as Joe Namath and their lifestyle became popular and were talked about and even emulated and glamorized. But those things pass and are usually limited to a certain segment of fans around the country. You could go to the youth of the country, the farm, the city, anywhere and Roger Staubach was a hero."

Schramm certainly has intimidated some players. He is the power, the structure and can be overbearing. He keeps saying he no longer will negotiate contracts. Yet, when it was Gil Brandt's job, he stepped in and changed Dorsett's contract. But when he did negotiate contracts with some veteran players he did so from a power viewpoint, often saying things to them that they weren't about to say to him. This is often the nature of negotiating but leaves some residue of ill feelings.

Staubach was one with whom he had no such problems." Tex can be very tough but, as far as I'm concerned, he was always honest and fair with me," Staubach explained. "He rewards fairness as he sees it with fairness. Oh, sure, he has the temper, but maybe sometimes he has good reason. We never had that much trouble with contracts."

Schramm remembered a conversation he had with Staubach over a contract.

"Well," Schramm said, "how much do you want?"

"Look," said Staubach, "I've talked to Fran Tarkenton and several other quarterbacks that were supposed to be making the big money. I don't think a quarterback should be judged by the size of his contract but by how well he plays."

Staubach recalled the conversation and added, "As a quarterback, I was one of the keys to the team. But I just believed I was well paid in the overall structure of the club. I signed my last contract for $230,000, with $600,000 in deferred money. If I'd gotten $100,000 more, I'd have felt guilty."

"It was a tribute to his wisdom that he always took deferred money, because he was starting to get into the real estate business," said Schramm. "He deferred money to cover any drops in the market if he should get into a bind on his investments. He was using that money instead of trying to get the top dollar up front and have it splashed all over the newspapers. He was taking care of the future and, as a result, seven years out of football, he heads a very successful company (the Staubach Company) that specializes in commercial real estate and has 125 employees."

"We have had our differences," continued Staubach, recalling when center Dave Manders was holding out for more money and Schramm was going to apparently let him sit.

"I went in to talk to Tex and he was mad about the situation. But he was candid. He'd say something like, 'Some of you guys are getting too big for your britches.' But we were having trouble at center and we needed Dave to be successful, to have a chance for the Super Bowl. But he listened to reason and talked to Dave and got him back.

"Oh, the Lee Roy situation was bad. I still disagree with Tex over the "Ring of Honor" deal."

Lee Roy Jordan played for 14 years, tying Bob Lilly for longevity with the Cowboys. He easily is the best middle linebacker the Cowboys ever had. He had 32 career interceptions, ranking behind only four defensive backs for that distinction, and remains the career leader in tackles, including 21 in a single game. He made the NEA Pro Football Writers All-Pro team in 1973 and was named All-Pro by *The Sporting News* in 1976. And he played middle linebacker in an era with Dick Butkus, Tommy Nobis and Ray Nitschke. Schramm somewhat jokingly will say that Bob Lilly, Don Meredith, Don Perkins, Chuck Howley, Mel Renfro and Roger Staubach were selected by a panel of judges to the "Ring of Honor," whose recipients have their names written on a ring going around Texas Stadium. Schramm might listen to suggestions but he IS the panel.

Schramm blows off steam and ordinarily doesn't hold grudges, or there would be a number of players to whom he no longer would be speaking, but time still hasn't erased his feelings regarding an incident with Jordan before the 1973 regular season opened. Lee Roy negotiated his own contract and felt vastly underpaid.

"I was like Bob Lilly and a number of people in those days," said Jordan. "We were just not brought up to beat our own drum. We'd go into Schramm's office and were intimidated by his power. He was so blunt, and we weren't used to hearing that. He'd say things like, 'Well, you're 29, 30, and we've got to start looking for somebody to replace you.' Hell, we were afraid to be very blunt, because we thought it might make us an outcast in Dallas and that people would look down on us. It wasn't true, but that's what we thought.

"One time in the late 1960s I asked for a raise, and Tex said what I wanted was more than Landry was making. It was about $50,000 a year. I asked Tom and he said that was true. So I just told Tom he was underpaid.

"I give Roger a hard time about the situation, too. Roger and Lilly were the highest paid. Roger didn't worry about the extra money, because he was getting a lot outside football. We got $100-$250 for a speaking engagement, and Roger might be getting $300-$400 in those days. But things were in proportion to what they made and that kept the rest of us down."

Jordan decided to play out his option in 1973 after few, if any, negotiations were held before training camp and no agreement had been reached. Some Cowboy players believe the Cowboys employ an unwritten strategy of waiting until a veteran gets to camp before seriously negotiating contracts.

"They'd brought in a bunch of linebackers, people like Rodrigo Barnes, who was destined for stardom," said Lee Roy. "They also had talked about moving D. D. Lewis into the middle. I thought they might negotiate if I reported to camp, so I went out there and worked. Here I was out there in two-a-days and the preseason playing out my option, taking a chance of getting hurt, and having no income in the future. There was a lot of pressure.

"I'd talked to Lee Roy Caffey, Ray Nitschke, Tommy Nobis and some of those guys and knew what was being paid middle linebackers. The season was starting. D. D. hadn't gotten much work in the middle, and those other guys didn't work out. I just got fed up and didn't show up for practice the Wednesday before we opened against Chicago. Schramm phoned me."

"What are you doing?" asked Schramm.

"I only play with a contract," said Jordan.

"I can't believe you're doing this," said Schramm.

"I tried to start negotiations six months ago. This is my last hurrah, my last chance."

"It wasn't so much Tex was rude," recalled Jordan. "It's just that we had a cool relationship."

"To me, one of the worst things an athlete can do is desert his team on the eve of a game when everybody is counting on him," said Schramm. "That's the basis of the ill feeling between us."

Lee Roy said Schramm signed him to a three-year contract which would pay him $75,000 in what turned out to be his final year. He's now successful in business, presiding over the Lee Roy Jordan Lumber Company. But he is not in the "Ring of Honor."

"A lot of people ask me about that," said Lee Roy. "I know it goes back to 1974 and the way Schramm feels. That's all right. I know what I contributed to the success of the Cowboys and the coaches know. I got the best out of my ability and was a good leader. I played against top competition and didn't chicken out in games that didn't count, like some of the players they have now do. Who knows? I might make it some day. Tex can't live forever."

"One of the things I admired about the New York Yankees is their selections of their Hall of Fame," said Schramm. "Guys like Ruth, Mantle, Gehrig and DiMaggio were in there. I believed we had to get our "Ring of Honor" started with people who made the most impact the first ten years. I don't think Lee Roy has priority over any of the people we have in there.

"Now that doesn't mean he won't get into it someday. You never can tell what the panel might do."

Roger Staubach is Schramm's greatest example of a guy who will find some way to win, of a person for whom things seem to fall into place. Roger could be having a terrible day but, when the game was on the line, he'd do a turnabout and make the big play. Twenty-three times he brought the Cowboys from behind to victory in the final period.

With 24 seconds left in the 1975 playoff game in Minnesota, he combined with Drew Pearson on a 50-yard touchdown pass that beat the Vikings, 17-14, and it became known in team annals as the "Hail Mary Pass." Actually, the pass was short, although Roger threw it as far as he could under the circumstances. Both Pearson and defender Nate Wright slowed down to wait for the pass. Pearson screened off Wright, who slipped and fell. Pearson caught the ball on his hip and lunged into the end zone. In a 1979 game with the Redskins, Dallas trailed 34-21 late in the final period. Roger threw for two touchdowns, the final one coming with 39 seconds left, as Dallas won 35-34.

On the other hand Craig Morton, the heir apparent to Don Meredith, played very well for Dallas but was just ill fated, somewhat of a puzzlement to Schramm.

"Morton was a tragic figure much of his career here," said Schramm. "It just seems some people are destined to win, and others to lose. I just haven't been able to put my finger on the reason."

In 1969 when Staubach was a rookie, Morton had stepped in for Don Meredith, who had retired, and was tearing up the NFL. Going into the season's fourth game against Atlanta, Craig was completing 73 percent of his passes and showed tremendous confidence. But he was hit by end Claude Humphrey after releasing a screen pass and fell on his right shoulder, suffering a slight separation. There certainly was a question about whether he should continue to play or undergo surgery. Landry said Staubach just wasn't ready. Morton said he'd been waiting four years to play and didn't want to come out. He continued to play, although his shoulder would be so sore during the week that sometimes he couldn't practice.

Surgery was performed after the season. While playing with the bad shoulder, Morton apparently changed his delivery and developed elbow problems the next season. This also required surgery.

"Craig showed a lot of courage after he hurt his shoulder," said Schramm. "But he wanted to play and knew the team needed him. Our doctors said he could play, but that he would be in pain. If they hadn't given the okay, he wouldn't have been allowed to play. Sure, you wonder what might have happened if he hadn't been injured and we'd have gone on and won the Super Bowl in 1970. It could have delayed Roger taking over for a while, but there's no way he wouldn't have been our Number One quarterback.

"I think the basic difference between Morton and Staubach was symbolized in our 1972 playoff game in San Francisco."

The preseason following the Cowboys' Super Bowl victory over Miami, a game in which Staubach was named MVP, Roger suffered a separation of his right shoulder in preseason. It was more severe than Morton's had been and required surgery right away. Staubach wasn't able to come back until near the end of the regular season and made only token appearances. He also was having shoulder and arm problems. Morton had taken over as the Number One quarterback again and helped Dallas make the playoffs. But the 49ers were leading Dallas, 28-16, with 1:53 left to play.

"Morton wasn't losing the game," said Schramm. "The defense wasn't playing well, and other people on the offense were messing up. Calvin Hill lost a fumble at our one and gave them an easy touchdown. Morton threw a touchdown bomb to Bobby Hayes, but he dropped the ball. Then when it all seemed over, Landry put in Staubach for Morton. The rest is history."

Staubach made a key run and threw for two touchdowns to give Dallas a 30-28 victory. In order to have a chance for the winning touchdown, Dallas had to recover an onside kick. Dick Nolan, then head coach of the 49ers, put receivers and backs on the front line of the kickoff return team, because they had better hands than the linemen. The kick went directly to wide receiver Preston Riley, who caught the ball, was hit and fumbled to Dallas.

"Something bad always seemed to happen to Craig and something good to Roger," said Schramm. "And it wasn't necessarily their making. Maybe it was their attitude, the way they thought. Frankly, I don't know. There has to be some reason that, when two players both have good ability, one wins and the other loses. Oh, Craig didn't have the talent of Staubach, but he was still a helluva athlete.

He was a smart, nice man. Hell, he took Denver to the Super Bowl against us (January, 1978) and had had a fine season. Then he ends up with awful statistics in the game. But the fact was our line rushed him off his feet. He didn't have a chance. Things went against him off the field, too. He trusted the wrong people and went bankrupt. Then look at Staubach.''

Danny White seems to be like Morton. He'll play well, and then, sometimes, things go against him in crucial games. "It was unfortunate for Danny to have to follow Staubach," said Schramm. "Nobody could have done that. There was going to be the natural comparisons. Danny is a nice, devoted guy. I think one play could have made the difference in his career."

In 1980 when White replaced Staubach, Dallas was badly beaten by Philadelphia in the NFC title game, one step away from the Super Bowl. White did not play well but had previously. He had taken a page from Staubach's book by bringing Dallas from a 27-17 deficit with four minutes left to victory in the first round of the playoffs against Atlanta. But the play Schramm is talking about occurred the following year in the NFC championship game against San Francisco.

Dallas seemed to have the game won, 27-21, but the defense couldn't hold Joe Montana and his passing game as the 49ers marched the length of the field. Montana hit Dwight Clark for the winning touchdown, 28-27. But as time was running out, White had moved Dallas to the San Francisco 40. One more first down and the Cowboys would have been in good field-goal range. The crowd noise kept Dallas from using the shotgun, so White had to get under center. He dropped back to pass, and Tony Hill was wide open for the first down. But Danny tripped, was trapped and dropped the ball and the 49ers recovered. He wouldn't have been in position to trip in the shotgun.

"I don't know if he saw the rush or not, or if he could have gotten the ball to Hill," said Schramm. "But if he had and we'd have won the game, we'd have been matched in the Super Bowl against Cincinnati. I don't think the Bengals were that good then. If Danny had been able to complete that pass, if we had made the Super Bowl and perhaps won it, then everybody would have been singing his praises and he'd have been riding on a crest of confidence."

The following season was shortened by the NFLPA strike. White made some statements that they ought to get on with the season. This angered some of his teammates. In the NFC title game White was knocked out, and Gary Hogeboom came in and did well, although Dallas was demolished by the Redskins, 32-17. The seeds of what became the Hogeboom-White controversy were planted. A contingent of players, writers and fans began to believe Hogeboom was the answer at quarterback, not White. He wasn't. Hogeboom was traded, and White seemed to be on top of his game again in 1986 until he suffered a broken right wrist at midseason. For that and other reasons the team fell apart.

Schramm thought for a while and added that he always will regret the team's other quarterback, Don Meredith, didn't stick around for the championship years.

"Here's a guy who took a beating and helped us get through the difficult, early years," said Schramm. "Then he retires at the age of 30. My god, he was only reaching his prime."

Meredith was outstanding in 1966, when Dallas first reached championship caliber and brought Dallas on a tremendous comeback, when it almost caught Green Bay before losing, 34-27, in the NFL championship game. With Meredith quarterbacking the Cowboys lost another last-second NFL title game to the Packers, 21-17, in the Ice Bowl the following season. In 1968 he only had to complete a third of his passes against the New York Giants in the season finale to win the NFL passing championship. But the game was meaningless, and Meredith partied with friends at George Plimpton's apartment in New York the night before and, as he put it, "I couldn't hit the ground with the ball the next day." He left after completing one of nine passes, and Morton came in to help Dallas win. The Cowboys were 12-2. They had defeated Cleveland during the regular season but were beaten by the Browns, 31-20, in the Eastern Conference championship game. Landry had pulled Meredith in the game and replaced him with Morton. Don had thought about retirement the previous year after the disappointing second loss to Green Bay. This time he thought about it and quit.

Actually, Schramm got along a lot better with Meredith than Don did Landry. Meredith was a fun-loving, laidback-type person who would smile on the outside, even when he was hurting inside. He would laugh and joke with Schramm, and they even cried on each other's shoulders on the sideline near the end of the surprising loss to Cleveland.

"Don had problems understanding Landry, and Tom couldn't figure him out," said Schramm. "Don just didn't always act serious about football, like Tom did, especially in those days. Playing quarterback was not his whole life. Tom couldn't understand his, well, flippancy.''

Sometimes Meredith would come into the huddle singing. Once during a big scrimmage game in Thousand Oaks, a Meredith pass was intercepted by Cornell Green. Meredith took off his helmet and began chasing Cornell. He held his helmet high as if he were going to try to bean Cornell and ran in a kind of a gallop, as if he were pretending to ride a horse. Green laughed. The fans laughed. Schramm laughed. Landry did not laugh. They did seem to reach an understanding in later years, and Landry did take up for Meredith when the fans and media seemed to be against him in 1965. Meredith was in a slump and, in midseason, people were calling for Landry to play Craig Morton or Jerry Rhome. After a long night of contemplation, Landry said Meredith would start the remainder of the year. Period. After that Meredith came on strong and led Dallas to the Playoff Bowl, a game for runnerup teams in those days.

Meredith played his last game against Minnesota in the Playoff Bowl of 1968, after Dallas had been beaten by Cleveland. He won the MVP award in the 17–13 Dallas win. On the trophy was a figurine of a football player. Somehow, the head broke off. "Figures," said Meredith.

"I tried to talk him out of retiring, but couldn't," said Schramm. "We knew that at the age he retired a quarterback is just coming into his own, maturing. I think Don would have matured and done even more than he did.

"I'm very sorry he didn't stay around long enough to win a Super Bowl. He deserved that and would have been recognized as one of the very best there was. He'd have became as famous for his ability, as he did for his personality on the Monday night football games."

After being retired for a season, Meredith phoned Schramm and came to talk to him in 1970. He mentioned that he would be interested in coming out of retirement but didn't want to get into a situation where he'd have to battle Morton for the job. He'd had enough of any quarterback controversies. But Morton had been the quarterback in 1969, and Schramm couldn't offer him any such situation.

"I think Don had just begun questioning why he'd quit in the first place," said Schramm. "But we didn't have any continuing conversations about it. We just talked that one time, and I don't know how serious he was. He just thought about it, we talked and that was it.''

Schramm said he liked Meredith and that maybe he did get a little close to him. "But in my dealings with him, we stayed away from subjects on which we might disagree. We knew what we could and could not talk about, so we didn't argue or have any problems. He'd always talk about our different worlds. Once we were talking about contracts or something and I said, 'If you were in my world, you would think this way.' Don looked at me, grinned and said, 'I don't want to be in your world. I want to stay in mine.' After that, he'd always kid me about my world and his.''

In 1970 the Dallas Cowboys seemed to be reeling and about to bottom out prematurely. The team appeared to be locked in some kind of psychological tunnel when it came to key games. Perhaps, it was the lingering disappointments of two straight last-minute losses to Green Bay in the NFL championship games. It could have gotten to the point where, subconsciously, they were holding back and trying not to lose, rather than attempting an all-out effort to win. Schramm, for one, does not believe the team would have suffered through the shocking losses to Cleveland in the Eastern Conference championship games in 1968 and 1969 had it not been for the Green Bay defeats. Green Bay had the experience and the best team in 1966, but Schramm and many other observers believe Dallas was the better club in 1967 and that only the elements in Green Bay, Wisconsin, that day stopped the Cowboys from proving it. Temperatures were 13 below zero at gametime and, with a strong wind, the chill factor was some 30 degrees below zero. Dallas was a wide-open team and, when the field became an ice arena, Landry had to abandon his best-laid plans.

The 1968 and 1969 clubs were better than the ones which lost the NFL title games to the Packers and yet they had failed miserably against the Browns. Prior to 1970 Schramm and Landry discussed the situation, and everybody began to look into his particular phase of the organization to try to find out what was happening to cause the team to play well in regular season and fall apart in the playoffs. The second major inner evaluation of the organization would not come again until the spring of 1986, when Schramm would become stronger in prodding Landry to make changes in his staff and looking into once successful methods which no longer seemed to work that well.

"There were no plans in 1970 to bring anybody new into the organization," said Schramm. "We evaluated our entire organization but this is no way included Tom Landry." Schramm and Landry had seemed equal catalysts but Schramm would take the initiative the next time.

In 1970 questionnaires were sent out to each player, asking opinions on all aspects of the club—the approach, the system, the coaches and their teammates. In exchange for candor the players received anonymity and were not required to sign the questionnaires. However, Roger Staubach later admitted that he'd skipped all the questions and simply put down that he wanted a "real" chance to play.

"On some of the questionnaires the players said the team was overly prepared for games," recalled Schramm. "Some criticized Landry's 'puritanism' and voiced negative opinions regarding some assistant coaches and even equipment manager Jack Eskridge. Players said there were too many cliques on the team, too many prima donnas, and that they were tired of trying to finesse opponents and wanted to try to plysically blow them out, as Cleveland had done to them."

In the early years Landry admittedly had more of a closed mind but, to his credit, he was becoming more flexible by this time. He also had begun to think more of individuals, rather than just people, as part of a team. He went more to a grind-it-out offense, instead of relying so much on the big play, a weapon which had made the Cowboys even more popular than the Los Angeles Rams during Schramm's days with that team. Landry moved backfield coach Ermal Allen into a new capacity of special assistant, in charge of scouting other NFL teams and grading all players in the league by performance levels. This included the Cowboys. Danny Reeves, a very popular player, was named player-coach. Reeves, it was felt, could more easily relate to the players, because he was closer to their age. In the past starters had remained starters even if their performance level fell off. But Landry decided if a player didn't live up to the level expected of him, he would lose his starting job until he did. This was to effect some of the offense linemen and also Bobby Hayes and Craig Morton. Each was benched, although each eventually returned to the starting lineup.

"Most of the complaints came, because we started a new off-season conditioning program," said Schramm. "At that time, pro football really wasn't a year-round job, and so the players kind of forgot about it during the off season and took other full-time jobs. But the competition was so close, and everybody was looking for the slightest edge and the job of being a professional football player, for all practical purposes, became a year-round.''

Alvin Roy, former Olympic weight coach and the man who had had great success in conditioning the Kansas Chiefs when they won the Super Bowl, was hired. He initiated an off-season running and weight program which was said not to be mandatory. But a list was kept of those who were there and the inference was clear.

The new approach did not seem to be working, as Dallas lost a Monday night football game over national television to St. Louis, 38–0, and slipped to 5–4.

It was before the next game against Green Bay on Thanksgiving, a traditional date for Dallas to play because Schramm figured the team would get more TV exposure, that Schramm got a call that seemed to put the team in more disarray than ever.

"It was the most shocking call I've ever gotten," said Schramm. "The Highland Park police department was calling. They said I'd better come on over to the station, because Lance Rentzel was there and had a serious problem.

"I went over there, not knowing the extent of the trouble. And then I saw Rentzel in the corner of this room. He had on slacks, a sport shirt, and his head was down. He looked like a beaten animal."

The police told Schramm that Rentzel had been identified and then picked up for exposing himself to a young girl. He'd called her over to his car, exposed himself and driven off. But a witness had gotten his license number.

"The police were prepared to make positive identification," said Schramm. "At that point there wasn't any denying of anything. The evidence was there."

The Cowboys had gotten Rentzel from Minnesota in a trade for a draft choice, and he'd proven to be an outstanding flanker, leading the club in receptions for two seasons, becoming a good blocker, and furnishing a threat opposite Bob Hayes that had not been there before. Rentzel beat out Pete Gent, who remained angry over the situation and was eventually traded to the New York Giants. Gent went on to become a successful writer, authoring *North Dallas Forty*, a best seller whose fictionalized characters were often thought to be real members of the Cowboys.

When Rentzel came to Dallas, there had been rumors that he once had an indecent exposure episode in Minnesota but that it was hushed up.

"We knew he'd had a problem in Minnesota, but we investigated the situation and were satisfied that he recognized his problem, was getting treatment and doing positive things to correct it," said Schramm.

The Cowboys tried to keep the Rentzel incident out of the media, but *The Oklahoma City Journal* broke the story prior to the Thanksgiving game, stating that Rentzel had been released on an appearance bond after being questioned in regard to indecent exposure involving a 10-year-old girl.

The night before the Packer game, Rentzel appeared before the team and, tearfully, said, "I've made a mistake in my life before, and now I've made a second one. The Green Bay game will be my last one for the Cowboys."

The players had taken a vote and unanimously wanted Rentzel to stay on the team. Schramm met with Landry and decided otherwise. The players felt Lance was part of the team and that just because he was in trouble didn't mean they shouldn't stick by him. Schramm, however, could see this as being not only a great distraction for the team but also as creating problems for Rentzel. Lance would take a lot of abuse, and Commissioner Rozelle could also step in and suspend him. He played in the 16–3 victory over Green Bay, which launched the club on a string that ended with the Super Bowl loss to Baltimore. After the Packer game, Rentzel again spoke to his teammates.

"I just want to thank all of you guys for sticking behind me. I've decided, though, that it is best I don't play again until this problem is straightened out." Schramm had been one of his advisors on this decision.

In early April of the following year, Rentzel pleaded guilty to indecent exposure and was assessed a five-year probated sentence, with the understanding he receive regular medical and psychiatric care. The Cowboys traded him to Los Angeles.

"He went to California and stayed by himself and wrote a book, *When All the Laughter Died in Sorrow*," said Schramm. "His marriage with Joey Heatherton had fallen apart, but Lance seems to be doing alright now. He'll call two, three times a year.''

Bobby Hayes, the other wide receiver, would also have serious problems and became the first of two former Cowboys to be sent to prison.

Bobby Hayes was a child-man. He had left Hell's Hole, a poor black section of Jacksonville, Florida, to became everybody's hero in the 1964 Olympics in Tokyo when he won the 100 meters in 10 flat and, taking the baton far behind, raced the United States to victory in the 400-meter relay. On his anchor lap Hayes was timed in 8.6 in the final 100 meters. When he took the victory stand to receive his Gold Medal, Hayes did not raise his hand with clenched fish in the symbol of Black Power, as John Carlos and Tommy Smith later were to do, when the national anthem was played, but said he got chillbumps and never had been so proud when he heard the "Star-Spangled Banner." After he joined the Cowboys, he said he continued to get chillbumps when the national anthem was played before a game.

Schramm, always intrigued with speed and in a position when he was with the Rams to see what a weapon it could be in pro foot-ball, had personally chosen Hayes as the team's Number Seven draft pick in 1964. The top prospects were gone, and Tom Landry didn't feel his input in the grab bag of players that were left was impor-tant so he went home. Gil Brandt also left to go to try to sign Mel Renfro, the team's top choice that year. The list of the remaining prospects was there, in order, but Schramm took it on his own to deviate from this list and pick Hayes. Bobby went on to become a catalyst in the 1960s, time and time again running through man-to-man coverages to catch long touchdown passes. Hayes, perhaps more so than anybody, was the reason the NFL defenses changed to combination and zone coverages to try to cope with super speed. When Landry took a tougher approach in 1970 and required his wide receivers to be adequate blockers, Bobby Hayes fell short. The new coverages frustrated him and, with the advent of Lance Alworth and, finally, Drew Pearson, quarterbacks began looking the other direction.

Hayes, in his frustration, made a childish statement that passers, even Roger Staubach, wouldn't throw to him because he was black. Nothing could have been farther from the truth, but some of Bobby's friends told him this, and he began to believe it. He was traded to San Francisco in 1975 and soon was let go by the 49ers. His days, excellent days in his prime, as a player were over.

In 1979 Bobby Hayes pleaded guilty to charges of delivering narcotics to an undercover agent and was sentenced to five years in prison.

"That was very tragic," said Schramm, who along with Tom Landry testified for Hayes prior to sentencing. "Bobby's biggest crime was that he was a person who always wanted to please people. As a result, he would do or say something that a person wanted to hear. He wanted to be accepted. Oh, he might have made that statement about quarterbacks throwing to white faces, but he didn't mean it and I'm sure apologized later.

"He was way ahead of his time as far as a sprinter making it as a football player. His intelligence was more street-wise in nature. He did not have the basic knowledge or, perhaps, intelligence to deal with life after football. He continued to try to do this or that to please people, so they would like him.

"I sincerely believe that had a lot to do with the drug deal. He did not really want to get involved in the associations that led to that. But he believed that if he did it would make him more acceptable to this or that person. He wanted to do whatever he could to make somebody like him, so they put an undercover agent in with him and, hell, he was trying to do something to please that guy, too.

"This is all going to sound stupid to somebody who did not know Bobby, but it's true. I testified that here was a man who did not intentionally do anything wrong, but one who wanted to be accepted and said and did the things that the person with whom he communicated (the federal agent) wanted to hear.

"But, hell, Bobby was a prominent person, a name, so that judge didn't want people to think Bobby was getting special treatment, so he gave him a strong sentence."

Hayes was a model prisoner. He was released after serving 18 months. While he was in prison Schramm arranged to get him a leave to attend a Cowboy reunion.

Thomas Henderson was a fun-loving, clever young man from Langston College, a small school in Oklahoma. He came to the Cowboys with an inlaid gold star in one of his front teeth and nicknamed himself, "Hollywood." His physical talents were immense. He was a linebacker but had such great speed that he was also used to take handoffs and run back kickoffs when the Cowboys used a reverse. He was a member of the "Dirty Dozen," the 12 rookies which helped revive the Cowboys in a 1975 season in which they became the first wildcard team to make the Super Bowl. That group also included Randy White. When people weren't talking about White, they were talking about Henderson—that is, when Henderson wasn't talking about himself. But he did it in a lighthearted manner.

"Something about the crowd makes me think, hey, they're all looking at me," he said. "With 80,000 in the stands, that means 160,000 eyeballs staring at me, unless there's some one-eyed people up there."

Henderson would make mistakes in the defense but also made a lot of big plays. Landry finally put him in the starting lineup, instead of using him only on passing downs and special situations, and he had a good season with the promise of much better things to come. But in 1979 he began to miss meetings and claim he was injured and couldn't practice. In one game he did not record a single tackle. Landry remained patient. During the 34–20 Cowboy loss to Washington over national television, the sideline cameras caught Thomas clowning. This incident did not go over well with the Cowboys, who did not find losing to the Redskins a laughing matter. Landry, as he had with Duane Thomas, reached the end of his patience and told Schramm to get rid of Henderson.

"When Tom gives them chance after chance, and then the negatives outnumber the positives, he lets them go," said Schramm.

Henderson's life went from 80,000 people watching to a place where people glance at your name, feel sorry for what might have been, and then who you were keeps paling until you're forgotten. The limelight becomes only a flicker and then goes out.

He was traded to San Francisco for a draft choice. The 49ers waived him. The crowning blow with Bill Walsh came during a stretching and exercising drill in practice. The players were on the ground, going through their routines, and then stood up when they'd finished. Henderson did not stand up. He was asleep. Thomas signed with Houston and was released again. It was then that he put himself in a treatment center for cocaine abuse. He said he'd been taking some form of narcotics for 14 years and had had a cocaine dependency for five years. When he left the center, Miami coach Don Shula, realizing Henderson was still a super athlete and might have straightened out his problem, gave him another chance.

Henderson injured his neck and failed to make the team. Henderson served a term in federal prison for a charge in which two women, one in a wheel chair, accused him of sexually assaulting them.

"Thomas Henderson could have been a dominating force in this league, even now," said Schramm. "You could sit across the desk and talk to him, and he was so clever and charming. You could watch him make great plays on the field and be amazed and then disturbed when he'd mess up so bad when you knew his capabilities."

Henderson contacted Schramm while he was in prison and told him he wanted to do something positive with his life, to tell people what cocaine had done to him and could do to them. Upon his release, he began going around the country lecturing on the pitfalls of using drugs and how they had ruined his career. He also wrote a book on his life and problems called, *Out of Control*. Schramm hopes Henderson continues to speak out against drugs. Others, such as Mercury Morris, have done the same thing in regard to their drug experiences. There has been a lot of talk . . . a lot of talk.

chapter nine

DRUGS, TOO REAL

During a two-week period in June 1986, a time that was too true to be real, a nice kid from the University of Maryland named Len Bias and Don Rogers, a young man just beginning his career with the Cleveland Browns, each died in cocaine-related incidents. Their deaths both diminished and, perhaps, emphasized winter's headlines of the New York Giants' fine linebacker Lawrence Taylor checking himself into a Texas drug rehabilitation clinic for cocaine abuse. Bias, 22, was the picture of health and, perhaps, the best collegiate basketball player in the country. He had been drafted by the world champion Boston Celtics, and a Great American Dream was about to unfold. He would become a millionaire almost overnight. After being drafted he partied with friends, used cocaine and died. Just like that.

"He was so healthy, in such great shape," said roommate Terry Long, who was at the party, "that it never occurred to me that he might die, that someone might die. You always think it will be someone else, not you or your friends."

The national toll-free helpline (800-COCAINE) receives some 1,200 calls per day. Dr. Arnold Washton, director of substance-abuse research and treatment at the Regent Hospital in New York City and research director of the helpline, estimates 25 million

Americans, a tenth of the population, have tried cocaine and that between five and six million use it once a month. Furthermore, he feels two to three million are seriously dependent. The drug is a stimulant, an anesthetic. It increases heart and respiratory rates, raises temperatures and restricts blood vessels. It overstimulates the brain, which can trigger seizures. Len Bias shuddered in a kind of seizure and died.

At first there was an attempt at a cover-up. Bias was a tremendous, law-abiding youngster who just wouldn't do such a thing. After the truth was known people said his death would serve as a deterrent to others. It was not for Rogers, 23.

In 1982 Tex Schramm proposed random drug testing in the NFL. But in the collective bargaining agreement that same year, teams were only allowed to administer a urinalysis in preseason physicals and to use spot checks during the season only if there was reasonable cause to believe a player was using drugs. "Reasonable cause" was an evasive term.

Gene Upshaw, an old adversary of Tex Schramm's and the executive director of the NFLPA, offered the union's plan, in which the urinalysis was retained as a part of the preseason physicals. Further tests could be taken by team doctors if "reasonable cause" was determined. Players testing positive would be treated at an independent facility, where they would be subject to random testing. If they failed any of these random tests at the facility they'd lose one-sixteenth of their annual salary. If they failed a second time they would be suspended, subject to review.

After the tragic death of Bias and Rogers, Commissioner Pete Rozelle chose to ride the crest of public sentiment and announced a strong plan. Besides the preseason checks, Rozelle wanted to subject players to two other random checks during the regular season for cocaine, heroin or marijuana use. First time offenders would be sent to rehabilitation centers, removed from the roster for 30 days and fined half a month's pay. Second-time offenders would be removed from the roster for 30 days and fined a month's pay. Potential lifetime suspension faced third-time offenders.

The NFLPA quickly challenged Rozelle for violating the collective bargaining agreement by unilaterally making a change in the drug agreement. Upshaw said if Rozelle did this in regard to drugs, he might do it on other issues. Rozelle said he would not. The players also said the plan constituted an invasion of privacy. It was after the threat of court action that Rozelle agreed to binding arbitration.

The key issue seemed to be "random testing" which would be unannounced and, by the letter of the wording, perhaps in violation of the Constitution. The Fourth Amendment protects the right of people to be secure in their person, their homes and against unreasonable search and seizures.

Schramm believes a professional athlete gives up certain rights because of the nature of his profession. He is a role model, a person who is paid an inordinate amount of money for his work.

Some players agree with him, and the ones who do not say it might be more beneficial to our society to, for example, give random drug tests to airline pilots who have the lives of hundreds of people in their hands. They say sports is not life and death, but a game. But Bias and Rogers were life and death. Another argument is that, if random tests are to be given to professional athletes, then why not to entertainers. They're in the public eye, and drug abuse certainly seems more prevalent in that field. However, entertainers do not generally have the clean-cut image of an athlete. Sportswriters around the country differ on the issue, some of them beating the drum against invasion of privacy.

"I wonder what would happen if they gave some of the so-called liberal minded columnists and reporters random drug tests," said Schramm.

He quickly dismissed the player's first suggested plan as "embarrassing and insulting to everybody, because it proposed nothing new and only limited the penalties for those caught using drugs. But that doesn't surprise me. The union doesn't have what you might call adult leadership in its executive committee." That leadership would be a subject he'd center in on during and after the 1987 strike.

Schramm said the committee's immaturity was very evident in the drug plan the players originally presented.

"Their plan didn't even address prevention of drug use," he continued. "My god, people are killing themselves with the drug, and we're worried about a union issue. I didn't think Pete's first plan, the one he went to arbitration with, wasn't nearly strong enough but, at least, it was a step forward.

"What the hell. I mean they're worried about the Constitution. I don't see the correlation when it comes to a serious problem and an alternative of unannounced testing. You know, if I'm hiring you to work for me, I have a right to set standards for your employment.

"They certainly bend the libel laws and the rights of an individual who is in the public eye. They say, well, a person is in the public eye, so he is subject to fair comment and criticism. They're treated different. The same should go for drugs. When you become a professional athlete and a public figure, you get special treatment, so you have to give up some things. There has to be a payback for this. I believe most of the people who come into sports know this and are willing to give up rights a normal citizen enjoys.

"In today's society there has to be a point where drugs just aren't acceptable. Why, it's against the law in the first place. And when you have a chance to control it and maybe even defeat it in an organization such as the NFL, then you've got the obligation to do it. Everybody has that obligation.

"Any plan that does not have random testing isn't going to be successful. I like the term unannounced testing better than random testing, which sounds like you're going to jump around and pick this guy, then that one."

Schramm believes the unannounced testing has to be administered by the league, an independent agency, and not by the clubs. "Nobody should know when they're coming to do the tests," he said. "The group just shows up unannounced, and sets up and gives the tests. I'm not sure I trust all the clubs to be discreet if they know when the tests are going to be held.

"I don't have the attitude that you can classify drug abuse as just a sickness that only deserves treatment, not punishment. Fear of unannounced tests will stop it. They say, 'Cure it by education.' That's naive. You'll cure it by education all right if they realize that once they get nailed their careers are over. Then they'll be educated."

Schramm doesn't believe the random testing will help the heavy users, because their addiction will eliminate them, forcing them to get help.

"Most of the people I've talked to or read about will say about the same thing. They'll say they started using cocaine as a social thing and kept doing it for about six months. They'll say they did not believe it was hurting them or anybody else. Then they'll say something happened to them, and that they just couldn't let go.

"The tests would catch the early user and deter him. Discover them doing it in the early months, and you can stop them."

Schramm, of course, would have much stiffer penalties for violators. First-time offenders would be sent for treatment at their own, not the club's expense. If they didn't have the money, it would be deducted from future salaries. A second-time offender would be suspended for a full season without pay. In order to be allowed to return after that year, he would be required to present as much conclusive evidence as possible that he had kicked the habit. A third-time offender would be banned from the NFL for good, without recourse or another chance.

Upshaw also complained that the drug problem was being "painted as a black issue by the league." From 1980-86 37 of the 43 NFL players linked to illegal drug use have been black. All seven players suspended by the league for drug use have been black.

"Leaders in the black community are aware that the drug problem in our league has mostly concerned their race," said Schramm. "It is disturbing and is a deeper rooted problem than any we can deal with at this stage, other than to try to stop it now. Generally speaking, it's environmental. We're trying to address a drug issue, not a black or white issue.

"When Gene says the league paints it as a black issue, he reminds me of his predecessor, Ed Garvey. Garvey was always trying to build his strength in the union through the blacks by attempting to make differences with the league a racial issue."

chapter ten

SCHRAMM VERSUS NFLPA AND AGENTS

During the first great confrontation between the NFL owners and the National Football League Players' Association in 1970, one of the strategies of the players was to try to wear out the opposing side's representatives. The players were in their 30s, and members of the owners' negotiation committee were 20 or more years older. Tex Schramm, who was chairman, was 50. The players believed they could mentally and physically fatigue the opposition and make inroads.

NFLPA president John Mackey and its director Alan Miller took Schramm up on his offer to go fishing in Bimini, the small group of islands in the straits of Florida in the northwest section of the Bahamas. Schramm borrowed Pete Rozelle's boat and they took off, feeling perhaps their talks could be more progressive, if private and uninterrupted.

"Okay, we can just stay up all night if we have to in order to reach some agreements," said Mackey.

"That's fine by me," said Schramm.

Miller and the players dropped off one by one in the early morning hours as Schramm sat there, sipping his Scotch and arguing. The longer they went, the more he came alive. They had miscalculated his staying power, which is not correlated to his age

but, perhaps, to his experience in such late hour sessions, and he
was the last one to go to bed.

The heated negotiations lasted from early April until after training camp had opened in August. The players had sought to neutralize
the power of Rozelle and gain $25.8 million for their retirement
fund and other expenditure increases. The owners offered $18.1 and
would not compromise the power structure of the league. The settlement was for $19.1 million and Rozelle retained his status and
the governing body of the NFL, its structure. Schramm was proud
of these things and also the fact that he was able to get the players
to agree on a four-year settlement, meaning four years of peace.
The iron hand of Rozelle was evident in the settlement. He kept
the negotiations together in a 22-hour marathon until the deadlock
was broken.

A strong indication of the way Schramm thinks and feels was
that, even after such an exhausting experience, he did not take the
advice of friends and go on a short vacation. He didn't even go
home to Dallas but caught a flight from New York and went directly
to training camp. He looked like a caricature of himself, his clothes
baggy from the loss of 15 pounds and his face very drawn. But he
felt it was important to get to camp and mingle with the players.
He had been the main negotiator for the owners, but the war was
over and he didn't want any lingering hard feelings about him from
the players. There did not seem to be. The first day he came to the
practice field players continually came over to greet him and shake
his hand.

John Mackey said Schramm was the toughest negotiator the
players had ever confronted.

"I was very proud of what we'd accomplished," said Schramm.
"Another interesting aspect of the negotiations was the appearance
of a young attorney from Minnesota. He was from a firm repre-
senting the players. After we'd agreed on all points, he was going
to draw up the legal agreement for the parties to sign. A couple
of months later when I received the bargaining agreement, it did
not represent at all what we'd agreed upon. All kinds of things had
been added, and changes had been made to benefit the players. So
we went back for another meeting to tell them the agreement had
been altered, and there was no deal unless it was written just as
we'd originally agreed upon. So there was another big fight before
we got it straight.

"The young attorney was Ed Garvey. He got Alan Miller fired and became head of the union. But that was how he got his foot in the door with the players. The truth really meant very little to Ed Garvey. To me, he represented a feeling you sometimes find in the Communist Party or a religious cult. The end justifies the means, no matter what you have to do.

"Garvey took the players out of the original context of their organization and into a full-scale union. In those days the players didn't like the term "union," and resented it when you used it to describe their association. They thought of themselves as an association of professional players. I remember saying at the time (1970) that they were going to be a union and might as well join the teamsters or something."

Schramm, who is back on the owners' committee but not its chairman, was used in an advisory capacity when the NFLPA struck in 1974. That year there were pickets in training camp and a clenched-fist salute.

"Garvey tried to split groups, even blacks and whites," said Roger Staubach. "He had many blacks feeling they were seeking social upheaval. Blacks haven't been treated very fairly in our society over the years, and they certainly could relate to taking such a stand—a revolutionary stand. It was as though we were going into a kind of black separatism. The association even came out with the clenched fist to signify what we were doing. That's the symbol of a revolutionary country. There are areas in society that need changing, but to equate them to professional football isn't apropos. Garvey and the NFLPA officials led the players to believe this was necessary."

Veterans began to filter back into camps, breaking the picket lines. Staubach reported before the third preseason game. Garvey commented that he'd have hated to "have been at Pearl Harbor with Staubach." He later apologized. Staubach was a Vietnam veteran.

"Garvey always used the racial issue to solidify the blacks behind the union by continually charging that management was prejudiced," said Schramm. "Anybody in the league or associated with it knew this wasn't true. The truth didn't matter. He wanted passionate support."

He added that Garvey did do a good job for the players but left a lot of hard feelings. He compared him to Marvin Miller, who took a softer approach in dealing with the baseball owners, but ended up gaining a lot more. Garvey left the union and entered politics, failing in an attempt to gain a state senate seat. Schramm said it wouldn't surprise him if Garvey returned to the NFLPA. "We forgot to drive a stake through his heart," he added.

During the following confrontations between management and the NFLPA, Schramm seemed to work more in the background but when, in the spirit of Garvey's so called "freedom issues," the NFLPA sought to change the basic structure of the NFL by going all-out for "free agency," Schramm took the bit in his mouth and jumped right back in the middle of the fray, something for which he received a lot of credit and also paid a price.

The visitors could not have picked a worst time to stop by Tex Schramm's office on their tour of the Cowboys Center at Valley Ranch but, of course, enthusiasm sometimes makes people oblivious to timing. Schramm certainly isn't a Hamlet-like figure, the opposite being true, but he seems to be subject, as Shakespeare put it, to the "slings and arrows of outrageous fortune." The forces of fortune were members of the NFLPA and union-inclined practitioners in the media who had targeted him as the symbol of the disaster that was the 1987 strike, one in which the players were publicly humiliated and financially devastated. He was but one of five members of the Management Council, whose chairman was actually Hugh Culverhouse, but Schramm was the person the opposition came after. The union had stated, if necessary, it would dismantle the system of pro football to achieve its demands of free agency. Schramm, a keeper of the flame as far as the integrity and structure of the NFL, took this threat personally, because the league is among the closest things to his heart, soul and being. So he had taken the baton, run both the opening and anchor laps and trampled some feelings on the way.

As he put it, "Hell, I went from a committee member to spokesman to proponent to architect to czar."

And some of his players such as Jeff Rohrer and, predictably, Tony Dorsett, had insulted Cowboy fans for supporting the replacement team. Rohrer had said Dallas fans were second-rate and not as knowledgeable as those in strong union cities. Dorsett, booed when he played in a replacement game, said he didn't care, because the fans didn't pay his salary. "Just who the hell does he think pays it?" asked Tex, cringing.

And the team had just lost and Victor Scott had been taken off the roster for treatment of an alcohol and/or drug problem . . . And it had been falsely implied by some media people that Tex had short-changed the replacement players that he had so supported and loved by taking back the original $1,000 retainer they'd been given. This wasn't true, but the facts somehow seemed to have been lost in the translation . . . And there were soon-to-explode rumblings from Herschel Walker and Tony Dorsett that one or the other should be picked as the starting halfback and be left alone . . . And he was worried about his grandson Shane, who so much reminded him of himself as a youngster, and the new baby his daughter had adopted was just coming home . . . And other NFL officials who had been just as strong, if not as vocal, in their feelings about the strike seemed to have become extremely quiet . . . And. . . .

So Tex Schramm was uncharacteristically subdued when his secretary Connie stuck her head into his office and apologized, but said, "Mr. Schramm, there are some visitors here who would like to meet you and see your office, but I'll just tell them to come back later."

He stared at the floor for a few moments, a weak smile crossing his face, and he said, "Oh, why not. Tell them to come on in."

He got up, smiling and extending his hand to greet three men and a woman holding a baby. He chatted and posed for pictures and assured them they were not bothering him in the least. They'd been touring the team facilities and told him how impressed they were. Finally, as they were leaving, one of the men asked Schramm if he would mind holding the baby and posing for just one more picture. Schramm held the infant as the man took a couple of shots.

"This is such a thrill, Mr. Schramm," said the man." Someday he'll really be proud of this picture." Schramm told them to come back. A visitor who had been in his office expressed astonishment, not only because Schramm had taken the time, under such trying circumstances, to visit strangers but also because, the way things were going, the baby hadn't wet on him. Apprised of the odds of such a thing happening, he laughed.

It is indicative that Schramm would take the role he did during the 1987 strike and also that so many players who supported the union would not only single him out as the enemy but also his team. Dallas is a right-to-work city, a weak union area, and the Cowboys are not a strong union team. As player rep Doug Cosbie put it, "We stayed together all of 15 minutes" as far as the union's stand was concerned. Randy White and Don Smerek crossed the line the first day, followed shortly thereafter by Ed Jones, Tony Dorsett, Danny White and Mike Renfro. And then Kevin Brooks and N' Newton crossed. In all, including the injured reserve and frin players, 21 turned their backs on the union. Teams such as San Francisco and St. Louis had more key veteran players forsake the union, but the Cowboys took the brunt of the criticism for not supporting the NFLPA. This happened because of the Cowboys' tradition and reputation and to Schramm because, once he had gotten into the battle, he was in it not only to win but to shake the NFLPA leadership foundation, so that it would give much more time and thought before calling another strike. In some form or other the NFLPA had called a strike each of the five times it had negotiated a contract.

Schramm is more accessible and outspoken than other leading NFL officials. Members of the media are used to contacting him, because he's chairman of the all-important Competition Committee, and they know they'll nearly always get a usable settlement out of him. He became the man to whom the media looked to get management's views. So everytime NFLPA executive director Gene Upshaw would claim this or that would happen, Schramm would contradict him. Upshaw, at one time or another, said the players were willing to stay out all year for free agency. He said, when the NFLPA struck after the first two games and the third weekend of contests were canceled, that those games would be made up. He said there would be no replacement games and that, if the league tried to play them, other unions would join the players to stop this from being done. When the replacement games were played, he said they would not count. He said the players would be paid for the time they were on strike and, finally, when the strike ended, that the players could come in on Thursday, instead of the Wednesday deadline the owners had set, and still be paid and play on the weekend. Schramm denied each of these statements; he was right.

Schramm's was the quote and the picture in the newspapers, and his was the voice and face on television. He was in all the papers that counted and was interviewed on the "Today Show" and a regular on ABC, NBC, CBS, ESPN and CNN. He was the salvation for some and the dartboard for others.

Schramm, Culverhouse (Tampa Bay), Dan Rooney (Pittsburgh),

Washington Grammar School Class Picture, 1929. Schramm is in bottom row, third from right.

Schramm, a senior at Alhambra High School.

Tex Schramm (on right) in his early high school days.

*Schramm near family's beach home
at Manhattan Beach.*

Early days in California—Tex and Marty.

Schramm (second row, second from left) at University of Texas pledge class, Phi Kappa Psi, 1939.

Tex with parents, Elsa Julia and Texas Ernest, at his wedding reception on April 15, 1942, at Marty's aunt's house in Alhambra, California.

Marty, shortly after marriage.

Tex and Marty at Marty's parents' home in Alhambra, California.

*Schramm, then General Manager of L.A. Rams,
and Pete Rozelle, his PR man. It never
rains in southern California.*

*Schramm in 1960 with Pete Rozelle during his
first year as Commissioner, and Bedford Wynne
at Wynne Ranch, Athens, Texas.*

*Field Scovell (left) of Southland Life Insurance Company,
Vince Lombardi of the Green Bay Packers, and Tex Schramm
getting ready to helicopter to boys' camp in Hawking, TX.*

Schramm with his prize marlin.

Schramm, proud winner of the 1978 Lombardi Trophy,
Dallas beat Denver 27-10 in the Super Bowl XII.

*Tex and Tom Landry breaking ground
for Texas Stadium, which opened in 1971.*

*Competition Committee Meeting. (Left to right)
Don Weiss, Schramm, and Don Shula.*

Schramm making point to official.

Don Weiss, Schramm, and Rozelle discussing NFL matters.

Schramm and Pete Rozelle.

*(Left to right) George Halas, Clint Murchison, Jr.,
and Schramm in early 1960s.*

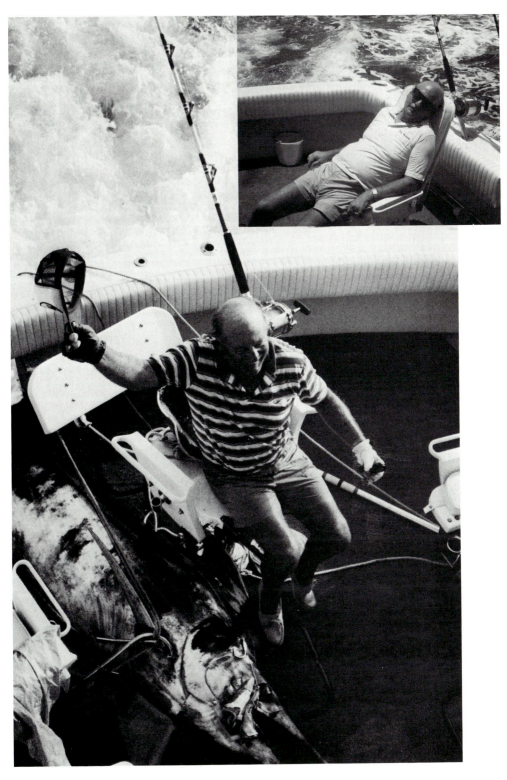

*Tex, celebrating a marlin catch on his boat, The Key
Venture, and (above) always alert on deck.*

*Schramm and wife Marty.
He's working a marlin.*

**Schramm surrounded by his wife and daughters.
(Left to right) Christi (Schramm) Wilkinson,
Mardee (Schramm) Smith, Marty Schramm
and Kandy (Schramm) Court.**

*Schramm and Phyllis George, former
Miss America, at NFL party.*

*Competition Committee. (Left to right) Paul Brown,
Tex Schramm, Don Shula, and Al Davis, who was later
taken off committee by Rozelle.*

Schramm as, of all things, a referee during ex's game.

Tex Schramm presents Roger Staubach to the crowd during his introduction into the Cowboys' Ring of Honor at Texas Stadium in 1983. Looking on are Bob Lilly and Frank Glieber. (Photo courtesy of Ron St. Angelo)

Schramm and Al Davis at Cowboys' Training Camp, Thousand Oaks, California.

Schramm striking Hemingwayesque pose during long fishing sabbatical.

Mike Brown (Cincinnati), Joe Robbie (Miami) and Charles Sullivan (New England), who was not active during the strike, composed the Management Council, with Jack Donlan as its executive director. During a strike the Council has the power to act for the league. It voted 5-0 to have replacement games, to play through the strike. This, more than anything, broke the NFLPA's back, limiting the strike to 24 days, whereas in 1982 when games had not been played, the strike lasted 57 days, with seven games being canceled and some $275 million being lost by both sides. The players seemed to almost single out Schramm alone for holding the replacement games and keeping them from gaining free agency.

"Schramm is the architect of scab ball," said the Giants' Joe Morris. "Schramm put us in a bad position. We (the Giants were 0-3 in replacement games) didn't try to build a great scab team, because management respected our veterans."

"He's a smart man but a moral-less person," said Giants' center Bart Oakes, who then predicted the union-supporting Giants would beat the Cowboys once the veterans returned. "If it's a close game I'll be surprised," he said. When the veterans came back, Dallas won again, also having beaten the defending Super Bowl champions in the second game of the year.

Ram quarterback Jim Everett called Tex "Mikhail Schramm," and Eagle quarterback Randall Cunningham said, "Tex Schramm had a game plan. He said, I'm going to go on strike. I'm going to get the best replacement players in here and try to get in front of everybody, because we know we're going to have an off year. So in the long run, Schramm knew the Cowboys were going to fall apart."

"The problem," said NFLPA assistant executive director Mark Murphy "is Tex Schramm."

"Tex Schramm made a marked team out of us," said Cowboy tackle John Dutton, who was waived at midseason. And Everson Walls commented, "People used to hate us out of respect. Now they hate us out of disrespect."

When the players were not paid nor allowed to play after they reported on Thursday, missing the Wednesday deadline set by management, Washington tackle Mark May said, "If Tex had nothing but replacement players instead of half his regulars, he would be the first one screaming his lungs out about being able to play the veterans. If he's calling the shots, the NFL and all the fans in the NFL have no choice but to watch those replacement games when the Redskins are willing to come in and give them their money's worth. At least in Washington we decide to fight a man one-on-one instead of fighting him when his hands are tied behind his back.''

The owners informally voted 23-5 not to let the players return that weekend unless they reported by Wednesday. Redskin owner Jack Kent Cook was one of several club officials who telephoned Schramm and were insistent about not letting the players return. Schramm defended the decision, although the players did not believe his statement, by saying, ''We had the deadline for several reasons. We wanted to protect the players from injury, which was a situation we consulted with the coaches about. We wanted to eliminate any competitive edge one team would gain over another from eleventh hour crossovers. And of even greater importance was our concern that the product we put on the field once the strike was over was truly representative of the caliber of play that our fans had come to expect from our regular players. We believed Thursday would be consumed in reassembling the team and that it would be necessary to have two full days—Friday and Saturday—for practice. Some players were not likely to be in playing condition. It was one thing to allow one or two players to join your team shortly before a game and another to expect an entire team to come back and be prepared to play crisply for 60 minutes. The fans would have expected them to be in top condition, going full speed and that would not have happened.

Washington, with only replacement players, beat Dallas, 13-7. The Cowboys played veterans Danny White, Dorsett and Renfro on offense and Randy White, Ed Jones and Smerek on defense. Schramm was angry, as were the fans, that Landry used White, Dorsett and Renfro all the way on offense for the first time instead of going with the replacement players, such as quarterback Kevin Sweeney, who had been the top passer in the NFL while the veterans were out and a very popular player. He believed the enthusiasm of the first two games would have carried over and given the Cowboys a victory. White and, especially Dorsett, were booed by Texas Stadium fans. The Cowboy offices received an abundance of letters from angry fans. Moreover, most all the calls Schramm received on his radio show were from people who felt cheated because they had paid to see players such as Sweeney, who had excited them with his fine long passing touch, and defensive lineman

Mike Dwyer, who epitomized the enthusiasm by leaping into the air and/or clapping his hands wildly whenever the defense would make a good play. And it did not help that the offense led by White and Dorsett could produce only one touchdown, whereas the Sweeney-led teams had scored 38 and 41 points in the two previous games, reminding Cowboy fans of the old days when their team was dominant.

"A strange thing happened in Dallas," said Schramm." Our fans adopted the replacement team. They liked the excitement and enthusiasm they showed. Certainly, the reason the fans booed Danny and Tony was because they wanted to see the replacement team finish the dream. I think it was a terrible thing that the team had come together, caught the imagination of our fans, performed at such a high level, and then wasn't given the opportunity to finish the story. Landry admitted the enthusiasm level of the team was different than in the first two replacement games. The heart was cut out of the team when he used those regulars on offense. I'd liked to have seen us go with the ones who had gotten us that far."

It was an unusual twist of fate that in the end, when the final replacement game was over, that it would be insinuated that Schramm had misled the players by withholding $1,000 from their final paycheck, which was $3,125 per game. Schramm had marketed the replacement team better than anybody, openly supported them and, certainly, felt a soft place in his heart for many of the players. Yet, Metroplex columnists such as Randy Galloway of the *Dallas Morning News* reported some of the players felt the $1,000 they originally received as a retainer had been misrepresented to them. It was clearly written in their contracts, and Schramm had instructed Gil Brandt and Bob Ackles to make sure it was understood that they were receiving an advance, which they could keep if the replacement games weren't held, and not a bonus. A bonus would have been illegal because it could have been construed as a monetary enticement to cross the picket line.

Schramm, visibly upset about the misunderstanding, had even checked with the league office to see if he might legally give the replacements gifts worth $1,000. He was told he could not. This fact and the legalities of the situation were buried in the stories written.

There also had been a lot of grumbling around the league that members of the Management Council had the advantage over executives of other clubs because they were more able to gauge the possibility of a strike. However, each team was notified at the same time to start signing replacement players and, in order to help the situation, the cutdown from 65 was extended an extra week.

Giants' general manager George Young said he didn't want to upset his veterans by going after replacements, so he had waited too late, and Viking general manager Mike Lynn said, "I just made a mistake. I didn't sign replacement players until three days after the strike." The Vikings and Giants, along with Kansas City and Philadelphia, were 0-3 during the strike.

As for the performance of the teams of Council members during the strike, Dallas, Tampa Bay and Pittsburgh were 2-1, whereas Cincinnati and Miami were 1-2. San Francisco, Washington, and San Diego were all 3-0.

Sure, Schramm might have been the stronger or, at least, the most outspoken proponent of replacement games, but the idea didn't even originate with him.

In 1982 replacement games were proposed by Lamar Hunt but didn't receive much support, and the NFLPA strike caused the league to lose seven weekends of games. Schramm, for instance, wasn't enamored with the idea, and Pete Rozelle was totally against it. But in the back of everybody's mind there had been a precedent. When the players struck during the preseason of 1974, the league had gone on with the games, using rookies and any veterans who wanted to cross the picket line. The College All-Star game had to be called off, but the preseason continued as scheduled and, after three games—there were six in those days—a "cooling off period" was declared and the veterans reported.

"We had learned some things and were determined not to let what happened in 1982 recur," said Schramm. "We learned that, as a strike progressed, more and more players began to disagree with the wisdom of it but had no recourse or alternative because the union's leadership was so committed.

"We also were aware that it was very damaging to the league to go through such a long period without any games. We lost the interest of the media, the fans, and everybody else as far as pro football was concerned. There were no games, and all you read about was the strike."

Because the NFLPA had struck to some degree each time the collective bargaining agreement expired, there was mounting support in 1987 to play through any walkout with replacement teams. The league did an extensive study pertaining to the dual relationship management had with players. The relationship of labor-managements in professional sports was different because, although the players had a certified union, they also had personal services contracts with management. In that particular area the NFLPA obviously relinquished any right to negotiate wages, hours and working conditions, as a union in the pure sense would do in nonsports management-labor relations. These were left to the individual and/or his agent. So when all aspects of this was diagnosed, it was decided the NFL could legally play through the strike. The Council vote was unanimous but, once again, there was opposition from Pete Rozelle, who said it would be a monumental public-relations disaster.

"I felt strongly it was what we must do and bet him a dinner it wouldn't hurt us that much as far as public relations, and that it might hurt us more if we had no games at all," said Schramm. "When he saw how far we (the Management Council) had gone, he became supportive."

"I wasn't thrilled," said Rozelle, "but I understood why they did it. This was the fifth strike, and they wanted a new approach. By the time I had consulted with them, they were going ahead with the games."

Exactly who lost a dinner to whom remains up for negotiation. Crowds in the strong union cities such as New York, Detroit and Philadelphia were very small, but they were larger in most of the South, especially in Dallas, which drew 40,622 for its first home game with replacements and 60,415 for its final one against the Redskins on Monday night. Furthermore, Dallas had a 17.7 television rating for the Washington game, meaning it was watched in 15,680,000 homes. The following game on ABC's "Monday Night Football," featuring the regulars of the Los Angeles Rams and Cleveland Browns, drew an audience rating of 16.3. The Cowboy game also was blacked out locally, meaning perhaps another three-quarters to one full point in the ratings. Denver drew some 60,000 for a game but had given away 10,000 tickets. The actual paid attendance when Dallas hosted Washington was the largest of any replacement game.

Average attendance for the replacement games gradually climbed from 17,070 the first week to 27,357 the second and 28,933 for the last games. Schramm believed attendance would have been better had it not been for harassment.

"People in New York will never accept this but, if you live in that city and its environs, you would naturally adhere to feelings toward the union," he said. "That's prevalent in your environment. So there was a lot of hooliganism going on in those union strongholds to frighten or deter people from going to the games. There were trucks blocking the entrances to the stadium in Philadelphia and threats. The police were letting people get pushed and shoved by those in unions. Some policemen didn't lift a hand to help the fans. What happened in Philadelphia is a disgrace.

"But, contrary to what the union leadership said, the games were played, they were carried by the networks, and they did attract varying degrees of attention. So many people in the media were against the games, but I don't think their negative attitude and writing reflected the feelings of the fans in many places, certainly not in Dallas."

When the veterans returned and Dallas beat the Giants, 33-24, in Texas Stadium the boos, mostly, became cheers again. Attendance, however, remained below capacity the remainder of the season, one in which the Cowboys again were up and down, and the passing was very erratic because White never regained full use of his wrist.

"The league was just fully recovering from the previous strike (1982)," said Schramm. "The crowds and television ratings were back up. Then the union unceremoniously struck again, and the pall returned over the league again. Now, it'll just take more time for everything to get back to normal."

The only thing upon which everybody—NFL management, the NFLPA, the fans and the media—agreed upon was that the replacement games, like them or not, greatly shortened the strike of 1987.

Tex Schramm also had been accused by members of the union of coercing some Cowboys to cross the strike line by pointing out they might lose their annuities. There was both more and less to this than met the eye. He had become extremely impatient with players holding out, and he reached the boiling point when Randy White missed the entire 1984 training camp in order to try to get a better contract. White was appeased with the promise of millions in deferred payments if he signed a contract that he would never again miss practice, a meeting, or game if he were physically able to be there. Dorsett, Danny White, Ed Jones, Doug Cosbie and Everson Walls also received such contracts with annuities. Randy

White crossed the picket line the first day, and Dorsett called him "Capt. Scab" and said he didn't think he could any longer be a co-captain with him. Dorsett crossed the line shortly thereafter when his legal advisor found out he might lose half of his $6.4 million in annuities. All but Walls and Cosbie followed.

"If a player wants security after he completes his career, we want security while he is playing," said Schramm, one of the first and few to devise such contracts. "Therefore, if we are to provide the security later, we want to know that the player is going to perform now. And it's a perfectly even trade off, which both parties have understood in each case."

NFLPA officials threatened to file suit against the Cowboys, claiming they had illegally forced veteran players to return during the strike. "We feel the Cowboys were gratuitously giving out improper advice," said union attorney Buck Briggs.

"The letters sent to Dorsett and other players were prompted by an inquiry by Tony, who had been told by his advisor that he should check into the possibility that he might be breeching his contract in regard to annuities," said Schramm. "I called our attorney, Bob Payne, and he confirmed this was a danger. I asked him to set down this opinion in a letter. I sent the letter to Tony in answer to his question. I sent it without any comment whatsoever. Then I instructed Joe Bailey to see who else might be in that same position and also to send them letters, without comment."

When Dorsett reported to play with the replacements, he didn't help his case with the fans when he said he didn't want to play in the games, that he'd get down on his knees at the 50-yard line and beg Landry not to play him, because he didn't want the yardage in his pursuit of Jimmy Brown's all-time rushing total to be tainted. After Tony averaged less than a yard per rush in the ninth game, Landry decided to go with Herschel Walker at tailback the remainder of the season, using Dorsett as the backup. On paper it had looked great having them in the same backfield, but it never seemed to work out well in a game, one diluting the other. Mostly, Walker wasn't getting to carry the ball enough, and he was the team's future. Schramm wholeheartedly agreed with the decision.

No matter whether you agreed with Tex Schramm during the strike nobody could accuse him of ducking an issue nor, for that matter, a confrontation—not even with his own players. Nothing really ugly happened when the Cowboy players walked the picket line. They tossed some eggs at the busses carrying the replacement players and yelled insults at veterans such as Randy White, and they also said some things about Schramm, but he certainly gave them a chance to voice their opinions to his face. One day while his union-supporting players were picketing, Schramm left his office and walked across the parking lot and placed himself in the middle of the strikers.

"I wanted them to know I was available and not sneaking in any back entrances or anything of that nature," he said. "I wanted them to know I would debate with them, yell with them, or whatever they wanted to do."

Schramm told the strikers they were being misled, getting a different message from their union leaders than actually was taking place. He said they were getting an optimistic view, but added, "There will be no free agency."

Some of the players yelled and some listened and, he explained "This is the most foolish thing (striking) I have ever seen or heard about. Strike is a last resort. You need union leadership that will act responsibly. You are not getting the facts from your union."

"Mr. Schramm," said Nate Newton, "I love you and you are a shrewd businessman and all, but if you were me, wouldn't you be on strike?"

Schramm answered not for such a foolish reason. "Tell Schramm," said a voice from nearby, "that if he busts the union, we'll sue the hell out of them."

"Who is that!" said Schramm. "Talk to me eye to eye."

"Hey, Tex," said Doug Cosbie, the one who had yelled at him, "You say free agency will only affect 15 percent of our players. Well, that won't bust you, will it?"

"Free agency won't work," said Schramm. "We found that out with baseball."

Schramm had several sharp exchanges with Cosbie and Jeff Rohrer. Before he left he'd talked about several issues and shook hands with Herschel Walker, who had not supported free agency but didn't want to alienate his teammates by crossing the picket line.

"I think it's good for us to be out here in this atmosphere, talking," said Walker. "There's violence out there . . . people throwing eggs and stuff."

"I hear there are some of you with bad arms," said Schramm, and there was some laughter as he walked back to his office.

The NFLPA's last stand in 1987—its final attempt to negotiate—came with an offer to the owners that the players would return to work if an agreement would be accepted for mediation and binding arbitration. The Management Council would accept mediation but never binding arbitration, something which has come back to haunt major league baseball. So the NFLPA did something it could have done from the first, without even staging a strike; it filed an antitrust suit against the NFL, seeking elimination of restrictive free agency, the college draft and other elements in individual contracts. While there was no collective bargaining agreements, dues were not automatically taken out of the players' salaries and sent to the union. Thus each player had to send the union $2,000 (reduced from $2,400) per year on his own. After what happened in 1987, some were reluctant to do so. Again, the players were embarrassed at every turn and they, in effect, lost 25 percent of their salaries for nothing.

"The way the union set up the strike and put it into action borders, as far as I'm concerned, on fraud," said Schramm, as usual throwing subtlety to the wind. "I base this on the fact that the membership was continually misled and affected dearly by the consequences."

Schramm was confident the NFLPA did not want to divulge that free agency would be its main issue in collective bargaining to members of the media and kept the bulk of the players in the dark.

"Obviously," he continued, "had they known, the majority of the players would not have struck over free agency. It became obvious that summer (1987) that their major thrust would indeed be free agency. Yet union leaders were making a concentrated effort not to convey this goal to the players. It wasn't until after the strike vote had been taken, the strike dates had been set, and the players had agreed to strike that the true reason for the strike started to emerge. And, even then, it was not presented openly by the union. The strike date was set before teams left training camp and four weeks before the collective bargaining agreement had expired. After the date was set, but not announced, it was impossible to get union leaders to the bargaining table. The union kept saying management was refusing to sit down and negotiate. This was not true. They kept saying we were backing off free agency, but unfettered free agency remained unequivocally the No. 1 stumbling block, and there was no way we'd give that up.

"The union had for years said all it wanted was free agency. We've always claimed this would escalate salaries. The players, in turn, would always say that by using financial responsibility we could stop this from happening. Well, after giving players free agency, baseball owners finally began using financial responsibility, which their players said they could do. Constantly escalating salaries were killing them, so they drew back on bidding for free agents. Then the baseball players charged them with collusion, and this was upheld. You're forced to bid. If you don't, you break the law; if you do bid you stand to go broke.

"Our players were so in the dark that members of our team asked me why we started signing people we cut in camp to options. I told them because the strike date was set before we left camp, and we were protecting ourselves. They seemed surprised."

Some believe a major problem was that Gene Upshaw, the executive director of the NFLPA, was simply overmatched on labor-management negotiations by Jack Donlan. Schramm, however, doesn't blame Upshaw for the union's staunch stand and attitude as much as the executive committee—Dick Berthelsen, Doug Allen, Marvin Powell and Mark Murphy.

"This is the same group that Ed Garvey put in place. I believe them to be revolutionaries who want to destroy the structure of the NFL and gain control of the league. That leadership, in my opinion, controlled Upshaw. I don't believe he was ever in control in the areas in which he was negotiating. Then he ended up taking the blame when everything went wrong, while the committee sat behind a closed door.

"The union's executive committee is made up of the most radical, militant, antimanagement group of former players. They are there because they're the kind of people who speak out and are often heard; yet they are the type that are without much knowledge or real understanding. In a regular union the leaders are the guys who have a heckuva lot of understanding and experience. So without fully understanding or having the experience, they're directing policy of a high-profile union.

"Listen, everybody loses in a strike. But maybe we learned something this time. In today's society a strike is not the answer to labor-management problems and the NFLPA, with an average salary of $230,000 (up from $90,000 since 1982), is never going to be looked upon as a union fighting for the survival of the working man. I still think the public wants its heroes to be heroes and not see them on some picket line and learn that they have more of a devotion to money than the game. It's been a terrible thing that the union and management situation developed as it has, because it doesn't portray a positive role in professional sports.

"It's sad, really sad, that the players lost a fourth of their salaries during a crusade by their leadership over something from which they'd never benefit nor, in the case of so many, even supported.

"There certainly is a place for a union, but the players—and I said this many years ago—must reassess their position. They must take a close look at their leadership and become more personally involved in order to make sure their ideals and goals are being accurately represented.

"Everybody wants that so-called pie in the sky, and you go to the people who offer it to you. The players must be represented by people who can make judgments not only in their bests interests but also those of the league. Eighty percent of their income comes from individual contracts, which has nothing to do with the union. So before they strike they should realize what they're doing affects only 20 percent of what they make.

"Sure, we took a tough stance in the last strike. So much was at stake. If you're in a fight you better not leave anybody to fight back. As Napoleon said, 'If they're going to take France they better take all of it.'"

The NFL would slowly but surely return to normal, and the bitterness and things which were said would pale in the reality that would be winning and losing. People even would eventually stop pointing fingers at Schramm regarding the strike, although they'd probably do so sooner or later over some other issue.

"I'd be lying if I said some of the criticism didn't bother me," added Schramm. "But that doesn't mean I don't feel just as strongly about what we did and wouldn't do the same thing again.

"Oh, what the players said didn't bother me that much. They made a decision to strike, and I made a decision to do what I believed was best for the league and the Cowboys. I would have to believe that's something the players eventually would understand. In the long run I would be more hurt and disappointed if my peers, if those in the league, did not understand my role."

Schramm walked a visitor out of his office, past a frame containing the words: "It is not the critic who counts, not the man who points out how the strong man stumbles or where the doer of deeds could have done them better. The credit belongs to the man who is actually in the arena; whose face is marred by dust and sweat and blood; who strives valiantly; who errs and comes up short again and again; who knows the great enthusiasm and spends himself with cause; who at best knows in the end the triumph of high achievement and who at worst, if he fails, at least fails while daring greatly; so that his place never will be with the cold and timid souls, who know neither defeat nor victory."—Teddy Roosevelt, 1895.

So much has changed in the NFL in the last decade and a half. First the union was formed and then came what Schramm sometimes refers to as "so-called players' agents."

If Tex Schramm were dictator of the world, he would have each tree shaken and some agents who fall out either deported to a faraway island or lined up and shot. He believes for the most part that agents bring a totally undesirable element to professional sports, and that the NFL and the country in general would be best served if they weren't around. The players, on the other hand, feel they need agents to deal with club officials in the same manner in which they believe they are dealt. So Schramm has, begrudgingly, learned to live with the Witt Stewart's and Howard Slusher's. He realizes that some agents serve a useful purpose and, whether they do or not, he will play their game to try, as they do, to get an edge. But, quite honestly, nothing outside of losing pushes him to the boiling point more than agents.

Schramm was totally disgusted with Witt Stewart, regarding Tony Dorsett's financial problems, and the summer of 1984 he would have loved to have seen Howard Slusher go up in smoke after he coaxed Randy White to miss training camp. In fact Slusher had him so upset that Schramm jumped a couple of reporters who were only trying to do their jobs. Ordinarily, he is more understanding of the media in situations regarding agents and players. Certainly, he seemed overly tolerant of the constant barrage during the daily Dorsett drama, when he was continually dogged by the press, who were asking him the same questions in the same and different ways.

But when a reporter asked him for the tenth straight day if he'd talk to Slusher about Randy White, Schramm shot back, "That's none of your business!"

"Lookit," said Schramm, "if a player gets a recognized, responsible attorney or financial advisor, that's fine. Slusher's an attorney and knows about finances, but isn't interested in the team, only the player. He might talk somebody into holding out for training camp or even a season, which obviously is hurting the team, but that doesn't bother him."

Schramm continued that he didn't believe most agents cared about the team nor the player but only about what they could make off a contract. "Agents brought an unfortunate dimension into sports," he said, "which goes beyond any service they might render. With the advent of the agent we have a third party who has no interest in the success of a football team.

"Now, both the club officials and the players obviously have a big stake in how well the team does, whereas the agent's only concern is getting as much money as he can for his client and himself, and he doesn't care whose toes he steps on, or what this might do to a player's relationship with his organization or his teammates.

"My own personal experience in the days before agents was that, when we negotiated with a player both parties had a certain responsibility. I always believed it was important that you had a sound salary structure on a team, wherein each player is compensated in relationship to his contribution. You compared what they contributed to the team to what each of their teammates contributed.

"When I negotiated with players for the Rams and later for the Cowboys, it was not on the basis of how little I could sign a player for, but how he fit into the team spectrum. In those days the only problem you had was that sometimes a player had an inflated opinion of his contribution. He'd project himself to a higher level than he actually was on.

"The player also was aware that he had a responsibility to the team and that he was going to have to face his coaches and teammates. So, if he were outrageous in his demands, it might have an effect on his acceptance by his teammates. This formed a kind of checks-and-balance situation.

The agent came along and changed all this, because he doesn't care about those things. The agent caused a helluva big change in the relationship between players and management. He just faces no consequences if a player holds out and misses time, even though it affects the preparation of the entire team.

"Another thing agents will do is tell a player they'll do this or that for him after he's signed and they've gotten their percentage. But they seldom do. Lookit, they've gotten their money and run. From this standpoint, I have strong doubts regarding any beneficial role that agents play in the overall picture. By and large, they're untrained people who are hustlers.

"The thing I'd like to see, as I've said before, is for a player to use somebody to advise him in legal and financial matters. I mean somebody who is versed in these things.

"But the typical agents . . . I tell you what they ought to do. Instead of taking ten percent of the guy's contract, an agent ought to be paid on the basis of how much more he can get a player than the player could have gotten himself.''

Schramm said, however, so many of them hustle and get ten percent of something they often don't deserve. He said, in fact, one agent, whose name he would not mention, told him he grossed $1.5 million off players' contracts in one year.

"Until recent years, you didn't hear much about the role the agent was playing in college sports," continued Schramm. "From my experience, I would say that in the past years 90 percent of the players coming out of college, the ones who were good enough to be drafted, received money from agents while they were still in school, before their eligibility was up.''

Schramm does, however, say some nice things, in a roundabout way, about some of the practicing agents. He probably would like Slusher, for instance, because of his legal and financial background, if he weren't so adamant about holding out for clients. He'll never forgive him for the time Randy White missed training camp. Slusher also was instrumental in having John Jefferson leave the San Diego Chargers while in his prime. Slusher forced a trade to Green Bay, and Jefferson never approached his former stardom. Sam Cunningham boycotted the Patriots on Slusher's advice and never was the same. Basketball star Gus Williams once sat out 13 months before Slusher got him what he wanted.

"Mike Trope has somewhat of a notorious reputation, but we've had no serious problems dealing with him," added Schramm. "I think he knows the psychology of different clubs. He knows the ones that are going to fold and the ones who aren't. He knows we'll hang in there with him, so we usually get our people signed that he handles.''

Schramm added that Tony Dorsett didn't get anything more by using an agent that he would have gotten had he talked to him about renegotiating or restructuring the contract without using an agent.

The somewhat astonishing financial mess Tony Dorsett found himself in isn't unusual by any means in professional sports. The most publicized case in history was that of a fine gentleman named Joe Louis, perhaps the greatest heavyweight champion of all time but a man who spent almost his whole life after leaving sports trying to settle with the IRS. To make ends meet Louis, who had turned from the slim, sleek Brown Bomber into a chubby, graying man, tried wrestling.

"There are a lot of brilliant, bright young men who achieve success at a very early age in many fields," said Schramm. "Unfortunately, what you have in professional sports are young men who went to college on scholarships but who are, by and large, totally lacking in experience in the real world. They're very immature in finances and business. Suddenly, they come upon large sums of money and are in no way prepared to handle it.

"All their lives things have been given them, and they've been treated well because of a special athletic talent they have. They've been so successful in all they've tried, which might be only football, and so they just assume they can transfer their talents and find that success in something else. They are naive enough to believe all they have to do is be themselves and can transfer their success from football to another field. They think the magic will never end. It's quite a blow to them when it does, when they are faced with reality. There's just something very tangible in maturity and experience, neither of which many of them have.

"They get all this money all of a sudden. Agents, other people prey on them. They're easily lured into this bad investment or that one. Some get into drugs. They do it for a lot of reasons, but I would imagine some of it has to do with the fact that they don't want the high feeling, the sound of the crowd to end. It ends.

"Most of them I've found live in a kind of *now* world. They don't worry about tomorrow and, hell, they blow their future, all this money that would have made them comfortable the rest of their lives. People have said to me, 'Why don't you tell them.' Hell, you can't tell them anything.

"Listen, we started a series of seminars in the mid 70s for our players. We invited special people to speak to them each week. We had experts in the stock market, insurance, investments and all phases of business.

"I still remember the first seminar we had. I'd brought in the head of a large brokerage firm, part of a top national chain, to talk to them. He spent 45 minutes explaining about investments, diversification of investments and how to make them in a prudent way.

"When he was through and opened it up for questions, the players only asked questions about highly speculative stocks. Instead of listening to a sound program, they wanted the quick kill, something that would have a chance, no matter how slight, of yielding 10 to 1, or 20 to 1 over a year.

"Subsequent seminars were very sparsely attended, and the program was finally dropped."

Schramm said it was very frustrating attempting to set up some kind of program to try to help the players get out of football with security and money. It was just too difficult to get through to them.

"So many," he explained, "insist on going into the restaurant business. I don't know how many people we've had who have gone broke in that business. But they are naive enough to think they can run a restaurant because they are football stars and have the following and the right personality. A restaurant is probably one of the most difficult businesses to run. Restaurant people, the knowledgeable ones, tell me the percentage of success in their business is very, very low. It's one of the most specialized professions there is and, yet, so many players think they can step right in and make it go."

Harvey Martin, Craig Morton, Mel Renfro, Drew Pearson, Rayfield Wright, Dave Edwards, Mike Ditka, and Tony Hill are a few of the Cowboy players who failed in the restaurant business. People such as Johnny Unitas and Bobby Boyd made a success in Baltimore, and baseball great Stan Musial still has a solid restaurant business going in St.Louis.

"I would imagine they had help from restaurant people," said Schramm. "The only player I personally know who made it in the business was Don Paul, whom I knew when he was with the Rams. Don was smart enough to start off in a partnership with one of the top restauranteurs in Southern California. He let the guy run the restaurant, while he watched and learned. He eventually bought out his partner, but by that time knew what he was doing."

Paul had been an All-Pro linebacker when Schramm was an executive with the Los Angeles Rams. His restaurant, the Rams Horn in Encino, was extremely popular and a place where Cowboy officials often ate while they were at training camp in Thousand Oaks. It was in the Rams Horn that Schramm and Paul often relived their old days with the Los Angeles Rams.

chapter eleven

REEVES AND THE WEST COAST

When Tex Schramm saw Dan Reeves for the last time in early 1971 in a New York hotel room, the contrast was striking. Reeves once had been a handsome, dark-haired man whose eyes had the proverbial twinkle of an Irishman. He was relatively small of stature, 5-9, but very dapper and had a kind of bounce to his walk. That last time they met the little Irishman, the man who had brought Schramm into professional football and had had the greatest influence on him, was a thin, shadow-like figure. He was near the end of his five-year battle with Hodgkin's disease and was gaunt, the lines of his face deep and drawn, and his complexion was ashen. His clothes hung loose on his body, as if they were on a coathanger, and his movements were slow and painful.

Dan Reeves was 58 but seemed 15 years older. And he was terribly troubled. There had continued to be problems in his marriage that were long-seeded and deep-rooted. Dan and his wife were devout Catholics and did not believe in divorce. He was in New York again to be treated for Hodgkin's and other forms of cancer, which had spread over his body. He also had just fired George Allen for the second and final time. He talked to Schramm that day about his problems, but did seem glad to have gotten rid of Allen once and for all.

Allen had been a problem almost from the outset of their relationship, but he had turned the Rams back into a winner, even if they never got the big cigar, never won a playoff game. Allen had taken a team which had not finished above .500 from 1959-1965 and posted a 49-17-4 record, twice winning the Coastal Division of the Western Conference. So Reeves, as much as possible, had tried to overlook some of Allen's tactics. Reeves believed a team builds through the draft and creates a solid base for the future if it makes the proper selections, a philosophy Schramm learned from him and also advocated. Allen immediately came in and began trading draft choices for older, veteran players, ones which could produce now but would fade in the daylight of the future. Allen also tried to assume more control of the team, making decisions that he had not been given authority to make.

It also was his method to try to establish an "us" atmosphere, meaning Allen, his staff and the players faced the world alone. This was not unlike the image the Raiders tried to create, but Allen would tolerate no nonsense. Once before a 1968 game, Allen told the team that Reeves had telephoned him to say the players were a bunch of washed-up old men who couldn't win.

"Reeves," said Schramm, "would not have done that."

Even after Allen had coached LA to a 10-3-1 record in 1968 and to a second place finish behind the Packers in the Coastal Division, Reeves fired him. Allen immediately rallied the players behind him and called a press conference with Roman Gabriel and some of the team leaders there to support him. Allen tearfully explained his position and how unfair Reeves had been. "I thought," said Reeves when asked about the press conference and Allen's tears, "that it was well done."

Reeves relented and rehired Allen. By 1970 the Rams had slipped to 9-4-1, future draft choices had been ransomed for older veterans, and even some of the players had soured on their coach.

"George tries hard to establish trust between himself and the players," Merlin Olsen once observed. "He makes you feel that he's for you all the way. After a while you find out he doesn't always tell the straight story. It was a gimmick. He'd say one thing and the front office would say another. After a period of years the negative influences came out."

In an attempt to gain public sympathy once again, Allen hinted Reeves had been extremely cold and unappreciative in firing him and that Dan had been slurring his words when he phoned him from New York. It was well known that Reeves had drinking problems on and off during his adult life, and Allen's insinuation was that Dan had been drunk when he phoned him. However, Schramm recalled that Reeves also was fighting throat cancer at that time, and it was difficult to understand him.

"Dan said that day I talked to him for the last time that he'd rather lose than to win with George Allen," said Schramm. "It was very sad to see him like that. He'd been a great influence on me. If you look back on the Rams in those days, I think you'll see some parallels with the Cowboys.

"He made the correct move firing Allen. George was a very selfish individual. He did want to create an atmosphere in which the team had only him and that everybody else was against it. I mean the owner, the public relations people, everybody. He certainly was effective as far as winning, but you find very few people who were ever associated with him that have any admiration for him as a person.

"His time always runs out. You keep trading draft choices for older players, and one day you just run out of them. You've depleted your draft and have nobody else to trade. When George leaves town, the team there usually is in a mess.

"No, I don't dislike George Allen. I usually don't dislike somebody I understand. If you understand somebody you just take them for what they are, who they are. Under those rules I like George.

"The reason he hasn't been able to get a job in the NFL after leaving Washington is that it's just difficult for an organization to live very long with the way he does business."

Allen lasted a lot longer with Reeves than he would have with Schramm.

"When I saw Dan in New York that last time, he had gone there to die. He knew it. I knew it. I remembered the first time I'd met him. He was only 34 years old then and a real go-getter. He'd contributed so much to the game and could have done even more. He did have the drinking problems but often would get off booze for long periods of time. There were times when he couldn't control the drinking and times when he could. He'd drink scalding hot tea when he was off liquor."

Schramm and others who worked for Dan Reeves saw his genius. But it was a flawed genius.

Daniel Farrell Reeves, the man who would create the proper atmosphere for Tex Schramm to form so many of his ideas, was the son of the founder of the Daniel Reeves' grocery chain in New York, one of the first of its kind in the country. Dan became heir to $11,000,000 when the 600-store chain was sold to Safeway. He had played football in prep school and continued his interest in the sport while attending Georgetown University. But he was slight of stature, weighed about 140 pounds and wasn't big enough to continue actively in the sport he loved. Besides, he also had become interested in other aspects of football, wondering just what it took to become a good football player, to develop a good team.

While at Georgetown Reeves became impressed with an unheralded halfback from nearby West Virginia Wesleyan and recommended him to the Boston Redskins of the fledgling National Football League. The halfback's name was Cliff Battles, who became one of the stars of the league.

After college Reeves moved into the New York Stock Exchange but retained his interest in football. He would see all the games he could and made a trip with his friend Fred Levy to watch the Cleveland Rams of the NFL play in the Rubber Bowl game in Akron, Ohio. The Rams beat Pittsburgh, 17-14, that day in 1941, and Reeves fell in love with the team. When he heard the Rams were for sale, he talked Levy into joining him in the purchase for the price of $125,000.

The Cleveland Rams suspended operations in 1943, while Reeves was in the army, but came back in all their glory in 1945, when they found a superstar in a rookie quarterback from UCLA named Bob Waterfield. Waterfield led Cleveland to the NFL title, beating Sammy Baugh and the Washington Redskins, 15-14, in Municipal Stadium.

The Rams had won the championship but lost $50,000 in the three-month season. Reeves began to look around for another home for his team. He was never one to be swayed by conventional ideas. He was very aware of the population boom in California, that young men had and were still going West, and also that the LA Coliseum, built in the 20s and enlarged for the '32 Olympics, seated upwards of 100,000 people for football. But Los Angeles was a college town, a haven for sports as played by UCLA and Southern Cal and that the opposition to professional football would be very strong there.

Reeves also investigated Dallas and talked to Cotton Bowl officials about an option on that stadium, but his major interest remained on the West Coast, where fans had strongly supported football, even if it were the collegiate kind. He knew that a 1926 exhibition game, featuring the Chicago Bears and Red Grange, had drawn 65,270 in LA. He also was aware two minor league teams—Paul Schissler's Hollywood Bears and Jerry Corcoran's Los Angeles Bulldogs—had good followings for their games in Gilmore Stadium.

Members of the Coliseum Commission were graduates of USC and UCLA and didn't want the pros competing with their schools for the football dollar. It was obvious that a pro team would bring in additional revenues, but members of the commission stood their ground, wanting to keep the Coliseum a sanctuary for amateur sports. By the spring of 1946 the commission seemed to be relenting somewhat and Reeves tried to apply the *coup de grace* by contacting the influential George Preston Marshall, the owner of the Redskins who had their training camp in the area at Occidental College. Reeves persuaded Marshall to sign a contract with the powerful Los Angeles Times-Charities, Inc. to play an annual exhibition game in the Coliseum. When the *LA Times*, sensing a great deal of money to be had for its charities, started pressuring the commission it relented. It would accept the Rams as a new tenant. Reeves also was supposed to have made a concession to the commission that he would sign former UCLA star Kenny Washington, who was playing minor league football in the area at the time. Washington, a black man, had played alongside Jackie Robinson at UCLA and become a popular figure in the area. Reeves had no problem accepting Washington, who along with Woody Strode, now an actor, became the first black men to play in the NFL in its modern era.

"I was home for summer vacation in 1946 when the Rams played the Redskins in the Times-Charity game," said Schramm, who was finishing his degree at the University of Texas. "I saw the game, and it was very exciting with the Rams winning on a last minute field goal. There was a big crowd there, and I think it was then that people began to like the idea of a pro team in Los Angeles at the Coliseum.

"Everybody was talking about what a gutsy move it was for Reeves. Hell, the move seemed logical to me. I didn't see the big deal. I thought the sun rose and set in Southern California. We had better college football than anybody else, year in and year out. We had the Olympics, the Rose Bowl, and the top track and field meets. To me, the rest of the country was backward, so why not move to Los Angeles.

"But I was still young. Later, I realized that it did take a lot of guts. Others were aware of the potential on the West Coast but were just afraid to be the first to try it. They wanted to see what happened to somebody else first. But the fans were there, the money was there."

Reeves had to overcome the stiffest opposition in convincing the NFL power structure that such a revolutionary move was feasible. The Maras in New York, Art Rooney in Pittsburgh and George Halas in Chicago were opposed. In those days teams traveled by train or flew prop airplanes and would go on road trips for as many as 16 days, playing two or three games before returning home. A trip to the West Coast would be too time-consuming and much more expensive.

"We reacted to a West Coast franchise as if the Indians were still lurking on the other side of the Mississippi," said Art Rooney. "Dan clinched the deal when he upped the guarantee for teams visiting the coast."

Reeves said he'd make up the difference, out of his own pocket if necessary, in expenses for teams coming to Los Angeles. Normally, a visiting team would get $10,000; Reeves said he'd pay $15,000. He got permission to move.

One thing Reeves hadn't bargained for was a new league, a new competitor for the Los Angeles sports dollar. The All-America Football Conference had formed and placed the Dons in Los Angeles on a direct collision course with the Rams. The Dons didn't have the Coliseum but featured popular Glenn Dobbs, running out of the singlewing, and fullback John Kimbrough, who had run rampant for Texas A&M in the Southwest Conference while Schramm was at the University of Texas.

"Actually, the Dons were more popular than the Rams for a while," said Schramm. (In 1948 the Dons were still outdrawing the Rams, averaging 41,096 fans to 33,796.) "But both teams were losing their tails. Cleveland was dominating the All-American Conference, and none of the other teams were really that close to them. The Rams were struggling along. What was needed was for one of them to come up with a championship club."

The year after Reeves brought his team to Los Angeles, he fired his general manager Chilie Walsh and assumed the duties of operating the club on a day-to-day basis himself. He also began looking for a publicity director in 1947, a man who could go around to the newspapers and get stories about the Rams printed. In his search he kept coming across the name of a young University of Texas graduate named Texas E. Schramm.

Schramm had spent a summer working for the *Los Angeles Times* while on break from the University of Texas. He'd made a good impression on *Times* sports editor, Paul Zimmerman, who became key in his landing the publicity job with Reeves.

Zimmerman also had known Schramm's father because of his association with the Southern California Golf Association, of which the senior Mr. Schramm was president.

"One day Tex's father phoned me and said he had a son who was interested in journalism," recalled Zimmerman, who retired in 1969. "He said the boy had worked for the Alhambra High School paper and was majoring in journalism at Texas. He wanted to become a newspaperman. He sent him over, and we hired him. He was an office boy, and then we used him to take dictation over the telephone. He also did some rewrite work for us. I let him do some extra things, because he was the son of a friend of mine. But he worked out well.

"He just seemed interested in everything. Tex made friends easily. He wouldn't get in anybody's way and just wanted to learn, so they kind of took him under their wings. And while he was at Texas, he'd sometimes send me a story on something which might be of interest to us. He was a hard worker, a fast learner."

Schramm gave Zimmerman the story that the Southwest Conference would have a tie-in with the Cotton Bowl. The Texas Longhorns of 1941 had finished with a 8-1-1 record and demolished a good Oregon team in the season's final game, 71-7. Coach D. X. Bible had been led to believe the Longhorns were going to be invited to the Rose Bowl, so he had shunned any other bids. The Longhorns, ranked No. 4 in the nation, had in fact rejected an Orange Bowl bid. Oregon State was to be host for the Rose Bowl but had only beaten Oregon, 12-7. The comparisons of the Oregon scores were too much to promote a Texas-Oregon State game, so the Rose Bowl settled on Duke, a safer choice. There also was a great fear that the Japanese might launch an air attack on the West Coast, so the Rose Bowl was moved to Durham, North Carolina.

"Bible told the team that the Rose Bowl committee didn't have enough confidence that it would show up well against Oregon State," said Schramm. "He was extremely angry. Even the Sugar Bowl had decided to hold off, because there was a chance it might get Texas. But everything got messed up, and Texas ended up without a bowl bid. Bible then steered the Southwest Conference toward a Cotton Bowl contract in which the champion always would go to Dallas. I just got the story, wrote it and sent it to Zimmerman.

"I think I must have made an impression on him. That story didn't exactly hurt my chances of getting the Rams' job."

Schramm was working as afternoon sports editor of the *Austin American-Statesman* when he received a somewhat urgent call from his father, who was in the brokerage business. His father had learned from someone in Reeves' firm that the owner of the Rams was looking for a publicity man. Tex told his father that he was interested in returning to Los Angeles. The news was passed on to the man in Reeves' firm, and Dan was then told about Tex Schramm.

"Dan Reeves phoned me and asked about Tex," said Zimmerman. "I told him Tex didn't have any experience in publicity, but that he was a helluva worker and liked to learn. I was honest with Dan. I don't know how much influence I had. I just know Dan hired Tex."

Reeves got in touch with Schramm at the Kansas Relays, which he was covering for the *Austin American*, and asked him to come to LA for an interview. Their first meeting was amiable, Reeves was impressed and hired Schramm for a salary of $4,000 a year.

"No, I didn't know anything about being a publicity man, but I was eager and willing to work and learn," said Schramm. "I'm sure people were surprised I got the job."

Some of the newspapermen in the Los Angeles area were interested in the job, which didn't endear Schramm to a segment of people with whom he'd be working.

"Reeves called me back and said he was hiring Schramm," said Zimmerman. "He asked me to do him a favor and help Tex as much as I could until he got his feet on the ground. I told him I would. You get a job . . . well, there are always people who wanted the job you get."

"I'm not sure I totally subscribe to the theory that you have to have a little luck to be in the right place at the right time,'' said Schramm. "I didn't know it at the time, but I'd laid the groundwork for getting the Rams' job by impressing Zimmerman.

"So I'd done something to put myself in the right place at the right time. I think that's been true of my entire career. What happens is that a person creates the right conditions and the right circumstances to be in a particular place at the right time.

"I've thought about it all in recent years and believe that's why I also got the job with CBS and the job with the Cowboys. I think, without even realizing it, I'd somehow merchandised any talent I might have and impressed this or that person, and it led to getting a particular job. It was a subconscious thing when I was younger, and I probably didn't even think about doing it. But I do know that a person can have talent, and it doesn't do any good if he doesn't merchandise it. Look at Elvis Presley. A lot of people had voices as good as his. But they couldn't merchandise themselves like he could. They couldn't package it like he could, so he became a great success."

When Schramm returned to Los Angeles, there were five major dailies in the city and a dozen columnists. "It wasn't easy to get stories in the newspapers," said Schramm. "We were in competition with the Dons, the colleges and a lot of other things for space on the sports pages. The newspapers didn't have a regular beat guy for teams then, like they do now. So every day I'd have to go to each newspaper and write a story about the Rams and give it to them, hoping it'd get into print. We'd go on the road, and I'd send wire stories to each paper, changing the leads, trying to find a new angle for each one. It was tough. Writing never came easy to me, and I really labored.

"I'm not just talking about stories. If you wanted a column, you also had to write something for the columnists. Sometimes, if they liked it, they'd just change it up a little and send it on in. But you'd try to do it in the guy's style."

One particular writer whose style was easy to emulate was John B. Old of the *Los Angeles Herald Express*. As with some other writers of the day, he was engulfed in cliches.

"He kept a card catalogue," said Schramm, "with different cliches in it. He'd see one, figure it fit a certain situation and use it in his stories. He'd also sometimes, well, make up quotes."

Old would use phrases such as "the helmeted heads of the Los Angeles Rams popped from the greensward in Jack-in-the-Box fashion" . . . "Remember, young fellow, there's no substitute for determination and know-how as you travel down life's highway" . . . "on the rack of emotional torture" . . . "cloudy but clear weather."

In Detroit Old supposedly talked to Lions' linebacker Joe Schmidt, whom he quoted as saying, "Shucks, we just pulled up our socks and played ball." Later in the same story, he quoted defensive back Jack Christiansen as saying, "Like Joe says, we just pulled up our socks and played ball."

A favorite drinking spot was Hudlow's, near where the Rams trained at that time in Redlands, California. In 1949 after Schramm had moved up to become an assistant to Reeves, he hired Tex Maule to replace him as publicity director. Maule was an excellent writer, who later would become a noted pro football analyst for *Sports Illustrated* and author of several books. Maule and Schramm had known each other at the *Austin American-Statesman* and hung out a lot together. Writers and columnists in the area began calling them "the co-Tex."

"We'd stop at Hudlow's for a few drinks before going out to dinner," said Schramm. "One day Maule had his typewriter there and started composing a John B. Old column, using all the cliches we could think of. We'd write this phrase down or that one and then giggle like kids. Then we'd make up a quote. We wrote things like, 'The Rams girded their loins for the onslaught of the Washington Redskins' and then make up some quotes. 'They put on their pants one leg at a time. We're playing them one at a time.' We kept drinking and damned if we didn't send the column to Old. It ran the next day and we were scared to death. Then Old called and said, 'Thanks, Tex. That was a great story.' We couldn't believe it."

"Tex caught on fast," added Zimmerman. "He had that same quality with the Rams that I'd seen in him when he was a kid working for me—the undying determination to learn everything he could—how to do this—how to do that."

"Schramm," recalled long-time *Los Angeles Herald-Examiner* columnist Mel Durslag, "didn't seem to have much of a temper back then. He was much milder, easier-going. He would come to the newspapers and was so conscientious and hard working. He always went out of his way to be fair to everybody. He'd been in the newspaper business, and I think that helped him have a sense of fairness. But, no, we never saw anything of his fabled temper then. No, we never did."

The Rams hardly were taking Los Angeles by storm, finishing 6-4-1 after the move from Cleveland, 6-6 in Schramm's first year of 1947 and 6-5-1 in 1948.

"Can you imagine how it looked to have a game with 14,000 people in the Coliseum, which held 100,000?" asked Schramm.

Reeves lost $161,000 the first year and $201,500 the second season, forcing him to try to make an arrangement with friends, in which they'd get a percentage of the club for $1 but had to agree to share any future deficits he had. When the transaction had been completed, Ed Pauley had 30 percent of the Rams with Hal Seley, Bob Hope and Reeves' original partner and friend, Fred Levy, holding minority shares. Reeves maintained a third ownership and, with Levy, held 51 percent, the controlling interest.

"When I first got there, Bob Snyder was the coach," said Schramm. "We had a good team but suffered a lot of injuries. Snyder wasn't exactly Dan's kind of coach. He'd put in eight hours, but Dan expected his coach to work 18. Snyder also was a wild man and liked his fun. In training camp there always was a question about whether Snyder or one of his players would be the first to sneak in after curfew.

"We won about half our games, but might have done better in fights. We got into a big brawl with the Chicago Bears, and a number of players were thrown out of the game. One of the Bears, Jack Matheson, tried to charge into our dressing room and continue the fight. Snyder's assistant coach, George Trafton, just held the dressing room door open while Snyder drew back and punched out Matheson. Then Trafton made this statement to the press."

"I could have done the whole thing myself," said Trafton, "but Snyder needed the work."

"During a preseason game we were playing terrible," continued Schramm. "At halftime Snyder went into this tirade and told the players that if something didn't change in the second half, there were going to be some new faces around. Well, the next day, Reeves fired him. That was my first inkling that the head coaching position with the Los Angeles Rams wasn't the most stable of jobs."

The Rams, however, even when they weren't winning titles, did establish a kind of identity that would not be easily forgotten. In 1947 Fred Gehrke, a halfback who also had been an art major in college, started experimenting with an insignia for the club. He showed a sketch of a ram's horn to various club personnel, and Schramm sent him home with one of the team's leather helmets. Gehrke painted the leather helmet blue and put a gold ram's horn on the sides. It was different, flashy for the times, but Reeves accepted the idea, and the helmet became an official part of the uniform, making the Rams the first professional team to use an insignia on its helmets, something that one day would be universally accepted.

The early Rams teams weren't exactly generating the kind of publicity Schramm had in mind, but Tex and Reeves got along well. Almost from the beginning of their relationship, Reeves opened the doors of the organization for Schramm, not just in dealing with the press, but in other aspects of the club's operation. Reeves was a great innovator in the drafting of college players, and this was something that interested Schramm most. Reeves first showed Tex the ropes and then sought his input into the system, which was far superior to any in pro football at that time. It was with the Rams that Schramm gained the knowledge and began exploring the ways and means that would help turn the Dallas Cowboys from an expansion club into one which would turn the corner after five years and put more consecutive winning seasons together than any other team in NFL history.

Scouting in the NFL in the 1940s and early 1950s was a matter of making a few phone calls to college coaches, getting newspaper clips of All-America teams and dissecting football magazines, such as *Street and Smith*, which had a complete if surface roundup of collegiate teams. Reeves had different ideas from the outset. He hired pro football's only full-time scout, Eddie Kotal, and set up a system that was the forerunner to modern scouting in the league.

"Philadelphia had a scout by the name of Marv Whitehead but, unlike Kotal, he only worked during the season," said Schramm. "Kotal worked all year around. He was on the road, actually looking at prospects first hand, something that was unheard of in those days. We also hired college coaches around the country to send us reports on the schools and the players on the teams they played against.

"Reeves was a great guy for me to work for in those days. He was very enthusiastic and receptive to ideas. I didn't get out and scout but was interested in the development of the whole system. I'd get ideas, and Reeves would listen."

One of the stones the Rams had left unturned was small colleges. Nobody else paid any attention to them either, but Schramm and Reeves discussed the situation and figured the time was ripe. Perhaps the competition hadn't been as tough, but superior athletes might be able to hold their own against anybody. The problem was finding a way to secure information and gauge the talent. Schramm came up with a plan of starting a Tom Harmon Little All-American football team, named in honor of the former Michigan hero and star on early Rams' teams.

Schramm went to Harmon and told him, "All you have to do is let us use your name. We'll do the rest. We'll gather all the information and, at the end of the year, give the players plaques. You sign the plaques, and we'll send them to the players selected."

The Rams got the names of all the small colleges around the country and sent head coaches forms, with Tom Harmon's picture on them. "We just asked them to vote for the best players who could be considered for the Little All-American team," explained Schramm. "We felt the best way to do this was to have all the coaches list the top five players they'd played against. This would give us more objectivity than if they chose their own players. We also had them fill in the height, weight and time in the 100-yard dash.

"Nobody had paid any attention to the small colleges before, so we got a helluva response."

Schramm's idea uncovered players for the Rams such as Tank Younger, the first black to be signed out of college as a free agent, and Dan Towler, the first black drafted by the NFL, and Andy Robustelli, one of the NFL's all-time greats.

"Everybody in the Rams' office was making calls and working on the draft," said Schramm. "We'd pick out all the guys who were fast and big, and then we'd start following up on them. We had books of information on the players and, just before the draft, we'd put them on a big board like the teams do today. Then we'd rate the players in order, from one to fifty, in regard to their athletic ability, regardless of position, college eligibility or military status. People who faced military duty were usually passed over by the other teams, but we also developed a scouting system regarding military teams and, as a result, got a lot of players signed as free agents. Among them were Tommy Wilson and Gene (Big Daddy) Lipscomb.

"We'd go into the draft with our books and lists, and the other teams would laugh. But, whereas the other clubs were hoping to get maybe two of the top players out of the first 25, we'd be getting nine out of our top 15 or six or seven out of our first 18. It was like shooting fish in a barrel.

"After a while teams began trying to copy us. Some of our methods are still being used today. In the early 1950's a number of clubs had gotten a copy of our scouting form and were making similar ones. One team even went so far as to make an exact copy of our questionnaire, which included a bunch of squares. But the team had no idea what the squares were for, nor how to make use of them.''

Reeves had such thorough information that he outwitted other NFL teams and drafted Norm Van Brocklin, considered the best quarterback prospect in the country. The Oregon star wasn't supposed to be eligible for the 1949 draft, because he wouldn't have graduated from college. But the Rams found out he could graduate in three and a half years instead of four and went ahead and picked him. Van Brocklin got his degree ahead of time, and LA had him. He became one of the NFL's best passers, although splitting time with Bob Waterfield. The Van Brocklin-Waterfield situation gave Schramm some early insight into the quarterback controversies that would be faced by the Cowboys.

Schramm, as assistant to the president, became a specialist in recruitment of players. Reeves called him, ''the most competent executive in the league.''

''Tex had a lot to do with the Rams' scouting setup and he was Dan's right-hand man,'' said Hamp Pool, a Ram assistant who became head coach from 1952-1954. ''I never did think Tex got the credit he deserved.''

''Dan put in the scouting system, and Tex was always striving to improve upon it, so he certainly had a hand in its success,'' said Bert Rose, former general manager of the Vikings and Saints and the man Schramm hired to replace Rozelle, when he was with the Rams. ''It's almost laughable how much ahead we were. By 1955 we had 100 assistant coaches from colleges around the country on our payroll. We'd pay them $50 twice a year to fill out reports. The Rams also were the first to hire high school coaches to grade films on potential draft choices. They'd come in at night, grade films and fill out reports.''

The Rams were finding and getting the best college talent. They had fine teams as a result, yet didn't achieve the continual greatness their drafts seemed to justify. This was a question that would bother Tex Schramm for years, and he wouldn't find the answer until after he'd left the club.

chapter twelve

THE BOMB AND THE NFL

The 1950s have been called the placid decade, although just below the calm exterior were signs of revolt from the establishment that would become prevalent in the 1960s. But with each new threat there seemed to be even more assurances that everything would be all right. There were hula hoops, white sport coats and penny loafers. Teenage boys wore their hair in ducktails and flattops, and we listened to the music of Bill Haley and the Comets, rocking around the clock. Frank Sinatra made his comeback in *From Here to Eternity*, and people sang along with Johnny Ray and Nat King Cole and sultry Julie London got our attention when she did "Cry Me a River." The brightest star of all was Elvis Presley who sang "Heartbreak Hotel" and "Blue Suede Shoes" and wiggled his hips in a most, at that time, provocative manner. He finally made the Ed Sullivan Show, but the king of nighttime television instructed his cameramen to only show Elvis from the waist up. The brightest star that fell was the introspective James Dean, The Rebel without a Cause, who was tragically killed in an automobile accident.

A young Marilyn Monroe emerged in *All about Eve* and married everybody's hero, Joe DiMaggio. We read timeless books, such as Salinger's *Catcher in the Rye* and Hemingway's *The Old Man and the Sea*, and words like suburbia, automation, and togetherness crept into our everyday vocabulary.

There was the great movement to the suburbs as people began to desert the cities for fresh air and commute to their jobs. GI's, home from WWII, could make mortgage payments on a three-bedroom track home with washer and dryer in the LA suburbs for $59.95 a month. And it was a decade that began with Korea and ended with Vietnam and one in which Senator Joseph McCarthy would rise with his Communist witch hunts and fall when he accused the army of harboring spies in hearings that were nationally televised. It was television, the new and powerful media, that would show McCarthy for what he really was, a man who destroyed lives—so many of them innocent—to further his own goals. He would die of natural causes, a broken man.

We liked action, at least to watch it, and went to see Westerns such as *Shane* and *High Noon*, and we watched *Gunsmoke* on television. Ah, television. It would become the medium that would take hold and change the leisure habits of a nation. Its growth was phenomenal. There were, for example, 1.5 million television sets in the United States in 1950 and 15 million a year later. Homes sprung up in suburbia, and they were closely followed by TV antennas, appearing almost overnight.

"The Fifties," recalled Tex Schramm, "was a decade in which everybody became watchers instead of doers. This was personified by the television sets that took over our dens and our living rooms. Television meant the end of minor league baseball as we had known it and also minor league entertainment. Why pay to see a stage show with one big name and no other major talent, when you could turn on your TV and watch the best entertainers in the world? I think this also signaled the end of regionalism. People started thinking more on a national scale."

What people feared most was "The Bomb," that man-made monster which could destroy us all. Yet, there also was a kind of fascination with its power, the speed of its destruction. Everybody talked about "The Bomb," and many built shelters against it in their backyards. So it was not surprising that "The Bomb" became a part of the NFL vernacular when the Los Angeles Rams showed just how exciting and devastating a long arched pass run under by a speedy receiver could be. The pattern of wide-open offense used by the Rams in the 1950s opened up pro football, gave it an identity and dictated the trend of the game that was to follow. The Rams used "The Bomb," the long pass, as an integral part of their attack and also began splitting small, speedy backs to the opposite side of the tight end and using motion to confuse the opposition.

There were quarterbacks, such as Van Brocklin and Waterfield, receivers like Elroy (Crazy Legs) Hirsch, Tom Fears and Bob Boyd, and a stable of running backs that possessed speed, power and quickness. They were Glenn Davis, Tank Younger, Deacon Dan Towler, Vitamin T. Smith and Dick Hoerner. It was said that the Rams were more dangerous inside their own 15-yard line than in that of their opponents, and Van Brocklin used to tell his defensive counterparts, "You hold them to three touchdowns, and we'll win by two."

George Halas, for one, believed he could pinpoint the change in pro football when the Rams were playing the Bears one afternoon. He watched as Waterfield dropped back behind his own goal line and arched a pass to Hirsch in front of the Bears' bench. Without breaking stride Hirsch ran under the pass and loped into the end zone on a 91-yard play in the Rams' 42-17 victory.

"That play," Halas later said, "demonstrated the big change that had come about in T-formation football. Almost without realizing it, we had reached the point where the pass catching end had replaced the running back as the long distance threat. There wasn't a back in the league who could have run 91 yards against us."

It was the Rams who helped turn the head of football fans toward the NFL and then, on a gray day in 1958 Baltimore beat the New York Giants in sudden death overtime. More than any other, that single game, watched on national television, brought pro football into our homes to stay. The picture of Alan Amache taking a handoff from Johnny Unitas and preparing to score through a big hole is part of sports' lore, and the Colts' 23-17 victory remains one of the best games ever played.

Ironically, the Colts originally had been the first NFL team in Dallas. In 1952 Ted Collins gave up on his New York Yankee football franchise, turning it back to the league, which, in turn, sold it to a Dallas group. But the first Dallas team, the forerunner to the Cowboys and Lamar Hunt's Texans, drew so poorly that NFL authorities dictated that the club should play the entire second half of the season on the road. The Texans, as the team was called, were the last NFL team to fail and the following year were sold to Baltimore, becoming the Colts. Officials of the Texans had gotten in touch with Dan Reeves' assistant, Tex Schramm, and tried to get him to become the team's general manager. He later said he made a good decision not taking the job, because he just wasn't ready. But the experience he was gaining greatly accelerated as Reeves, more and more, drank too much.

The Los Angeles Rams of the 1950s were the NFL's first glamour team, the first club with more stars than you could count. It was natural then that there was the Hollywood connection and, although there wasn't much to it, Schramm recalled that the Rams didn't particularly try to discourage the image.

"There are a lot of things in Southern California to distract you," he said. "So we took advantage of anything we had. We wanted to make the Rams Southern California's team, and that included Hollywood. We took advantage of what we had. We had star players and merchandised them. It was the same approach we used with the Cowboys later—to try to make everybody you can feel that they are a part of the team. You want the players to want to play for you. You want all the free agents to want to sign with you. You win and establish an image and then, when players come in, they're prepared to adapt to your ways because of that success. I think you can compare the Rams when I was there to the Cowboys—glamour, speed, the type of players."

Hirsch and Fears still rank among the best pair of receivers in football. Fears was a possession receiver, a move man after whom many later players patterned themselves. Elroy Hirsch was the speed, the glitter. He was the man at the end of "The Bomb" and became so popular that he starred in movies, including one about his life, *Crazylegs, All-American*. He also was featured in *Battlecry*, from which the song "Unchained Melody" was the background music. Elroy was constantly torn between the cinema and football and retired, only to be coaxed back by Schramm. Finally, he quit for the last time in 1954, and fans mobbed him on the field, leaving him to race to the dressing room, wearing only his jockey strap.

"The quarterback situation worked out only because we had such a talented team," said Schramm. "Of course, they both had a lot of ability but, as later with Dallas, some wanted one to play, and others wanted somebody else."

In 1951, the year the Los Angeles Rams won the NFL title by beating Cleveland, 24-17, Waterfield finished first in the NFL in passing, and Van Brocklin was second. In a single game Van Brocklin passed for a then NFL record of 554 yards against the New York Giants, who had a young cornerback named Tom Landry. Fears led the league in receiving, and Hirsch caught passes for 1,495 yards and 17 TDs.

"The only real significant thing I can remember about the quarterback controversy was that it drove Waterfield out of football at a very young age for a quarterback," continued Schramm. "He was 31 and had played only eight years and, as Meredith after him, was just getting into his prime.

"Waterfield was a very low-key, quiet person. But he was just one of those guys who could do a lot of things well and was just a winner. He led by doing, instead of talking. He was a good placekicker, and he never gave up, an attribute that Roger Staubach possessed. If somebody just won't give up, won't quit, then a lot of things can happen. In a game shortly after I'd joined the Rams, we were behind Philadelphia, 28-0, with 16 minutes left. Waterfield threw four touchdown passes to give us a 28-28 tie against a team that was on its way to the NFL title.

"Van Brocklin was one of the most accurate passers the game has ever known. He had a picture-book motion and pass. Back then he was just about like he was when he was coaching Atlanta. He was very outspoken and sometimes hard to handle. There were times when he'd be at practice and, for some reason or another, a teammate would make him mad. So he'd throw the football at the guy, smacking him upside the head.

"They were both excellent quarterbacks and they usually alternated, with Waterfield starting and then Van Brocklin coming in. And certainly it didn't hurt our Hollywood image that Waterfield was married to Jane Russell."

Jane Russell, a towering, busty brunette, had reached instant notoriety and stardom in Howard Hughes' controversial movie, *The Outlaw*, in which she appeared not to have a stitch on when she was under the covers with Billy the Kid, played by Dallasite Jack Beutel. The movie was so bold at that time that it was held up for release for three years. Russell wasn't actually shown nude in the movie but in the scene under the covers, little was left to the imagination.

Pete Rozelle recalls when he was a young publicity man with the Rams, he went to a party attended by players and some club officials. "I was just a little PR man with no sophistication. But my greatest thrill in those days was watching Jane Russell play pool at that party.''

Actor Loyd Nolan was president of the Rams' Booster Club, and Bob Hope was a minority owner. After Hampton Pool became head coach, Hope introduced him at a club function by saying, ''Hampton Pool? That sounds like a resting place for yachts.''

''We were a finesse team, but we had some hardnosed guys on defense,'' said Schramm. ''A lot of people thought Don Paul was dirty, but he was, uh, just tough and mean. After playing against him, Leon Hart, the Detroit Lions end from Notre Dame, called Paul the dirtiest player in the league. Don just laughed, thinking it was a compliment.

''Paul was always out there, like a lot of players in those days, whether he was hurt or not. In one game he suffered a broken jaw and left the game with blood coming out of his ear and his jaw all crooked. They were going to try to make some kind of protective thing so he could play the next week. It wasn't ready, so he played anyway, without anything protecting his broken jaw.

''Before the next game, our equipment man Bill Granholm came up with a kind of bird-cage looking thing to put in front of Paul's helmet. It protected the jaw, and I think that was the first time one of those big face guards, like the ones used today, was used. The next year you saw a lot of them.''

One night after Schramm had joined the Cowboys and begun training camp in Thousand Oaks, and Paul had retired from football into his restaurant business at the Rams Horn, they were talking and trying to figure out who was the toughest player they'd ever seen. Paul, of course, was a candidate, but Don mentioned Tex Coulter, the Texan who grew up in Masonic Home, an orphanage in Fort Worth. Coulter had gone to West Point and played for the New York Giants.

''We had this young guard out of Oklahoma named Stan West,'' Paul was saying. ''He was All-American and all that stuff. Somebody was hurt, and West was moved across the line from Coulter at the last minute before the game started. West knew Coulter's reputation and I just looked at him, feeling sorry for the guy. West saw me staring at him and yelled, 'I'm not going to be intimidated by that SOB!'

''On the first play he hauled off and hit Coulter in the face. Coulter just blinked, looked at Stan and said, 'So that's the way you want it, Okie?'

"On second down I followed a sweep to the other side of the field and heard this awful scream. I looked around, and there was West, holding his upper lip. I rushed over and, well, the guy had blood all over him. I pulled his lip loose from his teeth. A defensive player couldn't call time out, so West had to stay in the game. I just told him if we stopped the Giants on that possession, he could go to the bench. When we did, he was the first man off the field. He'd seen enough of Coulter.''

"The players in the 1950s wanted to play football," said Schramm. "They'd quibble about the salaries, but that wasn't a big deal. Football was the big deal. They loved to play the game. There were just management, players, coaches, and no third parties like the agents. There was a great balance between the club and players. The club had the obligation to treat players fairly, because if they didn't, there would be a morale problem. Players accepted the fact that they had to be treated in comparison to others on the team. Both sides were fair, because there were the restrictions on them.''

Schramm has a list of salaries from 1955. Coach Sid Gillman made $22,800; Van Brocklin, the highest paid player, $19,000; and All-Pro Don Paul, $8,500.

"We used to have more fun," continued Schramm. "We'd sit around and talk and tell stories. We don't do that anymore. We had a succession of Chicago Bears as coaches for the Rams, and they'd tell stories on George Halas for hours. Now, all you hear about are players' salaries and strikes and court cases.

"I'll always have a special place in my heart for George Halas. When I was young and just starting, I can remember at the NFL meetings when I'd be fighting and talking about an issue I felt strongly about. Some of the older guys would be jumping on me, and then Halas would take my side and the others would calm down. That happened when Halas was on your side.

"Halas, more than anybody, started the league and had the guts to make it go. He was, however, a ruthless competitor. He'd do anything to win.''

When Schramm was with the Rams, it was usually the Chicago Bears of Halas who stood in the way of a conference title. The Bears had the better team in the late 1940s but the Rams became more formidable in the early 1950s. In 1950 Chicago and LA tied for the conference championship, with the Rams winning the playoff game, 24-14. In 1955 the Rams finished only a single game ahead of the

Bears in the conference race. By the early 1950s the Detroit Lions with Bobby Layne and Doak Walker had begun asserting themselves as the challenger to the Cleveland Browns for NFL supremacy, but Schramm long remembered games with the Bears, on and just off the field of play.

"Once I was in the coach's booth with Red Hickey, a Ram assistant," recalled Schramm. "Hamp Pool was our coach, and Van Brocklin was the quarterback. Hickey was calling the defense the Bears were in."

"They're in a 5-3-2-2, uh, uh, a, a 6-2-2-2," said Hickey. Then he paused briefly and added, "Hell, they're playing with 12 men on the field. Tell Van Brocklin."

"Van Brocklin was such a stubborn guy that he would not go ahead and run the play so we could get a penalty," said Schramm. "Another time we looked down and saw Halas had 13 men on the field. He'd be pretty sneaky about it, slipping in an extra guy when the officials were talking or looking the other way.

"But I tell you, the Chicago Bears' goal line defense with 12 or 13 men on the field was the toughest I'd seen."

Schramm recalled that once a Rams' ball carrier was running past the Chicago bench, and a Bears' player stuck out his foot and tripped him. "Another time we were looking at films of our game and saw one of our players go out of bounds by the Chicago bench," said Schramm. "He started to run back on the field, and Halas just hauled off and kicked him in the butt. Our guy looked back to see who had done it, and Halas was standing there with his arms folded and with this very angelic look. He also was staring off in another direction, as if he had no idea what had happened."

When Mike Ditka left the Bears, it was because he got into a salary hassle with Halas. Ditka then made the classic statement, "George Halas throws nickels around like they're manhole covers."

"Halas would do anything to make some extra money," said Schramm. "We'd play in Chicago, and he'd sell standing room only space on the field behind our bench. I mean there were the Bears' fans, three deep, right by our bench. You look at the films and it's funny. The game would be in progress and this hot-dog vender would be walking out there in front of our bench, leaning over players to make a sell to the fans. When one of our coaches would talk to a player, the fans by the bench would lean in to listen. It was like one of those commercials where when E. F. Hutton talks everybody stops and listens.

"The Chicago police were beautiful, too. One day a Chicago fan sitting by our bench reached over and grabbed one of the Rams' capes our players used when they came off the field. The guy snatched the cape and took off running. Our trainer and one of the guys helping our equipment man started chasing him. They ran after him until he got to an exit gate. The Chicago cop just stood there by the gate and let the guy run on past. When our people got there the policeman wouldn't let them go out. Halas had them trained."

When the Bears played in old Wrigley Field, home of the Chicago Cubs, there was not enough room for one of the end zones when it was converted for football. So, one side of the end zone was sliced off because of the dugout and wasn't the official 10 yards. Chicago fans were actually in the bleachers at the very edge of the end zone lines. They were so close that they could almost reach out and touch the players. Once a fan actually reached out and caught a pass Elroy Hirsch was trying to get to. Schramm remembered fans picking up a bunch of snowballs and throwing them at the Rams' receivers when they'd run into the end zone. "Our guy would be looking back for the ball," said Schramm, "and splat, a snowball would smack him upside the head.

"They were so close, right at the edge of the end zone, that they'd chunk snowballs at the kicker and holder on extra points.

"George Halas was something. I think he considered all those things just part of having a home field advantage."

Schramm paused and seemed a little sad as he reflected back. "Things were just different then," he said, finally. "It was a lot of fun. The heroes were real heroes. People have asked me to compare the teams and the players in the 1950s with those of today, but you can't do that. It was as different as night and day. There is so much more sophistication in the game now. There's been so much advancement in training methods, for instance. You just can't bridge the time gap, except perhaps with the type of players and attitudes. I'd say Roger Staubach had the attitude of the 1950s player. He loved the game more than anything else. But the only way you compare players would be with others of their era and then measure the impact they had.

"As I've mentioned before, the leadership has changed, too. When I came into the league, the primary occupation of the owners was the football team. They had other things going, but the team was their main interest. People like Tim Mara, Art Rooney, George

Halas and George Preston Marshall had the common bond that they were struggling as a league. To be successful, they needed each other. The new owners who have come in feel no real bond to the other people who make up the league. They're as much if not more involved in other financial interests besides their football teams.

"At meetings we never sandbagged anybody in the old days. There was an unwritten rule that if something really offended a particular guy, then the league would not vote against him.

"One man I greatly admired was George Preston Marshall. He was the first to bring his team to Southern California for training camp. He was a great innovator, a very colorful guy. He got the idea of having a band for a pro team and formed that Redskin Marching Band that's so popular today. When he took his team to New York to play, he'd have the Redskin band march right down Broadway. Nobody had a team song as popular as "Hail to the Redskins.''

Marshall, who had made his money in the laundry business, was certainly a showman. He not only displayed his 150-member Redskin band but also had pom-pom girls performing. It was not unusual to see dancers or a chorus of singers performing during Redskin games. He believed the pageantry of college football could be adapted to the pro game. When he signed TCU All-American Sammy Baugh, Marshall immediately started publicizing him as a football-playing cowboy. When Baugh got off the plane in Washington wearing shoes, Marshall was aghast. He immediately bought Baugh a cowboy hat and boots before he met the press. Baugh said the boots hurt his feet. Marshall told him they did not. Marshall was flamboyant, outspoken. He married actress Corinne Griffith, and some believed Marshall had his team train in California so his wife could be closer to Hollywood. Before the Redskins played the Chicago Bears for the NFL championship in 1940, Marshall told the press, "The Bears are a team that folds under pressure in the second half against a good team. If they come here (to Washington) to play us for the title, they better be prepared to win by a big score, or they won't win at all." Chicago won, 73-0.

"In the early days of television in the NFL, Marshall also cleaned up," said Schramm. "He set up a network that had the whole South getting his games. He had no black players in those days and during pregame ceremonies, the Redskin band would march down the field playing 'Dixie.' He had a losing team most of the time, but still made more money off television than anybody. Now that's ingenuity for you."

Marshall's refusal to hire black players caused problems in the league, although he remained very stubborn over the issue. Pete Rozelle put pressure on Marshall through friends on Capitol Hill, and Marshall finally relented and traded a No. 1 draft choice to the Cleveland Browns for Bobby Mitchell in 1962, becoming the last NFL team to break the color line. Marshall had claimed that a black player would hurt his network in the South, but Mitchell became one of the Redskins' biggest and most popular stars.

"Do anything you want and say anything you want, but don't ignore me," Marshall liked to say.

"I came into the league admiring George Preston Marshall very much for his showmanship and ideas," said Schramm. "Sometimes I wonder . . . if I might be looked at by someone, as I looked at George Preston Marshall."

There was no doubt Tex Schramm had his eye on the Ram general manager's job. After serving two years in publicity, while helping in the scouting department and other aspects of the organization, Schramm did become assistant to the president, Dan Reeves. He was Reeves' right-hand man in all matters concerning the organization and, when Reeves' drinking got out of hand, Schramm, for all practical purposes, ran the Rams from 1951 until the time he left in 1957. But it wasn't until 1954 that he actually was given the title of general manager.

"Reeves taught Tex a lot," said Bob Oates, long-time *Los Angeles Times* pro football expert. "The odd thing is that Dan wouldn't give Tex the title of GM. That was something Tex deserved. It was a mistake. It didn't cost anything but would have solidified Tex's authority. When Tex got to Dallas and started the Cowboys, he didn't make that same mistake. He gave titles that distinguished the people who worked for him. For instance, Gil Brandt was head of scouting but also vice president. The title vice president carried more clout that just head of scouting. Tex realized something Dan never did."

"The first two or three years with the Rams, I didn't realize Dan had a problem because, at that time, he wasn't drinking on a daily basis," said Schramm. "But even then, he would disappear for a week or ten days, two or three times a year. They'd just say he was out of town, and I left it at that. Then I knew he was off on a binge."

Schramm became aware of the problem when Reeves started phoning him to get him to join him drinking. "He didn't do it halfway," said Schramm. "When he'd go on a binge, he'd do it for 24 hours. He was a young man then, in his 30s, and it was a sad thing to see. When you joined him, he didn't want you to leave and became very ingenious in concocting ways to keep you there drinking with him.

"I'd be with him and go home at two, three, four in the morning, and sometimes we'd have all-nighters. Then I decided I wasn't going to be drawn into that, so I stopped going with him. Yeah, it pissed him off."

Once Schramm and Reeves were returning home by train from Chicago, and Reeves suggested they get off and go up to Sun Valley.

"We've got to get back," said Schramm. "There's a lot to do and we're going on back home."

"No, we're getting off the train," said Reeves. "You work all the time."

"We can't. We have to get on back home."

Reeves, sitting across from Schramm, began to chant, keeping cadence with the train, "Nine-to-five, nine-to-five." But they stayed on the train and got home.

They were in the Shamrock Hotel in Houston during a league meeting, and Reeves had been drinking heavily. He wanted to go out and continue, but Schramm said he didn't want to go.

"We don't need to be going out," said Schramm, blocking the door.

"If you don't move," said Reeves, "I'm going to punch you."

Reeves actually drew back to hit Schramm and then, suddenly, dropped his arms and said, "Come on, dammit. Let me out."

They argued and Schramm hid Reeves' shoes under a pillow. Dan finally fell asleep after looking all over the room for his shoes.

"It was a shame because when he was sober he was a fine thoughtful man," said Schramm. "But he kept going in and out, drunk and sober. For all intents and purposes, he no longer was active after 1951 until after I'd left the team. I did everything a general manager would do. The only problem was that his signature had to be on checks. So I spent a lot of time trying to chase him down to get our checks signed."

After failing to attract a steady following and suffering financially during the early years in LA the Rams then became the team to see. The All-American Football Conference folded after four years, ridding the Rams of the troublesome Dons. The NFL assimilated three AAFC teams—the Cleveland Browns, Baltimore

Colts and San Francisco 49ers. The 49ers formed a natural rivalry with the Rams, and one of their games in the Coliseum drew 102,368 fans, a regular season record that still stands and isn't likely to ever be broken because the Coliseum no longer seats 100,000 for football, nor does any other stadium in the league. In 1952 the Rams set an NFL standard by drawing 977,744 spectators, and in 1954 averaged 61,060 per home game, more than any league club had done at that time. The average was later increased to 71,192.

Ram fans were avid; they were legion. One ticket buyer walked into the Ram office and said, "I'm in love. I'm going to get married this fall, and I'd like to buy a season ticket for my fiancee and myself."

As the receptionist began to make arrangements, the guy said, "Just one more thing. My girl doesn't know anything about football yet, and I've been following the Rams since I was 15. I'd like to concentrate on the games, so could you put her in a seat about 17 rows away from me?"

"There was a baby sitter that called our offices," said Schramm, "and asked if we might rope off a special section for sitters and kids. I also remember a psychiatrist prescribing Ram tickets for a patient who was subject to mild attacks of melancholia."

The Rams had booster clubs in Honolulu, Kansas City, Detroit, New York and London. They had two fans in Hillman, New Mexico, who bought season tickets and drove 900 miles to Los Angeles to see each home game.

The Rams drew because they were winners, had a team of matinee idols and played a wide-open brand of football. In 1949 the team won the Western Division, losing 14-0 to Steve Van Buren and the Philadelphia Eagles in the NFL championship game on a rain-drenched field, not conducive to Ram football.

Only nine percent of people owned TV's at that time, but people were becoming more and more intrigued with the medium. Reeves consulted with Schramm and came up with another revolutionary idea. They would use the relatively untapped new medium to gain more fans.

"Tex was in on a lot of decisions," said Bert Rose. "Dan once told me he would ask Tex a question, say about 5 P.M., about a new idea or some club matter. He said Tex never gave him an answer right away but would say that he wanted to think about it and get back with him the next day. Dan said that, when Tex would come into the office the next day, he'd have all the angles figured. Tex would say, 'If we do this, then this will happen. If we do that, then we can expect this.' Dan said Tex had anticipated everything and knew all the aspects and ramifications of the situation.''

"As far as television, we weren't completely sure what would happen," admitted Schramm. "We'd be the first NFL team ever to have our home games televised. But we worked out an almost fail-safe deal with a local television station and its sponsors. They would televise all our games at home, but they also would pay the difference in the gate receipts if our attendance fell below a specific figure that we had projected. We'd won our conference in 1949, so we figured our attendance would increase from 10 to 15 percent in 1950.

"So we were covered as far as any losses regarding actual attendance on home games. We also calculated that if we could just get enough people to see our games, a predictable percentage would begin to buy tickets. We wanted to reach the people who never had taken time to see a Ram game. If the game was there for them in their living rooms, maybe they'd watch it.

"I think we would have succeeded eventually without television, but it might have taken another 25 years. There were more people watching a single game on TV than we, the Rams, and all the colleges who played in the Coliseum would draw in an entire season."

Sponsors of the Ram games knew immediately they were in trouble. The first home game in 1950 drew just 16,919, and the Rams went on to average just 25,000 for the season. Schramm has always hated the look of an empty stadium and began trying various things not only to help the attendance but also, at least, to make it appear more people were there when the television cameras panned the stands. He began letting kids in free when accompanied by an adult and also began selling seats on alternate rows, giving the stadium a fuller look. The sponsors wished it had been fuller. At the end of the year, they had to pay the Rams $307,000 in revenue lost on tickets, which then sold for $3.90 each.

"You have to remember," explained Schramm, "that in 1950 we also had an outstanding team, but the fans were still staying away because they could see us on television. We tied the Bears for the National Conference championship and then didn't televise the playoff game. It drew 80,000 and we won (24-14)."

That year the NFL would institute unlimited substitution, opening the door for two platoon football, and also the season in which the Rams first would lose the NFL title game to Cleveland, which had tied the New York Giants for the American Conference title and beaten them in the playoffs. Paul Brown's team had dominated the AAFC in its four years of existence, with players such as Otto Graham, Mac Speedy and Marion Montley and the talk, as it later would be concerning Lamar Hunt's American Football League, was that the AAFC teams, even the Browns, were inferior to the established NFL powers. Cleveland proved that theory wrong and then played the Rams for the championship in Municipal Stadium, where game time temperatures were 27 degrees and a stiff wind was blowing off Lake Erie.

It was a game Schramm has not forgotten even today, not only because it would have meant the first championship for the Rams in LA but also because it concerned a team which had been adopted from a rival league. Los Angeles led 28-20 with 16 minutes left and, had not the usually accurate field goal kicker Bob Waterfield missed a 15-yarder, it would have been even more. Graham took the Browns to a touchdown, but when Los Angeles recovered a Cleveland fumble at the Ram 24 with three minutes remaining, the NFL title seemed within LA's grasp.

The Rams took their time but made only six yards on three running plays and had to punt. With 50 seconds remaining the Browns were at their own 32, trailing 28-27. Graham guided Cleveland into Ram territory, and Lou Groza kicked a 16-yard field goal with 28 seconds left to give Cleveland a 30-28 victory. Paul Brown has called it his most memorable game.

"To this day, that loss hurts me more than any game in which I've been involved," said Schramm. "It was more than just a Ram game. The prestige of the NFL was at stake. Cleveland was playing in the NFL for the first year after being the power in the All-American Football Conference. There had been so many arguments about the relative strengths of the two leagues. So the defeat was more devastating. In subsequent years it wouldn't have been so bad. But it would have been the same thing had the Packers lost to Kansas City in the first Super Bowl.

"And I felt we had the game won, that we were the better team, and it would have been the first NFL championship that I was involved in, that perhaps I had something to do with.

"It's odd how losses like that, the big ones, the devastating ones, leave a lingering, indelible impression on you. I can still see Groza kicking that field goal. Big losses do this to you, more so than big victories. Losses are more emotional. The defeats hurt you more than the enjoyment you get from the victories. Hurt is a stronger emotion than joy. Hurt digs at your forever.''

The Rams got their NFL title in 1951, defeating Cleveland, 24-17, as Van Brocklin combined with Fears on a 73-yard TD pass in the final period for the margin of victory. The winner's share was $2,108, the loser's $1,483. It also marked the first time a game was carried coast to coast on television. It went out over the DuMont Network, which paid $75,000 for the rights. And then in 1952, the Rams changed their television policy, blacking out home games and showing only road games in the Los Angeles area.

''When our attendance had gone down over 50 percent in 1950, we knew that televising home games wouldn't work,'' said Schramm. ''We'd gained more fans but also furnished such a strong example of what would happen if home games were televised that Judge Allan K. Grim in the U.S. District Court approved the entire blackout feature of the league's television contracts. The Grim decision was one of the most important ones ever made and is still in effect today. I testified in that case, and the thing that made it happen was that we actually had all the facts and figures and didn't have to cope with outside influences lobbying against us. Judge Grim just made the decision, and that was it.''

In the days before the Transcontinental Cable, network shows were shipped from New York around the country and shown a week later. A local LA station did do a live telecast of an atom bomb test in the Nevada desert but had to string a remote cable over the mountains.

''The way I remember it was that the program that signified the big breakthrough on the Transcontinental Cable was when General Douglas McArthur returned from Japan,'' said Schramm. ''He'd been fired in 1951 and was in San Francisco, and this event was televised back East. And that was the time he also made his big speech that went around the country. It was so dramatic and showed how effective television could be, and our lives were never quite the same again.''

Before a packed Senate and national television audience, McArthur went on to capture the imagination of a nation and ended his speech and career by saying, ''Since I took the oath at West Point, the hopes and dreams of my youth have vanished. I still remember the refrain of one of the most popular barracks ballads of that day, which proclaimed most proudly that old soldiers never die; they just fade away. I now close my military career and just fade away.''

The Rams achieved success but this didn't stop Reeves from playing musical chairs with his head coaches, a practice that would leave a lasting negative impression on Schramm. From 1946 until the time Schramm left the Rams after the 1956 season, Reeves would have six different head coaches. Adam Walsh, who had coached the Cleveland Rams to the NFL title, was fired by his own brother, general manager Chilie Walsh, after the team finished second the first season in Los Angeles. Reeves then turned around and fired Chilie Walsh, taking over the duties of general manager himself.

Reeves then hired Bob Snyder to be his head coach, but the Rams continued to drop in 1947, finishing fourth.

"My second year with the Rams (1948) we were on our charter flight, and Maxwell Stiles, who covered our team for the *Los Angeles Mirror*, was walking around the plane trying to find Coach Snyder," said Schramm. "He didn't see him and finally asked this gray-haired gentleman if he might be able to help him."

"Who was it you said you were looking for?" asked the gray-haired man.

"You know. The head coach," said Schramm.

"You're looking at him," said the gray-haired man, who was Clark Shaughnessy. After the preseason Reeves had fired Snyder and brought in Shaughnessy.

Shaughnessy's reputation would grow after he died in 1970. He had worked as a consultant with the Chicago Bears under George Halas. Halas hadn't wanted Shaughnessy to coach on the field. He treated him like a mad scientist, figuratively locking him up in a room and letting him work on innovations to be coached by others. Shaughnessy had made the T-formation popular in college and had coached Stanford to the Rose Bowl championship. He also came up with taking a back out of the straight T-alignment and putting him in the slot outside the linemen. And he devised sending the other back in motion, leaving only one man deep behind the quarterback. The quarterback could see how the defense reacted to the man in motion and adjust the play accordingly. Halas received a great deal of credit for these innovations, but Shaughnessy was the man behind them.

Shaughnessy also coached the Rams to a conference title in 1949, after a third place finish in 1948. "Halas had the right idea about Shaughnessy," said Schramm. "He was smart as hell but impractical in his coaching. He changed things every week and kept everybody confused. Even Bob Waterfield, a brilliant guy, made the statement that if Shaughnessy could write down 50 percent of the plays he'd given the Rams that season, he would learn the stuff. Otherwise, he said, to heck with it.

"We won the championship, because we had such great talent, not because of the lack of confusion. Shaughnessy was in his 60s at that time and was a sweet old guy, but he was like an absent-minded professor. He had problems even remembering the names of his best players."

Schramm recalled that, during a practice one afternoon, Shaughnessy was unimpressed with the effort of a big fullback, whom he apparently had mistaken for a rookie.

"That guy shows me nothing," Shaughnessy told an assistant. "Get rid of him. We don't need that kind around."

The big fullback turned out to be Dick Hoerner, one of the stars of the team. Hoerner that afternoon had been practicing on a badly sprained foot.

During a game Shaughnessy screamed at a linebacker on the field who had just made a mistake. He told an assistant, "Get that guy out of there! Get that Don Paul out of there, you hear me!"

"It turned out," said Schramm, "that Paul was standing right next to Shaughnessy on the sidelines.

"And Shaughnessy was always getting traffic tickets. He'd be riding around in his car, thinking about a play or strategy, and absent-mindedly run a stop sign. One time, he ran a stop sign because he was concentrating on diagramming a play on the condensation on the windshield of his car. He had to stand in line and wait to pay the ticket. He had plays to think up, things to plan, and so he asked one of the officers if he could just leave $500 on deposit for any future tickets. Hey, he was serious."

Schramm indicated a mistake Reeves made was that he always had an open ear for complaints from players, causing a great deal of internal friction. In spite of winning the conference title, there were many player complaints about Shaughnessy. So Reeves fired him, naming a Ram assistant, Joe Stydahar, who had been one of the Chicago Bears' famous "Monsters of the Midway," to replace him.

"Shaughnessy was still getting calls of congratulations for winning the conference when he was fired," said Schramm. "The newspapers and fans were for him, and everybody was up in arms. Then he made an awful mistake, something you can't do when you're in the public eye.

"One of the newspapers had sent a photographer out to his home.

While the guy was taking pictures, Shaughnessy said, 'I hired Joe (Stydahar), but when he gets through coaching the Rams, I'll be able to take a high school team and beat him.' Naturally, the photographer went back to his paper and told the writers. It was all over Los Angeles papers the next day. Suddenly, everybody was against Shaughnessy for saying something like that. That one statement, and Stydahar was popular, and Shaughnessy went to oblivion.''

Stydahar lasted only two seasons, in which he was in the NFL title game twice and won the league championship once. Joe weighed 280 pounds and liked beer, bourbon, black cigars and chewing tobacco. He'd established a reputation as a tough guy while he was in the navy.

''The story goes that Joe saw three marines in a Philippine port beating up a fellow sailor,'' said Schramm. ''So Joe joined in the fracas and, when he had finished he'd knocked out all three marines.

''He played during the days when nobody worried about losing teeth or anything else. After we lost the title game to Philadelphia, he stormed into the dressing room and started yelling.''

''No wonder you guys got kicked around!'' screamed Joe. ''Every guy on this team still has all his teeth!''

''Joe was smart at first,'' said Schramm, ''because he was good with the press and fans. And he also let one of his assistants, Hamp Pool, handle much of the strategy. Pool was a brilliant guy and served as both offensive and defensive coordinator.''

''To my way of thinking, Hamp Pool is the best young coach in football,'' said Stydahar.

Soon reporters became aware that Pool was the brains behind the Rams and began talking to him instead of Stydahar.

''I know Tex liked Hamp, but I always felt he knew what he was doing,'' said Zimmerman. ''And Hamp had his Boswell, too, in the Ram radio guy, Bob Kelley. Kelley was supposed to be objective in his broadcasts but he was always singing the praises of Hamp Pool.''

''Joe began to get paranoid,'' said Schramm. ''He started imagining Pool was trying to unseat him, to get his job. That wasn't true but it was what he thought.''

Stydahar began taking back responsibilities he'd given to Pool. Finally, he went to Reeves to try to get Pool fired. ''Either he goes or I go,'' Joe told Reeves. Soon Stydahar was gone, and Hamp Pool was head coach.

''Contrary to what has been written, Joe wasn't actually fired,'' said Schramm. "He had a choice. He quit because Reeves wouldn't get rid of Pool."

Joe Stydahar's last Ram team beat Cleveland, 24-17, in 1951 for the NFL title. He was gone one game into the 1952 season.

Pool lasted longer than his predecessors, from 1952-1954. His first team tied Detroit for the conference title, losing in the playoffs to the Lions for the right to play Cleveland for the league championship. The Rams were third in 1953 and fourth in 1954.

"Even finishing fourth we were still very popular," said Schramm. "I'll give you an idea of the popularity and marketability of the Rams. CBS negotiated separately with each team for TV rights. In 1954 CBS paid the Rams $100,000 for our games. Later when I'd gone to work for CBS, I found out the network had paid Green Bay just $5,000 for the same package."

Schramm liked Pool. They were close friends and often socialized. "Reeves taught Schramm about the organization, and Pool showed him the game as it was played on the field," said Bob Oates. "Tex was interested and learned. That's why he can sit in on a meeting of coaches and know what's going on."

"Hamp Pool was ahead of his time," said Schramm. "He had ¡ been the brains behind Stydahar. Hamp experimented with having a certain sound in the dressing room. The sound was supposed to irritate the players and make them perform better. He also came up with the personality tests to try to unlock the emotional aspects of a player's character. There was a lot of complaining about this at the time. He had performance charts in which each player was evaluated for each game. The players objected to this and, again, had Dan's ear. The odd thing is that, 20 years later, all the other teams were doing what Hamp had tried to do.

"He was a big help to me. We were a little short on coaching staff then, and I did a lot of things for him, because I was interested. I didn't coach but did draw up game plans. In those days, the game plan was about ten pages. I'd list all the players on the other team, with comments on how they played, their tendencies, what to do to beat them inside, things like that. I'd draw up the plan on stencil and memograph it."

Reeves was coming into the office less and less, and Schramm, running the team, made what was known around the league for years as "The Trade."

In an unprecedented move, Schramm swapped 11 Rams to the original Dallas Texans for Les Richter, an All-America guard from the University of California. To make the trade even more controversial, Richter had a two-year service obligation and wouldn't be able to play for LA until 1954.

"You could make a trade like that then," said Schramm. "In those days, so many of the teams had such poor reserve talent that they would make a deal to get help. The Rams had depth. You couldn't do something like that now, because the game has changed and teams aren't interested in getting a large number of average players for depth."

The Texans got Dick Hoerner, Tom Keane, George Sims, Joe Reed, Dave Anderson, Billy Baggett, Rich McKissack, Jack Halliday, Richard Wilkins, Aubry Phillips and Vic Vasicek. Hoerner had been a fine back, distinguishing himself as a member of the Rams' "Baby Elephant" backfield, but his best days were behind him. The 11 players together didn't approach the status Richter was to achieve. He was moved to linebacker and made All-Pro eight straight years.

Schramm also traded five Rams that were going to be cut to Art Rooney's Steelers for draft choices. One of the players suffered a broken hand in the last preseason game before the swap. Rooney still kids Schramm about the trade— "Ol' benevolent Schramm, always trying to help his friends. Those five showed up. One had a broken hand, and the other was limping." Schramm said he "gracefully forfeited the draft picks."

"Tex knew what he was doing and was popular with the press," said Oates. "But Pool was just out of place as head coach. He had trouble dealing with the press and public. He didn't feel at ease."

There was somewhat of a correlation between Pool and Tom Landry. Schramm liked Hamp for his intellect, innovative ideas, and willingness to try new things. Landry was the same way and, like Pool, Tom in his early years in Dallas was not particularly comfortable with the press. And like Pool he seemed preoccupied, which was thought to be a sign of coldness or aloofness by some of those around him and in the general public. But Schramm had control in Dallas, and Landry was given his time and space. He became excellent in dealing with the media and loosened up with the players, who began to understand him. The Cowboys knew, too, that they had best adjust to Landry, rather than he to them, because he was going to stay around. Schramm wasn't about to get rid of Tom, because of what somebody thought or said. This wasn't true of Reeves and Hamp Pool.

The players grumbled about Pool and so did his assistants. He felt pressure and made an attempt to show the emotion they said he lacked after the team lost to Detroit. Hamp came into the dressing room, stood over a table containing fruit for the players, and then slammed down his fist. He hit a bunch of oranges, which sprayed juice and seeds all over him. Instead of conveying emotion, he looked like a stand-up comic. "Reeves fired Hamp much against my wishes," said Schramm.

This was the first big clash between Schramm and Reeves, and almost led to Tex leaving the Rams prematurely. The Schramms were at home when Reeves phoned and told him to fire Pool.

Somewhat shocked, Schramm said, "No, don't do that. You can't fire him."

"Yes I can. Fire him."

"No."

"Tex, you better make up your mind whether you want to stay or go with him."

Reeves kept talking but Schramm wouldn't answer him. Reeves finally said, "Well, Tex, make up your mind."

"Fuck you," said Schramm, breaking his silence and hanging up.

Tex was so distraught that he left his house and walked for hours around the neighborhood. He didn't want to leave the Rams. He couldn't. The club was still ahead of its time in drafting, dealing with television, and in other organizational aspects. They still were getting good players, and Schramm wanted to help them get back to the championship game. So he knew he couldn't leave but remained angry at Reeves for a long time for having to fire Hampton Pool.

"Hamp had been in Northern California and, while driving back home, had stopped by our house," said Schramm. "I had to tell him Reeves wanted to see him and why. I'd never been so mad at Reeves before or after that. What a waste. What a stupid thing for him to do."

Pool later blamed much of his problem on his dealing with the press. "If I could go back," he said, "I'd work on my relationship with the media more. Schramm and Rozelle both talked to me and criticized me for my failure to have a better rapport with the press. They stressed it and said it was important. I didn't listen very well. I wish I'd paid more attention to them. I really do. Those two guys knew what they were talking about."

"Oh, hell yes, I think Reeves' drinking had something to do with his firing of Pool," said Schramm. "I don't think it was a completely rational move."

As a kind of consolation Schramm would hire the next Ram coach, and his choice would be a controversial one. He'd already brought the aforementioned Pete Rozelle into the National Football League, giving him his start toward the commissionership and placing him on a path toward the pro football Hall of Fame.

chapter thirteen

BRINGING IN ROZELLE

People began to line Park Avenue across from the Waldorf-Astoria an hour and a half before President Ronald Reagan was to arrive. The men and women in dark suits from Madison Avenue were there, some stopping and some marching on past to elsewhere, with great determination and purpose and not enough time to lose. People from Fifth Avenue had walked over in hopes of getting a glimpse of the man who would easily defeat Democratic candidate Walter Mondale and Geraldine Ferraro, the first woman to be nominated by either party as a vice presidential candidate. The people from Fifth Avenue had brought the smell of chestnuts roasting over a charcoal grill and of knishes or big pretzels. A man pushing a cart bumped a woman, holding a small child, and she suggested he do something unnatural and he, in turn, suggested she do the same.

Two mounted policemen rode near the edge of the crowd, where ropes had been placed to keep people out of the street, near the curb. Some people would duck under the ropes, and some were asked to move back and others were not noticed. Two cars with men who had the Secret-Service look rode up and down the street, studying the crowd. An hour before his limousine arrived, some had thought they had seen Reagan two or three times. And, then, all of a sudden he was there, getting out of the long, black limo, surrounded by the Secret Service and aides. He looked happy, younger than his years. He smiled, waved to the crowd which cheered and clapped and, just as suddenly, he was gone into the hotel.

Prime Minister Indira Gandhi had been murdered and terrorists had bombed a hotel, trying to kill Margaret Thatcher, and Kathryn Sullivan had been the first woman to walk in space as a mission specialist on the Challenger. VCR's were booming and Christmas sales would reach gigantic proportions. You could watch movies in the comfort of your home and see yesterday's television shows today. You read a lot about Michael Jackson and whether to give or not to give aid to the Contras, fighting the Sandinistas who controlled the government in Nicaragua. Terrorists were out there. Where and when would they strike next? "Old Calcutta," a remnant of the 60's sexual revolution, was still playing at the old Edison Theatre, drawing mostly tourists. Dustin Hoffman was playing Willie Loman in *Death of a Salesman*, the toughest Broadway ticket in town. Everybody who was or thought they were anybody had been Tom Stoppard's *The Real Thing* or William Hurt, who in 1986 would win the Oscar for his portrayal of a homosexual in *Kiss of the Spider Woman*, in *Hurlyburly*.

Commissioner Pete Rozelle was in his suite at the NFL offices down the street from the Waldorf on Park Avenue. He could not see Reagan from where he sat. Rozelle was surrounded by everybody you would ever need and was, as usual, cordial and relaxed around a visiting writer. He certainly seemed a man in place. This seemed such a long way, a far cry from where he had begun in the NFL and a status that he never dreamed he'd reach, not even until the moment he actually reached it.

Before Tex Schramm ever joined the Rams they trained at Compton Junior College, where a slender young man named Pete Rozelle was a student and did extra work for the team when needed. He was friendly, enthusiastic and ambitious. He went on to the University of San Francisco and happened to be there at the time the school had its one great shining moment in football. As Schramm, Rozelle had placed himself in the path of a destiny he did not then understand or even realize.

San Francisco went undefeated. It was coached by Joe Kuharich and had a number of players who would make it in the NFL, including Ollie Matson, Burl Toler, Bob St. Clair and Gino Marchetti. Pete was handling public relations for the school and, at that time, people were interested.

"After I came to the Rams, I struck up a telephone relationship with Pete," said Schramm. "They had a great team and a lot of players in whom we were interested. Pete would give us information on the San Francisco players and their opponents. I was greatly impressed with his hustle, his thoroughness. Certain people just make a good impression on you, and Pete was one of those."

When Tex Maule quit in 1952 to join the short-lived, ill-fated Dallas Texans, Rozelle immediately came into Schramm's mind as a replacement. The University of San Francisco had dropped football after fielding its undefeated team. Rozelle was greatly disappointed. "I was making $4,800 a year at the time," recalled Pete. "They'd also made me assistant athletic director to Kuharich, which qualified me to do things like making up the baseball schedule. I was raised in the suburbs of Los Angeles, so when Tex called to see if I were interested in the Ram job, I naturally was."

"I'm prepared to pay you $5,500," Schramm told him.

"I'm making almost that much now," said Rozelle. "Could you make it an even $6,000?"

"No," said Schramm. "Money isn't everything."

"Okay, I'll take the job."

Rozelle, however, recalled that he was doing all right financially. "I was picking up an extra $500 each year for handling publicity for the Pro Bowl game, which was being held in the Coliseum. Tex also knew some people in polo, and I got more money for helping promote that.

"I'd write about the Rams for all the newspapers in the area, then about the Pro Bowl. And then I'd try to write interesting stories about 10-goalers in polo. We had a couple of them in California. I wasn't a good writer like Maule but plugged away.

"It was obvious after I'd gotten to Los Angeles that Tex was assuming Dan's duties. Looking back, I don't think Tex was as intense then as he later became with the Cowboys. Maybe he was, but he just didn't have such a short fuse then."

Rozelle said the only trouble he had with Schramm was over an expense account. Schramm called him into his office to explain why he'd spent so much.

"Tex, you had this job," said Rozelle. "Don't you remember how much those guys (newspapermen) drink. We go over to Hudlow's, and they drink the place dry, and I have to keep up with them.'' Schramm remembered and okayed the expense account.

Their friendship grew and has been sustained over the years, because of mutual interests in football and fishing. Because of that close friendship, some officials in the NFL have called Schramm, "The Assistant Commissioner," and hinted that he gets favored treatment, although there are few facts to back this up. Schramm is outspoken, high profile, and does have more influence than anybody on league matters, because he not only is chairman of the Competition Committee, the strongest single body in the NFL hierarchy, but also because he works hard on league matters. Still, Schramm and Rozelle have had a number of clashes over league matters. And Schramm has also been known to let Art McNally, head of officials, and others in the NFL office know his thoughts.

"He generally refers to us as assholes," said Don Weiss, who works with Competition Committee and is a special assistant to Rozelle. "In the press box he'll blurt out all sorts of things against officials. Tex is one of the reasons we have public relations directors always announce before a game that this is a working press area and to please refrain from cheering, yelling, etc. We have representatives from the NFL office go around the league. When you're at a Cowboy game and something goes wrong against the Cowboys on the field, you'd better hide, because Tex will be looking for you."

Weiss recalled he was at a Cowboy game, and Schramm was strangely quiet. So Don walked over to where Tex was sitting and said, "What's the matter? Are you sick? You haven't yelled out once."

"I've reformed," said Tex. "I just sit and watch the games now."

"I felt a little uneasy, sitting there waiting to be attacked by Tex," said Weiss. "Then something went wrong, and I heard him yell, I felt everything was back to normal."

During a Cowboy-Cardinal game in which the lead kept changing hands, Schramm alternately screamed at officials, "You sons-of-bitches!" and "You cocksuckers!" Finally, as the game entered the third period, Cowboy public relations director Doug Todd stood up and announced to all in the press box, "Entering this period, the bleep-bleepers lead the bleeps of bleepers, 6-5."

Schramm watches games from the press box rather than a private booth, as most other NFL officials do. Early in his career with the Cowboys, he tried to watch a game against the Giants in Yankee Stadium from the bench. Near the end of the first half, he became so angry over a call that he found himself charging onto the field and grabbing an official.

"I was giving him hell," Schramm said, "and he looked at my tag (a sideline pass) and said, 'Anymore of that and you'll be out of the stadium.' So figuring discretion to be the better part of valor, I looked up at the private box where I knew Pete would be watching all this with his binoculars. And he was. So I gave him the finger.

"I have disagreed with the league office that not enough time and effort and modern means have gone into selecting and teaching officials. And not enough have been let go who aren't qualified. Improving the quality of people is the best thing we can do, because you can't take away the human element in officiating."

Nobody, not even the players, gets more uptight before a game than Schramm. "I feel myself getting tight several days before a game," he said. "I get so tight three hours before a game that that's the worst time in football. But when you're in a position like mine, where you work all year for something and then it all can go wrong because of a call, a bad bounce, a freak play, then it's hard not to react. It's just a play, just a game to 99 percent of the people. But it's my life. One little thing can have a lot to do with the whole success of your 365 days or even longer. So . . . every now and then, I do mutter an expletive."

Pete Rozelle got on the elevator by the press box in the Orange Bowl after Super Bowl V in January, 1971. Jack Fette, who had been on the sidelines and couldn't see what was happening, had made what most Dallas Cowboy observers felt was the worst call in an important game ever to go against the team when he awarded Baltimore the ball at its own one after Dave Manders obviously had recovered Duane Thomas' fumble. The call very well could have cost Dallas the game.

"That fumble worries me," Rozelle told another NFL official. "I hope it was the right call. It'll be a mess if it wasn't. I imagine we'll hear from Schramm." He did . . . for a long time.

"Tex doesn't call us to raise hell as much as he used to do," Rozelle said. "But I guess there hasn't been a key play in a big game lately, or he would have. He does get very angry, but you can't blame him if a call goes against the Cowboys that might cost them a big game."

Schramm and Rozelle were at odds when Rozelle took Al Davis

off Schramm's Competition Committee. They clashed over a reduced player limit and, no doubt, will lock horns again.

Schramm led a coalition against Rozelle in 1978 to stop a movement to alter the regular season schedule, establishing a four game preseason and a 16 game regular season, instead of the six and 12 setup.

"That became a bitter argument between us," recalled Rozelle. "Tex wanted to keep things as they were, because the Cowboys were doing well with six preseason games. Their attendance was good, and they were making money. Other teams were not. I needed one more vote for the change, so during a break in the meetings, I went to the newest owner, Edward DeBartolo, Jr. I told him that with 16 games in the regular season, we'd be negotiating a new television contract. I said there would be more meaningful games, more public interest and talked him into coming over to our side on the voting.

"Then we all went back into the meeting, and I noticed Schramm was just glaring at me. He later said he'd been watching me and knew exactly what I was doing."

"I saw you corner him," said Schramm. "Pick on the new guy who doesn't know any better, huh?"

"Tex can be a warm, friendly person," said Rozelle. "But the other side is his temper. He can become so angry over something he feels he has no control over."

Rozelle often seeks Schramm's council. It is not unusual to be sitting in Schramm's office when Rozelle calls to get his feedback on a league matter.

"Everybody in the league knows I'm close to Tex, and they assume I discuss everything with him," said Rozelle. "But he doesn't have that much time and neither do I. We're both working on so many problems. We don't have time to talk as frequently as we used to do."

"It doesn't bother me what people say. I've known Tex for 34 years. He gave me my start in football. We're roughly the same generation and both like fishing. I like Tex and his family, so it stands to reason that I'm going to see more of him than I do the other owners and club officials.

"There's no doubt Tex has been a big help to me and the league. Once I was down there, at his house, and sitting around the pool. We'd just taken Atlanta into the league, and I was trying to come up with a possible alignment. It was then that Tex thought of the four divisions of four teams each."

Since 1933 the NFL had had two divisions or conferences, with the winners of each playing for the championship. With the Falcons the league went into the 1967 season with 16 teams, so Schramm felt it would be logical to divide into four, four-team divisions. There would be two conferences or two divisions each. The division champions would play for the conference title. Thus, there would be another playoff game. This continued until the format in both the American and National Conference were changed to three divisions in 1970. In order to even out the playoffs, a wild card team was added and, later, a second one. Those were Schramm's ideas.

"He's had a lot of good ideas," continued Rozelle. "He's always been so conscious of the fans. It was his idea for the 30-second clock in each end zone, so the fans could see how much time a team had left between plays. He was the one who wanted the referee to have a microphone, so he could explain a penalty. Tex also was the reason we have the white borders on the field to keep the photographers and the players back.

"He reminds me of a later day example of the oldtimers who were so important to the development of the league. I mean men such as George Preston Marshall and George Halas. When people remember Tex Schramm, they should think of him as one of the great movers of the league.

"The Dallas Cowboys have been great for the NFL. They generate a lot of positive publicity. They're more responsible than any one team for selling NFL merchandise, and they have that weekly newspaper. They're very popular. By generating publicity and attention for themselves, they also do it for the league."

Rozelle laughs again when he thinks about Schramm's competitiveness. "He's intense, combative, competitive," said Rozelle. "I think that also characterized the oldtimers in the league. They had to be that way to stay in business. Tex is just the same way in another generation. He epitomizes the competitiveness for winning. I don't think I've ever seen a worse loser than Texas E. Schramm. He just won't accept defeat. Sure, he has a short fuse, but that's just Tex so you accept it."

Rozelle remembers when he married Carrie and took her to Dallas for a playoff game. The Cowboys lost to the Rams, 14-12, and there was a questionable call during a Dallas drive near the end of the game. The Rozelles and Schramms went out to dinner with Carrie, of course, being the only innocent.

"I told Carrie that it would be her first lesson in the NFL, her official welcome to the league," recalled Rozelle. "We'd no more sat down to eat than Tex started letting me have it about the officiating. He ranted and raved, and Carrie didn't know what to think. Marty kept trying to soften the situation, to slow him down, but Tex wouldn't stop. Then he jumped on Marty. Carrie told him he shouldn't talk to her like that, but you know Tex when he gets started.''

When they'd finished dinner and the Rozelles had gone back to their hotel, Carrie asked Pete, "If he's your good friend, just what are the other people you know like?"

"He has great pride in the Cowboys and the league," continued Rozelle. "Look at the Cowboy Complex he's built. It's the best there is. And that pride carries over into all aspects. For instance, when NBC gives scores over the air and talks about upcoming games, the network occasionally won't give the NFC teams but just the AFC. Tex will call us when this happens."

"Hey," Schramm will say, "just wait until NBC comes down here to do one of our games. I won't cooperate. I just won't cooperate with them."

Rozelle left the Rams in 1955 to join a private public relations group, and Schramm hired Bert Rose to replace him. But when Tex left the Rams in 1957, tiring of a dispute between the owners, and went to CBS, Reeves asked him if he had any ideas about his replacement. He told Reeves that Rozelle was the best man.

During Rozelle's reign as general manager of the Rams he obliged a request by Norm Van Brocklin by trading him to the Philadelphia Eagles, a team he'd lead to the NFL title in 1960. He'd also trade from the Rams Billy Wade, Frank Ryan, Del Shofner, Red Phillips and Jon Arnett. And then Rozelle dropped his own blockbuster, a la Schramm, before the 1959 draft. He'd continued his fascination with Ollie Matson, who had been a star at San Francisco when Pete was there and also was outstanding for the St. Louis Cardinals. Rozelle believed Matson might be just what the Rams needed and traded Glenn Holtzman, Ken Panfil, Frank Fuller, Ed Hauser, Don Brown, Larry Hickman, John Tracey, and a player to be named later and a high 1960 draft choice to the Cardinals for Matson. Matson, however, was in the twilight of his career and never produced in Los Angeles. Rozelle took much of the blame for his lack of success and the Rams, who had finished fourth in the conference in 1957 and tied for second in 1958, fell to dead last in 1959.

"Rozelle," said Schramm, "managed to destroy a great football team and lead it into the celler in just three years. But . . . I guess that's what qualifies him to be commissioner.''

Schramm had hired Rozelle for his first job in the league and had recommended him as general manager for the Rams. However, when Pete was elected commissioner in 1960, Schramm was too busy forming the new franchise in Dallas to take a hand in helping Pete get what was, to him, the ultimate job. But in the summer of 1985, when Rozelle was inducted into the NFL Hall of Fame, Schramm was asked to do the honors at a ceremony in Canton, Ohio.

Schramm called Rozelle a man of the times. ''We were fortunate to have Rozelle come along in 1960—a man familiar with the media—with television and the new era we were moving into. He had a lot to do with the tremendous growth our league experienced from the early 1960s to the present. In particular, he helped boost public awareness of the game. He knew how to deal with the media, with TV and he thought big. For instance, his thinking on the Super Bowl—'Let's do it with class and style and make it the best we can.' As a result, it has become the biggest single sporting event in the United States. A great deal of that comes from the leadership he's offered. Additionally, he has the personal qualities—he's had the knack for keeping the owners together, working toward a common end. When there have been differences of opinion, he has been the great negotiator. He's the man who does whatever it takes to get the right things accomplished.''

Later, Schramm confided that he should have said in his speech that Rozelle does the right things . . . most of the time.

One of the casualties of the decline and fall of the Los Angeles Rams was the first coach Tex Schramm ever hired— Sid Gillman. He also was the only coach other than Tom Landry that Schramm considered for the Dallas Cowboy job.

After Reeves fired Hamp Pool, he told Schramm to find a new coach. During his search Schramm came into contact with Bud Wilkinson, a household name because he'd built powerhouses at Oklahoma, Eddie Erdelatz of Navy, Bobby Dodd of Georgia Tech and Wally Butts of Georgia. From the professional ranks he considered trying to hire Paul Brown of Cleveland, a team that outdistanced the Rams for domination of the NFL in the late 1940s and early 1950s, and Buddy Parker of Detroit.

''When I talked to Wilkinson, he recommended a guy named Sid

Gillman for the job," said Schramm. "I'd never heard of him. He'd only worked at Cincinnati, a small college at that time. But he'd had some excellent teams. He'd also been an assistant to Earl Blaik at West Point. Blaik told me Gillman was an excellent choice. Red Sanders told me the same thing. Everywhere I'd turn, the name Gillman would come up.

"Some people told me the only reason he hadn't landed a head job at a larger school was because he was Jewish. Those things happened in those days, but I'd never thought about that. It never was a factor."

Schramm hired Gillman as the sixth head coach the Rams had had since coming to Los Angeles. Gillman immediately endeared himself to the players by seeking their advice in regard to curfews and other training aspects of the team. He also brought in new ideas. In college Gillman had been the first to alternate small units of specialists on offense and defense. He'd started the belly series off the T-formation, a tactic in which the quarterback would place the ball in the back's stomach and then sometimes withdraw it and roll out to give the ball to a trailing back. He had begun using zone blocking, having linemen hit the man nearest them rather than go after a specific man who might have moved too far out of their range. And in 1955, Gillman's first year, the Rams won the conference championship.

"Where has this been all my life?" said Gillman.

"Sid," Tex told him, "it won't always be this easy."

The Rams' old nemesis, Cleveland, bombed them, 38-14, in the NFL title game in which Van Brocklin threw five interceptions. This soured Gillman on The Dutchman, who insisted on doing things his way rather than seeking council with such people as the head coach.

The following season Gillman began using Billy Wade more and more to replace Van Brocklin, who was traded by Rozelle, with Gillman's blessings, to Philadelphia. By 1959 the Rams had fallen to last place, and Gillman was fired. He would go on to achieve great success in the AFL with the Chargers and serve a season in the twilight of his career as a special assistant to Tom Landry.

"If there's one thing I've learned, it's that there's no prototype for a winning coach," said Schramm. "All have their particular idiosyncrasies. A coach has to be able to do things his way without interference. There's no way to clone one, because so many of them win by doing things differently. The biggest mistake people in this business make is to try to find a coach who is like a Landry, a Shula, or a Lombardi. You can't do that. You find the best man you can and accept him as he is.

"Over the years it has been written that I tried to get Gillman for the Cowboys' job before Landry. That isn't true. I considered Sid but never even talked to him about the job. The only reason I even considered him was because of our past relationship. I knew how to work with him and what had to be done but, in the back of my mind, Landry was the only choice all along."

Schramm worked with Gillman through the 1956 season, when tension between the owners had placed him in a situation under which he could no longer work for the Rams.

By 1954 the difference between Reeves and his partners had reached the boiling point. After Reeves had sold interests in the club for $1, with the stipulation that his partners share in the deficit, the Rams had turned the corner financially and had begun to show profits by the 1950s. Ed Pauley, for whom UCLAs Pauley Pavilion was named, Hal Seley, and Harold Pauley wanted the team out of Reeves' control, but the way the ownership was set up they needed another vote, that of Reeves' friend, Fred Levy, the man who had joined him in purchasing the Rams when they were in Cleveland.

"The other owners used the fact that Dan was drinking a lot and not coming to the office to do his job as the reason they wanted to terminate him as managing partner," said Schramm. "Reeves and Levy always had retained control of the vote, so they couldn't do anything. Then Levy went over to the other side, and Dan lost a lot of his power.

"They wanted to dissolve the partnership. But there had been an old agreement that, if they couldn't resolve their differences, they would differ to the courts, and a third party could step in and bid on the club. They didn't want this to happen, so they settled the issue by making me, officially, general manager to run the operation.

"I was caught in the middle of the two factions. Pauley, Levy and Seley knew I was a Reeves' man, but I sincerely tried to have a fair balance, keeping the peace, although my tendencies obviously were with Reeves. Still, being aware of this, I made a special effort to represent each side as fairly and honestly as I could. In fact, I liked Ed Pauley.

"But what was happening was that I'd want a decision on some matter and go to one side to get it. That side would ask how the other side felt. If I told them, then they'd go the opposite way. I wasn't very happy, and it came to a showdown in 1956 before Commissioner Bert Bell. It was resolved that each side would have a 50-50 vote on any major issue. If the two sides couldn't agree then Commissioner Bell would make the decision for the club. The commissioner would become the independent mediator or arbitrator for the Rams.

"For me, that was just impossible. I couldn't live with that so I left."

More and more Schramm had become intrigued with television and the possibilities it offered for sports. He'd had feelers from CBS and finally took a job as assistant director of sports for the network. He stayed close to Reeves and Rozelle during the years he was in New York with CBS and watched as Reeves slowed down his drinking and was able to buy back controlling interest of the Rams. At the NFL meeting in 1960, his friend Pete Rozelle was elected commissioner.

"I was just a compromise choice," said Rozelle. "Paul Brown and Wellington Mara suggested me at the last minute when the owners couldn't settle on anybody else. I think I was the only one there at the meeting who hadn't antagonized anybody, so I was picked.

"I don't know what I might have turned out to be if Tex hadn't brought me into the league. I'd been sports editor of my high school paper and also at Compton Junior College. Being from Southern California, I suppose I thought, if I could ever work for the *Los Angeles Times*, that would be a pretty good deal. I'm just not sure. I'm just glad Tex hired me."

Shortly after Rozelle was elected commissioner, Schramm stood outside the meeting room, talking to Dan Reeves, who looked over as Rozelle walked past and said to Schramm, "But not for a quirk of fate, that would be you."

"But fortune seems to take care of things," added Schramm. "I would have been a totally different commissioner than Pete and, as a result, I question whether I'd have been as successful. Who knows at that time, if somebody had asked, I might have taken the job? But on the other hand, I had the unique opportunity of taking a new franchise, the only one to come into the league without benefit of the college draft, from scratch and building it into something to be proud of. That was something I'd dreamed about. I didn't inherit a team but built the Cowboys, which is something nobody can take away from me.

"Pete was great in his area. And I hope there are some who think

I've had something to do with the success of the league from my level.''

Schramm would build the Cowboys into one of the most successful franchises in sports history. But it would be the years at CBS that helped him put into perspective some of the mistakes the Rams had made. Why had the Rams, with the best players, been unable to dominate the league? He found the answers and also came up with a new way to process draft information. Texas E. Schramm would discover the computer.

chapter fourteen

LEARNING,
DOING AT CBS

Bill McPhail couldn't have been more surprised at what he was hearing. The mid-1950s were the infant years of sports on television but McPhail, the director of sports at CBS, had just made some headway with the network. He'd been told he actually could hire an assistant, something he'd sought for a long time. He telephoned his friend Tex Schramm, general manager of the Los Angeles Rams, to tell him the news. McPhail had been in public relations before going to CBS to try to get in on the ground floor of what appeared would be an exciting new era of sports on television. He'd gotten to know Schramm and their friendship had grown by that year, 1956.

"Guess what?" McPhail told Schramm. "They're finally going to let me hire an assistant sports director. The process has been slow but, at least, we're moving forward."

"Is that so? Well, congratulations," said Schramm.

"Well, it'll free me for a lot of duties and also give me somebody with whom to confer."

"Would you consider me for the job?"

"What? What are you talking about?"

"I'm serious. I'd like to have the job."

"I thought football was your whole life. Why would you want to get into television?"

Schramm told him he always had been interested in television, its vast possibilities, and that he no longer could work for the Rams because he was sick and tired of being caught between the Reeves and Pauley factions of the club ownership. He explained that they now had brought Bert Bell into the situation to make judgments when the owners couldn't agree and that he just wanted no more of the situation.

"I wasn't asked to leave," recalled Schramm. "They wanted me to stay, but I just couldn't function in that atmosphere. Television was exploding at the time. It was an exciting medium. I was getting into something entirely different than anything I'd ever done, but I wanted to try it."

"Shortly after I talked to him and he expressed interest, I hired him," said McPhail, who is now vice president of sports for Ted Turner's Cable News Network in Atlanta. "Tex didn't know anything about the technical aspects of television, but neither did I. And Tex was always a guy with good ideas and knew a heckuva lot about sports. It was good timing for him. Television was on the verge of a great growth period, and new ideas were welcomed."

People were getting hooked on Milton Berle on the *Texaco Hour*, and Sid Caesar's *Show of Shows* and *The Twilight Zone*. More and more, their leisure hours were spent in front of the big box with a little black and white picture. And the mid- and late- 1950s were a time of political upheavel. Khrushchev rose to power in Russia, and Castro came out of the mountains to oust Batista in Cuba. Russia launched Sputnik I and II, and we rushed to establish NASA, the National Aeronautics and Space Administration, to start a scientific exploration of space. Our first moon rocket launch failed, but we were on our way to catching up on the next frontier, space. The Beatnik movement began and there were signs of a sexual revolution, which would culminate in the 1960s. Eisenhower was reelected, Nixon was his vice president, and Martin Luther King emerged as the civil rights leader of the black community.

People were nervous about the Russians, integration and racial problems in Little Rock, mounting crime, and everybody in California knew New York wasn't a safe place and, why, you could even get mugged in broad daylight.

The Schramms were California people. California was where they were born, raised and had spent most of their lives. They had seemingly found happiness with the Los Angeles Rams. And now Tex was 37, starting a new career in a strange, foreign place.

"When we packed to leave for New York and the job with CBS, everybody was crying," said Schramm. "Marty was in tears, my daughters were sobbing. I bought a car from the Rams, and the damn thing blew an engine about halfway, in Arizona. We were stuck there while they were fixing the car. Marty and the girls had left heel marks all the way back to California."

While Marty and his daughters lamented California, Tex Schramm sat down and read a complete book for the first time in his life. It was a biography of, of all people, Wyatt Earp. The book was there, just there, so he bought and read it.

The Schramms found a home in Connecticut and almost immediately loved it. They liked their neighbors, learned to ice skate, and they fit into their new lifestyle perfectly. After a while none of the Schramms could remember why they so hated leaving California for New York. The second of their three daughters, Mardee, became a cheerleader and quickly found a boyfriend she liked better than the one she'd left in California.

At CBS Schramm quickly began making his mark. NBC was the sports leader in those days, and ABC didn't even have a sports department. NBC had a contract to televise college football but would let the other networks have three games each year to air what it didn't want.

"I was working with the Cotton Bowl in those days," said Bill Sansing, Schramm's long-time friend from the University of Texas. "We were exploring the possibilities of getting a long-term contract to have the New Year's game telecast. Schramm was the only guy I knew in television, so I contacted him. He was a big help. People don't know this, but Tex was very instrumental in putting CBS and the Cotton Bowl together in a relationship that exists even today."

"I thoroughly enjoyed those years," said Schramm. "I got to see all the great sports events, the Indianapolis 500, the Masters, the Kentucky Derby and all the Triple Crown and the top NBA and NHL games."

Schramm also was interested in a number of minor sports and wanted to find some way to try to get them on the air, but these sports were not strong enough to be featured by themselves.

"I was trying to figure out some format that might be acceptable," said Schramm. "There were a lot of people interested in minor sports but not enough to support a single one on TV. CBS had a program in those days called *Wide, Wide World*, in which news events and happenings would be shown from various places. I got to thinking that we could do the same thing with worldwide sports. We could have a program showing different sports events from around the country, going from one to another event and packaging the program.''

His idea turned into *Sunday Sports Spectacular*, which was the forerunner to ABC's ever-popular *Wide World of Sports.*

''I know Roone Arledge won't agree, but we had that type of a show a long time before he did it at ABC,'' said McPhail. ''As I recall, we ran into some conflicts with it, because we had Dizzy Dean's *Game of the Week* on weekends during baseball season, and that was more popular.''

Once McPhail and Schramm went to Philadelphia to have dinner with Commissioner Bert Bell of the NFL. ''If you wanted to see the Commissioner, you'd have to go to Philly, because that was his city and he'd never leave,'' said McPhail. ''Schramm and I had a suite together in a hotel there. I came in early after dinner and went to bed. Tex got in about 2 A.M.''

While McPhail and Schramm slept, thieves broke into their suite and stole all of Schramm's clothes and other belongings. Schramm had been expecting a call and gone to sleep, holding the telephone on his chest. When he woke up the cord had been cut. None of McPhail's clothes or other things had been touched.

''You were drunk, or you'd have heard them,'' yelled Schramm.

''You're the one who was drunk. I came home early. But at least they didn't take any of my clothes.''

''Your clothes are so cheap they didn't want them!'' yelled Schramm.

Tex Schramm's pet project, the one for which he's still remembered in the profession, was the first time the Winter Olympics had ever been televised. ''I thought it was a natural for television,'' said Schramm. ''It had all elements—speed, snow, scenery, man against man and also the elements.''

The people in power at CBS were not particularly impressed with Schramm's idea, and he had problems selling it to them. ''Oh, there was a lot of infighting when Tex proposed CBS go to Squaw Valley and do the Winter Olympics,'' said McPhail. ''It was a shocking idea at that time. The networks had done track and field but nothing like that. Of course, the way it turned out was that the show was more successful than even Tex dreamed and not only opened the doors for future coverage of the winter events but also showed how effective a new format he came up with could be.

"But there was a battle. Tex tangled a lot with the executive director at CBS, who knew nothing about sports. But Tex and I were always getting in trouble with our bosses. We'd get an idea and kind of strike out on our own and let them know about it later."

Schramm worked on the project at Squaw Valley for over two years. He made numerous trips there to try to get the tremendous scope of the undertaking into focus. He tramped through the area, devising, planning, trying to determine the best places for the cameras.

"We got the rights for the telecast, but then CBS just decided it wouldn't go on with my project and turned it over to ABC," said Schramm. "Then ABC changed its mind and gave it back to us. Finally, I got a go-ahead from CBS."

After Schramm supervised the laying of the television cables along the mountainsides at different sites, he started thinking of ways to cover the various events and yet still have continuity. He'd watched the network coverage of the Republican National Convention in which an anchor man was used. The coverage would move from the anchor man around the convention floor to various reporters and then back to the anchor. He was the focal point, the continuity.

"I didn't see why we couldn't use the same system for the Olympics," said Schramm. "Yes, I suppose that was the first time that it was done in sports. We looked around trying to find the right guy for the anchor spot. He had to be a person who could stay in control and keep the show moving. We finally settled on a guy who had a lot of talent, was up and coming, but certainly not a household name then."

Schramm's sports anchor man was Walter Cronkite. Tex also got the CBS people who had handled the convention to help. Then he added still another successful twist by assigning former Olympic competitors as on-the-scene commentators. Two of the first he got were skier Art Devlin and skater Dick Button. He had cameras and commentators at various event sites, such as speed skating, bobsled runs, ski jumps, downhill racing and in the hockey arena.

The network would win an Emmy for its Winter Olympic coverage, but Schramm had begun to make a name for himself in television even before that and had been offered the sports directors job at NBC and the challenge of directing coverage of the summer games in Rome, Italy. It was tempting but by that time he already had his mind on Dallas.

The CBS anchor room during the Olympics was in a building IBM had leased for its computer operation, which would be fed statistics, standings, etc. and put them in proper order. Schramm became intrigued with the way the computer could absorb so much information on so many varied Olympic events and then give a printout in such an organized form.

"I watched them work and made friends with some of the engineers," he said. "Finally, I started asking a lot of questions. I told them, for instance, the problems we had had in scouting with the Rams. We were getting so much data that it just couldn't be assimilated.

"I was curious if there was a way the computer could absorb all the draft information and arrive at a conclusion regarding the order in which players should be rated. They told me, of course, the accuracy would depend on the information put into the computer, but that it certainly could be done. I told them I'd be back in touch."

He would get back in touch after the Dallas Cowboys were formed and introduce the NFL to the computer, which would revolutionize the draft.

"The time I spent at CBS turned out to be one of the best things that ever happened to me," explained Schramm. "Besides enjoying the work, I was able to step back and look at what other teams were doing in football and to think more objectively about what we had done when I was with the Rams. We had the best players in the league and should have been winning the world's championship almost every year. But we didn't. We won it only once (1951), and I never could understand why. What were we doing wrong when we had the best players and good coaches?

"One of the things I concluded was that we were getting so many good athletes that we were almost totally ignoring the value of experience. For example, a guy like Andy Robustelli. He had been with us four or five years, and then here comes another player in the draft who probably had greater potential. We would keep that new guy and let Robustelli go just at the time he was becoming a great pro. We were getting a lot of talent, and we were continually upgrading it, but we were never letting it reach maturity. So when we'd get into tough games or against teams with a lot of veterans, we were losing. They'd draw on their experience, and we couldn't.''

At the time Schramm was working on the Winter Olympics, he actually had two jobs, one with CBS and the other as general manager of Clint Murchison's proposed football team in Dallas.

"The closest I ever got to being mad at Tex was when I was about the last person to know he was leaving CBS to join the Cowboys," said McPhail. "When you work for the network, you're always attending various functions and banquets. CBS always had a table at the big fetes and social events, and sometimes we'd invite guests. Tex told me he wanted to bring Tom Landry to a particular banquet. I couldn't figure that one out. Sure, Tom had gained a great reputation as coach of the Giants' defensive unit, but he wasn't exactly a well-known celebrity. I asked Tex why he wanted to bring Tom, and he said he just admired him. All the time, he was thinking about hiring Landry for his team in Dallas. But, no, I couldn't stay mad at Tex very long. I liked him too much."

Schramm had told the people at CBS he was leaving if, indeed, Dallas was awarded an NFL franchise at the league meetings. They said he could have his old job back with the network if Dallas didn't get the team.

"We wanted him to stay," said McPhail. "Money was never the issue. Tex just wanted to get back into football. If he hadn't, he could have had a brilliant career in television. We might have been talking about him instead of Roone Arlege all the time."

Marty and the girls didn't want to leave New York and move to Dallas. They were happy, had their friends and loved Connecticut because there always seemed to be somewhere to go, something to do. The girls felt the move would ruin their lives. And Marty remembered how hot it had been when they'd lived in Texas before. They'd been so young then but, when they left, she never imagined they'd be going back to the Lone Star State to live.

chapter fifteen

ORIGINAL MOVE
TO TEXAS

The first time Tex Schramm moved to the Lone Star State, it was not only to gain the proper tools and education to seek a career in journalism but also to pursue a place for himself on the Texas Longhorn football team, which he believed needed him, whether it knew it or not. Schramm had thrown his belongings into his Ford Tudor and made the long trek over two-lane highways, past Burma Shave signs, from his home in San Gabriel to Austin, the capital of Texas. His father, a Longhorn basketball letterman in 1912-13, had filled his head with tales of the state with its legendary pioneer ancestry, its many-splendored geography that ranged from the Gulf Coast to the mountains of the Big Bend, and of the great opportunities it offered. And when you are 19 it isn't difficult to fan the fires of adventure, because you believe the world is there for the taking.

The year was 1939 and the country was recovering well economically from the Depression. This was due in no small part to the sale of weaponry and war equipment to the European market. People talked about possible involvement in the war in Europe, but nobody really believed it would happen. England and France had declared war on Germany and Hitler, the little man with the fancy mustache, had moved his armies into Austria and Poland but the war, actual war, seemed so far away, just pictures in a newsreel on the silver screen. The "sig heils" of the Nazis echoed throughout Europe but could not yet be heard clearly in the United States.

People went to see a kid named Judy Garland in *The Wizard of Oz* and were shocked when, in *Gone with the Wind* Clark Gable actually used profanity on the screen when he told Vivien Leigh's Scarlett O'Hara, "I don't give a damn." Another Californian, John Steinbeck, reminded people of the Depression, the Dust Bowl, in *Grapes of Wrath*, and Orson Welles had frightened a nation of radio listeners with his graphic description of the landing of the Martians on earth. People were saying the almighty radio was getting out of hand.

They were singing songs such as "Flat Foot Floozie with Floy Floy" or "September Song" . . . "It's been a long, long time from May 'til December . . . and the days grow short when they reach September . . . ." Kate Smith, that lady of song, had just introduced what would become her trademark and a piece that would become a tradition in this country called "God Bless America," and the Austin Tex Schramm saw that year had a population of only 50,000 with the University of Texas showing an enrollment of some 12,000. Austin was a small city with a big university. It was a city in which the only prominent landmarks in its skyline were the Texas Tower, rising skyward as a monument to athletics as much as academics, and the state capitol building, whose granite glowed pink in the early morning sun. Most business was centered on or just off Congress in downtown Austin but, although there was no suburbia, the 40 acres of the University of Texas were almost like a city within a city.

Schramm would miss the ocean but grow to love the Hill Country, with soft-rolling hills, spring-fed streams and scenic oaks, cedars and pecans, and the Colorado River which snaked along the edge of downtown Austin. These places would become picnic areas, places to go and swim and be outdoors. He later admitted that he believed, having grown up in the California culture, which was light years ahead of Texas, that he might have an advantage somewhat akin to the all-knowing city boy moving into a country area.

"I enrolled and pledged my father's fraternity, Phi Kappa Psi, and it didn't take me very long to realize that I wasn't particularly held in awe because I was from Southern California and already had drunk a bit, smoked a bit and been around," he said. "Actually, I was just shit, because I wasn't from Abilene or some place like that. I'd also decided to continue my football career. I hadn't played much but figured, being from Southern California and all, I might have an advantage. I was due a rude awakening."

Even then the Texas high school system was a football factory, and Schramm's timing could not have been worse. The University of Texas had experienced some very lean years, including a 1-8-0 record in 1938, but Coach D. X. Bible had brought in what was called the best freshman class in the school's history. Among the 120 recruits were Jack Crain, Pete Layden, Roy Dale McKay and Malcolm Kutner, and they sparked a resurgence of Longhorn football. By 1941 this nucleus would form the Texas team that would be picked for the national title. It would be featured on the front of *Life Magazine*, which sold for 10 cents. Injuries depleted the team, causing it to finish 8-1-1, but many still consider it among the best of Longhorn teams in history.

"I was what they'd call a walk-on nowadays," said Schramm. "I was somewhat marked, being from California. I didn't even have a scholarship. Everybody around me was named Billy Bob or Tommy Glenn or something like that, and they'd all led their teams to state or district titles.

"I felt I had some ability and fairly good speed. I actually won the intramural 100-yard dash with a blazing 10.2. I do remember it was a world record at that time for a Californian from San Gabriel who went to the University of Texas.

"Oh, I played enough to get a letter sweater. I also played enough for it to change the direction of my football career."

Clyde Littlefield, who had played basketball with Schramm's father, was the freshman coach. Freshmen were not eligible for varsity competition then, but it was the custom for the frosh team to scrimmage the varsity, upon which Crain and some of the other stars-to-be were sophomores.

Schramm, playing tailback, slipped out of the backfield during one such of those scrimmages and made his way over the middle, where he received a short pass. Just as he caught the ball and was thinking about turning upfield, he felt himself involved in a massive, bone-crunching collision and then the world became an aching blur. He'd been clothes-lined by a defensive back and knocked into semiconsciousness.

When Schramm opened his eyes, Littlefield was standing over him saying, "Give me the ball, will you?" It was a tugging match. Schramm, not realizing completely what he was doing, would pull the ball back every time Littlefield tried to take it from him. It was his ball. Finally, Littlefield, not knowing that Schramm was somewhere in never-never land, jerked the ball loose, and Tex somehow made it to his feet and went back to the huddle. He felt sick at his stomach, his head ached, and things started spinning around him. He wasn't sure whether he was in Southern California or Texas. Finally, all he could think of saying was, "Time out! Time out!"

He ended up badly damaged, suffering from a torn rib cartilage, a concussion, and various other aches and pains. "I couldn't raise my arm, and even my eyebrows hurt," he said. "If you want to pinpoint it, I believe it was at that time that I decided my ability was lacking and gave up my football career to concentrate on becoming a journalist."

Schramm started working as a sportswriter for the University's *Daily Texan* and began closely following the Longhorn athletic teams from a safer distance.

Tex Schramm brought a strong interest in track with him to Austin. At that time the University of Texas, under Littlefield, had developed a world class track team, and Schramm and Bill Sansing, who was sports information director at Texas and with whom Schramm, the associate sports editor of the University's *Daily Texan*, was developing a close friendship, were determined to publicize track, making the Texas Relays more famous than even the Drake and Kansas Relays. They decided to attend the Drake Relays to see how things were being done there and got into Schramm's car and drove all the way to Des Moines, Iowa, with a stopover in Dallas.

"My home was in Dallas, and we went by my mother's house," recalled Sansing. "We were on a tight budget. I figure we probably had $15-$20 between us for the entire trip. My mother fixed us a big box of fried chicken to eat on the trip, and that probably saved us. We finally got to Des Moines and had this room in a downtown hotel. Our careers could have ended the first night there. The place caught on fire."

The morning of the track meet Schramm and Sansing had gone back to their room and fallen asleep. Sansing started coughing and woke up, smelling smoke.

"All of a sudden I heard all these sirens and commotion and went to the window," said Sansing. "I saw smoke coming from the floors below me, and people were gathering on the street outside. So I woke up Schramm."

When Schramm asked him what was the problem, Sansing said, "Tex, I don't know whether we should get out of here or not, but this place is on fire."

They went back to the window and, looking down, saw people climbing out of their rooms on sheets and dropping to the ground.

"Look out the door," said Schramm. When Sansing opened the door, smoke swept into their room. "Let's get out of here," said Sansing but, with smoke all over the room, he couldn't see Schramm. He called for him.

"Tex," he yelled, "where the hell are you! Let's get out of here!"

"I couldn't find him," said Sansing. "Finally, I made my way to the bathroom and there was Schramm, combing his hair. I couldn't believe it. We were about to be burned alive, and there was Schramm taking time to comb his hair."

They got out of the room, made their way down the hall to the elevator and out the building.

"A couple of years later, 1941, Schramm got the idea we'd do the Texas Relays up right," said Sansing. "We splashed stories about the relays all over the *Daily Texan*. You've never seen so much about one event. We made the relays our biggest story.

"We were in Los Angeles together for the last Olympics (1984), and the *Los Angeles Times* devoted everything to the events. We thought it was the greatest sports journalism of all time. Then I told Tex, 'Well, somebody has finally given the same kind of coverage to track that we did that time when we were on the *Daily Texan*.' "

You might say Jarring Johnny Petrovich was, in a broad sense, the first draft choice Tex Schramm ever made. Those were the days of the singlewing, and Petrovich was a triple-threat tailback who was tearing up Southern California schoolboy circles at Alhambra High, Schramm's alma mater. Petrovich was a couple of years behind Schramm in high school, but by the time he was a senior he'd grown to 6-3 and some 215 pounds, which was extremely large for a running back in the late 1930s, and was very quick and fast. He was one of the most sought after high school players in the country and could have had his pick of schools, but chose to stay at home and play for Southern California's Trojans.

At that time the Pacific Coast Conference had a go-getter by the name of Antherton as its commissioner. He promptly announced plans to put a stop to recruiting violations once and for all. After conducting a thorough investigation, Antherton announced in a well-publicized decision that he had found the Trojans guilty of illegal inducements in the recruitment of Johnny Petrovich. Petrovich was immediately declared ineligible and banned from playing for USC or any school in the conference. However, in those days, if he were granted a release by his school USC, then he would be eligible to play in another conference.

"You can see what a great job he did," said Schramm. "Here we are over 40 years later, and the same violations are still going on."

Schramm, of course, had kept abreast of the affair. He immediately went to see Coach D. X. Bible and told him about Petrovich, his credentials and noted that he might be just the tailback Texas needed. Bible explained that, before Texas could contact Petrovich, it would have to get clearance from Southern Cal. Tex became relentless in his pursuit of Petrovich for the Texas Longhorns. He phoned his father in California, and the senior Mr. Schramm talked to both USC and Petrovich. There seemed to be no problem, so Petrovich was given permission to talk to the University of Texas, if he so wished to go there.

Johnny wasn't sure, although he also wasn't in the best of positions. Schramm got his father to talk to him about Texas, and then Schramm made the trip to California for the *coup de grace*. He explained to Johnny that the Longhorns were on the verge of greatness and glorified all the virtures of the Lone Star State. He talked about the campus, about Austin with its history and many splendored surroundings, and the pioneer spirit of Texas. By the time Schramm got through with his selling job on Johnny Petrovich, the kid could hear music.

"When I went back to school the following fall," said Schramm, "Johnny Petrovich was in my little car with me. We drove to Austin. I even got him into my fraternity. I had little doubt in my mind he would become one of the greatest runners in the school's history."

Petrovich did all right as a freshman. Again, he was as big as a tackle and as fast as a halfback. But he wasn't ready to leap tall buildings.

"I went into the service, and Petrovich tried to play one more year but didn't do much. Then he joined the service, too. Oh, he had eligibility remaining after the war but never used it. After the war he played a little minor league pro ball but . . . I guess you might say he didn't live up to what I had anticipated.

"I'm still not sure what went wrong. Well (he grinned) you can't win 'em all.''

Schramm remained friends with some of the Longhorn football players, including Jack Crain, a young man from Nacona, who made All-Southwest Conference as a sophomore. He was known as the "Nacona Nugget," "Jack Rabbit," and "Cowboy Jack." Crain literally had exploded on the scene in 1939. Oldtimers still talk about his 82 yard run to set up a touchdown from the Arkansas 8-yard-line. It is said he reversed his field six or seven times. Then he capped the day by taking a short pass and racing 67 yards for a touchdown in the final 30 seconds to give the Longhorns a 14-13 victory over the Razorbacks. But Crain also was somewhat of a reveler. Many believed this might have kept him from achieving greatness, but others felt he was like Bobby Layne, who soon would follow him to Texas, and that he could party half the night and still be at his best the next day. Schramm was one of the ones who believed the latter.

One party almost cost Crain more than a lost night's sleep. One of his buddies in the caper was none other than Texas E. Schramm.

"We'd just beaten the Aggies, 23-0, on Thanksgiving, 1941, and Crain and I and some other guys went to Monterrey, Mexico, to celebrate," recalled Schramm. "I admit, we did drink a bit, and I remember getting very sick. I also remember we almost got our butts whipped."

It is custom in Mexico for *novios*, sweethearts, to meet in a park or the town square. The boys will walk in one direction, and the girls in the other. They'll meet and then pair off. Schramm and Crain thought it might be more interesting if they walked in the same direction as the girls, engaging in conversation, of course. Some harsh remarks by the Mexican boys were made in a language that neither Crain nor Schramm understood. When this didn't work, there were physical threats. Schramm and Crain understood this language.

"They let us know the best way they could that we were not a bit funny," said Schramm. "They also let us know that we'd better get our tails out of there while we were still able. We conferred briefly, thought about the better part of valor, and hightailed it out of there."

Near the end of the season, the injury-ridden Longhorns were tied 7-7 by Baylor and beaten by TCU, 14-7. But several key players returned for the big victory over the Aggies. Then the Longhorns simply destroyed Oregon in the final game, 71-7.

"If I'd still been around, even I would have gotten to play in that one," said Schramm. "Well, we partied again and celebrated much of the night. The radio woke me up the next morning. The celebration was over.

"*We interrupt this broadcast to bring you the following bulletin. Japanese air planes bombed United States military installations and ships at Pearl Harbor, on the island of Oahu, this morning in a sneak attack that resulted in serious casualties and extensive damage. Additional information will be reported as soon as available.*"

Halfway across the country that same Sunday, the Chicago Bears of George Halas were using the talents of George McAfee, Sid Luckman and Clyde (Bulldog) Turner to defeat the Chicago Cardinals, 34-24, and thus tie Green Bay for the Western title of the National Football League. The announcement of the Japanese surprise attack came at halftime of the Philadelphia Eagles, 20-14, loss to the Redskins in Griffith Stadium in Washington, D.C. Immediately, all military and government personnel began streaming for the exits, and only a few thousand people saw the game's finish. That was Sunday, Dec. 7, 1941, a day President Roosevelt said would "live in infamy." Reports confirmed that 2,403 were killed and another 1,778 were wounded at Pearl Harbor.

The Bears went on to win the NFL championship, 37-9, over the New York Giants, with the winners getting $430 each, and the losers, $288. After the game Halas joined the Navy. Only 13,341 fans had seen the game. Their minds were on something else. It was, after all, only a game, and the United States was in World War II, theater in the real.

chapter sixteen

WAR II AND PEACE

Tex Schramm is known for his undying devotion and loyalty to the Dallas Cowboys and the National Football League. But he also is an extremely patriotic man, who adhers to the seat of government—especially if it is in Republican hands—and will still stand at attention and get chillbumps when the National Anthem is played before a football game. In Schramm's time and that of his WW II generation, there was little gray area in war, such as we were later to experience first in Korea and to a greater extent in Vietnam. The good guys and bad guys were clearly defined. The oppressors and the warmongers were from Nazi Germany, Japan and, although somewhat reluctantly, Mussolini's Italy. There was little subtlety, for instance, in Hitler's goals to establish a so-called master race in the world and the expansion plans of those in power in Japan.

Schramm remains strongly patriotic but, as sometimes happens when discussions become overly critical about the Cowboys or the NFL, his opinions are clouded by the emotion of the moment.

Once Dallas Cowboy officials and a few newspapermen were having dinner at Westlake, one of those sprawling, ranchstyle suburban California communities where everything seems so precise that it appears to be a life-sized rendition of an architect's scale model.

The streets and buildings and even the nearby lake, from which the name Westlake comes, are all too perfect. The streets are too clean, the flowers too colorful, the people too tan. The Westlake Restaurant is by the country club and a ten to 15-minute drive from the Cowboys' training camp in Thousand Oaks. It is a place where the Cowboy contingent often goes to eat and also a restaurant in which Schramm, finding out that college coaches visiting the training camp had gotten faulty service, contacted the place's management and let them know in no uncertain terms that, if anybody in his organization or their guests didn't receive first class service, another eating establishment would be found. There were no lapses in service thereafter. Oddly enough, if Schramm had experienced bad service, he would not have complained nearly as much as he did when it happened to his guests.

That night we talked, as usual, about football this and that, and then the subject of Vietnam surfaced. There was a discussion about how the war divided the country, encouraged conscientious objectors, and how Vietnam veterans returning home, even those severely wounded, had not been treated as heroes, as those who came back from World War II were. Schramm remarked that things were just different when he was in the air force in WW II. He said the country was united, regardless of race, creed or religion.

I was there and could not resist remarking, "Well, right here in your native California, the government took Japanese-Americans out of their very homes and placed them in internment camps. These people were, for the most part, born and raised in the United States."

"You're commenting again about something you know nothing about," said Schramm, who ordinarily would have a point. He paused, his face becoming a little redder. I could tell his fuse was getting shorter.

Curt Mosher, now an executive with the Phoenix Cardinals, was public relations director for the Cowboys at that time and said, although he wished he had not, "I think he's right, Tex. I had this Japanese friend in the army, and he was very bitter about what happened to his parents during the war."

"You don't know either!" yelled Schramm. "You be quiet!"

Mosher looked down. Joe Bailey, who had replaced Tom Hardin as business manager, said diplomatically, "Tex is right."

"B.S.," I said. "How can he be right? That's stupid."

"What do you know!" roared Schramm. "Why, the Japanese-Americans understood. They didn't mind!"

The people around us had gotten quiet. The subject was changed quickly. The *Los Angeles Times* was a godsend the next morning. It featured a story in which former Justice Earl Warren remarked that the low point of his service on the Supreme Court came when he advocated placing Japanese-Americans in internment camps during World War II. We pasted the story on the door of Schramm's room in the dorm at training camp. The next day at practice, having read the story, Schramm laughed. You have to say this for Schramm; he's a man who can laugh at himself and his own quirks—to a certain degree. He might not think a situation is funny at the time but usually sees the humor later. This endears him to a lot of people who might not otherwise particularly like him. He saw the humor in what he'd said the night before, but I still wonder if he believed the Japanese-Americans didn't mind going to internment camps.

A madness of reason seemed prevalent as the United States entered World War II. Young men just out of high school and college students such as Schramm quickly enlisted, and the country as a whole mobilized against what seemed an enemy with overwhelming odds. Women joined the industrial force in factories quickly converted to wartime measures. Victory gardens sprung up, and ration stamps were issued for food. Stores lowered the height of their shelves so women, who did the shopping with men away, could reach various items. This was believed to be the introduction of self-service. Thousands volunteered for civil defense efforts, and a group of farmers in Wisconsin formed a "tank corps," using tractors.

As for many others, Schramm's life became a roller coaster. He not only enlisted in the air force but also called a young lady named Marty Snowden in Alhambra and asked her to marry him. After dating in high school and on and off while Tex was away at college, he had assumed she'd be waiting. She wasn't. It was Christmas 1941, and he explained to her over the phone his plans for the air force and that they should go ahead and marry. She said she was dating somebody else and was almost engaged.

There was a silence on the other end of the telephone. "Don't do anything," Schramm finally said, "until I get there. I'm coming to California before I go into service."

"You might say," explained Marty "that I was a mail-order bride. Tex came home and then left for the service. We agreed to get married. But his parents picked out a number of rings and sent them to him, and he chose the one he liked and mailed them back. Why, I think I even bought the marriage license."

When Schramm enlisted, Bill Nuckols was developing an aggressive public relations program for the air force at San Antonio's Randolph Field. He was in the process of assembling a group of young men to start a public relations campaign to try to draw recruits into the air force. Nuckols contacted Sansing to determine if he might know anyone who might help with this program. Sansing said he had just the right man, Tex Schramm.

"We eventually had eight or ten guys helping," said Sansing. "But Schramm and I were doing it alone at first. Shortly after he joined, we were placed in a room full of pictures, cutlines and envelopes. They told us not to come out until we'd prepared a publicity campaign."

"No," answered Schramm, seizing upon an assumption, "we didn't just sit there and sort out pictures and papers. We trained and marched and all those things. But I had the advantage over those guys from . . . Abilene and places like that, because I'd been in military school. I already knew how to march."

Sansing and Schramm both went to officers' training school and then their separate ways during the war, although both ended up back in Austin when it was over. However, Schramm later recalled that he was proud of Sansing for keeping up the spirit of the Texas Longhorns, even in Europe.

As the war ended Sansing was stationed at a small air base in southern Italy. And as fate would have it there were a lot of Texas Aggies in the area.

"You know how we always felt about Aggies," recalled Sansing. "Well, they were trying to have a big Aggie muster overseas and had guys from all over southern Europe coming. I just figured I should help—do something in the manner befitting my love for Texas A&M."

Sansing hired a bunch of Italian kids, paying them a cigarette each, and taught them the words to the Texas Longhorn fight song, "The Eyes of Texas." He had told the kids and their parents that the song was actually the Aggie fight hymn. So when the Aggies gathered and began celebrating, Sansing's kids came out and started singing "The Eyes of Texas" in broken English.

"I was the only Longhorn around, so they knew who had done it," said Sansing. "I took off. They chased me out into the countryside, and I finally got away by hiding in a haystack. Later, D. X. Bible read about the escapade in a story written by Weldon Hart in the *Waco Tribune*. Mr. Bible wrote me a letter and said he'd like anybody who did something like that to work for him."

Sansing accepted and became the first full-time sports information director at the University of Texas and renewed his friendship with Schramm after the war.

Schramm also took a round-about way back to Austin. He finished officers' training school and then joined the air transport command at Hamilton Field near San Francisco. Finally, he was transferred to Hawaii, which had been touched by the Japanese bombing but still remained as an almost paradise, virtually unspoiled by progress and the great influx of tourist trade. Schramm's unit flew people and supplies to and from Hawaii, en route to the mainland or destinations in the South Pacific. They could fuel tactical aircraft and move military personnel and supplies.

He loved Hawaii at first sight. He was near his beloved ocean again and, when off-duty, joined a friend in building a boat and using it to fish at a far, uncluttered side of the island. Over the years he often has returned to Hawaii. Once during the mid-1970s, he was asked if he'd ever considered leaving the Cowboys to run another franchise and answered no, at first, but eventually added, when pressed, that he might consider going to Hawaii if the NFL ever were to put a franchise there.

While stationed in Hawaii, Schramm used his ingenuity not only to further, in his small way, the progress of the air force but also to satisfy a yearning he had to see his wife and first child, named after her mother, but with a different spelling. Mardee.

"We were working out of a hanger that had been converted for processing people," he said. "It was inadequate. So I wrote a letter suggesting we build a new terminal for passengers and freight. I also recommended that a certain knowledgeable person be sent back to the United States to look at commercial terminals around the country and thus get ideas."

The person he recommended go back to the States was himself, and he closed the letter by writing, "Besides I'd like to see my wife and new baby." Permission was granted. Schramm saw his family and also designed a terminal that still stands at Hickam Field near Honolulu.

He remains proud of the terminal and once, when it was referred to as "just a cargo terminal," he snapped, "It was a passsenger terminal, too! Any fool could design a cargo terminal!"

It was strange. A guard was stationed near the cargo plane, which was on a distant ramp at Hamilton Field, where Capt. Texas E. Schramm was finishing his tour of duty, waiting for his discharge. The war had ended in Germany in early May, 1945. German radio had reported that Hitler had died while defending Berlin against the great Russian onslaught, although it later would be determined that the Fuhrer had committed suicide, along with his long-time mistress and later his wife, Eva Braun, while hiding in a bunker. The Japanese were still hanging on, although they had enlisted young men to fly one-way suicide missions in kamikaze planes. A bomb would be placed in the plane's nose and teenage pilots would try to crash the aircraft into enemy ships. President Roosevelt had died in office in April and Harry Truman, a stubborn man from Missouri, ascended into the top office in the country. Talk was that the war with Japan might go on for another year. And there also were rumors that Albert Einstein and a group of scientists had developed for the United States an atomic bomb that was capable of destroying an entire city.

"We had no idea," said Schramm, "that our country was ready to use an atom bomb. I later found out, due to the name of the operation, that the cargo plane they wouldn't let any of us near that time at Hamilton Field was part of the contingent taking the atom bomb across."

On a gray dawn of August 6, 1945, the war, for all practical purposes ended, too, for Japan. The Enola Gay dropped an atom bomb on Hiroshima, destroying the city and killing some 92,000 people. Truman had given his okay and launched the world into the Atomic Age. Three days later an A-bomb was dropped on Nagasaki, killing 40,000. The Japanese surrendered on Sept. 2, 1945. The war was over.

Texas Edward Schramm was discharged from the air force and returned to Austin and the University of Texas. Actually, they'd discharged the right man under the wrong name. His real middle name was not Edward, but Ernest.

"All my life I'd been kidded about my name being Texas," said Schramm. "People would say, 'Oh, you must be from Texas.' I'd say no, and they'd just grin and stare. I didn't mind that. What I minded was that my real middle name was Ernest, which sounded sissy, so I just made up Edward and substituted it. All my high school, service and University of Texas records have me listed as Texas Edward Schramm. It wasn't until after I came to Dallas that I decided to confess."

NFLPA leader Ed Garvey, a heated rival of Schramm's, found out his real middle name and always addressed him as "Texas Ernest Schramm." Schramm said Garvey knew how to humiliate a guy.

The war had ended, and people were trying to pick up the pieces of their lives. Joe Louis was heavyweight champion. He had enlisted in the army when the war started and become a popular figure among armed forces personnel. Juan Peron had been elected president of Argentina and would fall in love and marry a young actress named Eva. More than one million would enroll in American colleges under the G.I. Bill of Rights, and people were singing "Tenderly," "Ol Buttermilk Skies," and "How Are Things in Glocca morra." *The Best Years of Our Lives*, a movie which depicted the complexities faced by three veterans returning to civilian life, garnered most of the Academy Awards. It starred Frederick March, Dana Andrews and a double amputee war veteran named Harold Russell. It would be Russell's only acting role and one for which he won an Oscar for Best Supporting Actor.

People had begun to talk more about space, about what might be out there in our universe, and Kenneth Arnold, pilot of a private plane, recorded a sighting that has periodically affected our imaginations to this day. While piloting his small craft near the Cascade Mountains in Washington State, Arnold said he saw nine very bright objects flying in what appeared a chain formation. He said each object was about the size of a DC-3 and going at a high speed. When asked to describe the objects, he said they looked "like saucers skipping across water." Newspapers across the country adapted that phrase to read "flying saucers." Thus began the flying saucer craze. What Arnold apparently had seen were high-altitude weather research balloons called skyhooks. They would rise over 120,000 feet, and helium gas would cause the balloons to flatten out from a cone shape to a near circle when they soared into dense air . . . like a saucer. Skyhooks, equipped with cameras and radio gear, also were launched from European bases over Russia. They were easily detected, and the results were spotty but they were the beginning of our spying system from the sky. In 1947 we had begun to worry about the Soviet Union and its plans to take Communism throughout the world.

There was never a time quite like when Tex Schramm returned to the University of Texas in the fall of 1945. The return of 10,000 veterans swelled enrollment, and the student profile changed drastically. Veterans, many with families and in their mid-to-late 20s, joined 17- and 18-year-olds just getting out of high school to widen the age range of the student body as never before. Austin was not ready for the great influx of students. There simply were not enough places for the students to live, especially veterans with children. People just would not rent to those with children and/or pets.

An ad appeared in the *Austin American-Statesman*, that read:

"Is this you? Is there someone in Austin that feels a child is not an outcast of society? If so and you have a two bedroom house or apartment, let us show you our daughter. If you think she will not demolish your property, you will not only have reliable tenants but also honest friends. A veteran. Phone 6876."

The ad was taken out by Tex Schramm, who even then could show the subtlety of a sledgehammer. Schramm had brought his wife and baby daughter to Austin and found only a small walk-in apartment not much bigger than a closet in which to live. Marty recalled that they had to step over the bed to get to a hot plate, upon which they did their cooking. But the ad was effective, and soon the Schramms rented a nice garage apartment on Red River, across from Memorial Stadium.

Schramm's plans for a journalism degree had received a somewhat surprising setback. Before the war he had worked for the *Daily Texan*, for which he was supposed to receive class credit.

"You had to write x-number of stories for the *Texan* and turn them in at the end of the year for credit," recalled Schramm. "When we all went into the service, the understanding was that we'd get the credits when we got back. At that time Paul Thompson was head of the journalism department. So when I got back, I was given an 'F' in that particular writing course. I'd written all sports stories and he didn't like that. I thought that was unfair. But after that I got 'A's' in journalism courses.

"And after the war Dewitt Reddick was head of the journalism department. He was a tremendous guy. I was taking a full load of classes and working a full shift at the *Austin American-Statesman*. I had a helluva time trying to stay awake in some of the classes, but he understood. He gave me a lot of credit for things I was doing for the *American-Statesman*, figuring logically that I was getting good on-the-job training. Reddick also didn't mind that I was only doing sports stories. Now I won't say much for Mr. Thompson, but that Reddick was a helluva guy."

Schramm also received some other welcome help in school. This came from his wife Marty, who unlike Tex, is an avid reader. The fact is Schramm can't be still long enough, can't maintain his concentration long enough to finish a book. So, of course, Schramm enrolled in a course on the novel given by the English Department at Texas. Marty read the books, summarized them for him, and he took the tests. He passed the course or, rather, Marty passed it for him.

Schramm had been hired by then sports editor Wilbur Evans to work 4 P.M. to 1 A.M. for the *Austin American-Statesman*. Tex had some experience, not only having worked for the *Texan* but also one summer vacation for the *Los Angeles Times*. And, while Schramm was at Alhambra High, he had been sports editor of the school paper and also a stringer or correspondent for the Times and old *Los Angeles Examiner*.

During the war Evans had been hired by the University of Texas to research its athletic history. When he met Tex, he remembered coming across the name of another Tex Schramm, a basketball letterman, during his research. Tex told him that was his father and the reason he had come to the University of Texas.

"I hired Tex because of his great enthusiasm and knowledge of sports," recalled Evans. "Having been in the air force, he was very mature. He already had a wife and daughter, and we became close friends."

After Schramm became general manager of the Cowboys, he would return the favor, hiring Evans as the team's business manager. At Schramm's urging, Evans would later become publicity director of the Southwest Conference and eventually the first chairman of the Cotton Bowl Selection Committee, a post he held until retirement in 1980. He died in 1987.

"Schramm was no great shakes as a writer when I hired him," said Evans. "But he worked hard and had a quick, brilliant mind and good ideas. We just had an excellent staff."

Besides Evans, the sports staff included Weldon Hart, a fine writer who had come over from Waco; Jimmy Banks, who later would work for the *Dallas Morning News* and author of a number of books; Tex Maule, a former trapeze artist who also would become an author and later make a name for himself as the pro football expert for *Sports Illustrated*; and Jack Gallagher, who was to become a leading sports columnist for the *Houston Post*.

Those were the days of sportswriters of rhyme and legend. They worked hard for salaries of perhaps $25-$30 a week, played hard, drank hard and practiced their trade in open-air press boxes and crowded, smoke-filled newsrooms. They worked for tough, no-nonsense, if sometimes shortsighted editors such as Charley Green of the *American-Statesman* or Buck Hood, the managing editor of the same newspaper.

During the time Schramm had worked for the *Los Angeles Times*, he had observed how that paper used a vast network of correspondents to call in game results and scores from every nook and cranny in its area.

"I just decided we could do the same thing with the Austin paper," said Schramm, who recalled that when he was in high school the Los Angeles newspapers had paid him $1.00 and sometimes $1.50 to call in results of games from the San Gabriel-Alhambra area.

Schramm contacted people throughout Central Texas and set up a network of correspondents. He had been such a sports nut that he could name the players picked for the All- American team each year by the Helms Foundation, then one of the most prestigious selectors for postseason honors in football and basketball. So Schramm decided to give out awards for athletes in Central Texas and called it the "American-Statesman Foundation."

"Well, it got the paper a lot of attention," said Evans. "I wanted to reward him for his work, so during a banquet the newspaper held each year, I presented Tex with a check for $100 and Charlie Green went crazy. Charlie Green counted pennies like most people did $20 bills. He called me into his office and chewed him out for giving Schramm the money."

"To make matters worse," said Schramm, "I came out with this column advocating horse racing and paramutual betting in Texas. I had the background in California, having worked at the track and been around racing. So it seemed logical to me that Texas should have racing. Geeze! Green called me into his office and had a fit."

"In case you are blind, can't hear, read or see, perhaps we should get something straight young man," Schramm recalled Green telling him. "This newspaper, as are most all Texans, is diametrically opposed to paramutual betting. This state is against it. And so here, on my very own newspaper in the capital of Texas, you write that we should legalize horse racing. I can't believe this. I simply can't believe this."

"So," recalled Schramm, "I didn't write anything else advocating the legalization of horse racing."

Schramm loved to tinker with page makeup. The fact is he still notices and comments on the way newspapers are made up. But in those days, you not only made up the paper but also edited copy and selected where each story would be placed. One night Joe Louis would retain his heavyweight championship, and Schramm, of course, planned to lead with the story. "It was our big story," said Schramm. "Well, I had everything laid out and all ready, waiting for the fight to end. Then I'd put in pictures and the story. We had three wire services then—the AP, UPI and INS. I planned to read all three coverages of the fight and pick out the best story.

"Suddenly, the fight ended, and all hell broke loose. Stuff started moving on the wires like crazy. Here would come a lead from this guy and then a first add [first addition to the lead] from another one. I'd start to go with something and then something else would move. I had wire copy on the floor, the desk, around my neck and in my pockets, trying to sort it out. It was a nightmare but, somehow, I got something in the paper, even if it turned out to be an AP lead, an INS first take and a UPI second take. But next time I picked which wire service to use and was ready."

Green was explosive, but Hood liked to lecture—sometimes impromptu—the younger staffers. "The worst thing about that," said Banks, "was that he'd get you just about the time you were getting off. He was known to have a few drinks and sometimes would be pretty far gone when he'd call you into his office. It would drive you crazy. He'd be about half coherent and then say, 'Get what I mean?' You always said you did, because you wanted to go."

"Hood drank all right but I always got along fine with him," said Schramm. "I think I even learned some newspapering. He was tough, but seemed fair."

Gallagher was a kind of free-wheeling writer in those days. He knew better than to advocate horse racing in his column, but once did criticize the local boxing and wrestling scene. He so angered one of the boxers that the fellow called the *American-Statesman* office and said he was coming to whip Gallagher, who was about 5-9, 150.

"I'm coming to get him," said the boxer. "What does he look like?"

Banks described Gallagher as big and mean. When Gallagher heard about the irate caller, he substituted a picture of Primo Carnera in his column the next day. The boxer never called back.

"Those were," said Schramm, "exciting times."

Nobody had much money so the social scene for the *American-Statesman* sports staffers usually centered around gatherings at each other's homes, such as Schramm's garage apartment. You'd usually bring your own bottle and they'd talk sports and listen to a small radio set, which was advertised as genuine plastic. They'd have a beer or five at Scholtz' Beer Garden, which still is a landmark in Austin, or go on picnics at Barton Springs or Bull Creek. Sometimes after work or during a break, the staff would gather for coffee at the PK Grille, where a gentleman named Freddie ran the cashier and made sure the customers' cups stayed full. Decades later, Freddie was still serving coffee to staffers of the paper. There were street cars then, and the only hotels downtown were the Driskill and Stephen F. Austin. There also were a couple of movie theaters downtown but, mostly, there was sports.

"Tec was very busy," recalled Marty. "He really threw himself into his job, just as he always has done. He was very restless even then. I know he was gone a lot, covering a track meet or this or that event.

"In fact, he went to a track meet with Wilbur in Corpus Christi when we were about to have our second daughter. Tec saw the city limits sign and decided to name the girl, Christi. We'd planned when we married that I'd get to name any boys we had, and that he'd get to name the girls. Well, we had three girls, and he named them all. So you see, he was getting his way even back then."

The Texas Longhorns had begun a golden age of sports after Schramm returned to Austin. With the likes of end Hub Bechtol, center Dick Harris and a young singlewing tailback from Dallas Highland Park named Bobby Layne, the Longhorns were 10-1 in 1945, including a 40-27 victory over Missouri in the Cotton Bowl, and 8-2 in 1946. The basketball team, led by Slater Martin, who became one of the few SWC All-Americans, and John Hargis and Al Madsen, became a powerhouse and would post a 26-2 record in the 1946-47 season, ranking third in the nation and beating such household names in the sport as City College of New York and Wyoming before eventually losing to Oklahoma, 55-54, in the NCAA playoffs. The baseball team won SWC titles in 1945, 1946 and 1947, and the track team was one of the best in the nation.

Layne, who died in 1986, not only became a legend at Texas but in the NFL. His reputation for off-field activities was exceeded only by his play on the field.

"You have to understand the times were different then," said Schramm. "There were a lot of older guys coming out of the service, such as Bobby. They'd been away and wanted to catch up and have a good time. But Layne was always ready to play. He was just a helluva player. He wasn't what you'd call a picture-pretty athlete like, say, a Bob Waterfield. But Bobby was a winner, and I think the statement Doak Walker made best summed him up . . . 'Bobby Layne never lost a game. Time just ran out on him.'

"A lot of people might have forgotten, but he had an unbelievable record as a pitcher for Texas. He didn't have that blazing fast ball or anything but was, once again, such a great competitor. He just wouldn't let you beat him."

In baseball he never did. Layne had a 28-0 record. Before a key game against Texas A&M, Layne injured his foot with seven stitches needed to close the cut. The doctor told him to stay off the foot for a few days, but he went ahead and pitched against the Aggies, throwing a no-hitter.

"During the spring of 1947, just before I graduated, Blair Cherry had taken over as head coach for D. X. Bible and added a different form of attack," said Schramm. "He installed the T-formation, which was perfect for Layne. Bobby had never been that good of a runner but was smart, a fine ball-handler and passer."

Using the T-formation for the first time in the fall of 1947, the Longhorns posted a 10-1 record, beating the Harry Gilmer-led Alabama Crimson Tide, 27-7, in the Super Bowl. The only loss was

14-13 to Doak Walker and SMU. The Longhorns had had a chance to win that one in the final minutes. Texas faced fourth and one at the SMU 32. If it made the first down, it had a chance to score or at least try a field goal. But as Layne turned to hand the ball off, the fullback wasn't there to take it. The fullback had slipped in a mud puddle and temporarily lost his balance. By the time he regained his balance, the Ponies had closed the hole and stopped him. The fullback was Tom Landry.

Layne went on to star for Detroit and Pittsburgh. It was while he was playing in the twilight of his career for the Steelers that he stopped the Cowboys from reaching a milestone in their history in 1960 and then aided them in doing so in 1961. Dallas seemed to be on the way to winning its first game ever that first year, but Layne rallied the Steelers to a fourth period comeback and a 35-28 victory. In the 1961 league opener in the Cotton Bowl before 23,500 fans, Dallas middle linebacker Jerry Tubbs, now an assistant coach, intercepted a Layne pass in the final seconds of a game that was tied, 24-24. Rookie Allen Green, who had missed two earlier field goals, kicked a 27-yarder to give Schramm's team its final regular season victory ever, 27-24.

Schramm knew Layne at Texas but didn't remember ever meeting Tom Landry. "I knew of him," said Schramm. "When he came to Texas everybody was talking about what a fine passer he was. But he broke his right thumb and couldn't throw anymore so they moved him to fullback and also used him as a defensive specialist."

When they were at the University of Texas, neither Schramm nor Landry had any idea they'd enter pro football in their current capacities. Landry hoped to play pro ball for a while, which he did, and then go into engineering. Schramm still had his sights set on a journalism career. Both he and Pete Rozelle imagined that they might one day go back to Los Angeles and work for the *Times*.

"Oh, I don't think any of us had any idea Tex would turn out to be what he is today," said Jimmy Banks. "It just wasn't something we took all that seriously in our part of the country. College football was bigger, more important to us.

"The Austin paper carried very little about pro ball. But I do remember Schramm would talk a lot about it. I'm just not sure anybody listened."

"When I was growing up in California, my father took me to the games of the minor league Los Angeles Bulldogs in the West Coast League," said Schramm. "We'd also go see the Chicago Bears play exhibition games in Los Angeles. As I said before, the Redskins trained in California, and I was a big fan of theirs.

"The top college players didn't go into pro football back in those days. It wasn't necessarily the thing to do. But I thought it was a helluva deal. The program then was so much more wide open. The pros passed a lot, lateraled a lot, and they could kick the ball so much better than college players. And then when Dan Reeves moved the Cleveland Rams to Los Angeles, I was hooked."

Schramm was home on summer vacation between his junior and senior years when the Cleveland Rams moved to LA. "The Dons of the All-American Football Conference were in Los Angeles, too, so I was a fan of both teams," said Schramm. "That, of course, changed drastically when I went to work for Dan and the Rams.

"That seemed the ultimate for me. When we left Texas, I never dreamed we'd ever go back there to live." Dallas was just a place then, and Tex was only slightly familiar with multimillionaire H. L. Hunt, not even knowing he had a son named Lamar.

chapter seventeen

LAMAR AND THE AFL

It wasn't until the AFL-NFL merger in the spring of 1966 that Tex Schramm first emerged from the shadows of pro football's power structure, where he already had been working efficiently but generally unnoticed. It was Schramm who not only inaugurated merger discussions but who, in conjunction with AFL founder Lamar Hunt, secretly set up points of negotiation and the guidelines for one of the most important happenings in professional sports history. Their cloak and dagger meetings led to a coupling which would propel the NFL into its modern era and not only give us "Monday Night Football" but a game which has become sports biggest event— The Super Bowl.

Schramm's Cowboys had battled Hunt's Dallas Texans for the city's sports dollar, and so Schramm personally knew the man who went up against the NFL Establishment. Tex, however, came away from the Cowboy-Texan conflict and the merger discussions with a much different impression of Hunt than was generally shared by the public and media.

Hunt was believed by most to be a nice, easy-going, unassuming man who just happened to be rich. It had been duly noted that he had been rebuffed in his attempt to bring an NFL team to Dallas and thus was forced to establish his own league. He was the son of H.L. Hunt, once believed to be the richest man in the country, and whose income had been reported to be $1.5 million a week. Lamar was a bespectacled young man who, at 30 years of age in 1960, was estimated to have a personal wealth of $50,000,000. Yet Lamar dressed in suits bought off the rack of department stores and flew second class whenever possible and was even known to borrow money from sportswriters to buy a soda pop. He was friendly, quietly charming and likeable. Lamar Hunt had the perfect image to mount a white charger and challenge The Establishment.

"I obviously have emotional reasons to cloud my perspective," said Schramm. "But I see Lamar Hunt as one of the most selfish, commercial people I've ever met in sports. He has been able to sell people on a facade that he creates for himself as being Mr. Nice Guy, just a good ol' boy with money. He has created an image of himself as a person who would unselfishly do anything for the betterment of sports, as a guy who only wanted to see pro football come to his hometown.

"That's a bunch of bull. He was scheming all along to start his own league, and when he saw a chance to get out of Dallas for a better financial deal, he cut and ran, so I hardly think he was all that interested in his hometown as he led people to believe."

Hunt first had become intrigued with owning an NFL team in the late 1950s. The Chicago Cardinals, owned by Violet Wolfner and managed by her husband, Walter, had been losing a great deal of money. Hunt inquired about the possibility of purchasing a majority interest in the Cardinals and moving them to Dallas. He said the Wolfners told him they weren't interested in having the club relocated at that time but might be later. He said he then got in touch with George Halas, chairman of the NFL expansion committee, and asked if the league planned to add any new teams in the foreseeable future. Hunt indicated Halas said the NFL would not expand in the near future. The next interest Hunt showed was for a team in a league he founded.

Schramm said a lot of truths came out later in the $10 million antitrust suit Hunt and the AFL brought against the NFL, charging it with monopoly and conspiracy in expansion, television and signing of players. It was much the same thing the USFL would try in 1986. Judge R. C. Thomsen ruled against the AFL and stated that, although he surmised the NFL had moved up its debut in Dallas by a year (from 1961 to 1960) for business reasons (to combat Hunt's Texans), neither the Cowboys nor Texans had done very well, which "may indicate that the city is not as good a location for pro football as was generally believed."

"Lamar admitted in court that he went to see Commissioner Bert Bell—a nice, sweet old guy—under the guise of buying the St. Louis Cardinals," continued Schramm. "He knew at the time he wanted to start his own league. But he was after certain information from Bell about the league and operating a franchise. So he made a list of questions on an envelope or a scrap of paper about the things he wanted to find out and stuck them in his pocket.

"Bell, thinking Lamar was buying the Cardinals, was very open. At one point during their meeting, Lamar excused himself and went into the men's room, so he could check his list and make sure he hadn't forgotten to ask anything. Hey, this was a man who was getting help from the NFL commissioner under false pretense, so he could use what he found out to start his own league. That doesn't sound like an All-America boy to me."

Schramm said Hunt then got Davey O'Brien, the former TCU All-America who had played for Bell with the Philadelphia Eagles, to go see the commissioner to try to get more information. Hunt later explained he told O'Brien to advise Bell that he (Lamar) was starting a new league and that the commissioner said it would be good for football. Bell, who was somewhat preoccupied in his later years, died of a heart attack in the fall of 1959, before the NFL draft and meetings that were to be held regarding expansion.

Schramm said the late Clint Murchison, Jr., who was awarded the NFL franchise for Dallas, offered Hunt the majority interest in the team. "Clint even told Lamar he would withdraw from the franchise and that he, Lamar, could take it over," said Schramm. "But Lamar was obsessed with starting a new league, so Clint's offer didn't get a great deal of consideration."

Minnesota Viking president Max Winter later said when he told Lamar and a gathering of prospective AFL owners that Halas had told him the NFL would expand by four teams, Lamar seemed very happy about that information and said that he expected his group would get together and decide which ones wanted to become partners in the expansion franchises. Later, Lamar said he went ahead with plans to start his own league because of his loyalty to his prospective partners in the AFL.

"The truth, as I see it, was opposite of what just about everybody thought," said Schramm. "It was Clint who was only interested in getting a pro team for his hometown and not Lamar. You also have to take into consideration that, in three years, Lamar was perfectly willing to abandon his home city when he made a more lucrative agreement with Kansas City. Clint never would have made that decision, no matter what.''

Besides Hunt's opposition to Schramm's latest project, instant replay, the Chiefs' owner also riled Tex when he said it wasn't fair for Dallas to host a Thanksgiving game each year.

"It should be shared by all teams," said Hunt. "It's an unfair advantage to allow Dallas to continue to play the Thanksgiving Day games at home. One, the visiting team always has to travel on short notice. Then, two, with ten days off before the next game, it gives the Cowboys a chance to really build for the home stretch in the season. Dallas also gains by exposure on Thanksgiving."

"Oh, Lamar's always agitated by something we've done," said Schramm. "He tried to get the Thanksgiving game moved around at a league meeting and received very little support. He even admitted that he didn't expect the game would do very well in Kansas City.

"The league office asked us to play the Thanksgiving game in the first place. I took it because of added TV exposure and also because I believed it could become a tradition. I'd seen how important the Texas Aggie game was on Thanksgiving when I was at the University of Texas. The league decided to move the game around in 1974 and 1975 so tried it in St. Louis, but it didn't do very well. So people at the league office came back to me to host the game again. I said, fine, but if we started playing on Thanksgiving again, I wanted to keep doing it. That would make only Detroit and Dallas having a game that day. So we do get good ratings but I'm not sure about the great competitive edge."

Through 1986 Dallas had a winning percentage of 78 on home games during seasons when it hosted the Thanksgiving Day contest. The winning percentage on Thanksgiving was 74. However, for games following the holiday contest, with the extra days of rest, the Cowboys had a winning percentage of 84.

"What you have to realize is that Lamar lives in Dallas and has to sit there and read about us every day," said Schramm. "I can understand his frustration but can't think of anybody who deserves it more."

But Schramm said he bore no ill feelings toward Hunt during the years the Texans and Cowboys battled for the Dallas sports dollar, because all was fair in a situation like that. "With the popularity we have now, most people have forgotten or don't realize that the Cowboys weren't a very popular team when we first came to Dallas," he explained. "We started out way behind as far as the general public was concerned and had a long, long way to go."

Clint Murchison had tried for years to get an NFL franchise for Dallas but, like Lamar Hunt, had failed. In 1952 when the original Dallas Texans, who would be relocated in Baltimore, were in town Murchison talked to Commissioner Bell about acquiring the team, which was going under, and requested a 24-hour period to have his accountants look over the team's books before making a final decision. The Texans were owned by a group headed by Giles Miller, who was in the textile business. Except for the performance of its stars, such as Buddy Young and Gino Marchetti, the Texans were a disaster, both on the field and at the box office. "Bell refused the request," said Schramm, "because he wanted to let his friend Carroll Rosenbloom have the team." In 1954 he seemed to be in position to buy the 49ers, hoping that once he got into the inner circle of the league, he could get a team for Dallas. But NFL officials found the man who had put together the deal for Clint unacceptable. Clint then backed out, refusing to turn on the man who had helped him.

However, in late 1959 rumors were flying that the NFL would be willing to grant Murchison an expansion team at the league meetings in January, 1960. George Halas told Murchison the NFL might be willing to expand to Dallas in 1961. But Hunt's team was going to play in 1960, and Murchison didn't want to wait, giving the Texans an extra year to get established. Just before the league meeting, there remained a great deal of opposition to expansion. Murchison wasn't sure he'd even get a team but knew he had to start making plans, just in case.

Tex Schramm, who had left the Rams for CBS, had turned down a number of offers in professional sports while he was with the network, including jobs with the Detroit Lions, NBC, the Detroit Pistons and Montreal Alouettes. NBA executives also had interest in him for their commissioner. But Tex was waiting for the right opportunity to get back into the NFL and apply some of the knowledge and new perspective he'd gotten on pro football while at CBS.

"I kept hearing rumors about Dallas being awarded an expansion team, and that was what I really wanted," said Schramm. "I mean, I wanted to start something from scratch and build it into a success."

Bill Sansing had left Dallas and was working in New York, so Schramm contacted him and asked if he knew anybody who might know something about the proposed franchise. Sansing suggested Field Scovell, an official for the Cotton Bowl Association and a leading sportsman in Dallas. Schramm had met him, and Sansing knew him well.

"I called Field from Schramm's kitchen, and he got in touch with Bedford Wynne, who—along with Todde Lee Wynn and Fritz Hawn—was a partner in the proposed franchise with Clint," said Sansing.

Wynne told Murchison about Schramm's interest in the team. Murchison then contacted Halas, who strongly recommended Tex, having been impressed with his work for the Rams. Although Schramm was only 39 at the time, Halas told Murchison he couldn't find a better man to run the Dallas team.

"I flew down to Dallas and couldn't have been more impressed with Clint," said Schramm. "I told him some things he didn't want to hear and I think, in the end, that attracted him to me. I explained to him that the Cardinals probably could be bought for $2.5 million and that he'd be better off going that direction than paying $500,000 for the new franchise."

"With the new franchise you're going to lose $2.5 million before you ever get a football team that will draw," Schramm told Murchison. "You can get an established team that has some good players and have a chance to be competitive from the beginning."

"That's ridiculous," said Murchison. "The most we can lose is $200,000 or $300,000."

"No, that's what is going to happen."

Schramm recalled Murchison still didn't believe him. "He said all you've got to do is this and this, and the losses wouldn't be all that bad. I then told him I had a little book that I'd kept with the Rams and that I could show him the things he was talking about were only a small part of the operation.

"But Clint wanted the new team, and so did I. I also explained to him the things I felt were necessary to have a successful franchise. The most important one was that the ownership not be involved in the operation of the club. I'd seen what happened in Los Angeles and didn't want to be in that kind of situation again. The biggest temptation is for an owner to become friends with the players, which Reeves had done. If that happens, then the players start complaining to the owners about the coaches, and there's a problem right away. There has to be one line of authority, the owner to the general manager to the coaches to the players. You can't have a situation in which somebody can jump that line of authority. I had a lot of ideas and explained my whole philosophy to Clint and also that, besides salary, I wanted to be a part of the ownership. We covered all areas, and I felt good when I left. Ten days later he phoned me and said, 'Let's go.' ''

Murchison hired Schramm in October, 1959, for a salary of $36,500 per year and offered him a stock option in which, as long as he remained with the club, he could purchase as much as 20 percent of the stock at 1960 prices. If the club were successful, Schramm would become a millionaire.

If Dallas got the expansion team in January of the following year, the NFL draft already would have been held. Realizing then that Dallas would not be able to draft any college players Schramm started looking for ways to make the best of the situation. He told Murchison he should try to sign SMU star Don Meredith to a personal services contract. He knew Lamar Hunt also would be aware how important it would be for a franchise in Dallas to have a player like Meredith, who had been a collegiate star in the city and had a following, and wanted to beat Hunt to the punch. He explained to Clint that they'd work out something later to get NFL rights to Meredith.

Murchison not only heeded this advice but went a step further and had a friend, New Mexico Senator Clint Anderson, sign New Mexico University running back Don Perkins to another personal services contract after helping convince him Dallas would be a good place to be.

Each contract was, of course, contingent on Dallas getting a team. Perkins and Meredith turned out to be the backbone of the team, and each is now in the exclusive Cowboy Ring of Honor. As it turned out, Halas, sympathetic to the plight of the Dallas franchise, drafted Meredith and then let him go to the Cowboys for a future third-round draft choice.

After the NFL draft was held in November, Schramm attempted to get standard league contracts, so he could start signing free agents in December, two months before a decision would be made on expanding to Dallas, but Austin Gunsel, the acting commissioner after Bell's death, refused the request. Schramm wasn't about to be stopped. He managed to get a copy of the official NFL contract and had counterfeit copies printed.

"I had to do something to get us started, because we would miss the draft regardless of what happened," said Schramm. "I had the contracts made up and then got in touch with Dan Reeves. I made a deal with Dan to pay the Rams $5,000 to let us use their information on players who were not drafted, the ones who would become free agents."

Schramm made Eilene Gish his first secretary and Gil Brandt the first man he hired for a team that might never exist. He used Brandt and also enlisted the services of his old friend Hamp Pool to go out to try to sign as many free agents as they could to the counterfeit contracts. If a player signed the contract, they'd also sign another piece of paper, stating that if Dallas did not get the franchise, the contract would be void.

Brandt was a self-made man who had done some work for the Rams in the scouting department while Schramm was there. Tex remembered him as an extremely hard-working guy who could get things done.

Gil had attended the University of Wisconsin, but the only actual football experience he had was as high school quarterback. While in college he became intrigued as to just what it would take to make a good football player at each position. So he wrote various colleges and universities, identifying himself as a high school coach, and asked to get copies of their game films. He dissected the films and learned the qualities of good players at various positions. After college he had started a baby photography business. He put cameras in the hands of nurses at three hospitals in Milwaukee. Each hospital would add $3 to the patient's bill and keep 25 cents. Gil got the rest. So, working two hours a day, five days a week, he had a lucrative business going and could devote his spare time to scouting football and learning everything he could about the game. One of his neighbors while he was growing up in Milwaukee was Wisconsin All-American Elroy Hirsch, who had gone on to star for the Rams. Hirsch helped Brandt get a part-time scouting job with Los Angeles. He'd also done part-time scouting for the 49ers, and then Schramm called.

Brandt was able to sign 28 free agents to counterfeit contracts. This became one of the deciding factors in Dallas being awarded a franchise, another being the fact that Murchison agreed to let

George Preston Marshall have his song, "Hail to the Redskins," back.

Marshall didn't want expansion until 1961 and threw a roadblock in the path of Murchison. However, George Preston, who loved his marching band and the Redskins' team song, had had a falling out with band director Barney Briskin, who had co-authored the song with Marshall's wife, Corinne Griffin. Briskin, angry at Marshall, got in touch with attorney Tom Webb and asked him if he were interested in rights to the song. Webb figured it was a joke on Marshall and said he was. Incidentally, Webb was Murchison's attorney in Washington, D.C., so Clint ended up talking him into giving him rights to the song. Murchison then offered to let Marshall have the song back if he'd vote for an expansion franchise in Dallas. Marshall agreed.

In a somewhat little known fact, Schramm almost pulled off another coup before Dallas was even voted into the league. "Things were happening fast," said Tex. "Kodak had its All-America team in New York for some festivities, and I went there to see what I could do. I found Billy Cannon, the great LSU All-America and probably the most sought-after college player in the country. I actually convinced him to sign with us. Then I called my old friend Pete Rozelle, who was still general manager of the Rams, and told him what I had done. I figured we'd sign Cannon to a personal services contract and worry about details later. Pete said the Rams also were interested in Cannon."

"What the hell do you think you're doing," Rozelle told Schramm. "You start messing around like that, and I will see that you never get a franchise."

Schramm backed off, and the Rams signed Cannon. Later, a court declared the contract invalid, and Cannon was freed to sign with the AFL's Houston Oilers.

"If Rozelle had left me alone, the NFL, and the Cowboys, would have ended up with Billy Cannon," said Schramm.

Dallas was awarded the franchise in the January, 1960, meeting, and each existing NFL team was allowed to freeze 25 names on its roster of 36, and the Cowboys were allowed to pick 36 players from those remaining. Dallas could pick no more than three from each club so, in effect, the Cowboys ended up mostly with has-been's, unwanteds, club house lawyers and never-will-be's. Murchison and his partners paid $50,000 for the expansion franchise and $500,000 for veterans in the players' pool. Cost of the team was $550,000;

in 1985 it would be sold to a group headed by Bum Bright for $60 million.

"I lived in New York and kept hearing about a Giants' assistant, Tom Landry," recalled Schramm. "People were calling him a young genius for what he'd done with the Giants' defense. For the first time anybody could remember, the crowd was giving the defense a standing ovation, instead of the offense."

Paul Corley, a friend of Murchison's in Dallas, also recommended Landry to Clint, who phoned Schramm and asked him what he thought of Tom. Schramm said he already was considering Landry for the job. Schramm talked to Landry, a native Texan and former Longhorn star who already had been approached by the Houston Oilers.

"Tom was an NFL man, first and foremost," said Schramm. "He also wanted to live in Dallas, so I hired him. He was the only person I'd actually ever talked to about the job. From what I understand, the Maras told him he could become head coach of the Giants when Jim Howell left, but he wanted to get back to Texas, and he liked the challenge."

Landry, then 35, became the youngest head coach in the league. He was most impressed when Schramm told him that he'd be in charge of all matters pertaining to the field of play—the players, trades, final decision on draft picks—and that Schramm would reign over everything else. The lines were clearly defined and drawn, although Schramm in 1986 clearly began to exert more pressure and use his power of persuasion to bring about changes in Landry's domain.

And Murchison was the perfect owner, one who would not interfere with the operation. He was a man who hired the best people he could and left them alone to do the job. Over the years other NFL executives had often called Murchison the perfect owner for whom to work. But Schramm had something to do with this. He had told Murchison this was the way it must be for the team to be successful before he ever took the job in Dallas. Schramm laid the foundation upon which he could work, and Clint readily agreed.

The original Cowboys were hardly glamourous, on or off the field. They worked out at Burnett Field, a minor league baseball stadium. Rats roamed the locker rooms and gnawed at the players' shoes. The training room was set up in what had been the ladies' rest room, where the walls were painted pink. The executive and coaches' offices were in a single room in the Automobile Club Building on Central Expressway. Hunt's Texans, on the other hand, had their own field and offices.

"When I first came to Dallas," said long-time ticket manager Kay Lang, "there were three people in this long room—Tex, Tom and Gil. It hardly was a first-class arrangement and seems amazing when you see what they've got now at Valley Ranch."

Kay was another part of Schramm's LA connection. She had been an ice-skating champion who had performed in the Ice Follies. She'd left the Midwest to seek fame and fortune in California and was skating and working part-time in the Pan Pacific Auditorium helping sell tickets when the Rams asked her boss, Billy Jordan, to help them set up a ticket office. He brought Kay along to help, and she stayed with LA until Schramm hired her.

"I was supposed to help out for three weeks and ended up staying in the business for 39 years," she said. "I knew Tex then but not as well as after I came to the Cowboys. To tell you the truth, I think that fabled temper is something he's adopted for himself. He wasn't that way in LA. It's an image he's built. But he's done it for so long that now he really does have the temper. I just don't think it came naturally."

Lang became the first woman to hold a managerial job with an NFL franchise. A headline in a Dallas newspaper announced her hiring with the words: Cowboys Hire Woman Ticket Manager.

"Tex and I have had our ups and downs, but I love the man," said Kay. "I'd classify him as a hardnosed pussycat. He's both arrogant and lovable.

"I know in staff meetings he intimidates a lot of people. Some people actually are afraid of him. He makes you explain things. You say this or that and he'll say, 'Why?' You better be ready to explain yourself before you make an important statement."

Schramm and Lang had a terrible argument when the club converted from manual to a computer-ticket operation. Lang tried to get in touch with Schramm while he was in training camp in order to get a decision regarding ticket processing. She couldn't reach him, so she talked to then vice president Al Ward, and they agreed to go ahead with a certain process. When Schramm found out, he was furious. He phoned Kay and raved for a few minutes and then asked her why she hadn't checked with him first.

"I couldn't find you, so I talked to Al."

"That's a helluva note. That's why I'm general manager, and he isn't. I make those decisions."

"He talked awful to me, and I started crying," said Kay. "I told him he could take my job and shove it, and then I disappeared. I was hiding out at my sister's house, because I knew he'd be trying to find me. When I finally went home, sure enough, the telephone rang and it was Tex."

"Hi, Katy, how are you?" said Schramm, as if nothing had happened.

"Hi."

"Why don't you come in and talk to me when I get back from camp?"

"I refused but finally went to see him, and we ironed everything out," said Kay. "He was very sweet and cordial."

She paused and, after reflecting, said, "I don't think his temper or outbursts bother women who work for him. They usually end up loving him. You get used to hearing his booming voice and, again, he can be so sweet and understanding. You know all the trouble Duane Thomas caused him. Well, after Duane had gotten out of football, he phoned for tickets. Tex told me to give them to him. Another person whose name I won't mention was down on his luck. Tex hadn't seen the guy in a dozen years but gave him some money. He's like that."

He helped one of the young women in the office who was having marital and financial problems. Another employee with whom Schramm had only slight and indirect dealings had physical and mental troubles and even attempted suicide. Through the long and often frustrating road to recovery, Schramm made sure the man continued to be paid and also took care of his medical expenses.

"The general public never hears about that side to Tex," said Gil Brandt. "Maybe it's time they did."

It wasn't just the Dallas Texans of Lamar Hunt that the Cowboys had to battle when they first came to town. Other facets of the community didn't welcome the team. As was the case with the Los Angeles Coliseum, the Cotton Bowl was a bastion of college sports. It staged the annual New Year's Day game, the Texas-Oklahoma classic and was the home field for SMU. The Mustangs had fallen on hard times, and their supporters and officials greatly resented the pros coming to town and playing in the Cotton Bowl. Hunt, a friend of Mayor Robert Thornton, was able to get first options on games in the Cotton Bowl, so the Cowboys were forced to alter their schedule, sometimes playing on Saturdays and sometimes on Fridays.

SMU athletic director Matty Bell, who had coached the Mustangs during their heyday with Doak Walker, was furious. "I don't like it," he said. "By playing on days other than Sunday, it just shows the pros don't care for colleges and will do anything for selfish reasons. Friday night traditionally has been a high school football time, and Saturdays have been for colleges."

Hunt, with the prime Sunday afternoon dates, came up with a number of promotions to give away free tickets. One was Barber's Day, in which any fan wearing a barber's smock got in free. And then he had a Texans' Teen Salute, in which he let in free any youngster presenting a stub from a Friday night high school football game, an obvious slam at the Cowboys.

"People got so angry that they even turned on Roy Rogers, King of the Cowboys," said Schramm. "We brought him in for our first game and had him ride in a car around the Cotton Bowl. Fans started throwing ice at him, and we had to get him out of there. I'm surprised Lamar Hunt didn't have a day where ice throwers at our games got in free to see the Texans."

The Texans and Cowboys went head-to-head for three years and, actually, Hunt's team was more competitive in the weaker AFL, posting a 25-17 record and winning the league title in 1962, whereas the Cowboys were 9-28-2. Attendance figures were close, but both sides were losing a lot of money. When Hunt took his team to Kansas City, he'd reportedly lost $3,000,000.

"The Texan's' attendance figures were misleading, because they gave away a lot of tickets," said Schramm. "We didn't. The only give-away we had was that we'd let an adult who bought an end-zone ticket bring in five kids free.

"We just had a basic difference in philosophy. We knew we had the product, and all we had to do was eventually be successful on the field. Once we became competitive, we'd be all right. People knew about the NFL teams we were playing. So we just dug in for the long haul. Never once did I have any doubts we were going the right direction and that we'd have a winner.

"I also was confident we were in a good area. I felt all along, that you had to have good college competition and interest for a successful professional franchise. SMU was having some problems, but college football in the Southwest Conference was very hot. And everybody in Texas was brought up on the sport. We had a ready-made audience once we got the right product. I'd also determined that the ticket sales for the original Texans (in 1952) were higher than the Rams had in their first two years in Los Angeles. The first Texans just didn't have the money to withstand the losses and we did.

"Clint was great during all that time. Once with a game six days away, he wanted to know how many tickets we'd sold. I told him seven—we'd sold seven tickets."

"Well," replied Murchison, "why would anybody want to buy tickets now anyway? It's too early."

The Cowboys and Texans and the NFL and AFL battled over collegiate players. The Cowboys signed 84 percent of draftees mutually sought by the Texans and the AFL. Schramm had moved to get Meredith before Hunt knew what was happening, but the Cowboys lost a draft pick on E.J. Holub, the Texas Tech All-America center, because they didn't know he'd already signed with the Texans.

It was rumored that Hunt also had signed TCU All- America Bob Lilly, so other clubs stayed away from him on the early draft picks. Cleveland, picking twelfth was going to take offensive tackle Jim Tyrer, but Paul Brown guessed correctly that he'd already signed with the Texans. Schramm then rushed over to the Browns' table in the draft room and offered Cleveland his No. 1 pick in 1962 for that twelfth choice. The trade was made, and the Cowboys chose Bob Lilly, who had not signed with the Texans.

"One of the big things then was to have babysitters," said Schramm. "Each league would hire people to stay with players they wanted to sign, so the other league teams couldn't get to them to try to talk them into signing with them. We were looking for Buck Buchanan and couldn't find him. We found out Lamar was hiding him in an apartment complex he owned. I remember Blackie Sherrod also lived there.

"We thought we had Otis Taylor. We were hiding him in a motel room in North Dallas, and our babysitter was in adjoining room, guarding the door. So Lamar found out where he was and had somebody crawl through the window and talked Taylor into leaving."

The Cowboys and Chiefs also waged almost a two-year court battle over Jimmy Harris, who turned out to be a mediocre defensive back. In those days, mediocre backs could start for either team. Harris, who had played at Oklahoma, was with the Rams, but decided to sit out his option year of 1959. The Texans signed him, contending that, since his option year had passed, he was free to play for another team.

Schramm, believing Harris was in violation of his NFL contract, traded the Rams for rights to Harris and took the Texans to court to try to get him. The standard NFL contract has an option clause in which a team with which a player has signed has an option to retain his services for one year after the contract has expired. Schramm maintained that Harris had to "play out his option" and could not sit it out, and that he thus belonged to the Cowboys. Commissioner Pete Rozelle nullified any contract Harris might have, other than the one with the NFL, because he had not been active during his option year. The option clause was upheld in court, and the Texans let Harris go to play with the rival Cowboys.

"That became a landmark case," said Schramm. "It proved once and for all that you have to play out your option year." Harris played one year for the Cowboys and then was gone, but Schramm felt satisfied because he'd proven a point.

"Things were going bad for both the Cowboys and Texans," said Schramm. "At first Hunt proposed to play us in a 'Loser Leave Town' game, but we refused. We had nothing to gain by such a game and, besides, we weren't going anywhere. Then the joke going around town a year or so later was that the two teams should play and the loser had to *stay* in town.

"After the Texans continued to draw poor crowds while winning the AFL title (1962), Lamar called and set up a meeting with Clint and me. He just said, 'If we move, what will you do? How do you feel about it?' There was never any discussion or thought about the Cowboys leaving. Clint made it clear to Lamar that we would not move. Then, once again, Clint offered Lamar a partnership in the Cowboys. He even said he'd give him an option to become one of the Cowboys' owners at no cost. But Lamar didn't want that. He wanted to go to Kansas City, where he worked out a better deal with the city."

Hunt later said he took his team out of Dallas, because it was a question of how long the Texans could lose money and still make economic sense. Kansas City had offered him free use of Municipal Stadium for two years if he signed a seven-year lease. Sports leaders also pledged to sell 25,000 season tickets. The figure turned out to be about half that amount, but it was much more than the Texans had sold. He probably also felt he might be caught in the Hobby

Law, which said that after five years the IRS could rule teams were hobbies and not businesses and thus could require owners to pay taxes on all write-offs. Both Murchison and Hunt had been writing off club losses as tax deductions.

"Lamar's team had an emotional following," said Schramm. "Feelings like that linger. We even had a sportswriter named Sam Blair who wore a red Dallas Texan sports coat to our games long after the team had left town. We just had to live with those who favored the Texans until we started winning. When we reached the .500 mark in 1965, those things started taking care of themselves. We had become a very exciting team and had captured the imagination of the fans in Dallas."

Some revolutionary ideas that had been nurturing in Schramm's mind since he worked for CBS helped Dallas become a winner more quickly than it would have otherwise.

chapter eighteen

GETTING COMPUTERIZED

Tex Schramm had begun exploring the possibilities of using the computer in the college draft almost from the outset when he came to Dallas, but it would be the mid-1960s before the system was solidified enough to use it extensively.

"By the time we had organized and set up our scouting system and it was operating efficiently, I found we were having some unusual problems," said Schramm. "The more efficient we were, the less efficient we became. We were gathering too much information on too many players. We would start with, say, 2,000 players in their freshman year in college and steadily accumulate information on them. By the time they were seniors, the number was down to 500 or 600. That total was reduced to 300. Then each of the 300 was read, graded, and ranked. Since it took at least an hour to read and evaluate the information on one player, it became obvious at once that no one could judge the 300th player as efficiently as the first.

"Then the individual ratings varied because of the qualities the rater considered most important. For instance, I was always hooked on speed. If a player could run a 9.4 in the 100-yard dash, I'd overlook a lot of his other faults. Others tended to give priority to character. A player who had a good character rating would get special consideration from Tom Landry, even if he might fall short in other areas. Coaches and scouts had various prejudices. Some believed a Big Ten player was automatically good. Some were prejudiced against small college players.

"When I kept seeing the mass of information we had to digest and the difficulty of getting uniform reactions from the people who had to go over it, I knew we had to find a quick, dispassionate judge, and that was what I had in mind all along—the computer."

Schramm contacted the people he had befriended at IBM during the Olympics, and they put him in touch with a man named Salam Qureishi, who was with the Computer Science Division of the Service Bureau Corporation, an IBM subsidiary in Palo Alto, California. Qureishi, who was born, raised, and got his BA and MA degree in Aligarh, India, knew absolutely nothing about football. He was somewhat familiar with cricket and believed American football to be the United States' version of soccer. Schramm, on the other hand, didn't know a volt from an amp and sometimes struggled to put the proper light bulb in the correct socket. This unlikely pair would change the method of operation of NFL scouting departments forever.

"What we had," said Schramm, "was an Indian who knew nothing about football, and coaches who knew nothing about Indians. Fortunately, Tom Landry reluctantly agreed to cooperate, or we never would have been able to go on with the program."

There were times when it seemed illogical to go on, but Schramm gets an idea and often pursues it far beyond mere stubbornness.

Qureishi went to work with college coaches around the country, and they came up with more than 100 characteristics affecting their judgment of talent. At that time, even the most sophisticated computer system could work with only about 80 variables, so it became obvious the number had to be cut down. The physical qualities, such as height, weight and speed, did not count, because they could be measured, so no evaluation was necessary. Eventually, after years of work five intangibles were settled upon. They were character, quickness and body control, competitiveness, mental alertness, and strength and explosion.

"The next thing we looked for was as accurate a measurement as we could get of all these qualities to feed into the computer," explained Schramm. "I think the computer was about to blow a fuse trying to figure out what different descriptions meant. For instance, a coach we dealt with from Alabama might describe a fullback as a 'monster,' and one from Nebraska might call him 'a bull.' You ask a coach how quick a player is, and you get answers like 'quick as a cat' or 'quick as two cats.' The answers were practically meaningless for our purposes. Our next step was to employ assistant college coaches throughout the country and ask them hundreds of questions to try to find the descriptive phrases or words to best evaluate the five basic characteristics and be meaningful to coaches everywhere.''

Schramm enlisted the services of SMU psychologist Dr. Robert Stoltz to help in the study which took years. Eventually, they determined a more clear, concise, common meaning for the descriptions the coaches were giving and developed a language of terms to which they could all relate. The Cowboys then were able to devise a questionnaire, to be filled out by all scouts, using these common terms. It was worded in such a way that the scout had to think in only these specific descriptive terms. The questionnaire had 15 options, all in the form of statements. Declarative sentences described a facet or a particular skill or characteristic of the player being evaluated and asked the scout to evaluate these things, grading a player from one to nine. Nine was used, because it was discovered the human mind was not capable of judging degrees on a scale with more than nine ratings. Thus, the system was designed to fit the scale of the human mind. If a player was given a nine, it meant he exactly fit the description in the statement. If he was given a five, he "moderately" fit the statement. A rating of one meant that he was nothing like the description.

The term "wave drill" was common to all coaches around the country and is an exercise to test agility. One statement in the questionnaire says, "His movement is awkward in wave drill." So when a coach or scout is asked to rate a player on agility, he has something concrete to go on, instead of just saying a guy is "quick as two cats."

Besides rating basic qualities, scouts also rank players on specific skills of their particular positions, again using key words and phrases that have a clearcut meaning to everybody concerned. Offensive backs, for instance, are graded from nine, meaning exceptional and rare ability, to one, which is poor, on seven different aspects. And finally, a player is ranked one to nine on his likelihood of making the NFL. A nine grade would mean the player was a cinch to make it, and a one would give him no chance at all.

"It took us years to come up with the dimensions that define a player and to shave down the descriptions," said Schramm. "Then there was another problem. How did we assay the qualities of the scouts who were feeding the information into the computer?

"As was the case with Tom and I, each scout had built-in prejudices, some of which were subconscious. And some might be harsh graders, whereas others would be lenient. We went over reports from each scout individually and checked them with what the other scouts had given a particular player. Then when we saw what the results were, we could determine a particular guy's prejudices and assign him a value. This value, or weight as they call it, also was fed into the computer."

In the old system of scouting, there would be hundreds of looseleaf notebooks crammed with data on players. The process of extracting this data was so time consuming that it had to be started in the spring before a player was to become eligible for the draft. Updating the list at drafttime was impossible. With the computer, you could get a list of the top 100 draft choices in a day.

In the early 1960s there was great secrecy surrounding scouting systems, especially concerning the Cowboys who were trying to go into new areas. In 1961, before the computer was even used, Schramm tried to broaden his team's system by forming the first scouting combine, Troika. He asked the Rams and 49ers to join him but didn't want anybody else in the league to know what was happening. Dan Reeves of the Rams, general manager Lou Spadia and owner Vic Morabito of the 49ers, and head of the scouting department Gil Brandt had a secret meeting in Schramm's home to discuss the situation.

Art Modell happened to be in Dallas at the time to try to sign a college player and decided to drop by the Schramm's for a visit. He walked in on the session.

"What is this?" he said. "This looks like a meeting of the Mafia."

"Everybody began coming up with excuses as to why they were in town," said Schramm. "Modell still suspected something but didn't know what. Years later he learned he had broken into a meeting to form the first combine."

Schramm also attempted to keep the Cowboys' interest and work with the computer behind closed doors in the beginning, but invited both the Rams and 49ers to join the program in 1963. The New Orleans Saints became a part of Troika when they came into the NFL in 1967.

I wasn't trying to help the other clubs when I asked them to join us," said Schramm. "But we needed a bigger sample for our computer. We weren't getting enough reports from just our scouts. With the other teams, we got three or four times the amount of information, which should have reduced the margin of error. But only about 40 percent of the information we got became common knowledge among the combine teams. The other 60 percent the clubs kept to themselves."

Soon the other NFL teams joined combines called Blesto and Sepo. They also began using the computer to dissimulate scouting information and help form game plans.

In recent years Dallas, Chicago, Detroit, Philadelphia, Pittsburgh, Miami and Minnesota have composed membership in the Blesto combine, whereas the other 19 teams are grouped under the National Scouting Combine. National charges each team $50,000 to share the information and rating of college players. Three or four teams go right down the line with National's ratings when they draft. Some clubs are so dependent on National that they do very little in the way of scouting.

"Sure, it saves us money being in a combine," said Schramm. "But we're still using our own scouts, and we're still interpreting our own material. One of the gravest dangers facing pro football in the future is the growing tendency to share what should be competitive jobs. You can't share anything that influences the competition on the field. In our scouting we remain highly competitive in all but the purely mechanical aspects. Some groups now are sharing totally, and that's wrong. When you do that you abrogate your basic responsibility to compete. So I have obvious misgivings about total sharing of scouting information."

Schramm says the Cowboys are still working to be more accurate in rating a player coming out of college and that there are still many more doors to unlock.

"You go back 30 years, and we were scouting in a very primitive way," he explained. "Now we're refining our methods of testing players and use of the computer and are much more advanced and sophisticated. But the challenge of unlocking new doors is still there. We have a long way to go. Somebody far in the future will look back on what we're doing now and think we're primitive."

He explained Dallas is trying more and more to find a way to judge a player's emotional capacities to accomplish great goals. He added that the Cowboys also want to be more accurate in measuring the physical ability it takes to become a great success in football.

"We're deeply involved in research right now," he said. "For instance what combination of physical tests best predict the success of a football player? Somewhere there is a better way to determine exactly what characteristics best interpret into success at a particular position.

All scouting information is evaluated, and Tom Landry is given a list of the top 100 players to read. Several weeks before the draft Landry will meet with Gil Brandt, Schramm and members of the scouting department, and the prospects will be ranked in order of the Cowboys' preference. Schramm, Brandt and the scouts all have input in the ranking order, but Landry makes the ultimate decision on who the Cowboys pick. He usually goes home after the sixth round, because the order has been established and the prospects, theoretically, have been taken. However, Schramm has more than just made himself felt in the draft.

Again, it was Schramm, intrigued by speed, who picked Bobby Hayes in the seventh round in 1964 after Tom Landry had already gone home for the day. He opted for Herschel Walker in the fifth round in 1985, and of course, there was Roger Staubach, the man who made more difference than any in the history of the team.

Schramm, along with Brandt, was also behind what turned out to be a coup on a tenth round throwaway choice that year. He went for navy star Roger Staubach. Staubach still had one more year of eligibility and four years' obligation to the navy, and no player had ever bridged that gap before and returned to be successful in the NFL. When Schramm learned that Hunt also was interested in signing Staubach, he devised a plan in which the team would pay Roger a certain amount of money each month while he was in the navy. Staubach liked that idea and signed with the Cowboys and later, of course, he became a once-in-a-lifetime player. It also did not hurt Schramm's cause that his old classmate at Alhambra High School, Alan Cameron, was athletic director at the Naval Academy and a person Staubach looked up to. Had it not been for Staubach, it is unlikely Dallas would have won two Super Bowls in the 1970's and taken Pittsburgh down to the final minute in two others.

Dallas also was able to get Mel Renfro with its No. 2 pick in 1964. Brandt had fanned rumors that the Oregon star might be damaged property because of wrist damage which had occurred during a domestic squabble in which his wife had cut him with a knife. It appeared at the time that the severe laceration might cause permanent problems to the wrist. The Cowboys also had taken almost four hours—allowed in those days—before making their second pick, again causing speculation that they might be doing some serious checking on Renfro. But the Cowboys knew Renfro would be all right, and the four hours actually had been spent working out a deal for Buddy Dial.

The 1964 draft accelerated the Cowboys on their way to success. They got a Hall of Fame player in Staubach, an All-Pro in Renfro and a game-breaker in Hayes. But, had not Schramm let his emotions get in the way, the draft would have been even better, perhaps the best in club history.

Dial, a native Texan who had starred at Rice, had continually killed Dallas when he played for Pittsburgh. He was a fine clutch receiver, a man who could make the tough catch over the middle, and so when the opportunity presented itself, Schramm sent the team's No. 1 draft choice to Pittsburgh for Dial. Buddy suffered through a series of injuries with Dallas and never materialized as even a receiving threat, much less the star that he once had been.

"We'd already agreed to terms with the man who was going to be our first round choice," said Schramm. "He wanted to play for us and was all ready to sign. Then we decided to trade the pick for Dial. I've been kicking myself in the tail ever since. The guy we were going to get was Paul Warfield."

Dallas was having great success signing free agents in those days, but Schramm, somewhat tongue-in-cheek, although not completely, said, "One of my regrets is that Cleveland (Pussyfoot) Jones didn't make our team. We signed him as a free agent, and he looked good in practice but only lasted three preseason games. He was 5-3 1/2 and weighed only 160. Do you realize we could have had the first Spud Webb?" And Dallas also had come up short with the perpetual immortal (to himself), Rufus (Roughhouse) Paige.

Paige was a baldheaded, potbellied man who was, at 39, older than Tom Landry. He had been a halfback at Princeton and never stopped hearing the crowd noises that weren't there. He also was a friend of Murchison, who had met him in prep school. For years Paige had talked about how he'd never had a real opportunity to show what he could do. He remarked that he "had the feet of an antelope and the cunning of a rat."

Murchison, never one to resist a joke, signed him to an NFL contract for $13,000 and sent him to the Cowboy training camp. Schramm took one look at Roughhouse and couldn't figure out what was going on. He knew things were tough in those early days, but not *that* tough. Then he surmised Murchison must have been behind the whole thing. Schramm didn't want to hurt Roughhouse's feelings, so he gave him a uniform, allowing him to have his picture taken and to go through all the preliminary things with the other players. But all that time Schramm was plotting to get even.

Schramm finally told Roughhouse that Clint had invited him to Spanish Cay, the Cowboy owner's private island and get-away in the Bahamas. Roughhouse gratefully accepted the invitation. Schramm knew Murchison had planned a holiday on the island and that Roughhouse would be just the person he didn't want to see. Tex arranged passage for Roughhouse. When he arrived, Clint wasn't there yet. His wife was and became somewhat puzzled as to why her husband would invite such a man to visit them. But, knowing Clint was somewhat unpredictable in such matters, she accepted Roughhouse as a special guest. For two days he enjoyed the good life, the liquor and food and scenery and felt that his new career as a professional football player wouldn't be all that bad. It was said that Murchison aged three years on the spot when he arrived and found Roughhouse, grinning and extending him a hand of welcome. As cordially as possible, he sent Roughhouse to Nassau, the closest spot where he could catch a plane back to the mainland. And, at least, Roughhouse, so to speak, had had his shining moment in the sun.

The first time the Cowboys used the computer extensively for the draft was in 1965 when they chose Craig Morton as the No. 1 pick, Malcolm Walker as No. 2, and got a small college player named Jethro Pugh in the eleventh round. All became starters. The only reason Morton didn't remain with the team was the advent of Roger Staubach, but when Dallas traded him to the New York Giants for their top pick, the Cowboys used it to get Randy White. Walker was the starting center, and Pugh was an outstanding tackle for 14 years. The fact that he played in the shadow of Bob Lilly kept him from making the Pro Bowl. The computer also helped steer Dallas toward picking Calvin Hill and Duane Thomas as its top choices in 1970 and 1971. Yet, once again, a player such as Danny Reeves, now head coach with the Denver Broncos and an outstanding halfback with the Cowboys, was ignored in the 1965 draft and signed as a free agent.

Much of the Cowboys' success over the years had come because, in spite of picking late in the draft year in and year out, the club had been able to come up with outstanding players and sign unknown free agents who gained success. The club, with its computer information and network of scouts, and somewhat covert operations, plus the success of Brandt in making friends with college coaches around the country, was just ahead of the opposition until the late 1970s, when other teams seemed to catch up and malfunctions developed in the drafting philosophy.

Schramm began to look into the situation a few years ago. Only 14 selections in the first two rounds since 1978 were still on the team in 1985. Only six starters had come out of the five drafts before 1986, and only one first round choice, defensive end Jim Jeffcoat, had won a starting position since 1983. Middle linebacker Eugene Lockhart, a sixth round selection, was the only starter out of the entire drafts of 1984–85. It should be noted, however, that two top picks, Robert Shaw and Billy Cannon, could have become stars had not they suffered career-ending injuries. Shaw (1979) had been projected as a Pro Bowl center but had to quit in 1981 after a severe knee injury. Cannon had become a starting outside linebacker his rookie season (1984), but after a neck injury, doctors advised him not to try to play again. He later sued the Cowboys. Dallas just didn't have much luck with the Cannon family.

However, unlike in the early and mid-1970s, Dallas just wasn't coming up with good young players to replace those who were retiring. Furthermore, the Cowboys had passed on chances to make selections such as Dan Marino, Mark Duper, Vernon Dean, Neil Lomax, James Wilder, Mike Singletary and Chris Collinsworth. The Cowboys had made miserable No. 1 choices in Larry Bethea, a tragic figure who failed to live up to expectations in six seasons with the team and, suffering from a drug problem, took his own life in 1987, and Rod Hill, a defensive back taken in 1982 who, in spite of being a tremendous athlete, just could not play football very well. Dallas also had picked a mediocre player, Aaron Kyle, No. 1 in 1976 and Howard Richards, released in 1987, as the top selection in 1981.

Cowboy coaches do not believe a mistake was made in taking Kevin Brooks as the first choice in 1985, but the jury is still out at this writing. There also was a great deal of optimism when the team had the No. 12 selection in 1987, the highest pick Dallas had had without trading up since the early 1960s, and chose Nebraska defensive lineman Danny Noonan. Because of age, defensive linemen Ed (Too Tall) Jones and John Dutton have reached the end of their careers, and Randy White is getting closer. It is crucial the team find more than just adequate replacements if it is to compete at a higher level.

"Since we started having success and thus picking late in the draft, we'd lapsed into what I consider a human weakness," Schramm explained. "Usually the very solid players that you know are going to make it are gone in the early choices. We were passing over good football players when our picks came up and gambling on the ones who, if they turned out, just might become great. We were looking at the ones with great athletic ability and figuring, if they made it, they'd be the type players to take us to victory in the Super Bowl.

"We also might have been reading more into a player's potential than actually existed because we wanted to believe it. As a result we'd pick a guy who had potential, but whose odds of being successful were too great. We lost some perspective, looking for the super athletes.

"Then all of a sudden we'd passed over the good, solid college players too long and had begun to lose the nucleus of our team through injury and retirements. Rod Hill was a good example. We brought him into Dallas, and he worked out for Gene Stallings. He was sensational. He had all the quickness, the agility, the moves, the speed, the subjective things. But, the way it turned out, he just wasn't a football player.

"I felt we had to start making decisions like an army lieutenant might. Say, you were going on a secret mission or up the hill to capture an enemy. You're allowed to select two guys to go with you. You know who is the best shot, who is the smartest, etc. But, hell, you're going to pick the two guys who are the damnest fighters you know, because you'll have a better chance of surviving with them. You've got to do the same thing with football players. At some point you just say, we take this guy, because we know he's a player.

"There's been some difficulty too in finding players who fit into Landry's system, which is very demanding. But the system is successful, so we have to try to find a certain kind of player. We've had some guys, such as Mike Walter (No. 2, 1983), who have gone on to play elsewhere (San Francisco). He fits into the 3-4 defense used by the 49ers but just wasn't suited for our 4-3 Flex Defense. There were less demands on his ability in the 3-4. Now Coach Landry is planning to begin adding some new defensive alignments to go with the Flex, so perhaps a player like Walters would fit in more easily. I'm not in any way suggesting that we should have changed our defensive system sooner, but just want to point out that, besides some other miscalculations we made, we also had to find a certain type player.''

Brandt got most of the credit when the draft went well. He took most of the blame when it went wrong. Certainly, the media was on him and believed validity was added to their opinions when Schramm hired Bob Ackles, general manager of the very successful British Columbia Lions of the Canadian Football League, in the new job of pro personnel director. Brandt had also performed the duties of that post. Ackles had come up through the ranks with the Lions, often had visited training camps in the NFL and knew key people in the league. Schramm said he wanted a fresh outlook in the organization when he hired Ackles in 1986. He wanted Brandt to concentrate completely on scouting college players, while Ackles would scout and evaluate NFL players for possible trades. Gil also was freed from the job of signing players, that job going to Schramm's possible successor, vice president Joe Bailey. It appeared Brandt was being demoted, but Schramm quickly came to his defense.

"Most clubs had two people for the jobs, but Gil had been handling both," explained Schramm. "I had told him for some time I was going to try to free him from his other duties, so he could completely concentrate on college scouting. Obviously, we need to strengthen that area. Also, when you negotiate contracts for a period of time, animosity develops with some players, and I thought we best could avoid that by starting with the clean slate that Bailey could provide.

"I wouldn't say our drafts in recent years have been an embarrassment, but they have been disappointing. You can't put the total blame on Gil. We've all been at fault. He has the most input, using the information he gets from his scouts. But remember, we all sit down and rank our choices and put them in order on the board. Landry approves the choices. And he makes the final decision on which player we pick in the early rounds, based on some often times very lengthy discussions.

"Theoretically, we're not supposed to do anything but scratch the names off our list as they're taken and then make our choice from the name that comes up next. If we deviate from this, Tom is the arbitrator and the final judge, as it should be.''

Dallas has deviated regarding quarterbacks in recent years, because Landry and his coaches felt the team was set at the position. In 1979 Dallas picked Shaw as its No. 1, Aaron Mitchell No. 2 and tight end Doug Cosbie, a top player, No. 3. That was the year Roger Staubach retired, but the Cowboys believed they were more than covered with Danny White and Glenn Carano. So, although Dallas had Joe Montana listed ahead of Cosbie and could have taken him, Landry wanted Cosbie. In 1983 the Cowboys felt secure with White and Gary Hogeboom and passed on Dan Marino, whom they had ranked higher than the No. 1 selection they made, Jim Jeffcoat. Of course, other teams also passed up Marino, who was the fifth quarterback taken in the draft that year.

"We've gone back and checked the information we had on the people like that, which we've passed up, and determined everything was in our reports but that, perhaps, we were just interpreting them wrong. Gil now has more time to look into matters like this.

"I'm sure he didn't like some of the things that were said about him in the press, about his power being taken away, but he understood what really was happening."

Schramm and Brandt continue to look into the Cowboys' drafting system in hopes of trying to bring it back to the status it once held. One positive sign was when the team made Mike Sherrard, the UCLA receiver, its No. 1 choice in 1986. There was no question he could play, although his career was interrupted or, perhaps, finished when first in training camp in 1987 and again during off-season in 1988 he suffered a broken tibia in the same leg. The Cowboys, however, appeared to have strengthened the receiving corp even more by drafting Miami's Michael Ervin in 1988. Nebraska defensive lineman Danny Noonan played well enough in 1987 for the coaches to feel he could be outstanding. Of course, the Cowboys also made up for a number of bad high-draft selections when they were able to get Herschel Walker as a future in the fifth round in 1985. Walker seems to be a player in the category of Roger Staubach, Bob Lilly, Randy White and Tony Dorsett. Dallas had slim to no hopes of finding another back the caliber of Dorsett, who is in the twilight of his career, until scoring a coup by getting Walker.

Nobody was particularly surprised that Schramm suddenly took a hand in trying to correct the draft problems, because that always had been one of his expertise.

chapter nineteen

MIDDLEMAN IN MERGER

The signing wars between the AFL and NFL had reached a peak in 1966 with a combined total of $7 million being spent to sign draft choices. The NFL was signing 75 percent of the common draftees, but teams in both leagues were losing money. There had been informal discussions between various owners in each league, proposing that the NFL might agree to take in certain teams from the AFL, much as it once had done with the old All-American Football Conference, but no steps had been taken.

In February of 1966, Tex Schramm decided it was time to do something about the problem and began to take matters into his own hands. Many NFL officials, including—as it turned out—Commissioner Pete Rozelle, believed the AFL would eventually fold, but the new league had been given a financial infusion when NBC signed it to a $36 million television contract, beginning in 1965. Something else was happening that went entirely against Schramm's nature.

"Players were no longer being drafted for their ability and potential but whether you believed you could sign them," said Schramm. "This was especially true in the AFL, where money teams, such as the Jets, Chiefs and Oakland, with Davis as an adept infighter, were getting most of the good players. It was happening in our league with teams such as Pittsburgh, and it even influenced our thinking in the 1966 draft. We'd very rarely lost a player to the AFL. That year we liked Illinois running back Jim Grabowski, but since he was one of the first players to start using an agent, we knew it would cost a lot of money to sign him. In those days of competition with the AFL, teams from both leagues would bid on players before the draft. If you thought you could sign them, then you'd draft them. We tried to sign him but failed, so we didn't draft him. Green Bay wanted him, too. The Packers had a lot of money in those days because, after forming a corporation in 1923, they could not declare a dividend and had a lot of money lying around. So we were a little afraid and pulled back and picked Jim Niland instead. The Packers, of course, got Grabowski. I could see something developing in which the teams with money were going to get better, and the others would fall off. Once you take away the competitive aspect of the game, you destroy the package."

Schramm talked to his old boss in Los Angeles, Dan Reeves, telling him some of his ideas regarding a possible merger with the AFL. Reeves liked Schramm's approach, so Tex then got in touch with Commissioner Pete Rozelle. He explained to Pete that he wanted to initiate talks with an AFL man with some power. He said he wanted to keep the talks quiet. Rozelle told him to go ahead, as long as he was kept posted on the discussions. Schramm said his contact would be Lamar Hunt.

"If you want to get something done, you go to the guy who has the power and also a devious streak," explained Schramm. "In the type situation we were getting into, that might be beneficial."

Schramm planned to present his basic plan to Hunt and, if there were no grounds to talk, then the NFL would launch an all-out war against the AFL.

"My original plan was for the Oakland Raiders and New York Jets to move out of those cities, where they would be in conflict with the 49ers and Giants," said Schramm. "They would be given some kind of compensation by the other AFL teams for moving. The possibilities were that Oakland might move to Portland and the Jets south, perhaps to Memphis.

"I saw the Bay Area and New York as major stumbling blocks for a merger. I also was aware that there were powerful political forces in those two areas who might try to stop such a move. I felt one way to passify the city of Oakland for losing the Raiders would be to make the 49ers a Bay Area team, splitting its games between San Francisco and Oakland.

"I first went to see 49ers part-owner and GM Lou Spadia, and we sat in the backyard of his home in Palo Alto and talked. He didn't like the idea. You have to understand there's a lot of animosity between the two cities. San Franciscans think Oakland is the pits. We kept talking and, finally, he reluctantly agreed." Schramm also talked to Giants' owner Wellington Mara, who didn't like the situation but would go along with it if everybody else did.

Schramm then contacted Hunt, who said he'd be flying from Kansas City to Houston for AFL league meetings and that he'd stop over in Dallas and meet Schramm at Love Field, the major Metroplex airport before Dallas-Fort Worth Municipal Airport was built.

This was the beginning of the great cloak-and-dagger sequence. Schramm and Hunt, two powerful and easily recognizable figures in professional sports, met like spies in the shadows of the statue of a Texas Ranger in the Love Field terminal. They chatted, looking around to see if anybody was watching, and then hurried out to Schramm's car in the parking lot. So plans for the biggest merger in sports history, the one which would end the war in professional football, began in Schramm's car in a parking lot. Schramm laid out his basic plan and Hunt was receptive.

"He seemed enthusiastic but was noncommittal," said Schramm. "I told him what it would cost the AFL, that Rozelle would be the commissioner of the combined leagues, and that the AFL would have to compensate Oakland and the Jets for moving. I emphasized that we needed to keep the whole thing quiet because, if too many owners found out, it would be leaked to the press and might blow the whole thing up. He agreed. We made plans to meet again later.

"I think the fact that Lamar and I first met when he was on the way to Houston for the AFL meetings is significant, because it was during that meeting that Al Davis was elected commissioner, replacing Joe Foss. Davis always has said that he was the man who forced the merger when he went after some established NFL players, but that just wasn't true. The wheels were already turning before he came into the picture and, in fact, Lamar was smart enough not to tell him about our discussions, because he knew Al would try to stop the entire process."

Davis went after NFL stars in retaliation for Wellington Mara, with Pete Rozelle's approval, signing kicker Pete Gogolak, who had played out his option with the AFL's Buffalo Bills. Legally, he was free to sign with anybody, but both leagues had a hands-off policy regarding the other's players.

"Everybody had been smart enough not to do that," said Schramm. "Mara really threw a wrench into the negotiations. I had gone to see Rozelle and told him we had a deal, and then the Gogolak thing broke. I found out Pete actually had approved the deal. I remember Vince Lombardi got up at a meeting and really dressed down Mara and Rozelle for the Gogolak signing."

Al Davis had launched his signing war, talking John Brodie, Roman Gabriel and Mike Ditka into jumping to the AFL after they'd played out their options in the NFL.

The situation among the NFL inner circle who knew about the merger meetings was becoming very tense. The thing which surprised Schramm most was that Rozelle, with whom he'd be conferring after each meeting with Hunt, was actually against the merger.

On a spring day in 1966 Tex Schramm sat in on a very emotional meeting in Washington, D.C., of the NFL's most powerful men. They were Vince Lombardi, Art Modell, Billy Bidwell, Carroll Rosenbloom, Wellington Mara and Lou Spadia. Schramm had gotten Hunt's okay of the basic outline for the merger and, in spite of some opposition from Mara and Spadia, the group had finally agreed that the merger must come about. But a major roadblock remained. It was Commissioner Pete Rozelle, who didn't believe the AFL could continue even though it had a large television contract with NBC.

"The basis of the meeting was that Pete had to make a decision because we were going for the merger," said Schramm. "Pete just believed if we could hang on for a while, the AFL would self-destruct. The AFL had a lot of teams in trouble but, hell, so did we."

Schramm went to talk to Rozelle, the man he had brought into the league, in the Commissioner's room in their hotel suite. The late Marshall Leahy, a league counselor, was the only other person in the room.

"It was one of the most crucial nights of Pete's life," said Schramm.

"I was at a meeting, and we reached a decision," Schramm told Rozelle.

"What about the merger?" asked Rozelle.

"It was decided that if you're not going to lead us in the merger, then we're going to go ahead without you," Schramm said.

Rozelle felt betrayed to a degree and became very emotionally upset. Finally, he relented and said he'd go along with a merger. After Schramm talked to him that night, nobody, with the exception of Tex and Hunt, worked harder on the merger than Rozelle. But the strong assumption was that he'd been in favor of a merger all along.

Tex Schramm went to Lamar Hunt's home for another meeting in early May. Hunt indicated he'd gotten an okay from Sonny Werblin of the Jets and Wayne Valley of the Raiders to move their teams.

He met Lamar's new wife, Norma (Knobel). Their home was about half furnished. Norma told Tex that her husband had said they could finish furnishing the house just as soon as ticket sales in Kansas City reached a certain point.

The secret meetings were putting a lot of pressure and stress on Schramm, who had continued to do a balancing act with Spadia and Mara, both of whom kept saying they weren't satisfied with this or that. Once Lamar was supposed to phone Schramm at his home at 7:30 P.M. sharp. The call did not come, and Schramm became very nervous. The telephone finally rang twenty minutes later, and Schramm grabbed the receiver, thinking it was Hunt. It was Clint Murchison. Tex nervously explained what was happening and that he had jumped a foot when the phone rang. Clint apologized and hung up. The phone rang again a few minutes later. Schramm grabbed it again. "Boo," said Murchison, hanging up.

When Schramm went to a meeting in Washington, he knew he'd be a day or so late getting back to Dallas, so he told his wife to tell anybody who tried to reach him that he was going to the Preakness.

"I thought some reporter might try to reach me and think something might be up when I didn't come directly back to Dallas," said Tex. "So I made sure I watched the Preakness on television, so I'd know what happened."

"We started going over each point, and Mara kept insisting that we'd never get away with making the Jets move, because there was such strong political influence for them and that the merger under those circumstances would never get through Congress. I had learned that we'd probably have the same problem with Oakland, so I finally just said, "Okay, then we'll go the other way. Those teams will stay where they are, and we'll compensate the Giants and 49ers. We agreed the AFL would have to compensate the 49ers $8 million and the Giants, $10 million. Mara still wasn't completely satisfied. He kept saying he had to have somebody to fight Joe Namath's popularity in New York.''

Werblin, very smartly, had used $427,000 of the Jet's share of the $36 million television contract to sign Namath, a rebel and an extremely popular figure in New York.

"Then we decided that no matter where the Giants finished in the standings, they'd be given the No. 1 pick in the coming draft with the stipulation it had to be a quarterback or that they could only trade the choice for a quarterback. They later traded it for Fran Tarkenton. There weren't many complaints about what the Giants got because everybody wanted the merger.''

Rozelle flew to Dallas and went to Schramm's home over the Memorial Day weekend. "Nobody was supposed to know I was in town,'' said Rozelle. "So I hurried over to Schramm's house, hoping I wouldn't be seen. We were going to write down the points of the merger, but when I got there Tex didn't even have a typewriter. We had to borrow one from a close friend of his.''

Schramm cautioned Marty and his daughters not to say anything about Rozelle being in town. His daughter, Kandy, then a teenager, watched the proceedings. She saw her father and Rozelle set up the typewriter and a table out by the pool.

"Look,'' she said, "there's Sneaky Pete.''

"She's called me that ever since,'' said Rozelle.

Hunt agreed to meet Schramm and Rozelle in Washington, D.C., to finalize plans. "It was like a CIA operation with the characters being members of the Keystone Kops,'' said Schramm. "We set up dates in Washington, D.C., for Pete to meet with Senator Philip Hart and representative Emanuel Celler and also for Pete and Lamar to get together. A lot of rumors were flying, and we were afraid some alert reporter would find out what was happening, so we took a suite at the Sheraton-Carlton Hotel under the fictitious name of Ralph Pittman. I don't remember why we used that particular name.''

Schramm told Lamar, "When you get to the hotel, go right up to the suite. Don't register under your name, whatever you do.''

"We were already in New York in the hotel suite when I realized I'd forgotten to give Lamar the fictitious name,'' said Schramm. "I called the desk clerk.''

"Uh, lookit," said Schramm, "if a Lamar Hunt comes in and asks for Pete Rozelle or Tex Schramm , tell him they are in the Ralph Pittman suite. What? Oh, I'm registered there, but my name is Tex Schramm."

There's no telling what the clerk thought. But by pure coincidence, Lamar arrived at the hotel just as Schramm, Rozelle and the attorneys were returning from a meeting with Senator Hart. Otherwise he might never have found them. They went up to the infamous Ralph Pittman's suite, and about midnight, June 6, 1966, the merger plans between the NFL and AFL were finalized. The major parties involved then flew to New York, where they'd get better exposure, and made the announcement at a press conference.

At the press conference Schramm sat on one side of Rozelle and Hunt on the other. A brash radio reporter seated up front kept shouting sarcastic questions at them. "It was Howard Cosell," said Schramm. "And he never changed. Nobody knew him at the time.

"After the press conference Sonny Werblin was at Toots Shore's and made a statement to reporters that the merger was the biggest mistake the AFL ever had made and that he never would have given in to the NFL. I found that odd, although I've never said anything about it. But Hunt had said Werblin had agreed to move the Jets out of New York to accommodate the merger."

The basic points were: Rozelle would be commissioner; the leagues would play a world championship game in 1966 and the ensuing years (Hunt later would name the game the Super Bowl); the existing franchises would remain at their present sites; there would be a common draft in 1967; two franchises would be added by 1968, one by each league; the AFL clubs would pay an indemnity of $18 million ($8 to the 49ers, $10 to the Giants) over 20 years; interleague preseason games would be played in 1967; and a single schedule would begin by 1970.

"In the ensuing four years when we were putting all the pieces together for the complete merger in 1970, I found out Lamar had not gotten many of the agreements from the AFL people that he indicated he had," said Schramm. "These particularly concerned the Raiders and their coexistence with the 49ers and the aforementioned agreement with the Jets. Lamar also had not told me he was conferring with Ralph Wilson (Buffalo) and Billy Sullivan (Boston) all along. I felt I was completely honest with him but that he had not been with me. However, if in his mind that was the price of making the deal, then so be it.

Spadia thought he had a deal in which he would have an advantage over Oakland in scheduling and first option on using the Transcontinental Cable, which was difficult to get in those days. He thought it had been agreed upon by Oakland that the Raiders never would play at home games when the 49ers were there and that there would be no telecasting of Raider games in the Bay Area when San Francisco was at home. Lamar said all these things had been agreed upon.

"But Wayne Valley (Oakland owner) said he'd never even talked to Lamar about that situation. We had to all get together and work those things out in a very emotional atmosphere. When we asked Lamar to explain, he just shrugged his shoulders.

"Lamar's team did very well for years. He got a big boost and advantage when the leagues were at war, because he had the money to sign top players and a guy like Don Klosterman to get them for him. He could overcome problems with money that most of the other AFL teams could not. So the Chiefs were very competitive and went all the way to the Super Bowl championship. But when the nucleus of the players he'd gotten those years had retired, and the reality of operating within a system in which everybody has the same equal chance, the Chiefs didn't do so well. They started losing, and Lamar fired Hank Stram and has been firing coaches ever since.

"Looking back on everything, Clint Murchison did fall on hard times physically and then financially before his death, but he had 25 years of enjoyment and success with the Cowboys in his hometown," added Schramm. "That's where he always wanted to be. I think that's more than Lamar ever had."

After the merger Schramm and Hunt flew back on the same plane. Lamar had tried to get a seat in the second-class section, but it was full, and he had to go first class and ended up sitting by Schramm, who always flies first class. There was a drink limit of two on the flight so, knowing Lamar wasn't a drinker, Schramm talked him into ordering two Scotches and giving them to him. Tex, then, would have four drinks.

"You drink that much, and you'll get drunk, Tex," said Lamar. Schramm just smiled.

chapter twenty

FIGHTING A COLOR LINE

In the early 1960s there was a more important battle taking place in the country than one which concerned professional football, and its impact is still being felt today. It was one of freedom, of the civil rights movement and one to put prejudice into its proper perspective. Tex Schramm and his organization would not only be drawn into that battle but also, in a very attention-getting way, make their own social statement. Schramm had seen prejudice against black people while he was with the Los Angeles Rams, but he had to come face to face with it in Dallas.

The country's racial strife, which had lain dormant for so long, simmered and then erupted into violence as the Freedom Riders, a mixture of white and black liberals, moved into the South to test integration. But they never came to Dallas, Texas.

Dallas was a high-profile city and certainly one which experienced the same racial problems of its sister cities in the South, and yet, it never became a target area for the civil rights movement. Atlanta Mayor Andrew Young, a lieutenant for standard-bearer Martin Luther King, recalled, "We never really thought about Dallas." Apparently, the NAACP believed Dallas could be coaxed, rather than shocked into actual, instead of theoretical integration. The city had kept its racial differences mostly under control but the problem was there, like a slum in the shadows of downtown skyscrapers. It was there, as in most places, because one generation adhered to the prejudices of the previous one, of its fathers and fathers' fathers. It was there for no other reason than it always had been, because it was the way most people believed things should be.

As late as 1960 the water fountains in downtown Dallas were clearly marked for "Whites" and "Coloreds." Blacks, then referred to by both races as "Coloreds" or "Negroes," traditionally went to the back of the busses and streetcars and, if the city's transportation became too crowded, were expected to stand up and give their seats to whites. "Coloreds" could not stay in hotels frequented by whites nor eat in restaurants where white people went. They could not go to the amusement area at Fair Park nor attend the State Fair there, except on a particular day set aside for them. They attended separate schools, which were inferior, and as late as 1959 one of the city's leading hospitals, St. Paul's, would only treat black patients in the basement.

Blacks staged pickets in 1960, such as the ones in which they paraded in front of the downtown H. L. Green retail store and the Picadilly Cafeteria, for nine months. No arrests were made and the closest thing to the violence that was to be experienced around the country didn't occur until 1968, when Ernest McMillan and Mathew Johnson, both members of the Student Nonviolent Coordinating Committee in Dallas, led a raid on a white-owned store in predominantly black South Dallas. They threw items on the floor and smashed goods in protest of the store's lack of black employees and inequality in prices and quality of goods sold to blacks and whites. McMillan and Johnson were arrested and given ten years for destroying groceries valued at $211. The extremely harsh sentence seemed to serve as a deterrent for similar acts that might have followed.

The particular problem in sports was of housing, of securing room and board for visiting black athletes. This first seemed to become an issue when Syracuse running back Jimmy Brown was not allowed to stay in a hotel in Dallas with his teammates and was relegated to a lesser place in Fort Worth, when his team came to play TCU in the Cotton Bowl classic of January, 1957. TCU won the game, 28-27.

Schramm was very aware of race problems in the NFL when he first began organizing the Cowboys. He recalled that when the Rams would put up their draft list, an asterisk was placed by players who were in the military and by the name of black players. "And when I was publicity man for the Rams, I'd been in Dallas in the late 1940s to do advance work for the Salesmanship Club game," he added. "I had my publicity packet, with pictures and stories of the Ram players. Everybody wanted to know about Bob Waterfield and Jane Russell. They were quite an item then. But I'd go to the newspapers, and the sports people would start thumbing through the pictures and come on the one of Kenny Washington. They'd pass it around and chuckle. No, I don't think they were bigots during those times. They'd just never been exposed to the black player before. No, I don't recall Kenny's picture being used in any of the newspapers.

"Our team stayed at the Stoneleigh or Melrose hotel but Kenny had to stay someplace else, in a hotel for blacks in Fort Worth or in some black person's home. When we had the team meetings at our hotel they had to go through the kitchen, up the service elevator, to get to our meeting room. They couldn't just walk through the lobby like the white players. Nobody said anything about it because, right or wrong, it was a way of life then, the way things were.

"But there was no way we could live with something like that when we (the Cowboys) came to Dallas, so I wanted to do something about the situation right away."

In those days the Dallas power structure was the all-powerful Citizen's Council, a group made up of 250 heads of corporations who controlled the city's work force and paid 80 percent of its tax bill.

Dallas had been a somewhat unlikely metropolitan giant. Unlike Houston or Galveston, once Texas' largest city, it was not near the coast, so did not have access to the vast shipping industry. John Neely Bryan, a lawyer and trader, had settled the site of what was to become the city when he opened a trading post on the Trinity River in 1841. In 1855 a group of French artists, writers, scientists and musicians formed a community around the trading post, but most of them moved into the township when their settlement failed. The city just kept growing, because it was centrally located. It grew into a banking, fashion, manufacturing and transportation center. It also became the center of one of the world's leading cotton markets and headquarters for more oil firms than any other city in the country; three-fourths of the nation's oil reserves lie within a 500-mile radius of Dallas.

The city has steadily grown and become the second largest city in Texas, the nation's seventh largest, and with the great influx of people from the Midwest and East, it is now growing faster than ever in both industry and culture. And the Citizen's Charter Council almost single-handedly directed this growth from the late 1930s until the mid-1970s, when its candidate for mayor lost an election for the first time, being defeated by an independent named Wes Wise, who had been a sportscaster on a local television station. The Citizen's Charter Council remains powerful but is, perhaps, in the autumn of its strength.

When Schramm met with community leaders, he told them there was no way he could run a successful National Football League franchise in a city in which blacks had to be quartered separately from whites. When teams came to visit, it would be an embarrassment not only to the team but to the city.

"Listen," said Schramm, "there's one thing I want to make clear. I was not a crusader for black rights. I was not motivated by any social issue but by the success and happiness of our football team. We simply could not have separate quarters for black players. I told them at that time we had to have a hotel where all players on visiting teams could stay, that we just couldn't function with the restrictions on black players. Everybody seemed to be upset when they heard this."

Actually, the Council already had begun working on the racial problem, although perhaps Schramm furnished one of the pushes needed to put the wheels for integration of hotels in motion. The city's fathers were well aware of the winds of change, and the Council already had appointed a 14-man biracial committee (seven blacks, seven white) to meet secretly with Roy Wilkins, president of the NAACP. They began laying down plans for integration which was to begin a year and a half later in 1962. Something had to be done. The Dallas Independent School District had lost a five-and-a-half-year battle to stop school integration, as specified by the Supreme Court's 1954 Brown decision. School integration would actually begin in the fall of 1961. The city leaders didn't want the school children to bear the brunt of integration, so they began laying the groundwork. The secret plans were revealed 17 months later and included integration of the Fair Park amusement area, which was adjacent to the Cotton Bowl where the Cowboys would play, and the lifting of segregation in most downtown restaurants and lunch counters, some hotels and department stores and transportation facilities. Black leaders did become upset when H.L. Green's, S.H. Kress, the Union Terminal Cafeteria, bus stations, the State Fair and Parkland Hospital reneged on promises and continued to practice segregation.

But the path had been set and when the integration policy was unveiled in August, 1961, President Kennedy called Dallas leaders to Washington, praised their ideas and cited their integration policies in his drive to ease racial tensions in the Deep South.

Schramm could not wait until 1961. His team was playing in 1960. "I knew they were still using separate facilities for black players on visiting Cotton Bowl teams," he said. "So I talked to Cotton Bowl officials, Jimmy Stewart and Field Scovell, and was told that black players on teams coming to Dallas to play us would have to stay at this hotel for blacks in Fort Worth. I said that couldn't be done.

"The hotel people were a closely knit little group in those days. They had a way of keeping each other in line. If one hotel did something the others didn't approve of, they made sure everybody in town knew about it. This was a kind of unwritten threat, a type of blacklisting. Somebody had to give in. Something had to be worked out."

The Dallas Hotel Association was aware change was coming, but wanted to put it off as long as possible, to make it as easy for themselves as possible. The group knew in 1959 that the city had lost 14 major conventions, resulting in losses of $1 million in revenue, because of the DHA's segregation policies. In 1985 the *Dallas Morning News* obtained an unsigned memo from the confidential files of the association. It was dated in 1960 and stated open accommodations were needed "not only to increase the corporate income to the hotels and other business places in Dallas, but this practice would be in conformity (*sic*) with Democratic practices in other areas. Moreover, a very small number of Negroes will take advantage of the open policy of the hotel, as room rates would be the excluding factor."

"One hotel finally broke the barrier," said Schramm. "It was the Ramada Inn by the airport (Love Field). Management, at the hotel's headquarters in Phoenix, agreed to let blacks stay at the Ramada Inn, if other hotels would lay off them, regarding the issue. The other hotels agreed, and so we had a place where blacks could stay with their teammates.

"I imagine that was the first time this ever happened in Dallas. The next hotel to open its doors to black players was the Sheraton at the Southland Life Center."

In 1967 some Cowboy players, such as Renfro and Perkins, would complain that the team's black and white players were segregated at hotels on road games and in training camp. Schramm would change the policy, making it mandatory that rooming lists be made up alphabetically. Neither the whites nor the blacks would particularly like that. So they would be allowed to pick their own roommates. In most all cases, blacks ended up rooming with blacks and whites with whites.

But in 1960 Schramm had helped knock down the first wall of integrating hotels in Dallas. And then he helped change a longstanding Cotton Bowl practice of having a special section where blacks had to sit. For Dallas Cowboy games race would not dictate where a person sat. There would be other racial issues that would come up, and he would play a part in solving these, too, although with his background he was not particularly prepared for the job.

Tex Schramm was like so many people of his generation who grew up almost oblivious to the plight of the black man in the United States. He was raised in California, a more progressive and liberal-minded state than those South of the Mason-Dixon line, and therefore was not exposed to the bare, cold reality of racism. He was from an affluent, upper middle class environment and was shielded to a great degree from prejudices.

But sometimes people make a difference, because they are in a particular place at a certain time. Perhaps, they do not exactly pick up the gauntlet, but they make a difference just the same. Schramm learned about some of the problems when he was with the Rams, and Dan Reeves had brought in the first black players to enter the NFL since the 1930's. Because of who he was, Schramm made himself felt with the Dallas Cowboys, who certainly were a factor in easing integration not only in their home city but in Texas as a whole. And Schramm was a part of the executive branch of the NFL, which allowed the black athlete to showcase his talents and come to be thought of as a star, a player and not as a so-called Negro or colored player.

He became more aware of the existing prejudice when he joined the Rams because the team was faced with it, had to deal with it when it signed Washington and Strode and, later, Dan Towler and Paul Younger. Prior to that he just never thought much about the issue.

"When I was growing up in Southern California I, honestly, wasn't aware of any social issues regarding race," he said. "There

were blacks in the Los Angeles City School District but not particularly in the outlying areas, such as Alhambra and San Gabriel.
We had a couple of blacks in high school, but I didn't think anything
about it one way or another. They were just going to school like
we were. Obviously, the great concentration of the black population was in the LA area, not the smaller outlying cities such as where
I lived. We were in the California Interscholastic Federation and
didn't play the LA city schools, which had most of the black athletes.

"When I went to the University of Texas, once again, I never
thought about nor was faced with that many racial problems. I don't
recall seeing any blacks mistreated while I was in Austin or the
service, but I'm sure it was happening. It was just never an issue
I had to face. I do remember, however, that I was brought up being told never to use the word 'nigger.' This was very engrained
in me. My mother said we just didn't use such words. I was shocked
when I heard the word used in Austin, and I still am when I hear
it today.

"Certainly, I was cognizant of the problem when I came to the
Rams. We'd go on a road trip, and Kenny couldn't stay in the hotel
with the rest of the team. They couldn't eat in the same restaurants.

"But they never said anything about the problems or what was
happening that I recall. It was just the way it was. If they had complained to management, I'd have known. I do remember once we
landed in Chicago to play the Bears. It was a typical situation. A
bus met the plane and picked up the players to take them to the
hotel. Kenny got off the plane and there, waiting for him, was a
pretty lady in a big car. Kenny was just smiling and waving goodbye to everybody as they drove off. I don't think Kenny minded
not staying in the hotel with the rest of the team.

"I'm not saying this was right but am just trying to explain the
times and some of the things that happened. Another time when
we played an exhibition game in Little Rock, Arkansas, the blacks
naturally couldn't stay in the hotel with us. Our coach Joe Stydahar
was getting a little edgy at the time. As we've discussed, the Ram
head coaching job wasn't the most solid of positions. We'd lost
the title game to the Eagles the previous season, but beat them in
that particular preseason game, so the players were celebrating.

"The players had a big party, which Joe didn't know about. One
of the players phoned back to the hotel to check to see why one
of his friends wasn't there. But Joe had told the switchboard
operator to put through any player's calls to his room."

When Stydahar answered the telephone the player, thinking it was his buddy, said, "Hey, get your tail over here. We're having a helluva party."

"No," snapped Joe, "this is Joe Stydahar, and you get your ass back here to the hotel and that goes for the rest of your friends. You're all fined $100, and it'll cost you another $100 if you're not back in 30 minutes."

"Joe," continued Schramm, "went into the lobby and sat down. As the players came in, he'd say, 'That's $100!' If he was especially mad, he'd say, 'That's $150!' That was a lot of money then.

"We flew in those old DC-7s then, with a kind of lounge in the back. The press flew with us, and they'd heard about the fines, so Joe had a press conference in the lounge on the way back home. Bob Oates, with the Los Angeles Examiner then, questioned Joe about the fines."

"Joe, you're saying you fined 28 players anywhere from $100 to $500 each?" asked Oates.

"That's right," said Joe, "and you can quote me."

"Then that would come to almost $4,000," continued Oates. "That's an NFL record for fines."

"Stydahar seemed puzzled," said Schramm. "Then he got all red in the face and pointed a finger at Oates and yelled, 'That part's off the record!'

"The funny deal about the whole thing is that the seven black players on our team weren't fined. They couldn't stay in the hotel, so Joe didn't know how late they came in."

Washington's career lasted only three years, ending in 1948, and Strode only played the 1946 season, but the Rams made history again by becoming the first NFL team to sign a player from a black college. But Paul (Tank) Younger wasn't just another player, and Grambling wasn't just another black college. Younger was not only a mainstay as a running back for the Rams but also was a fine linebacker.

"The Rams didn't make a big deal out of signing Younger either," said Schramm. "I can remember stuff being written and said about Jackie Robinson when the Dodgers got him in 1947. But nothing was particularly written or said when we got Kenny or, later, Younger (1949) and then made Deacon Dan Towler the first black to be drafted by an NFL team. I can't remember Dan Reeves or anybody there saying we were going to sign a black player or draft a black player. Of course, I admit we didn't mind, because we realized the competitive advantage if we used black players and nobody else did. But, then, the NFL was small potatoes in those days compared to the Major Leagues, and not that many people noticed. We were fortunate. The ones we signed were damn good players, and we wanted them on our team."

Younger was later to agree. "Nobody said anything to me about being black," he explained. "There were only three other blacks in the league the year (1949) I came in. Emlen Tunnell was with the Giants, and Bobby Mann and Mel Triplett were with Detroit. As far as the Ram players and officials were concerned, I was treated just like the other players. Sometimes the press would mention the racial situation and, really, that was the only time I was aware of it. I was just a player trying to make the team."

Schramm recalled Younger had received some advice from legendary Grambling coach Eddie Robinson. "Robinson," said Schramm, "told Tank to run out each play in practice 20 to 30 yards. Ordinarily, a back will run ten yards at the most during practice and then come back to the huddle. But Robinson told him, 'The longer you have the ball under your arm, the longer the man (the coach) is watching you.' "

Younger didn't have any problems with the Rams, but there were racial tensions elsewhere, although he said they were not that serious. In an exhibition game in San Antonio Younger and a black rookie, who was cut, were stopped at the gate by a guard. He refused to let them inside until Ram assistant George Trafton interceded and let the guard know in no uncertain terms that they were part of the Ram football team.

"The only thing I remember anybody in our organization kidding Younger about was that he was tipping off which direction our plays were going," recalled Schramm. "If the play was going to the right, he'd roll his eyes in that direction. If it was going left, he'd look that way. We finally got him looking straight ahead."

Younger and Towler, who formed the core of what was known as the Rams' Baby Elephant backfield, both turned out to be Pro Bowl players. Towler was named All-Pro three times, and in 1951 Younger not only was one of the club's top runners but also made All-Pro as a linebacker. The NFL had adopted free substitution in 1950, a move that would soon lead to platooning for offensive and defensive units, but some of the multitalented players such as Younger continued to play both ways. Younger went into coaching after his career ended, and Towler, a minister, often visits Schramm and the Cowboys during training camp.

At the same time the Rams were breaking the modern-day color barrier in the NFL, Paul Brown was doing the same thing with Marion Montley with the Cleveland Browns in the All-American Football Conference. Other teams in the AAFC followed and, when the league folded, a number of black players moved into the NFL.

"I don't think any sports team did more than the Los Angeles Rams to break down racial barriers," said Schramm. "The Rams did it and made no big deal out of it. We were fortunate in getting such quality people as Washington, Strode, Towler and Younger. They handled themselves with dignity in tough situations.

"Sure, there were hotel problems, but by the time I left for CBS in 1957 things were getting better in many parts of the country. The hotel people had begun to realize they could integrate in a fairly safe and controlled-type situation by bringing in pro football teams.

"It was just done. No complaining. Maybe that was the great thing about people in the 1950s. In a quiet way they made everybody aware of prejudice and that things shouldn't be that way. You know, to me, some of those players we had with the Rams were among the real pioneers for integration.

When the Cowboys began operation in Dallas, the living areas in the city were as clearly defined, if not as clearly marked, as the drinking fountains in the downtown area. Blacks simply could not live in certain parts of town, nor were their children welcomed to schools in particular areas, regardless of the school district's integration plans for the fall of 1961.

But once again these issues were settled in court and through pressure applied by organizations such as the Dallas Cowboys.

There were no riots, deaths, no violent uprisings in Dallas, so it was somewhat ironical that the only racial riot that Schramm was near began on a long, hot, sultry early August night in 1965 in Los Angeles, the city he believed was much more immune to such things than places in the South. The Cowboys were in training camp and coming to Los Angeles to play the Rams in the Times-Charity game. It was delayed a day and almost cancelled because of the Watts' riots.

Watts is a southwest Los Angeles black ghetto with some 90,000 blacks in a 20-square-mile area. It is inhabited by prostitutes, narcotic addicts, dropouts of all ages and a seemingly endless line of people who have given up hope for a better life. That summer night a Los Angeles policeman chased a young, allegedly drunken black driver into Watts. There were rumors of police brutality when officers arrested the youth. A lady barber had come out of her shop to talk to the police making the arrest. She had on a barber's smock, and many bystanders thought she was pregnant. Some said she was shoved by the police. A crowd formed around the policemen, and other officers came. Soon people in the crowd started throwing rocks at the officers. Pent-up emotions that had simmered for so long erupted and, before the violence had ended six days later, 35 people, including 28 blacks, had been killed and countless people injured. Damage due to looting and arson was estimated at $200 million, as more than 600 buildings were burned. Los Angeles, a city which would have a black mayor named Tom Bradley seven years later and a place which was felt to be more stable racially than other large metropolitan areas, had experienced one of the worst race riots in history.

After the delay and the aftermath of Watts, only 31,579 showed up for the Times-Charity game, easily the smallest crowd for the annual preseason game in the Coliseum, located in the general Watts' area.

Dallas continued to have racial problems, even if they weren't of the volatile variety. Gil Brandt recalled bringing the team's prize rookies of 1960, Don Perkins and Don Meredith, back to Dallas before they went to training camp after playing in the College All-Star game.

"I took them to the Highland Park Cafeteria," said Brandt. "Suddenly, this woman came up to me, looked at Perkins, and said, 'I'm sorry, we don't serve Negroes in here.' I've never been so embarrassed in my life."

Perkins handled the situation well and suggested they go elsewhere to eat. But less than a month after the Watts' riots, Perkins became upset and threatened to retire when his son was refused admittance to a private school in North Dallas. Schramm stepped into the situation, sided with Perkins, and using diplomacy and his own particular brand of coercion, got the boy admitted to a school that satisfied both Don and his wife.

It also was Perkins, one of the players Schramm greatly admired, who prior to training camp in 1968, his final year with the Cowboys, made widely quoted remarks that concerned inadequate housing in Dallas for black athletes. At that time some branded him a troublemaker, whereas in actuality he was a thoughtful, personable man who was liked and respected by all who took the time to get to know him.

"Even if the remarks attributed to Don can be considered controversial, he definitely does not fall into the mode of a troublemaker," Schramm said at the time. "He is just such an honest and forthright person that it would be difficult for him to look anybody in the eye and say something he did not really believe. And there *is* a problem."

Some of the actions taken and statements made by Schramm in those days didn't exactly endear him to a certain segment of the population in Dallas, because he was walking a thin line between alienating too many people in the city's power structure and also trying to influence racial changes he believed must come about for the betterment of his football team and the NFL. Sometimes he would straddle the line for a while but, as is his nature, he'd eventually jump into the middle of the fight for the side he felt was right. This was never more in evidence than in the case of Mel Renfro, who took the unequal housing issue to court.

Renfro, from Oregon, said he was not prepared for some of the prejudices when he first came to Dallas. "Two days after I got to Dallas (1964), I walked into a restaurant and saw a sign which said, 'We don't serve coloreds.' After a while you'd get snubbed in a place, and then people would find out who you were, that you were a Dallas Cowboy, and then they'd start being nice to you. But I tell you about Schramm. He did more for integration in Dallas than anybody I knew about."

Schramm and his aides had worked with Mac Pogue of Lincoln Properties to secure acceptable housing for the team's black players, most all of whom lived in predominately black sections of South Oak Cliff and Hamilton Park. But even in the late 1960s, almost a decade after the birth of the team, apartment owners and managers, real estate agents and private sellers were still using discriminatory practices against blacks to keep them from moving into certain parts of town, especially the affluent sections of North Dallas where, ironically, the bulk of the season ticket holders lived. Blacks had been able to move into houses in certain white sections which had been repossessed, but that was an exception to the rule.

Renfro tired of the problem and joined his wife in filing a suit in U.S. District Court, charging racial discrimination and violation of the Fair Housing Act of 1968 against builder C.C. Freeman, realtor Mildred Broyles and salesman Garnett Sherill of the Ricon 20-unit apartment complex in North Dallas.

Renfro recalled that he went to see Schramm and told him what he was going to do. "Tex wasn't especially overjoyed about it. He agreed with the way I felt, but believed we had to go about the change more slowly. But when he saw that I was determined, he kind of looked away for a few seconds, staring out the window. I started to walk out of his office, and he said, 'Don't do it.' And then he said, 'Okay, if you do it, we're behind you 100 percent.' I got some hate mail. I'm sure he did, too."

Schramm not only backed Renfro, but saw to it that the Cowboys absorbed costs for all litigation.

The Renfros were represented by State Senator Oscar Mauzy, and the case was tried in the court of the late U.S. District Judge Sarah T. Hughes, who had received national attention when she swore in Lyndon Baines Johnson as president after John F. Kennedy had been assassinated in Dallas in 1963.

The Renfros, who had three small children, said they had looked at one of the Ricon duplexes on October 3 and were told by Sherill, a salesman for realtor Broyles, that they could return on October 6 and sign a lease for the unit of their choice. Mrs. Renfro also testified they were told there would be no restrictions regarding children. Mel phoned his wife from Philadelphia, where the Cowboys were playing, and told her to go ahead and rent the duplex. She said she called Sherill on October 5 and was told the policy had been changed, that they could not lease a unit unless it had been sold and the buyer okayed the transaction. She contacted Ms. Broyles and said the realtor told her that there had been *no* change in policy, that this had been the builder's policy all along, and that the management also did not accept small children. Mrs. Renfro then said Ms. Broyles told her how much she enjoyed watching Mel play football. "This," she testified, "made me extremely angry."

When the Renfros returned to the property, they said the "For Lease" signs had been replaced by "For Sale" signs.

Murray W. Miller, a white teamsters' union representative, testified he was at the Ricon units three days after the Renfros and told a salesman he was interested in leasing a place. He said he explained he had small children and was told that this didn't matter. He also testified that the Ricon agent showed him a particular unit and said others like it were available.

Schramm went to court and testified in behalf of the Renfros, explaining that such things as housing discrimination could destroy the Cowboys as fast as anything. He added, "This type of thing can have a very strong effect on our team. Mel has been very concerned about this. His mind has been on this issue as much—if not more so—than it's been on football." The Cowboys were becoming very popular by that time, and this seemed to outweigh prejudice as far as public sentiment.

Judge Hughes ruled the defendants had been leasing units to white families with three children and had changed their policy between October 3 and October 5. She enjoined them from leasing or renting any vacant units in the complex, unless the Renfros had had the right of first refusal. The Renfros had asked for $10,000 in damages and were awarded $1,500, but the point was made.

Perhaps the results would have been the same had the complainant not been a star for the Cowboys, been backed by a man such as Schramm and received a great deal of publicity. But these advantages did not hurt the Renfros' situation. The case and the things that were said brought attention to the housing segregation practices in North Dallas. Some private owners still will not sell their homes to blacks, but real estate agents, apartment managers and owners no longer can get away with the practice. The case apparently caused some people to see themselves as they were in regard to prejudice, rather than as they had perceived themselves. It also brought to light the hypocrisy that was being practiced. The black players made a big difference on the fan's favorite team, the one that represented their city and thus them. They cheered them on one hand but did not want to live near them on the other. For a number of years now black players or former players such as Drew Pearson and Harvey Martin have been living in North Dallas.

John Wooten, the All-Pro guard who blocked for Jimmy Brown during the heyday of Paul Brown's powerhouse, was hired by Schramm for the club's scouting department. Wooten, a strong and active black rights advocate, noted recently, "Now when I go south of the Trinity River into the Dallas black community, the leaders there scream at me, because most of the blacks on our team live in the North Dallas vicinity. They feel they've deserted their community."

Tex Schramm had just rushed from a radio interview in his room to the practice field in Thousand Oaks and was walking along the sidelines, talking to this person or that and commenting on some of the rookies who might make the team. He was shaken from his train of thought when he was reminded that there were those who have written and stated the NFL teams were still prejudiced to a degree, because they have no black head coaches. Schramm, who sometimes has been known to aim and fire without considering a bullet might ricochet and strike an innocent bystander, turned red and, then trying to control his anger, said, "The thing you have to goddamn understand about the NFL is that winning comes first. Your priority is to get the best qualified people to coach. When somebody in our league thinks a black head coach can help them win, then you will have a black head coach. People were making the same assumptions about black quarterbacks, even after Houston had Warren Moon. But when Philadelphia believed Randall Cunningham could help it win then he was in there. When the Redskins thought Doug Williams could win for them he took over at quarterback.

"But nobody is going to create jobs artificially for black coaches without proper backgrounds. And just right now there aren't enough black people who have the inclination or background to become a head coach in our league.

"It's very irritating that a certain segment of blacks and people in the media want to blame the fact there aren't any black head coaches or many higher executives on a racial issue. They don't take the time—as many journalists often don't do—to get the facts straight. Where are all the black sports editors and lead columnists?

"To be an NFL head coach today, you must serve your apprenticeship. You might start at the graduate assistant level and work your way up through the college ranks, proving at each stage that you can do the job, and then come to the pros. That's what a guy like Paul Hackett has done. It's very time-consuming but things are so sophisticated these days, with the computer and other innovations, that it has to be done this way. It's difficult for a pro player to go back to coaching in college. Certainly, there are pros who can serve their apprenticeship in the NFL, but that doesn't happen as often and only to a talented few.

"I think what happens to a lot of black people who might have made good head coaches is that they see more opportunities for immediate success in other fields. I find this disturbing.

"Listen, I don't think there's a team in our league which wouldn't welcome more black coaches, because players of their race make up half the teams. You get a good black coach, and perhaps he could help the whole staff relate more effectively to the black players.''

Cowboy running back coach Al Lavan is black and so is Larry Wansley, a former FBI agent that Schramm hired as director of player counseling. Wooten, who aspires to become an NFL executive, believed by accepting Schramm's offer to join the scouting department, he'd have a better chance. Drew Pearson asked Schramm for a job in the spring of 1985, and Tex urged Tom Landry to hire him as an assistant receiver coach. However, Drew tired of meetings and watching film, and he coached only one season.

Schramm will take offense when the NFL is criticized for any racial imbalance in the coaching or executive departments, but the difference is that he's trying to do something about it.

"About seven years ago, Tex and I were talking, and he said he had a program in mind that might help,'' recalled Wooten. "I think the fruits of that program are already being felt. Look over there.''

Wooten, standing ten yards from Schramm at the practice field, pointed toward a group of black coaches—Eddie Robinson and his staff from Grambling. They were watching the Cowboy coaches and taking notes.

"Hey, lookit,'' continued Schramm, his temper more under control, "everybody is looking for good, intelligent black coaches. It would help like hell to have some good ones, but they are hard to find at this level.

"I started asking around. The obvious progression for many would be to come from small black schools, to the larger universities, and then to the NFL. I was told, with some exceptions of course, that many of the small black colleges were just way behind in their methods of coaching. They just didn't understand some of the terminology that other coaches in larger schools were using. There had to be some way to try to change that.''

"You see how everything is organized here,'' said Wooten. "Everything is planned. Everybody is doing something. It's the same way in the big schools. I can remember in the old days, going to a small black school. The head coach would be showing, say, the tackles how to do something, and the backfield players would just be standing around, jiving. The coaches weren't being given the opportunity to learn. They lacked facilities, money, opportunity and exposure.''

Schramm reasoned that there had to be a way to give these coaches better training. He discussed the situation with his Competition Committee. It was suggested that perhaps the NFL could sponsor a clinic, say in June, for black coaches from smaller colleges. Schramm told the committee, "I think it would do them a helluva lot more good if they could spend a week in our training camps. They would have access to our coaches, meetings, observe the way things are being done and also talk to the players. That's much better than some superficial clinic."

It was pointed out to Schramm that the small black schools wouldn't have the money to send their coaches to NFL training camps.

"Hell," said Schramm, "we'll pay for it."

Expenses would be higher for some black schools than others. So Schramm suggested that all NFL teams pool their bills for hosting the black coaches and then divide the costs equally. Rozelle liked the idea. Schramm's committee presented the plan to the owners, and it was adopted in 1979. There are about 48 black schools which now take part in the program. They visit various NFL camps on a rotating basis each summer. And the total of black assistants in the NFL reached an all-time high of 39 in 1987.

Schramm continually complained the NFL was being unjustly accused of not giving blacks the opportunity, but was trying to do something to correct the problem. He's like that sometimes.

Eddie Robinson stood near the end zone of the practice field, surrounded by assistant coaches Ron Taylor, Ernest Sterling, Fred Collins, Billy Manning, Melvin Lee, Ed Stevens and Eddie Robinson, Jr., his son. Robinson in 43 years as Grambling head coach surpassed Paul (Bear) Bryant in 1985 as the all-time winningest coach in NCAA football history.

He is a black man from a small college who kept up with the times and knew the proper techniques and teaching methods, but he pointed out that Schramm's program was one of the greatest things that ever happened to schools in his category.

"This is the fifth year we've been in the program," he explained in 1985. "And I can already see the benefits. Our conference (Southwestern Athletic Conference) is better coached and better played than it's ever been, and this program has a lot to do with it. The quality of coaching, from head coaches to the lowest assistant, has improved greatly because of the program.

"It gave the NFL a chance to meet our coaches and for us to see how they operate. Both parties gained from this. We benefit now, and the NFL will benefit in the future. It will get more black coaches, because they will have learned early the proper techniques and advanced styles of play."

Robinson had each of his assistants critique each Cowboy practice and would meet with them each night to discuss what they had seen. Each coach would visit with and watch the Cowboy assistant in his particular area.

"I have seen so many changes over the years, and this is the most progressive," said Robinson.

In the early years at Grambling Robinson did everything himself. He taped ankles, sold hot dogs at games, tore ticket stubs at the gate, and even led the Grambling drill team through halftime activities. He also recalled making sandwiches for his team to eat on road trips and driving the bus to get them there.

"Nobody paid any attention to us, so after a game I'd even write up the stories and give them to the newspapers," he added. He became reflective and stared at the distant mountains, as if he were trying to see those times again.

"Oh, I'd had some success but never applied for another job," he said. "Carroll Rosenbloom did talk to me once about the Ram job, but we never got down to a serious discussion because, for one thing, I like it where I am. It's like a family. But some of these assistants I have will get the opportunity to go on and maybe even become an NFL coach.

"The thing I tell them is that they have to learn what they can and then be more aggressive. Just jump right in there and apply for the job. There's some good black coaches now, but they just sit back. James Harris (former Los Angeles and San Diego quarterback) is one. He never applied for a head job. He's smart, quickminded, and he could do it."

Schramm and Robinson talked after practice. Robinson told him, "This is a great program. My coaches and I have been to camps of the Bears, Eagles and Chargers but, believe me, this is the one we wanted to come to. We wanted to see how coach Landry and his staff did things."

Schramm told Robinson about the time Joe Stydahar waited in the hotel lobby and fined all the players as they came in after curfew,

explaining none of the blacks got fined because they weren't allowed
to stay in the same hotel in those days. Robinson laughed and then
told the story to his assistants.

After practice Schramm, as he often does, was holding court with
members of the media in his suite at the dorm where club officials
stay during camp. The ever-present, after-practise J&B Scotch was
in his hand. While the iron was hot, so to speak, he continued his
discussion of black quarterbacks in the NFL.

"There is no doubt that black athletes generally make better
players at certain positions, such as receiver, defensive back and
running back because of their speed, quickness and agility." he said.
"Quarterback is a position of leadership. There is no team in the
NFL who cares whether it has a quarterback who is black or white,
as long as he does the job and shows leadership qualities.

"Obviously, Cunningham and Williams had those leadership
qualities. Williams especially proved he had all the qualities it takes
and I'm sure we'll find more black quarterbacks taking over in the
coming years."

"I'd like to see more black leaders with the Cowboys. We'd had
some, but there just hasn't been a Roger Staubach or Lee Roy Jordan type—I mean a player who'd just take over, and the others
would follow him. I'm not sure what the answer is in regard to
leadership. I don't know if it can be traced, generally speaking, to
a social or environmental background or what."

Schramm believed Reggie Collier, whom Dallas drafted in 1983
but had to wait until 1986 to get after he fulfilled his USFL obligation, would make an outstanding quarterback. He was fast, quick,
had a strong arm and had more athletic ability than any quarterback on the team. But his concentration and work habits were
strongly questioned in 1986, and when the coaches felt he failed
to respond during the 1987 off-season, he was cut. Reggie Collier
is black.

Football players and other top athletes in cities such as Dallas
did a lot more for integration than they are generally given credit
for. They did not do what the Freedom Marchers did nor those civil
rights leaders who threw themselves under the wheels of their beliefs,
but they made a difference just the same. They played the game

and came to be accepted as players, as stars and personalities, rather than as blacks or this or that.

Black players in the 1960s, such as Don Perkins, Frank Clarke, Mel Renfro, Pettis Norman, Bobby Hayes and Cornell Green, and those in the 1970s, such as Drew Pearson, were very important in the acceptance of the rights of black people in Dallas.

Two young white kids came up to Drew Pearson when he visited training camp. They got his autograph and, later, when they were playing catch, one of them pretended to be Pearson. He was not viewed by people as black but rather as an extremely talented man who was nice and always had time for kids. He was soft-spoken and showed class and dignity, and personified the great American story by getting the most out of his God-given ability, by coming from an unknown free agent to an All-Pro. It would have been very rare for white kids to feel this way about a black athlete in the early 1960s.

Nineteen-sixty was not that long ago, really, and only seems so because of the racial changes that have taken place, not because of the years that have passed.

chapter twenty-one

SCHRAMM AND LANDRY

One of the great constants of the Dallas Cowboys' organization from its inception in 1960 until the 1980s has been the working relationship of Tex Schramm and Tom Landry. It has survived through frustrating years, heartbreaking and soul-searching losses in big games and prospered in Super Bowls and an unprecedented NFL succession of winning seasons. There was and still is a mutual respect, but a key reason they have been able to work together without friction is that their roles were clearly defined by Schramm and Clint Murchison when the team was first organized. Schramm would be the overseer of the organization itself and any and all things pertaining to the Cowboys that were not directly related to the field of play. He would establish salary structure, set policy and have the final say on anything that did not involve coaching or actual competition on the field. Landry would control these things and make the final decision on trades, draft choices, and the hiring and firing of assistant coaches. Suggestions might be made, but no pressure would be applied. And to either's knowledge they've never have had a serious clash.

This situation changed as Murchison faded from the picture and Schramm, who emerged as the clear-cut top man in all aspects of the organization, saw definite signs that the team was on the decline because of malfunctions in the drafting system, which once had been a leader in its field, and perhaps because of some stagnancy in the direction of the coaching department.

When in 1984 the Cowboys lost 14-3 to a Buffalo team that had the worst defense in the league and failed to make the playoffs for the first time since 1974, Schramm became furious and then began to think about changes that might be made. In 1985 Landry probably did his best coaching job when the Cowboys won the NFC East championship, but Schramm fumed when the team seemed to quit and was embarrassed by Chicago, 44-0, and by Cincinnati, an average team, 50-24. When Cincinnati was ahead, 43-10, Landry called two straight running plays in which Tony Dorsett netted three yards. In the press box Schramm was heard to say, "That's right. Let's establish our running game *now*."

But everybody agreed that the Cowboys seemed to be able to win when they had to, including two victories over the New York Giants, their chief rival, and the Washington Redskins. Then when they had to win in the first round of the playoffs, Los Angeles beat them, 20-0. Dallas suffered six turnovers and allowed Eric Dickerson to rush for a playoff record of 248 yards while getting thrashed by a team whose quarterback, Dieter Brock, completed only six of 22 passes for 50 yards.

"We are not going to play with the same deck again," said Schramm after the game.

Schramm seemed more and more to be looking over Landry's shoulder and, although he denies this, moved into an area that had been solely Landry's domain.

They'd first had the conversation in 1984 when the Cowboy NFL record string of nine straight playoff appearances (Dallas held the old record of eight) had been broken. The younger generation of assistant coaches Landry had trained had left the team with Danny Reeves going to Denver, Mike Ditka to Chicago and John Mackovich to Kansas City, and Schramm believed, quite simply, that Tom Landry needed some new, younger people on his staff— people who would bring in new ideas and get Tom's undivided attention when they expressed them.

Schramm told Landry his feelings and also said he was concerned about the age gap between too many of his coaches and the players. Landry had good, respected, proven people on his staff but, at that time, Jim Myers was 64, Dick Nolan 54, Ernie Stautner 59, Jerry Tubbs 51, special assistant Neill Armstrong 60, and Gene Stallings and offensive coordinator Jim Shofner both 50. Schramm did not want any of these people fired but said that Landry should bring in a younger coach who might have some impact. '

Landry agreed some changes had to be made, that the team certainly had been slipping in recent years. But he said he'd spent a lot of time coaching younger coaches who then went elsewhere and did not feel he had the time, in the twilight of his career, to educate a new coach in the system.

"The ones I have are talented and know the system," said Landry.

"I know that and don't want to get rid of anybody, but maybe we can just switch somebody around," said Schramm.

They continued to talk, and Landry finally said he wanted to try it with the same staff for a couple of more years, adding, "Then maybe after two years, I'll quit, and everything will resolve itself." Schramm said, okay, but continued to worry.

In 1985 Landry seemed to win the NFC East with mirrors. The offensive line, linebackers and parts of the secondary and the wide receiving corps sometimes seemed to be held together by glue and gum. Yet Dallas was able to beat superior Redskin and Giant teams twice. But Schramm was extremely upset regarding the lopsided losses to Chicago, Cincinnati and Los Angeles. He also was angry when the Cowboys lost their final regular season game to San Francisco, which was going to the playoffs as a wild card team, 31-16, and when some of the players said the game didn't really matter, because they already had made the playoffs. A victory also would have given them the home field advantage, but some players also said that didn't matter.

"If you don't want to go out there and win, then why play the fuckin' game," Schramm was overheard saying.

Publicly, he was more diplomatic. "It looked like we had a team that said, 'Don't get too concerned about this one—wait for the big one.' Then you get to the big game and rely on the stakes to be the motivator, rather being concerned about losing or being fearful of becoming embarrassed. We slipped into a certain syndrome—when we had to turn it on, we could. That attitude didn't always work. We have to get back to basics, that competitive athletes play for the sake of winning. The thrill comes from competing and winning. You cannot rely on external things to motivate you. Money can't be relied upon as the motivating factor. Don January was quoted as saying that nobody chokes over money but everybody, including Jack Nicklaus, chokes over titles."

Schramm began turning the wheels of change after the team moved into its new headquarters at Valley Ranch, although this was not symbolic, because symbolism isn't an integral part of Schramm's repertoire. As mentioned, he hired Bob Ackles in the new job as personnel director and handed vice president in charge of administration, Joe Bailey, the duty of signing players. Gil Brandt was freed to concentrate only on college scouting. And he found Tom Landry a new offensive coordinator.

"Tom Landry is an extremely intelligent man and knew some changes had to take place," explained Schramm. "If he could have gone to the Super Bowl with the same team in 1985, using the same coaching staff, then it would have been a sensational accomplishment. It's only human nature, if you've had unprecedented success, to try to keep hanging on to what you have.

"I'd been trying to take a more active interest in assistant coaches. I just don't believe Tom pays any attention to people on other staffs around the league. That's his nature. He blocks all that out, concentrating on the game and its preparation. Others had suggested people when we were looking for assistant coaches in the past."

In this case Schramm had had his eye on 49ers offensive assistant Paul Hackett for some time. He checked around the league and kept hearing good things about Hackett, who coached the quarterbacks and assisted Bill Walsh in developing the very successful 49ers passing attack. It had appeared Hackett might get the head coaching job with the Houston Oilers but, when he didn't, Schramm acted. He called 49er officials and got permission to talk to Hackett. Schramm then told Landry of his plans and said he would like Tom to meet Hackett when the coaches gathered in New Orleans during the testing of college players for the scouting combines.

"Hackett was the kind of person I was interested in," said Schramm. "He was smart, had a helluva lot of enthusiasm and had developed a fine reputation as a quarterback coach."

Hackett, 39, was given credit for helping mold Joe Montana into one of the NFL's best quarterbacks. Prior to going to San Francisco, he'd been an assistant at Cleveland. It was there that he worked with Paul McDonald, who beat out Brian Sipe and led the Browns into the playoffs. He previously had coached McDonald and Vince Evans while an assistant at USC, and as quarterback coach at California he had a great influence on Steve Bartkowski, who had experienced a mediocre junior year and decided to pass up his final season of football to concentrate on baseball. Hackett helped change his mind and Bartkowski was great in his senior year and became the top NFL draft pick.

"Tom was in a bad position, because he'd have to move Jim Shofner to another area," said Schramm. "But he agreed to meet with Hackett. Tom also said that either this season or after next season I should, in effect, start looking for his replacement and think about facilitating a reasonable transition. I don't know another man in Tom's position who would have done that. Not many people would want to bring in somebody who might be his replacement. But Tom is not selfish. He cares about the organization and wants to see it continue to be successful.

"I never promised Hackett anything, but he's smart enough and ambitious enough to recognize he's putting himself in a position that could make him a very likely candidate to replace Landry. He's got enough confidence in himself, so I suppose he feels he can sell himself by the time Tom retires. Sure, he's gambling coming here, but the gamble is to be the head coach of the most famous team in the league."

Landry visited with Hackett and the implication in the media was that the whole thing was his idea, and Schramm would just as soon have kept it that way. But when Landry made the announcement that Hackett had been hired as his offensive coordinator at a press conference, he was asked what he knew about Hackett. Tom, honest to a fault, said he knew nothing about him and that the first time he'd ever met him was in New Orleans. It then became obvious that Schramm had been suggesting the moves.

Shofner was offered the job as special assistant but resigned, later joining former Cowboy assistant Gene Stallings, who had become the head coach of the St. Louis Cardinals. Before he left Shofner said he was surprised at what had happened, noting Dallas led the NFL in passing yards in 1985.

"I thought we were on the right track," he said. "I don't know a quarterback in the league who could have taken this team to the Super Bowl." Shofner indicated Landry was trying to force him into semiretirement and that he was far from ready for that.

Landry said nothing. Schramm did. "Lookit," said Tex, "he was our quarterback coach. That's the area where we had all the dissension with Gary and Danny. Sure, he didn't make the decision on the quarterbacks, but it was his job to keep down the problems. When Landry decided to go with Hogeboom in 1984, Shofner should have had him ready to play. As far as having a good season because we led the NFL in passing yards (in 1985), well, we might have had the yardage, but we failed in key situations. When you get the hell beat out of you like we did against Chicago, Cincinnati, and Los Angeles . . . getting shut out in the playoffs, then you have problems. Hell, that isn't success. Maybe it's success for him, but it isn't for us."

Landry later said Schramm's unprecedented input in hiring an assistant coach didn't bother him, although some observers believed it had. "I've reached the point, with my longevity, that I'm not going to coach a lot longer," said Landry, who appeared to pinpoint his retirement when he agreed to three-year contract in 1987. "Therefore, Tex needs to be in a position to take an active role in looking at what is available and what will happen if I step down. There's a transition period. I don't know how long that period will be. But I'm a Cowboy and interested in what the team is going to do when I leave. It's important that Tex be in a position to do that. He hasn't interviewed or hired a coach in a long time."

Landry, who had designed and engineered the Cowboys very successful multiple offense and passing game, was not only ready to listen but also to accept Hackett's theories.

"We're trying to improve ourselves in every area," said Landry. "After all these years, we need a fresh look. This is the first time we've taken that fresh look at our organization, and we're trying to do what's best for the future."

Hackett is a proponent of the Don Coryell/Bill Walsh philosophy of the passing game, the one whose basic theories are also used by Joe Gibbs, in which you do not attack a particular defensive alignment. You do not care which defense a team is using. You have your plays and you run them, regardless. A quarterback looks for his No. 1 receiver. If he's covered he looks for No. 2 and, if there's time, No. 3. If a receiver can't be found and he runs out of time, a guy like Joe Montana will step forward and break out of the pocket. When he does this, the receivers know to adjust their patterns, and he often buys time to find them open. Coryell, in Dan Fouts, had a quarterback who wasn't that mobile. So, failing to find receivers, Fouts often would just throw the ball away.

In the Landry philosophy, also employed by Don Shula, you attack a particular defense your opponent is using. A quarterback reads the defense, the coverage, and knows which receiver will be open.

The philosophies obviously were diametrically opposed, but Landry believed he could gamble the first year, 1986, because he had a very intelligent and experienced quarterback in Danny White. White not only was able to phase Hackett's philosophy into the passing game but also could read specific defenses as Landry had taught him. So he became the leading passer in the NFC, and Dallas began that season with a 6-2 record. And then Danny White was there no longer.

The Cowboys, as Schramm had so hoped they would, seemed to have taken a firm hold on the present while reaching for the future. There was age on the team and some personnel problems, but he believed if the team could somehow get through the transition years with a winning record, then there was no telling how far it could take the string into the future. Few, outside of Schramm and his immediate organization, believed this was possible, but a young man named Herschel Walker stepped in and not only brought a new enthusiasm but also seemed to add the spark to not only have a winning season but perhaps even more. Dallas upset both New York and Washington the first half of the season, finishing 6-2 with losses only to Atlanta (37-35) on a desperation pass that a Falcon receiver took away from two Cowboy defenders and to Denver when Danny White was injured.

On the first Sunday in October the Cowboys played the Giants in the Meadowlands in a game which was expected to propel the winner into the final half of the season. In the second period linebacker Carl Banks blitzed and untouched, as a number of rushers seemed to be against the Cowboys that year, crashed into Danny White, who extended his right arm, hit a helmet or shoulder pad, and suffered a fractured wrist. His season was over. However, many believed that Steve Pelluer, who had a stronger arm and was more agile, might step in and do even better than White. Pelluer wasn't as brittle and could better move away from tacklers, which a mediocre Dallas line could not keep out. In spite of Rafael Septien missing two field goals, one a chip shot, Dallas trailed 17-14 but was in a position to win, at least tie, in the final three minutes. Pelluer dropped off a screen pass to Dorsett, who ran 30 yards for a first down at the Giants' six. The play was called back for holding by tackle Phil Pozderac. All seemed lost but then Pelluer found Timmy Newsome for another 30-yard gain inside the New York ten. The celebration was short lived. Pozderac was caught for illegal procedure. End George Martin said he knew, because of the tremendous crowd noise the officials could not quiet, Pozderac couldn't hear the snap count and that he raised his hand, giving the impression the ball had been snapped and Pozderac jumped. New York was no better than Dallas that day but, thereafter, it was better than everybody.

The coup de grace, for all practical purposes, seemed to come the following week. Dallas had never dominated a team more than it did the Los Angeles Raiders in the first half. But the Cowboys had been able to take only a 13-3 halftime advantage. Pelluer had run 25 yards for a touchdown, which was called back for Glen Titensor's holding, and Everson Walls had carried an interception 47 yards for a score, only to see it nullified by Ed Jones' infraction. The Raiders won 17-13 when Jim Plunkett lofted a 40-yard pass which Dokie Williams out-leaped three defenders to catch in the end zone. It also was during this game that it became apparent that the ankle Herschel Walker had injured against the Giants would plague him much of the rest of the season and that Tony Dorsett's knees, both of which were operated on after the year, would be a problem.

Pelluer, who had begun with such promise and excitement, was hit so much so often by rushers and became so confused that he ended the year looking like a punch-drunk boxer. And Dallas went 1-7 the second half, finishing 7-9, breaking the string of 20 winning seasons and slipping to its worst record since 1964. Schramm thought that was it, that the team had hit the bottom. But that would happen in 1987.

Each week before the final five losses, Tom Schramm would express confidence the team would come back in 1986. It was as if he was trying to will it so, because the 20-year winning streak was on the line, making it one of the most important seasons in Cowboy history. He would be down after a loss, regain his confidence during the week, and then be gripped by the disappointment of another defeat. By season's end, he didn't even seem angry; he just didn't have much left. He could not *make* the Dallas Cowboys win.

"The popular game by the end of that season was to point out things that Landry should have done and things that proved he had done a poor job," said Schramm. "These opinions came from people who had no idea what was going on internally with our football team. This would, of course, get even more serious in 1987. But writers would criticize and say this or that the year we were losing our winning string, but they had no fucking idea what should be done.''

A season that had begun on what Schramm calculated as a necessary gamble ended with feelings of what might have been, the most haunting refrain in our language. This was doubly important because, had the team hung on in 1986, the failure of 1987 might have been avoided.

"It was a tremendous gamble that first year Hackett was here to take two extremely intelligent people such as Paul and Landry and mesh their philosophies on offense, trying to take the best of both. But, if we were going to stop the trend, to try to improve and remain competitive with the top teams, it was a gamble we had to take. We might have done it, too, if we hadn't lost our engineer (Danny White) in midflight.''

The entire off-season had been spent developing a different offensive philosophy and building so much of the attack, once again, around Tony Dorsett at halfback and using Timmy Newsome as mostly a blocker at fullback. An intriguing problem developed when Schramm brought Herschel Walker to camp. He not only turned out to be a super runner but also an outstanding receiver, a talent Cowboy officials did not know he had. He was spotted that first year at tailback, fullback, flanker—as the man in motion and continually came up with big plays. But he still was spending too much time on the bench. The coaches never really solved the problem in 1986 and it, oddly enough, carried over into 1987. Finally, at midseason Landry made Walker his starting tailback and demoted Dorsett to a backup role. This helped the offense but likely would not have made any difference in 1986 when the Cowboys lost their streak of winning seasons.

"That year we were continually trying to find ways to use both Tony and Herschel," recalled Schramm, "and then a third force stepped in and put us on an entirely different track when White was lost in the Giants' game. Steve Pelluer stepped in and did a good job. We were the best team on the field that day and made two plays in the final minutes that could have won the game but both were called back.

"It was just the 'Year of the Giants.' They had hung on to win some games, especially ours, and then they got better and better. The type of breaks they got against us can propel a team to the Super Bowl.

"What happened the following week against the Raiders mirrored the Giants' game. Two big plays (touchdowns) were called back. So our momentum was stopped, White was out for the year and both Tony and Herschel, the Tabasco, were among the walking wounded.''

Schramm and other observers still believed Dallas could make a run at the division title and, certainly, have another winning season because of their confidence in Pelluer, the third-year quarterback from Washington. He seemed to be making up for his lack of experience and knowledge and blocking by improvising and scrambling, which was, of course, a magic word in Dallas, making fans think of Roger Staubach. But there probably won't be another Staubach and, besides, Roger played with a far superior team. And Pelluer finished as only a shadow of the promise he'd shown. That shadow continued to be there in 1987.

Hackett told Schramm after the 1986 season that, if he could have had the vision, he would have suggested to Landry that they junk the new offense and go back to the old one with which Pelluer was more familiar after White was injured. Landry agreed this was what they should have done.

"Landry became frustrated in attempting to call plays the last half of the season for a young quarterback who was having difficulty executing a new offense," explained Schramm. "He couldn't call plays the same way with the new 1,2,3 receiver philosophy. He was used to adapting to the defense, saying we'll run this, because this and this will happen.

"And Danny could see in a split second that the No. 1 receiver wasn't going to be the man he threw to and immediately go to No. 2. Steve was taking a half second longer, waiting to see what would happen, and then coming back to No. 2. By that time he was getting hit or trying to run away from trouble. The more he got hit, naturally, the more he was conscious of the rush. So we had difficulty executing, and our offense stopped putting points on the boards. And after a while, as often happens, our defense then came apart.

"People were asking why we didn't make the change when Danny first was injured. Well, it looked like Steve was going to do the job. So why change? Then we started shrinking our offense to accommodate him, and things kept building up against him, and it was too late to change.

"It was a dirty trick of fate that all these things happened, because it looked so much like we were going to do it, to keep the streak of winning seasons alive. The really tough part is that we had a

losing season and Coach Landry, myself, and others in the organization believed we had a better team in 1986 than we had in 1985 when
we won the division.''

Landry and Schramm both saw playoff potential in 1987, but
Mike Sherrard was lost in training camp with a severely broken leg
and Danny White's wrist problems continued, and sometimes he'd
lose control of the ball. The team had chances to win all its games
and did beat the Giants twice, but then it lost in overtime on
Thanksgiving to Minnesota, missing a chance to return to the
playoffs for most practical purposes, and then it fell apart, just fell
apart, in losing to Atlanta, 21-10, the following week. The Falcons
had the worst record, the worst offense and worst defense in the
NFC at that time. Only 40,103 paid to see the game, the smallest
crowd in the 17-year history of Texas Stadium.

Schramm had felt the low point had been reached when Dallas
was upset by a mediocre Detroit team earlier in the season and voiced
some of his strongest public criticism of Landry to date when he
said, ''There's an old saying, 'If the teacher doesn't teach, the student doesn't learn.' ''

He said, however, the loss to Atlanta was *the* absolute low point
of his years with the Cowboys. He was put in an even more difficult situation when owner Bum Bright had done something Clint
Murchison never would have done. Despondent over the loss, Bright
said in an interview with Steve Pate of the *Dallas Morning News*,
''I get horrified sometimes at our play calling. I've heard we're not
using certain players because they haven't been brought along yet.
Maybe the problem is we can't utilize the talent of certain guys (he
was speaking of Danny Noonan and Herschel Walker) because we
don't have anybody to direct how to use them. It doesn't seem like
we've got anybody in charge that knows what they're doing, other
than Tex Schramm . . . He is the best general manager in the NFL.
I don't want to do the coaching, and I don't want to try to run
the club, but I'm not satisfied with the results we get. We can't go
along like we are.''

Asked if he would support Schramm if he decided to change
coaches, Bright added, ''I'll support Tex in anything he wants to
do with the team. I've got all the confidence in the world in him.''

The statements, of course, put Schramm in another awkward position. When asked about Landry, he said at that time he was not
''even going to recognize the question. And there's one thing you
don't do in sports and that's to give votes of confidence. That has
become a joke, the first kiss of death.

"When you start trying to break down and isolate where the problems were (in 1987), you have to remember that, during our successful years, everyone shared in our success. The administration received credit for creating the proper atmosphere. The coaches certainly got credit for the job they did and the players for what they accomplished on the field. When you're not having success, you've got to start up that same ladder."

The tension did ease somewhat when Dallas won its final two games against Los Angeles and St. Louis, teams which could have made the playoffs by beating the Cowboys. Dallas finished 7-8 but the two victories helped the year end on a positive note. Schramm felt better about his team but knew more had to be done to make it competitive with the best clubs in the NFL.

Tex had begun to try to institute changes in 1986 by attempting to shed what some believed was a kind of stagnancy, a leave well-enough alone attitude that comes with winning. He did begin to change that. He had succeeded in initiating a change in the coaching area, but he had to walk a fine balance in his relationship with Landry. By 1987 the line didn't seem quite so fine as he weighed the disappointments of another losing season and tried to put it all into perspective and see what else must be done to get Dallas back among the elite teams. Certainly, he thought more about Landry, a man so different from himself that they have no relationship outside of football.

There are few people who are more opposites than Tex Schramm and Tom Landry and, yet, they have worked successfully together since 1960, and the dividends are the club's great accomplishments. Landry's stated priorities are, in order, God, family and football. Schramm's first two are football. Landry certainly is very competitive and wants to win. He tries to win under the rules of the game and the guidelines of his life as a Christian. He believes God wants a person to do his very best and Tom does. But, unlike Schramm, he does not linger on losses. They do not tear him apart because, with his faith in God, he is able to put them in perspective. Perhaps that is why in 1988 he went into his twenty-ninth year as head coach of the Dallas Cowboys, whereas won and lost records, ulcers, alcohol, and other tension and nerve-related problems have taken their toll on his contemporaries.

Losses gnaw at Schramm and crucial ones become, for a while, almost like death. He is profane and vocal about his feelings, whereas Landry remains reserved and can count the profane words he has used the last 20 years on his fingers. They do not think alike, feel alike and do not socialize, meeting only under the auspices of the football team.

"We have no relationship outside of football, but we have been able to work together successfully," said Landry. "Tex has very strong feelings and is outspoken about the way he feels regarding our place in history. That's a matter of difference in our personalities and what our priorities are. It doesn't mean anything to me to be remembered in football. People are always asking me how I want to be remembered and, honestly, I have no feelings about that whatsoever.

"Sure, I've seen Tex mad and witnessed his temper, but it passes. It doesn't linger, although the residue might bother some people. I've never been the object of his temper. Sure, I'm a Christian, and his use of profanity bothers me, but the same thing can be said about some of the players and other people I'm associated with."

When it was suggested to Landry that Schramm's use of profanity was more of a speech pattern and that he does not literally mean some of the words he uses, Landry thought for a few seconds and said, "Well, that's the pattern of speech in much of our society today. Certainly, one reason it's used is that people really don't know what they're saying, what the words really mean. The profane words are just an expression. God is very forgiving. He has to be for somebody like me to have a chance to get to heaven."

After Schramm worked out a deal in which Clint Murchison before the 1985 season sold the Cowboys to a group headed by H. R. (Bum) Bright, Landry did express the opinion that both his and Schramm's situation could change.

"It's really hard to say what might happen with new ownership," he said. "Time will tell. You can't be sure how tough these new owners might be. Clint was a different type of person. In bad times Clint always believed we'd come out all right, which we did. Bum Bright didn't get where he is by taking care of everybody along the way. He's a tough cookie, and I don't know what pressures might be asserted on somebody like Tex if, say, we continued a string of losing seasons. I don't think we will. We did have 20 winning years in a row, and that's never happened in the league before. Everything is fine when you produce. If you don't you never know what will happen."

Landry appeared somewhat prophetic when Bright, who had remained quiet about a losing situation, became vocal when the team lost to Atlanta in 1987, criticizing the coaching. "He owns the team and has a right to say anything he wants," said Landry. ". . . I could step down but made a commitment to build the team back up, and I'd like to step out after that situation happens. But who knows?"

Schramm has always said the respect he has for Landry, both as a coach and person, is obvious. Landry and Don Shula, considered by many as the top two coaches in the NFL in modern times, trail only George Halas, who coached for 40 years, as winningest coach in the NFL. Landry has won Super Bowls with two different casts of players and would like to do it with still another team, although this isn't prevalent on his mind, as it is Schramm's.

"His success speaks for itself," said Schramm. "Sure, over the years I've been like a lot of people. I'd look down on the field and second-guess some of his decisions. But in the long run I usually got the answer, because he'd be right.

"At this stage Tom is doing the same thing I am, fighting age. I can last longer than he can because, in my capacity, I don't have to direct things on the field, making split second decisions. But there just isn't anybody who can be as sharp in so many areas when he's 62 as when he was 42. Of course, you often can offset any shortcomings that occur with age by knowledge and experience. I suppose the great proof of that is we have so many presidents in their 60s or, as is the case now, their 70s.

"Still, there is a time when somebody in Tom's position just isn't as innovative or as pliable as when they were younger, and it becomes more difficult to devote all the time to the job that's needed. So you have to get outstanding assistants to take some of the burden off. Look at Paul (Bear) Bryant. He had great assistants and continued to do well into his late 60s.

"I just believed Tom needed to bring in some young chargers to go with the more experienced guys on his staff. If you notice, that's what I do in my capacity. I try to continually bring up younger people, so I can get their input, hear their ideas and get a different perspective." The most prominent of those younger people Schramm has brought along is Joe Bailey.

Among the Key West, Florida business ventures that Tex Schramm became involved in was his beloved marina, where he kept his boat, Kay Venture. He'd go there six or seven weeks a year and fish, and he also made friends with other fishermen who docked at the marina, which he originally purchased with broadcasters Curt Gowdy and Frank Gifford and Clint Murchison. Schramm loved to talk to anybody around the Cowboy offices who would listen about the marina.

Schramm always attends Tom Landry's weekly press luncheon, at which the current status of the team and the upcoming game are discussed. At a luncheon during the 1980 season, a very official-looking man appeared at the door, carrying a briefcase attached to his arm by handcuffs.

"My name is Jack Mann, and I'm from Washington, D.C." he said, interrupting the luncheon. "Mr. Schramm, I'd like to speak to you in private."

Schramm was, of course, puzzled and, solemnly, the pair went to the back of the room where their conversation could only be heard in whispers. The man informed Schramm that he was a White House envoy. He said he had been sent from Washington to deliver a document of utmost importance and secrecy. He unlocked his briefcase and handed Schramm the document. Tex gasped. The document informed him that his marina had been commandeered by the U.S. Government as a military outpost following a recent discovery of a Soviet troop buildup in Cuba. It stated that President Carter's wife, Rosalynn, had looked over Schramm's property and suggested to her husband that it might be of strategic military importance. Schramm, who was far from a Carter man, much less a Rosalynn man, was too flabbergasted to become angry. He turned white and walked to his office, followed closely by the envoy, who said he was under orders to remain at Schramm's side until he officially was told to do otherwise.

The pair was sitting glumly in Schramm's office when Joe Bailey, vice president in charge of administration, walked in and asked just what was going on. Schramm was very evasive. Bailey looked at Tex and then at the envoy, telling the man, "There's something about you I don't like."

Saying that, Bailey suddenly pounced on the man and began wrestling him around the office. Tex began yelling at Bailey to please stop, but Joe continued to struggle with the man, trying to throw him out of the office physically.

"Joe, stop!" said Schramm. "You don't understand! It's all a mistake! You're making a mistake!"

"I know what I'm doing!" yelled Bailey, seeming to get the best of the struggle as he moved the man near the door.

Then from outside the door, Schramm heard laughing. It was

publicity director Doug Todd, who literally was bent over laughing. Then Bailey and the man started laughing. Schramm, dropped his shoulders, fell back into his chair, and joined the giggling. Todd and Bailey had hired a part-time actor and set up the gag, and Schramm had fallen for it, swallowing the whole hook, line and sinker.

A sense of humor notwithstanding, Joe Bailey, the man who would seem most likely to replace Tex Schramm, has a very different demeanor than his boss. He is only 40 and has a cleancut-boyish aura about him and is not given to outbursts of temper and vented frustrations when things are not going well. Outwardly, he is easy going, but this is misleading because he also can be very tough if he has to be, and his competitiveness rivals Schramm's. He is more easily definable than Tex Schramm.

Outside of Schramm and Brandt, Bailey has the longest tenure on the administrative side of the club. Technically, he began working for the club when he was 13. His father, Dr. Joseph Bailey, was a personal friend of Murchison's and also served as one of the team's physicians. When the doctor would come to training camp, he'd bring Joe along with him. So Joe served as a ballboy, equipment room assistant, a driver who took players to and from the airport and whatever was needed. He attended North Carolina on a football-baseball scholarship, but a badly injured knee ended his career. After graduation he went to work for Merrill Lynch in his hometown, Washington, D.C., but was still very interested in sports and wanted to get into the field in some capacity. His father contacted Tex, who hired his son for the Cowboy scouting department in 1970. Schramm suggested he further his business education at the SMU graduate level and he did, later becoming business manager of the Cowboys and then being promoted to Vice President-Administration in 1978.

Bailey had become Schramm's right-hand man by 1980 and, in order to prepare himself even more as a possible replacement for Tex, attended the Advanced Management Program of the Harvard University Graduate School of Business in 1985. Earlier Schramm also had steered him away from taking the general manager's job with the USFL's Los Angeles Express. If Tex Schramm has the final say-so in the new ownership alignment, Joe Bailey could well be his replacement.

"Tex is somewhat unique in this day and time," said Bailey. "He loves the Cowboys, and he loves the league. I'd say he's greatly sacrificed his family, his personal life and his friends in order to do this.

"His outbursts and explosions have never bothered me. A lot of leaders are sometimes basically insecure. They have an outward facade of strength, but inwardly they have doubts, just like the rest of us, and sometimes become explosive because they fear making mistakes.

"Tex has a basic way of solving problems that is a little unusual. He'll walk around the problem and look at it from every conceivable angle and make sure he understands it 100 percent. Then he tries to find a solution. If he isn't comfortable with that solution, he won't act. This is diametrically opposed to the basic business practice of looking at a problem, then making a decision, right or wrong. He has a very vivid imagination and a good perception of what the cause and effect of certain actions are going to be. I'd correlate this to a chess game in which you're thinking four or five moves down the line. Tex will know what those four or five moves are going to be.

"He also overcomes what is a problem with so many executives. They're isolated. Tex isn't. He keeps in touch with the consumer. He talks to them, wants to know what they think."

Schramm is very proud of Bailey's preparation and ambition in the organization. He wants people who work for him to have greater goals; he wants Joe Bailey to want to become general manager. And even today he appreciates Bailey's sense of humor, especially the prank concerning the marina. Schramm can still appreciate the humor, even though the marina and other business plans in Key West fell apart because they became part of the fallout in the terrible and swift decline of Clint Murchison.

chapter twenty-two

A CHANGE OF OWNERS

On a spring day in 1983 Tex Schramm, who was preparing to go out of town, received a telephone call from Clint Murchison, who asked him to come over to his home. Murchison's adobe brick home was surrounded by a 24-acre wooded area in plush North Dallas. However, although the house was very large, it was very inauspicious looking and understated in keeping with Murchison's personality.

As he drove to Murchison's house that day, Schramm wasn't really sure what to expect. He knew Clint's health was deteriorating, slowly but surely, but the situation never had been explained to him, and he had not asked.

When they talked Murchison started discussing evolution. He explained that during the early evolutionary process animals had in the back of their heads very small brains which controlled their gait or equilibrium. He said that, as the animal grew more and more intelligent and became man, the brain became larger.

"But," said Murchison, "that small part in the back of the head remained. I've got problems with that particular part of my brain, which gives me speech and equilibrium problems. I've been to doctors everywhere and have been told there is no known cure, that

I will go through a slow but irreversible deterioration. It won't be fatal, and I'm told that the process will level off at a certain plateau.''

Thus, Murchison said, he wanted to sell the Dallas Cowboys and would like to entrust Schramm to find a proper buyer, one who would continue to allow the club to operate as it always had. He said he did not want to divide the club up among his heirs and those of his late brother, John. He believed this would be totally unruly and that one of the eight would, perhaps, want to sell his share, while another might not. He also didn't want to create a situation where it appeared he was selling the club because of failing health, which of course he was.

When Schramm left Murchison's home that day, he not only was greatly saddened but felt a great weight because of his responsibility to find just the right ownership, one which would not interfere with the club's operation. He had to try to get Murchison as much money as possible but also had a responsibility to the other people in the organization.

"It was such a sad thing," said Schramm, "to see him in a situation like that. I hate to use the term unique to describe our relationship, because the connotation of that word is one of a kind. But our relationship was very close to that. We totally understood each other but didn't have to continually define our parameters. I knew exactly how he felt, what his priorities were and acted accordingly. And he knew mine.

"Clint was able to live with the common perception that he had no voice in the decision-making process as far as the football team was concerned. In reality, he did, because I knew the way he thought, his perception, and his approach. It just wasn't necessary to pick up the telephone and say, 'Clint we have this problem. What should we do?' I already knew what he would do.

"When something exceptionally tough came up, I counseled with him but that was about all. For 25 years he viewed the Cowboys as a super fan, from a fan's standpoint and as being an asset to the community. He saw the team furnishing a recreational outlet and release for people because it *was* a game. He kept it in that perspective."

Schramm smiled when he recalled how each year he'd show Murchison the bottom line from the profit-and-loss statement. "I can't remember a single time he questioned me on that bottom-line figure. He was more interested in talking about the team we put on the field.

"And he was always such a positive factor when times got bad for us. After a big disappointment, he'd say something to make you laugh."

When Dallas lost in the final minute to Green Bay in its first championship game in 1966, the whole organization was saddened, but Murchison said, "Oh, well, we didn't want to give them too much too soon."

Schramm continued. "Murchison was the total opposite to the stereotype owner in professional sports—I mean the one who gets involved in everything whether he knows anything about it or not, the guy who comes raging at players and coaches after a loss.

"Oh, sure, he had a lot of pride, especially when we played in Washington, because he had so many friends there. Losses hurt him, too, but he didn't take them out on anybody around him. I'm not like that. We lose, and I bite everybody's head off."

Once after a big loss, Schramm went with a group to eat at a Mexican restaurant. Schramm, still fuming about the game, ordered chili. When the gentleman of Mexican heritage brought the chili, Schramm tasted it and barked, "This isn't chili, and you're not a Mexican!"

Rumors had circulated for a few previous years that Murchison might be in failing health, but nobody knew to what extent and that he was suffering from a debilitating nerve disorder that by 1986 would confine him to a wheel chair at 62 and cause his speech to be very difficult to understand. When word did get out that Murchison was suffering from a degenerative disease and the story reached the media, his creditors attacked from all directions.

His father, Clint Murchison, Sr., who had made his money in oil, had set up a partnership for sons Clint and John. Clint was the wheeler-dealer, as his father had been, and John was the conservative, striking a fine balance. John died in 1979 and by 1981 Clint was in court, because John, Jr., had sued him in a dispute over the handling of assets in trusts set up for the family. The suit was settled out of court for $20 million.

In 1984 *Forbes Magazine* ranked Murchison as one of the nation's richest men, with a worth of over $250 million. The year before the magazine said he was worth $350 million. Basically, Murchison had investments in oil, gas, real estate and banking, but when the oil market declined and trouble developed with other highly leveraged, speculative investments, his empire began to tremble. Most of his assets were not liquid, and when creditors heard of his declining health, they called in loans. Murchison had to file for bankruptcy under Chapter 11 and began selling assets. He paid back. It has been estimated that, with the sale of his assets and insurance policies, some $400 of the $500 million he owed creditors would be paid back.

But his island, Spanish Cay, his home and acreage were sold as was even his box at Texas Stadium, the home of the Cowboys that he had built in Irving after Dallas city fathers failed to support him in plans to construct a new stadium in the downtown area. The Cotton Bowl at that time was in ill-repair and remains in a poor area with a high crime rate. Texas Stadium, one of the finest football facilities in the country, opened in 1971.

The small, be-spectacled, crewcut founder of the Dallas Cowboys, who had been such an opposite of the caricature of the Texas rich, died on the 30th day of May, 1987, overcome by pneumonia which compounded complications of the nerve disease.

Schramm was deeply shaken by his death for days and will continue to be so, just below the surface, for a long time. "His was a very, very sad ending for a great person," said Schramm. "He gave our organization something very unique. There have been other organizations with great coaches, great management and great players, but none has achieved what this one did for 25 years. I think it was his support that made it possible. Sure, he didn't interfere with the operation. But he gave support and backbone to the people in the organization, which allowed us to have the confidence to perform at our best.

"This created an atmosphere that I believe in the end developed into what has been known as the 'Cowboy style,' a way of doing things in a prestige manner. That was Clint's way, first of all, and it permeated to the Cowboys. We'll miss Clint. There was nobody like him."

But back when Murchison asked Schramm to find a new owner for the Dallas Cowboys, Tex knew he wanted somebody who came as close as possible to having the outlook and attitude of Clint.

By mid-November, 1983, everybody knew the Cowboys were for sale, and Schramm began screening prospective buyers who seemed to have the qualifications and financial status he was looking for.

"The thing I had to do was try to put together a deal in which Clint and the others in his family would get top dollar, without having the club in debt to an extent that it wasn't reasonable for projected future income and profits," said Schramm. "Most of the people I talked to wanted to put up minimum money and borrow the rest on the club. That wouldn't do. You do something like that, and it puts you in a tenuous situation whenever you face tough times, such as caused by escalating payrolls, strikes, future television situations and things like that. If the principal owners aren't extremely strong financially in their own right, then the future stability of the team would be in jeopardy. Like I said, just about everybody made proposals involving heavy financing with the team as collateral."

The first serious bid came from George Barbar, a developer from Boca Raton, Florida. Barbar, after he didn't get the team, said Schramm mislead him, telling him he was a front runner as far as purchasing the club.

"That's not true," said Schramm. "He was advised all along where he stood. He appeared to have a lot of money and resources. The first thing that made me reluctant was that he'd be an absentee owner. When I brought this up, he said he'd get involved in ventures in Dallas. His associate said he had as much as $70 to $80 million in a Swiss bank. I just believed his financial statement didn't coincide with a person of the magnitude of wealth that I was looking for.

"I liked him, but some of the things he said bothered me a little. Sometimes people who don't get what they want believe they have to say something to the effect that it wasn't their fault. I'm used to that, so I just forget it."

Just before Christmas, 1984, Schramm took the advice of an associate and contacted H. R. (Bum) Bright, 64, who among other things had interests in savings associations, oil, gas, and was then chairman of the board of regents at Texas A&M University. His corporate assets were estimated at $500 million and his personal assets at $125 million. Bright looked over the Cowboys' books and decided he did not want to tie up $30 million of his own money to become the majority owner. The NFL had a policy, not a rule, that one person had to have 51 percent ownership of a team.

Two well-known Dallas financiers and sportsmen, W.O. Bankston and Vance Miller, then entered the picture and seemed to have the inside track. They were respected and lived and worked in Dallas. The things that bothered Schramm about them were that they wanted to put up half the money, borrow the rest on the team, and that they became very high profile.

"They let everybody know their desires to buy the team," said Schramm. "I don't know if they felt, by doing this, they might add some pressure to sell to them or what. But there were a number of stories written and interviews done with them." The last thing Schramm wanted was a high-profile owner, something Murchison never was.

Schramm contacted Pete Rozelle and got permission to have a limited partnership, rather than a situation with a single owner who had 51 percent ownership. Rozelle agreed with the stipulation that Schramm become the operation manager of the team and hold voting rights in NFL matters. The NFL owners also said they must have right of approval over Schramm's successor. They didn't want to get into a situation where there might be a conflict of interest, so they delegated this right to Rozelle. If Schramm left the team Rozelle would have to approve the person who took his place.

Schramm went back to Bright with this new proposal. Bright agreed to purchase the team for $60 million and add another $25 million to obtain the Texas Stadium Corporation. He would invest 17 percent of the money in the team, while maintaining responsibility for operations. He would head an 11-man partnership. Schramm believed he'd gotten the best deal under the circumstances.

"Tex Schramm is a very able person and knows the business well," Bright said after the sell. "He knows the people and is effective with them. He has full authority to run the club, hire and fire players, coaches, administrative people, secretaries and do everything necessary for the continued success of the organization. He's a high class person. Our relationship is very good. I've delegated matters pertaining to the club to him. As general partner, it's my prerogative to delegate. I can't consider any time I might step in. It would be ludicrous for anybody to think they could add to Tex' direction. There will be none of that. It was a condition of the limited partnership."

Actually, had Schramm sold the team to Barbar or Miller-Bankston, it would have been more advantageous to him. Each of them had agreed to give Schramm ten percent stock in the club at no cost. Bright would not. So Schramm had to pay $1.8 million for three percent of the team. Murchison originally had given both Schramm and Landry stock options in 1960, and each had sold them back to the team for a considerable profit in the 1970s.

And even in the end Murchison had taken care of the original employees of the team. Before the club was sold, he raised

Schramm's salary to $400,000 per year and gave him a $2.5 million bonus. He gave Landry a $2 million bonus and Brandt one for $500,000. Schramm, in turn, raised Landry's salary to $650,000 and Brandt's to $225,000. Murchison gave the bonuses not only as a reward for long service but also as an enticement for them not to leave the team when it changed ownership.

"I believe I fulfilled my obligation to get Clint the best deal and put the club in a situation where it would be operated as it had been," said Schramm. "Those were my top concerns. I wanted somebody with class who would see the team had a fighting chance to continue to be successful and somebody with a great sense of pride. Bum Bright had those attributes and was very, very solid financially. He seems the perfect choice."

Schramm had sold the club and made sure it would continue to operate as it had. He'd launched changes in the team's scouting philosophy and, taking matters personally into hand, signed Herschel Walker, who could be a franchise player. There had been a feeling in recent years that he had been more concerned with league matters than the Cowboys, an organization that seemed to be in such good order that it could operate itself. And then it didn't.

"If I hadn't thought something needed to be done, you surely don't think I'd have spent so many weekends during the off-season in the office do you? I'd have been in Key West fishing."

When Schramm finally lets go, finally gives up his job and leaves the rest to historians, that's probably what he'll do—just get on his boat and go fishing.

chapter twenty-three

WAVES IN FISHING

Key West is a 4-1/2- by 2-1/2-mile coral island less than 100 miles from the mainland, and when discovered it was called by the Spanish, "Cayo Huesco,"or Bone Island, the name originating because human bones were found there. It is the southernmost city in the continental United States, and some 30,000 residents are a blend of Spanish, Bahamian, New England and Southern cultures. Over the years it has become a haven for those who would be, are or were writers, artists, fishermen and smugglers. The city has had its ups and downs with hurricanes, the Depression and municipal bankruptcy but today remains a popular tourist spot with visitors and professions pertaining to marine life, especially shrimping and fishing, the main sources of its income.

It is a quaint town of streets lined with poincianas and where the real seems to meet the unreal, with restoration of the fishing village it once was, snuggling comfortably with boutiques and, of course, the great physical beauty of the surrounding emerald and aqua seas, the lush tropical foliage and coral beaches. Key West once was called the "American Riviera" by visitors and "The Conch Republic" by the natives. The conch, a colorful spiral shell from which edible flesh can be extracted with great difficulty and which is also used for decoration, is prevalent on the island. The saying is that it is more difficult to get a native off Key West than the edible part of a conch out of the shell. If you are born on Key West you are called a conch and if not something else.

There is a certain naughtiness or provocativeness. People go to dinner in cutoffs and, generally women especially wear only those clothes necessary to avoid arrest. Both natives and visitors gather each night at Mallory Square to celebrate the setting of the sun. There sometimes are tightrope acts, fire eaters, and always applause as the sun sets.

Tennessee Williams, for whom a local playhouse was named, had lived in Key West, and President Harry Truman had what was called his "Little White House" there. John James Audubon did a number of paintings on Key West, and Jim Harrison, Dan Gerber, Thomas McGuane and Jimmy Buffett, who was rumored to have come to town with less than $1 in his pocket, composed the literary-musical Mafia of the 1970s. But the most famous man, and the first writer to discover the island was Ernest Hemingway, who lived on Whitehead Street in a house that now is a museum. It also was Hemingway who made Sloppy Joe's famous because he drank there and held court.

We sat at a table by the open door of Sloppy Joe's, where walls are covered with all sorts of pictures of Hemingway and two reasonably bad oil paintings of half-naked native women. It seems odd, really, that Tex Schramm is probably the most famous deep-sea fisherman out of Key West since Hemingway.

Norman Wood, who could care less that Schramm is president of the Dallas Cowboys, is one of the best friends Tex has, because they have a strong common bond in fishing—to be studied, talked about, contemplated and done. Norman, a real estate man and developer, came to Key West over 30 years ago, married a "conch," and was once introduced by his father-in-law to Hemingway. At Sloppy Joe's they laughed about a Hemingway story, so many of which are told, retold and will always be told in Key West.

Hemingway supposedly began an affair with journalist Martha Gelhorn, who would become his third wife, at Sloppy Joe's. She had come to Key West to interview him, and they became involved almost immediately. His wife, Pauline, heard what was going on and tried to think of ways to keep her husband. While Hemingway was away on one of his long trips, she had a swimming pool built for him in back of their house. The cost in 1938 of the pool was $20,000, more than Hemingway had paid for their house. When he returned to the island and learned the price tag, he told everybody who would listen that Pauline had spent his last penny. She, in turn hearing what he had said, had a penny implanted near the pool and inscribed around it were the words, "This is Hemingway's last penny."

Hemingway went off to live with Martha in Havana, while Pauline stayed at the house with their two sons until her death. Hemingway came back after her death and worked in a small studio in back of the main house, which had been leased. He also returned to Key West shortly before he killed himself in the summer of 1961. The bulk of his work was written in Key West, and descendents of the many cats he owned still roam the grounds.

We could watch Key West go past through the open door at Sloppy Joe's. Generally, tourists sat at the tables and regulars sat at the bar. A fairly drunk gentleman at the bar, wearing faded jeans, tennis shoes, a T-shirt and a captain's hat surveyed the people around him. He had white hair and beard, sprinkled with red. He said he'd known Hemingway, as do so many natives of Key West, some of whom were not even born when the writer was there.

Two barely clad young ladies and a man got up from a table and walked outside to take pictures in front of Sloppy Joe's. The man with the white hair and beard and captain's hat got off the bar stool and walked outside and offered to take a picture of the three of them. He did and they thanked him and talked for a few minutes. They walked on down the street. He started in the other direction, stopped and then followed them.

"He's a former sportswriter," said Schramm, grinning.

We left Sloppy Joe's and drove past partially built condos and the golf course that were supposed to be a part of a very ambitious project Schramm had in mind and then drove to his boat, the Key Venture, which was docked at the marina he once had a large interest in. The city had a dump near the golf course. "Those asses," Schramm had muttered when we passed.

The high humidity, which can make Key West seem much hotter than temperatures indicate, was not that bad in early morning as we stood drinking coffee on the deck of the Key Venture, a 53-foot Hatteras fishing yacht. It is the Cadillac of fishing boats and could not be much larger and still retain maneuverability for serious fishing. The sea before us was relatively calm, swaying the docked boat ever so slightly, and pelicans, seeming oblivious to any and everything, sat very still on top of the surrounding pilings. The pelicans did not seem to know they didn't own the marina. Schramm was waiting for his captain, retired Navy man Jack Kondziela, who had stopped on the way to have sandwiches made for lunch at a Key West delicatessen. Four other boats, including Norman Wood's Petticoat, were docked at Oceanside Marina. Schramm just shook his head as he looked around. The marina once had been filled to near capacity.

In the late 1960s and early 1970s, Schramm had spent a great deal of time fishing in the Bahamas, coming out of Murchison's island, Spanish Cay. Often he was fishing with his friend Pete Rozelle.

"Pete and I have this saying," explained Schramm. "We say nobody has fished in the greatest fishing places in the world and caught less than we have. Once we went to this place in northern Michigan, one of the few remaining virgin fishing places in the country. It originally had been set up for Henry Ford to go there. Anyway, the fish had been waiting there for 5,000 years for somebody to catch them. Pete and I went there and didn't catch a single one."

In the mid-1970s Schramm began looking for a place for himself, somewhere with good climate in the winter and one that he could get to easily from Dallas. He looked around the Bahamas, in the Caribbean, the Virgin Islands, Jamaica, and around Mexico. He determined he wasn't a "manana" person, and the political climate for Americans wasn't good in some of the other places.

Sportscaster Curt Gowdy told Schramm how much he liked Key West and suggested Tex try there. Schramm liked the climate, the accessibility and the location; he could easily go into the Bahamas for fishing. He began looking for a house in Key West and began fishing out of there. The charter captain of the boat Schramm was using told him he thought both the boat and the marina could be bought for a good price. So one day Schramm was sitting on the boat, which turned out to be the Key Venture, listening to the owner tell him how he needed to sell, and six months later, Tex was a part owner with Clint Murchison and with minority partners Frank Gifford and Curt Gowdy.

Manny James was the attorney for the former owners who worked on some of the details of the sale. He later got into trouble over the sale of drugs and served time, although the money he made was never located. As soon as James was free again, he began living on a huge sailboat. The story around the marina was that, when he finished the boat, he was going to sail off into the Bahamas, where he might have stashed the money, and never come back.

Most of the dope smuggled into the United States comes in along the 8,426-mile, indented Florida coast, with the bulk of the remainder being brought across the 2,067-mile border with Mexico. A boat can carry enough gasoline to get to Colombia, from which most of the cocaine comes, from Key West. The Coast Guard now has slowed down the pace of smuggling somewhat by employing the new, faster hydrofoils, but custom officials claim that smugglers are so sophisticated that they have their own intelligence and counterintelligence corps. Smugglers often use decoy boats to watch the reaction of the Coast Guard before making a move. If the Coast Guard chases the decoy south, the boat with contraband will go north.

There also is a kind of laissez-faire attitude around Key West; you do me a favor, and I'll do you a favor, and we take care of our own. During one of Schramm's visits to Key West, a trial was underway in which a dozen local officials, including the deputy chief of police and two veteran detectives, were accused of racketeering. Residents of Key West often refer to friends as "Bubba," so the trial was dubbed "The Bubba Bust Trial." Government prosecutors also said police chief Larry Rodriguez was an unindicted co-conspirator in the case. Both city officials and Rodriguez were angered by this statement and were quoted as saying that the chief had done absolutely nothing wrong . . . since he took office two years prior to the case. When a local jury actually convicted the 12, it was applauded by surprised editorial writers in the local newspaper.

Often dope is packaged in a bail, wrapped in a trash bag, and dropped at a designated point in the waters off Key West for a pickup. "We've seen the bails out there before," said Schramm. "If you call the Coast Guard, a smuggler might pick you up on the radio and beat them there. They also might blow you out of the water. So if you see a bail, you're smart to just take off out of there."

The previous week we had seen some of the new hydrofoils and the gray bulks of a navy destroyer, a cruiser, and a frigate with a helicopter pad on its back. We'd also seen tankers flagrantly flushing out oil, a practice frowned on by the government. Then one Sunday we were out most of the day and didn't see a single

Coast Guard boat. "I guess,"said Schramm, "the smugglers take Sundays off."

Gowdy and Gifford both lost interest and pulled out of Schramm's marina, which he'd purchased in 1976. Tex not only had plans to keep the marina but also put into action some other ideas, which he wishes he'd forgotten. He talked to Murchison, and they decided to go on with plans to build a 200-acre resort in Key West with 597 luxury condos and cottages surrounding the local golf course, which they'd turn into an 18-hole championship layout. They also decided they'd renovate the marina. Norman Wood joined them in the venture. Revenue from the sale of the condos would provide money for the development of the entire project, and Murchison agreed to furnish injections of capitol when needed. Clint also guaranteed $21 million to kick off the project. When Murchison's health problems became known, there was a massive run on the bank by his creditors, and his financial empire crumbled. He then chose not to proceed with the building of the living units. There were suits, countersuits and the entire project came to a standstill. The City of Key West was appointed as receiver for the project, taking it out of the hands of the developers, and everything is tied up in litigation.

"I put my share of the marina into the development, and now all I have in Key West is the boat and an interest in a small condo development," said Schramm.

Schramm established his reputation in and around Key West not as president of the Cowboys nor as a developer but rather as a blue marlin fisherman, something for which he has a great passion. When he first started coming to Key West, he began to ask around to try to find someone who might have the same intense interest in the fish as he did. He was told that man was Norman Wood, so Schramm went to meet him. That meeting would eventually bring Key West into the mainstream of billfishing.

"Oh, I was always a Cowboy and a Dolphin fan, or rather a Don Shula fan," said Wood. "So I knew who Tex was before we met, but I never dreamed he was such an avid fisherman. After we became friends I started going to Dallas for some of the games and had a chance to observe him there, just as I had as a fisherman. And I can tell you his devotion to fishing is just like his devotion to the Cowboys.

"I remember a few years ago when he was coming here to fish after the Thanksgiving Day game, something he usually does. I hadn't heard the scores but asked somebody, and they said Dallas had lost. I said to myself, oh God, they'll be trouble now. He can be tough to deal with after a loss.

"But I tell you, Tex has a good heart. He has all the patience in the world, showing somebody how we fish. I've also seen him give away some of our lures to strangers. He's just that way. If somebody is interested in something he knows about he wants to help them. We fish on the same boat and we're together, but we go out on our own boats and there is a lot of competition."

Once they went out in separate boats and bet $100 on who would catch the biggest marlin. Nothing under 500 pounds would count. They kept lowering the standards as the day progressed and, in late afternoon, determined the winner would be the one who caught the biggest fish of any kind. Wood won by bringing in a 5 1/2-pound mackerel to Schramm's 4 3/4-pounder. "We probably spent $4,000 between us on the excursion that day, but Tex only got upset about losing the $100 to me. It kills him to lose. He hasn't forgotten that yet."

"I don't play cards or do things like that, because I don't have the patience to sit down and learn the games," said Schramm. "I just don't like to play another guy's games, because he's making the odds. But I've always been around fishing and loved it. The competition is there, too. Don't let anybody fool you. You go out there, and other boats are around you and you know damned well you're competing against them, because you can hear them on the radio. When you get a strike, you'll hear them say something like, 'Hey, you scared us there for a minute. We thought you really had a big one.' You're always competing when you go out."

Schramm became an innovator along the Florida coast, because he was most responsible for introducing artificial lures, originally known as Kona heads, into the area. Everybody in the Bahamas and off the Florida coast fished for marlin with dead bait. Schramm kept looking for new methods and strategies and once, when he was in Hawaii for the Competition Committee meetings, he heard of a somewhat legendary captain named Bobby Brown. He tried to get on one of Brown's charters, but he was booked solid. So Schramm told him, "Lookit, I don't care if I don't get a fish. I just want to come along and observe." Brown was so impressed with Schramm's interest that he let him come along. Schramm later invited Brown to join him in the Hemingway Billfishing Tournament out of Barlemento, Cuba and Brown agreed to come, bringing with him a selection of artificial lures, plastic skirts attached to heads.

They had two days to practice but, after a day and a half, had caught nothing with dead bait. Brown got out the artificial lures, and they began using them. For an hour and a half, they caught nothing and then, in a short period in late afternoon, they brought in three marlins. Schramm was not only hooked, so to speak, on the lures but also by the pattern in which they were placed in the water. They used a four-lure set, typically taking one flat-line lure on the third wave behind the boat, the second flat on the fourth wave, and two rigger lines trolling overboard on the fifth and sixth waves, with a teaser dragged close to the boat on the second wave. From below this is supposed to look like a school of fish. Another advantage of the artificials is that you can go twice as fast, traveling from island to island at ten to 12 knots, whereas the dead bait breaks apart if you go any faster than five or six knots.

Schramm later modified the artificial lures and, using the plastics, his boat caught six blue marlins in one day and another time, brought in a dozen in two weeks. "We caught six in that one day near San Salvador and the other boats, using dead bait, caught none," said Schramm. "We were becoming a legend there, for a while. We were three, four years ahead of our time. A year or so later, you'd go out and 90 percent of the people would be fishing with artificials. But that's changing too now. I guess fishing is like football—you have to keep moving forward."

Fishermen, trying to find the best of two worlds, began taking dead bait and, with the use of brine or formaldehyde, hardening it so it wouldn't come apart. When you get a hit, fish will come back to bait, whereas with artificial bait, you usually just get one chance. This method was having some success.

By the summer of 1987 Schramm's boat had brought in over 80 blue marlin, tagging and releasing them. In the boat's cabin there's an artificial lure mounted on the wall. It's in Dallas Cowboy colors and has Cowboy helmets for eyes. It's the original lure Brown brought from Hawaii, and its successors have been used to hook more blue marlin than any other lure Schramm's ever used. The biggest was caught by Wood on Schramm's boat. It was 13 1/2-feet long, 64 inches around. There were no scales around big enough to weigh it, but the marlin was estimated between 800 to 1,000 lbs.

Had Schramm not always insisted that his Competition Committee meet in ideal vacation spots such as Hawaii, he might never have come in contact with Bobby Brown and learned about the artificial lures.

chapter twenty-four

MOST POWERFUL COMMITTEE

It wasn't clear what the men were doing, but passersby on the nearby beach had no problem using their imagination. The men stood very close, almost eye to eye, and sometimes they seemed to be trying to hug one another and, at other times, grab the front of each other's shirt. Then they would bend down, straighten up, and one even got on his knees. It was broad daylight, and the man stood on the lawn outside a hotel on Maui in the Hawaiian Islands. It's disgraceful, the nerve of people these days!

Actually, the men were Don Shula, Paul Brown, Eddie LeBaron and Tex Schramm, physically trying to work out the fundamentals and techniques of the new liberal blocking rules that the Competition Committee would present to the league in hopes of changing what was considered a dangerous trend for a defensive-dominated National Football League.

"I shudder to think what people thought we were doing," said Schramm. "But we were so involved in trying to demonstrate what might be done with the changes we were considering that we didn't realize that people going by on the beach would be watching us. Those on the Competition Committee have to become very involved in what they do."

It was Schramm's feeling from the first that the Competition Committee conduct its business in exotic or resort places such as Palm Springs, California; Acapulco; Hawaii; or Jamaica. They stayed in the best hotels or in the homes of John Connally or Sen. Loyd Bentsen when they were in Jamaica.

Once when they were staying at Connally's house, a group of musicians contacted them and offered to furnish a night's entertainment. This was all set until members of the committee found out this same group of entertainers were suspected to be the same ones who had been coming down out of the mountains and robbing and murdering people.

Commissioner Pete Rozelle enjoys kidding committee members, saying, "It's a tough life. They made a major decision today on the sand."

Schramm said when Al Davis was on his committee he wanted life to be even better. "He always wanted special treatment," said Schramm. "Once when he was checking into a hotel in Acapulco, he called a bellboy named Alfredo aside and handed him $100."

"Now take care of me while I'm here," Al told Alfredo, who happily agreed.

The next morning Al phoned the desk and asked for Alfredo. "Who?" asked the clerk. "You know, Alfredo." The clerk asked him to wait a minute. When he came back on the phone, he said, "I'm sorry, sir, but Alfredo did not come to work today."

"And," said Schramm, "he never came back again. He took the money and ran.

"There were two things I wanted when the committee was being formed," said Schramm. "The first was that I get the very strongest, most powerful people possible, and the second was that we paid our own expenses to meetings, so we wouldn't have to be couped up in some meeting room. We were going to be together almost constantly, suggesting, arguing and trying to reach decisions, so I wanted us to be in a comfortable, relaxed atmosphere. I don't think anybody can deny the results have paid off."

When the AFL and NFL merged in 1966, Schramm was charged with forming a committee which would examine all football issues from rules to roster limits to waivers and, in its way, form guidelines for the direction in which the game would go. That first committee, chaired by Schramm since its inception, was made up of Paul Brown (Cincinnati), Al David (Oakland) and Vince Lombardi (Green Bay). Jim Finks, when he was at Minnesota, and Eddie

LaBaron, until he left the Atlanta Falcons, and former Green Bay coach Bart Starr were later replacements. Schramm's present committee includes Shula, Brown and Bill Walsh (San Francisco). It makes recommendations which are presented to the league and requires 21 of 28 votes for approval. Because of the prestige and power of the committee, its recommendations are seldom turned down.

Schramm is closer to Shula than anybody else on the committee. "He's one of my good friends," said Shula. "It seems odd now that, when we first met, we didn't have a very good relationship. They were having that Playoff Bowl (for runnerup teams) in Miami, and there was a big party. I kept hearing all this stuff about the Cowboy mystique, and Tex asked me something . . . I can't remember. I said something snotty back to him, and he just walked away. That was one of the most stupid things I've ever done.

"For the last ten years, we've been good friends. I've really gotten to know him. I admire him as much, if not more than anybody else in the league. For so many years now Tex has been one of the best kept secrets in the league as far as his contributions to the NFL. There is no question our game is much the better, because of some of the things he's done.

"I just hope he's remembered like he should be, as a great contributor to the league. Listen, if there is anybody in management or ownership who deserves to be in the NFL Hall of Fame, it's Tex Schramm."

"Virtually all the major changes in the league were initiated by Tex," said NFL executive director Don Weiss. "It continues to amaze me how he can take an idea and formulate it. He has as fertile a mind as anybody in our league and the great ability to grasp all facets of a situation. I don't think anybody in our league is more familiar with all aspects of the operation than Tex."

Bob Oates of the *Los Angeles Times*, a dean of pro football writers, said, "Schramm's innovations in the league and as a general manager and his run of winning years identify him as the number one front office executive football has had in this country." Following Schramm, he picked Pete Rozelle, Al Davis, Vince Lombardi and Paul Brown. He also added Schramm to his all-time, all-sports list which included Charles O. Finley of the Oakland Athletics, Red Auerbach of the Boston Celtics, George Weiss of the New York Yankees, and both Walter O'Malley of the Los Anegles Dodgers and Branch Rickey of the Brooklyn Dodgers.

Members of the committee usually play golf wherever they are.

The most avid, competitive golfers were Paul Brown and Vince Lombardi. Schramm recalled once when he was playing in a foursome with them. As they were approaching the green, a member of the group behind them went ahead and hit, the ball barely missing Lombardi.

"Vince was just furious and charged back down the fairway and really let them have a piece of his mind," said Schramm. "He was still red in the face and fuming when he got back. When we got to the next green, those people came up in a cart."

"Mr. Lombardi," said one of the men, "we want to apologize. We didn't mean to hit into your group, and we're very sorry."

"Vince smiled, forgivingly, and was at peace again, and then one of the women jumped him," said Schramm.

"We're sorry," she said, "but there's no excuse for the language you used. It's disgraceful, and I'm going to report you."

"Lombardi became furious again," said Schramm. "We went to a par three hole, and he was so upset he missed the green completely. When he finally got to the green, smoke was still coming out of his ears. And the people showed up again."

"What the hell do you want?" snapped Lombardi. "I've had enough of you!"

"Here's your pitching wedge," said the man. "You left it back on the last green."

"He didn't know what to say," recalled Schramm. "The rest of us had to turn around, because we were laughing so hard. But there's another side to the man. Marie and Vince and Marty and I spent a week together in Hawaii. We had a room overlooking the ocean, and the Lombardi's were in another section. Each night they'd come to our room, and we'd sit out on the balcony to watch the sunset. He loved it and was very sentimental. When he was dying, one of the last things he talked about was the sunset."

Given his own inclination toward outbursts, it might be assumed that Schramm would alienate members of the committee. But he also can be charming and has powers to conjure and ways and means of subtle manipulation. Everybody has ideas and input, but the conclusions the committee reaches mostly bear the stamp of Tex Schramm.

"Everybody on the committee loses his temper at times," said Shula. "But we forget it and go on with business. I think there's a mutual respect. There's nothing wrong with heated arguments if you feel strongly about something.''

"Tex," said Joe Bailey, "is a good politician. Members of the committee might think they're acting as a group, but I doubt if they are. Tex has this quality that allows people to become very powerful. He just isn't overpoweringly egotistical, especially when it comes to the league. He knows precisely what he wants to accomplish, what can be accomplished, and goes about getting it done. He's very methodical. He gets things done, but if somebody else wants to take credit, in order to keep the peace, he'll let them. But he's the one who got it done. You take a person who doesn't need a lot of credit for their well-being or peace of mind, and they can be extremely effective. He's ingenious on the committee.''

One of the proposals the committee was considering in recent years was the use of micro transmitters, by which a quarterback could communicate with a wide receiver when the crowd noise was so loud signals couldn't be heard. This has been experimented with preseason games and had been tabled for discussion in the league meeting in early 1987 but was set aside once again.

This was something Brown thought about when he was coaching the Cleveland Browns in 1954. He had the helmet of quarterback George Ratteman rigged with an AM radio speaker and thus transmitted plays to him from the sidelines. Ratteman recalled that once, when he banged his helmet, he picked up a transmission between a radio dispatcher and a taxi for a man who needed a cab outside the stadium.

A popular story goes that Brown dropped the idea after the Giants were able to pirate his signals to Ratteman. A Giant assistant would overhear Brown's instructions and transmit the information to middle linebacker Sam Huff. "I think Huff made 40 tackles that day," Brown was said to have remarked.

Schramm says the main opposition to the use of micro transmitters comes from teams which have domed stadiums, where crowd noise can be a definite advantage. Others who oppose transmitters feel quarterbacks can take undue advantage by communicating with receivers who are downfield, telling them to change direction of their route. But Schramm believes the bugs can be worked out and can foresee the day when transmitters not only will combat crowd noise but also do away with the huddle, a dead part of the game, because coaches can electronically send plays from the sidelines, as Brown once attempted to do.

An indication that Schramm—once convinced—will fight just as hard for something he wasn't originally enamored with is the use of instant replays, a subject which became one of the major controversies of the 1986 season. He was against the concept for years but, when modern technology made it more feasible, he led the charge for its acceptance. In the 1970s when television viewers began to see obvious mistakes by officials through the network's use of instant replays, the subject was talked about and its possible use explored. At that time Schramm said use of the process by the NFL would be too unwieldy and impractical. He mentioned how expensive it would be to place 12 to 14 cameras on all NFL fields where games were being held and also the finances and difficulty in getting the people to monitor the system effectively. In 1984 league officials discussed the possibility of using the instant replays that the networks showed its audience. If 20 to 30 million people can see and recognize an official's mistake, then why can't an official in the press box watch the telecast and correct such an error?

"I wasn't in favor of that idea, because we'd be totally dependent on the director of the telecast," said Schramm. "We'd have our man in the press box monitoring the telecast, but he'd only see and thus be able to make a decision on the plays that the director decided to show again. From a competitive standpoint, it wouldn't be fair. You might have a replay on one close call and not on another. But the Competition Committee wanted to recommend it, and I originally decided there wouldn't be a lot of harm to try it. Then I started thinking there had to be a better way, a way which would be more fair."

Schramm contacted Lee Martin, and they began to experiment with equipment and methods the NFL might use for its own instant replay, a system in which the league official in the press box could rerun any play on which he thought an official might have errored. They worked out a method in which the league could set up two feeds from the network, one from the sideline and another from the end zone, and instantly replay any situation as many times as needed. This was tried in the preseason of 1985 and voted in by a 23-4 margin, with Pittsburgh abstaining, for 1986. The New York Giants, Kansas City Chiefs, Denver Broncos and St. Louis voted against the proposal. Schramm and Art McNally got together and worked out the way the system would be used. Pete Rozelle called Schramm the "Godfather of the Instant Replay."

The replay would concern only facts, not judgement calls such as holding, clipping, unnecessary roughness, pass interference, etc.

It would be used when there was a question about whether a receiver was out of bounds when he made a catch and/or was in possession of the ball. It would be used to determine whether a player fumbled before he hit the ground. An official's call would be overruled only if the instant replay showed "indisputable visual evidence" that he had been in error. Otherwise, the play would be ruled "inconclusive" and be allowed to stand as it was originally called.

Originally, if an official in the press box who was viewing the play on two monitors detected a mistake, he would instruct a communicator nearby to contact the umpire via a paging device on his belt. By use of a walkie-talkie, the umpire would be informed if a reversal was called. The referee would then use a wireless microphone to explain the reversal to the crowd and players and coaches on the sidelines. But problems developed early. The press box official would not communicate quickly enough with the field, and another play would start before he made his decision known. And there were other misunderstandings and problems.

Early in the 1986 season detractors from instant replay gained some ammunition when Denver scored on a 79-yard touchdown against Pittsburgh in which there was a lateral pass and then a forward pass. The field official ruled the lateral had gone forward, and thus the play was no good. The instant replay showed clearly the pass was legal, but the official in the press box was unable to gather his thoughts together quickly enough to inform the umpire before another play started. This happened on Monday Night Football before a national television audience, all of whom saw that the play was legal.

The Raiders' Dokie Williams caught a 12-yard pass near the out-of-bounds marker in the end zone. Replay official Jack Reader ruled the pass was incomplete but, when the information "pass incomplete" was replayed to umpire John Keck, he thought he'd heard "pass is complete," and the touchdown was allowed to stand. It got the Raiders back into a game which they later won.

During the season the terminology and communication system from the press box to the field was changed. If the official in the press box reversed a play, he would say "reversal confirmed" or, if not, "reversal inconclusive." The method of communication was changed from a buzzer and walkie-talkie to a direct earphone plug from the man in the booth to the umpire. The system worked much better thereafter.

But a number of people, including Lamar Hunt, again spoke out against the instant replay, saying that it was taking the human element out of the game and was causing more problems than it was solving. Officials from Houston, Philadelphia, Cincinnati and the Rams also expressed concern. However, in various polls, such as those taken by CBS and *USA Today*, the public expressed a desire for the replay to be retained, 66 percent to 27 percent or less, over two to one.

"This was something that took us into an unknown area," said Schramm. "Any time that happens, there is going to be some opposition. In fact, that's often the criteria for opposition. Some people are against most any kind of changes and, I sometimes think, Lamar Hunt is against anything I'm for. But that's his problem. Some still say we're trying to take the human element out of the game. Hell, because you use a photo finish in horse racing doesn't mean you're taking the horses out of the sport.

"There were and are some bugs to be worked out of the system. The first year we had errors of omission in which an official's mistake on the field was detected but, through technical problems or, perhaps, lack of response from the man in the press box, we were unable to correct these mistakes. The plays stood as they had been called on the field even, as in the cases of the Denver-Pittsburgh and Raider-Kansas City game, if there were errors in judgment. But, remember, that's the way those plays would have been called without instant replay."

Schramm started pushing after the season to stop using league people and retired officials in the press box for instant replays. He sought to have replay officials become a regular part of the crew which worked a game. "If the official in the press box is part of the crew, the other people will start seeing him as a help to them instead of an ogre up there trying to catch them in a mistake. It's just a matter of finding the right officials. You find some who are better suited as line judges and others as field judges. We have to find the ones who are quick and good at reviewing the instant replay and giving their decision.

"Some people such as Lamar, who want to create a mounting opposition, say there is a mounting opposition," said Schramm. "That's one of his favorite methods."

Schramm spoke confidently that the instant replay would be retained for 1987, but he was concerned when he went to the league meeting where a decision would be voted on. It wasn't so much the "no" votes that he knew Hunt and Brown would cast as it was the abstentions.

Schramm needed 21 "yes" votes to get the instant replay system retained, and so those who passed on their votes might as well have cast a "no." There was a great deal of bickering and posturing at the meeting, and various factors came into play. Cardinal owner Billy Bidwell changed his vote from "no" to "yes," because he didn't want to be known as the person who cast the deciding vote to kill instant replay. Then when it became obvious that the league would vote to retain the system by a 22-6 margin, one over the required number of affirmative votes, Bidwell changed his vote again to "no" on philosophical grounds.

Wellington Mara made a strong, spirited plea in a speech against instant replay, citing the traditional feeling of the opposition that the game was being taken out of human hands. When a reporter asked Schramm if Mara had indeed made a very impassioned plea, Schramm said, "There's a difference between an impassioned plea and a persuasive argument."

Some changed their votes in favor of instant replay when it was decided that it would be voted upon for one season and not two. Pete Rozelle, who had been ambivalent on the issue in 1986, helped sway voters when he came out strongly for the retention of instant replay, and a letter from game official Ed Marion, supposedly expressing the feelings of the officials on the matter, seemed to backfire.

"If it hadn't been for the commissioner, I'm not sure we've had gotten it passed, but Ed Marion, official No. 26 in your heart, wrote the letter saying how the game officials didn't want instant replay. This seemed to have the opposite effect than expected. It angered some of the owners who felt that the officials were trying to run the game and tell them what to do.

"I will say this . . . anybody who doesn't want instant replay is only postponing the agony, because it's going to come to all sports. I include baseball, in spite of what Peter Ueberroth said, that the sport was never going to use instant replay. It takes somebody like that, who also tells us baseball is now free of drugs, to make a statement that this sport will *never* have instant replay. I find it ridiculous not to use something that will help you, that will cut down the margin or error.

"Our younger generation has been brought up in a world of computers and such advanced technology in communications that it has little tolerance for people who don't want to make use of advancements in the field. They don't like to hear you say, 'Well, we can't do it, because it wasn't done in the olden days. They've got the right idea.''

Reminded that he was a member of the older generation, which often is at odds with the younger people, Schramm added, ''Well, I never did accept my age group.''

Tex Schramm has advocated many other changes which worked almost immediately, not only altering the direction the game was taking but also making it more exciting for the majority of fans. In the early 1970s he advocated and got accepted by the league the moving of the hash marks closer to the middle of the field, so teams would have more room to work on both sides. He also pushed for and had accepted changes that would aid in the fan's enjoyment of the game, such as use of the referee's microphone, the wider markings for the sidelines, the designation of the 20-yard lines in color and the use of larger down markers. Since he has been head of the Competition Committee, the group has spearheaded moves to number players by position, making it easier for fans to identify them, taken away the defensive lineman's use of the head slap and come up with the ''in the grasp'' rule which was designed to help protect the quarterback, who seemed more and more to be missing games due to injury. And it was Schramm's idea to install the 30-second clocks so everybody, including the quarterback, could see how much time was left for a team to run a play.

But the most significant changes came in 1974, and Schramm had major input in all of them. There had been concern around the league that the average scoring in games had dropped from the mid-40s to the low 30s, because the defense had become the dominant force. Schramm received a mandate from members of the league for the Competition Committee to come up with rule changes to stop this trend.

''Everybody was concerned that the premium on the game was playing strong defense and being conservative on offense and not taking any chances,'' recalled Schramm. ''That was personified by the George Allen type of football. But scoring and exciting offense had been the trademark of pro football, and we wanted to get it back.

''The committee worked out a package of nine major changes and, when we went to the league with our plan, I told them they'd either have to accept all or none of them. Everybody was going to have ideas on one thing or the other, but we believed we had come up with a balance that would, as a whole, have a significant effect on the game. Of course, we got it passed, and the scoring was back up that same season, although some defensive people were angry, including those on the Cowboys' staff.''

Those changes are still in effect, and many of them have been followed by the NCAA. Basically, the goalposts were moved back to the end line, and kickoffs were made from the 35 instead of the 40 yard line. Field goals thus would have to travel ten yards farther, and kickoffs had a better chance of being returned instead of routinely being downed deep in the end zone or kicked completely over the end line. In order to discourage field goals even more, it was ruled that missed kicks outside the 20-yard line would be returned to the line of scrimmage rather than being called touchbacks and being given to the defending team at its own 20. This would cause teams, more and more, to go for first downs in opponent's territories rather than attempting a field goal. Only two outside men would be allowed to go downfield before a ball actually was punted, giving the return man a much better chance to run the ball back, rather than always being surrounded when he fielded the ball.

Defensive players were allowed to bump a receiver only once, rather than continually trying to knock him out of his route, and it became illegal to block or cut a receiver at the line of scrimmage. Holding was reduced from 15- to a 10-yard penalty, and receivers no longer could throw "crackback" blocks below an opponent's waist. And sudden death overtime was adopted for all games.

In 1978 the scoring was going down again and, once again, the Competition Committee looked for ways to change the trend. Schramm believed this would change if people in skilled positions, such as quarterback and wide receiver, were allowed more leeway to exhibit their skills. He led the way to liberalizing blocking rules in which offensive linemen would be allowed more freedom to use their hands and arms. That was what Schramm and members of his committee were experimenting with that day on the lawn outside their hotel in Maui.

The committee recommended, and got passed, rules in which offensive linemen no longer had to keep their arms in contact with their body and thus could reach out to try to stop a rusher. This would cause less pressure on the quarterback. Contact could be maintained on a receiver *only* within a five-yard area of the line of scrimmage, thereby eliminating the chance of him being hit deeper in his route and knocked off course. Furthermore, a seventh official was added to watch the action over the middle, where defensive backs often got away with illegally handling receivers, especially tight ends.

"We did little more than legalize what had been going on in blocking techniques on many clubs all along," explained Schramm. "We also gave the fans a better chance to see the performance of wide receivers. This helped get the scoring from the 41- to the 43-point range, where we want to keep it. But the defense always finds ways to catch up. They're using different tactics to put more pressure on the quarterbacks."

"What might be considered some drastic and revolutionary changes have been made in our game," said Weiss, NFL Executive Director. "Tex is probably the most willing person to consider change. So many people see that we have a successful game going and don't want any changes. They don't want to mess with it. But Tex will and does."

"There's nothing wrong with change," said Schramm. "We need to keep changing our game if we're going to stay on top. We're doing that. Our league has been on top and stayed on top. You get arguments, but the facts speak for themselves."

In a poll taken by CBS in conjunction with the *New York Times*, 53 percent of the sports fans interviewed said they preferred watching football, whereas 18 percent picked baseball. In 1982 the NFL signed a five-year, $2.1 billion television contract with the three networks and a three-year, $1.4 billion contract with the networks and ESPN in 1987. Schramm believes the contracts, especially the five-year one, are very significant in not only the belief in the stability and progressiveness of the league but also in its integrity.

"Television isn't a benevolent charity," he said. "When the five-year commitment was made, the networks had never made a deal that far down the line. And it was done with an unprecedented amount of money. The networks were convinced pro football would provide the country with the most reliable form of entertainment. They didn't know what games would be played nor what time slots they'd have to clear. They were investing in the structure of the NFL. I'd say that was unparalleled. It was based on the conviction that we have an intelligent league that will continue to provide competitive teams and an interesting, honest game."

There has been and probably always will be rumors and hints of fixing scandals in sports. In the case of collegiate basketball there appeared to be some foundation for the rumors but, as far as professional football it has only been innuendo. It would appear if you could reach an official or key player, a game certainly could be fixed. Schramm disagrees:

"I don't believe you can successfully fix a major league baseball nor NFL football game. I don't know what happened during the old Chicago Black Sox scandal, but baseball wasn't that big then. Today I don't think that could happen. Are you going to pay the pitcher to throw a game? If he isn't doing well, the manager would have him out of there. The shortstop? Maybe he won't get the key ground ball.

"It's a case of mathematics. There's too many players involved on a baseball team and even more for football. I'm not casting aspersions at any other sports, such as basketball or boxing or tennis. I'm just saying it would be so much more difficult with a 45-man team like you have in football or a 24-man baseball squad. In basketball you have the 11- or 12-man rosters. Mathematically, it would be easier to fix tennis or boxing. The more players you have, the less chance you have of fixing a game. You might get one or two on a team, but it would take more than that, and pretty soon you'd approach the wrong guy. There's just too much at stake financially and, generally speaking, it takes character to last in the big leagues."

"Tex just has a tremendous, never-ending pride in the league and what it has accomplished," said Weiss.

"I take more pride in the Competition Committee from a league standpoint than any of the other things I might have helped accomplish," added Schramm. "If there's a tough problem, the league gives it to the committee, and we solve it. Our recommendations and findings take up 80 percent of the time in league meetings. I think we've done a helluva job to keep the game current with the times.

"We get things done . . . even if we have to go to Maui to do them."

"When we were meeting in Maui, I took a couple of fishing trips with Tex to Kona," added Shula. "One time I caught a Maco shark but, when it hit the side of the boat, I almost jumped in Schramm's lap. Another time I got sick and threw up. Tex is right at home on the ocean. I can't say the same for myself.

chapter twenty-five

LOOKING FOR THE BIG ONE

The Key Venture was about 300 yards from Sandy Point on the southern tip of San Salvador, one of the southeasternmost islands in the Bahamas, when the giant fish exploded from the water, which turns from aqua to dark blue near the shore. It sent spray for 20 yards around it and tail-danced as it seemed almost suspended in air, if for ever so brief a time, and then crashed back into the ocean.

Everybody on the boat began yelling and taking their places in the kind of thrill and excitement that can't really be felt unless you've experienced it. The fish had taken the line on the outrigger on the port side and run some 250 yards before slowing down and leaping through the surface of the water in a majestic show of power.

"Shit, we've got a big one!" said Tex Schramm, removing the pole out of the holder on the side of the boat and taking it to the fighting chair and planting it in the gimbal as he sat down and mate Greg Sherertz began adjusting the harness, which would keep the fish from dragging Tex off the boat. There! To the left! The fish jumped once, twice and three times. It was a blue marlin, the bill fish for which Schramm is always looking.

"Come on, baby!" he yelled toward the fish.

"It's big, real big!" said Capt. Jack Kondziela, halting the boat. "Maybe 400, 500 pounds!"

Schramm had felt the thrill many times but, with a blue marlin that size, it was as if he were going through the whole experience for the first time. There would be a fight, a real fight, but he liked that. He'd been right again. He believes the particular stretch of water just off Sandy Point is the most productive blue marlin area in the Bahamas or Southern Florida. Other boats had gone to try their luck near St. Thomas.

The line moved back across the boat, and the fish dove or sounded, diving to the bottom of the ocean. Then it came back up and Schramm lightened the drag, slacking off a little. To everybody's surprise he'd brought the fish to the side of the boat in less than an hour.

"It must be 15 feet long," said Kondziela.

Sherertz reached out and grabbed the leader line, but this seemed to bring life back to the fish, which quickly took off again. Sherertz let go. Had he tried to hang on, the hook might have come out or he could have lost his hand. The fish dove again. Every muscle in Schramm's body seemed to be straining. His wife, Marty, stood behind his chair, keeping it lined up with the fish and also wiping off his face and cleaning the salt spray from his glasses and giving him sips of water when he called for them.

The fish dove and Schramm couldn't raise it. They were at a stalemate. Everytime he tried to raise the fish, line would come off the reel. "We're going to have to plane him up," said Schramm. Kondziela edged the boat forward in little spurts, trying to get Schramm a better angle on the line, which went straight down into the water near the boat. If Kondziela moved the boat too fast, the fish might take the line right off the reel.

"Okay, you ready," said Schramm.

"Ready," said Kondziela, and the planing began. Kondziela put the boat in reverse and Schramm reeled as fast as he could to get in as much line as he could. This process was repeated with Tex only able to get a few feet of line at a time. But he was inching the fish to the surface. Two hours later the fish was beside the boat and they got two gaffs into it but still had problems getting it aboard. Finally, the three men pulled it through the hole in back of the boat and Schramm leaned against the side of the boat, exhausted. It had taken him 3:45 to bring in the fish.

Schramm usually just tags a fish and releases it but had to bring this one in to be weighed because he was competing in the first annual World Cup Tournament, his tournament. He'd been think-

ing about holding such a tournament for a few years but finally
got it underway in 1985. The rules were simple. It was a one-day,
Fourth of July tournament for blue marlins only. Each boat had
to pay $1,000 to enter but could fish anywhere in the world. With
14 entries, there was $14,000 for the winner, and results would be
relayed to a committee boat by radio-telephone.

There had been controversy from the outset. Two boats going
out into the Gulf from Texas had contacted officials and requested
permission to fish on Friday, instead of the Fourth, because a storm
which could reach hurricane proportions was expected on the holiday. Schramm had checked with other people in the tournament
and made a decision.

"The commissioner had to make his first ruling," he said. "Rules
are rules. They had to fish that day, no matter what, if they were
going to compete in the tournament."

At 10 A.M. the first report of a catch came from the committee
boat. "I'll be damned," said Schramm. "It was one of the Texas
boats. They hooked a big blue marlin they estimated might weigh
275 pounds. Sonuvabitch." Actually, the marlin turned out to weigh
361 pounds, but Schramm said it was just as well he didn't know
because it would have scared him even more. He didn't bring his
fish in until 6:30 P.M..

The Key Venture headed north toward Cockburn Town to weigh
the fish and passed on the way a single, insignificant looking marker
on a bluff on the beach. It read: "On this spot Christopher
Columbus first set foot on the soil of the New World. Erected by
Chicago Herald in 1891." There also is a marker on the other side
of the island which also signifies Columbus' discovery, something
we are told about as children and which remains with us all our
lives. In actuality Columbus had no idea where he stepped on that
October day in 1492. He thought he was in the Indies and had found
a back way to India, and the general feeling is that he came ashore
on the east, not the west side of San Salvador. Actually, Don Juan
Ponce de Leon first discovered America, the Indians notwithstanding, when he stepped ashore in Florida 21 years later. He was lost,
too.

Anchorage is excellent in the harbor at Cockburn Town. It's well
protected by prevailing trade winds, and the build of the land pro-
vides a good lee or shelter, and the reefs break up the seas coming
around the island from both the north and south. Schramm had
telephoned ahead to Jack (Hacksaw) Reynolds, the former Los

Angeles and San Francisco linebacker who has a house on San Salvador, and told him he was bringing in an extra large fish, so preparations could be made to weigh it. Natives gathered around when he brought in the fish. There isn't much in San Salvador. Perhaps 200 to 300 natives live there along the porverty line. Natives make crudely mixed bricks, there's a diving operation and a single hotel. There's also only one bar, and you must go downtown to use the telephone. A boat comes once a week to bring supplies, and most of the people are either very young or very old, because those of working age have gone to find jobs in Nassau. Scuba diving is extremely good, as is fishing. A few years ago a developer came to the island with plans to build a golf course and resort quarters. Nobody seemed to have particularly noticed until he had disappeared that he failed to pay any of his bills. One day he was just gone, leaving the project in early stages of development and owing the Bahamian government $80,000 for electrical and other bills. Officials not only didn't know where he had gone but many could not remember his name. Schramm said he had noticed that, when a car or anything else broke down on the 12-mile by six-mile island, it stayed where it was.

"They just seem to walk away from whatever is broken," he said. "Nobody moves anything."

There seemed to be a Keystone Kop atmosphere when they tried to weigh the fish, with everybody telling everybody else what to do, but under Reynolds' leadership it finally weighed in at 537 pounds. After this was verified and certified by authorities, Reynolds handed out plastic baggies to the natives. He then gave two men knives and within ten minutes nothing was left of the fish but its head and tail. The natives headed home with blue marlin for dinner.

Schramm easily had won his first tournament with the Texans finishing second. He'd also promised the winner two Super Bowl tickets but sent them to the Texans, because he was impressed with their nerve in going out in the storm.

"I am," proclaimed Schramm, "a benevolent commissioner."

Late one afternoon the pelicans were gone from pilings near the Key Venture, docked again at Oceanside Marina in Key West. People in Malory Square were preparing to celebrate the setting of the sun, and Tex Schramm's newest son-in-law, insurance man Bill Wilkinson, stood near the stern on the deck of the boat. Bill is the second husband of the Schramm's No. 2 daughter, Christi. Her son Shane, 12 at that time, is the one Tex likens to himself when he was growing up. Shane is a little hyper, wants to get on with things, and doesn't like to wait around. Daughter Mardee and her children Todd and Jamie Anne, then 16 and 12, also were visiting, as was youngest daughter, Kandy. Schramm had supplied his grandchildren with fishing equipment, and they were off fishing from the dock. Tex had just gone inside the cabin to talk to his wife and daughters.

"I'd heard so much about Tex and his reputation," said Bill. "I'd known Christi for a year before I got up enough nerve to go to meet him. Here I was a 38-year old man and had to take two friends with me when I went to meet him for the first time."

Mardee, married to former University of Texas basketball player Jim Bob Smith, a broker, came out from the cabin later and recalled her father had been somewhat intimidating to boyfriends the girls had had over the years, but that it was more in countenance than action.

"He's just like a big old friendly lion, full of growl and no bite," she said.

Marty laughed when she remembered. "Well, you know the way Tex can look and how booming his voice can be. I'm sure the young men were a little nervous because of that and also who he was. But after they got to know him they'd relax. The same, I'm sure, was true of all our son-in-laws at first, but now he's friends with them. They fish together and go to sporting events.

"Tex was never one to change diapers, and when the girls were growing up he was gone a lot, especially during the time he was with them Rams. But when he was around, he was a softy with them. Sometimes I'd have him talk to them if they'd done something wrong. They'd always say they were scared, but I know they weren't. They probably were more afraid of me than him."

The most unusual thing was when Schramm was thrown into the world of horses because of Kandy's interest. Sometimes they'd keep Kandy's horse in the backyard, and once it stepped on Schramm's foot, causing him to limp for a week. But to his credit he was a good sport. When Kandy wanted to take her horse to a show Tex obliged. He rented a horse trailer, hitched it to the car and drove her. So here was Tex Schramm, president of the Dallas Cowboys, arriving at the show and trying to park among all the elaborate trailers with one marked, "Rent both ways. Save money." He also could not figure out how to back up the trailer. You usually turn the car the opposite way to back a trailer. Schramm is the fartherest thing from a horseman. He doesn't even wear cowboy boots. So he looked a little out of place but did leave the show with a strong feeling that the manufacturer of the trailer had made a terrible mistake and the vehicle could not be backed up properly. Kandy later did some barrel racing in the rodeo and met and married builder and rodeo performer Greg Court. Their horse trailer backs up just fine.

Tex Schramm sat on the bridge of the Ken Venture, guiding his boat. He looked in the direction of the sun, flashing brightly off the water. Even with sunglasses the glare was making him squint and he was quieter than usual, becoming very reflective for him. The sea was a little rougher than usual and the boat rocked as it rose and fell with the waves.

"I certainly don't look forward to retiring," he said. "I don't honestly think I'll ever retire in the sense that people retire and play golf and fish and do the things they've always wanted to do. Hell, I *am* doing all the things I've ever wanted to do!

"I feel just as competitive and haven't mellowed a bit with age. We lose a game and there I am up at 3 A.M. with a J&B in my hand, thinking about the game. That's just the way I am. I can't change. I can't be anybody else."

He thought briefly about the early years, the time he first had come to Dallas, and how the team had started from scratch and been turned into a winner.

"It was so exciting and exhilarating in those days," he said. "There were disappointments, but we were establishing something. It was one of the most fulfilling times of my life. I sometimes wish my whole life had been like it was in the 1960s.

"What! No, I wouldn't mind doing it all over again . . . if I were a younger man."

Yet, the challenge today seems even bigger because perspective has changed. In the early years the Cowboys were building something, slowly but surely taking solid, calculated steps toward becoming an elite team. Now they are trying to regain their status among the best teams in the NFL. He thought about the new look Paul Hackett had brought, and the new blocking techniques Jim Erkenbeck had installed, the addition of a spark for the future with Herschel Walker, and about how the team did appear to have turned its drafting philosophy back in the right direction. But now there was a quarterback situation that had to be solidified and, although there had been numerous turnovers, there was still some age in key positions on defense.

"We've tried," he said, "to begin making the changes that, hopefully, will make us competitive with the best in the league once again."

But the string of winning seasons was broken in 1986, and the losing trend had continued in 1987, and Schramm was aware that the team could experience other losing years before building a contender again.

"Nervous? Hell yes, I'm nervous," he said. "This team is going through a transition period and when Tom Landry retires, there's going to be a helluva another big adjustment. I feel confident we can do it, that we can regain the tremendous success we've had before. It's just that I can't stand the thought of us continuing to go backwards. All other greatly successful NFL teams experienced a number of losing seasons after being on top. I just don't want us to do that."

He continued to look out at the ocean and admitted, "You can be assured I know this is the biggest challenge we've had with the Dallas Cowboys . . . Oh, to be 40 again." As he thought about what was ahead, the great challenge, there almost seemed to be a transition on his face. He actually appeared to look younger, but maybe it was just the glare of the sun off the water.

INDEX

A

Ackles, Bob, 147, 271
Allen, Doug, 154
Allen, George, 161-63
Amache, Alan, 177
Anderson, Dave, 195
Anderson, Senator Clint, 251
Aquire, Mark, 76
Arledge, Roone, 216, 219
Armstrong, Neill, 302
Arnett, Jon, 206
Auerbach, Red, 337

B

Baggett, Billy, 195
Bailey, Dr. Joseph, 316
Bailey, Joe, 36, 102, 230, 271, 304,
    315-17, 339
Bailey, John, 90
Baker, Stephen, 79
Banks, Carl, 307
Banks, Jimmy, 238
Bankston, W. O., 323
Barbar, George, 323
Barnhill, Malcolm, 25
Bartkowski, Steve, 304
Battles, Cliff, 164
Baugh, Sammy, 184
Bayless, Skip, 45, 46
Bechtol, Hub, 241
Bell, Bert, 210, 216, 247, 252
Bell, Matty, 257
Berry, Ray, 7
Berthelsen, Dick, 154
Bethea, Larry, 269
Bias, Len, 133-35
Bible, D. X., 223, 226, 241
Bidwell, Billy, 22, 74, 276
Blesto combines, 265

Boyd, Bob, 160, 177
Braman, Norman, 78
Brandt, Gil, 6, 24, 31, 34, 49, 90, 95,
    106, 128, 147, 185, 252, 255,
    256, 266, 271, 272, 291, 304
Briggs, Buck, 151
Bright, Bum, 34, 254, 311, 313, 323,
    325
Briskin, Barney, 253
Brock, Dieter, 302
Brookshire, Tom, 108
Brooks, Kevin, 144, 269
Brown, Bobby, 333, 334
Brown, Don, 206
Brown, Jimmy, 84, 102, 151, 282, 294
Brown, Larry, 110
Brown, Mike, 74, 145
Brown, Paul, 74, 79-81, 189, 207, 210,
    258, 290, 294, 335, 337
Broyles, Mildred, 293
Bryan, John Neely, 283
Bryant, Paul (Bear), 314
Butkus, Dick, 117
Button, Dick, 217
Butts, Wally, 207

C

Caffey, Lee Roy, 118
California Lutheran College, 12, 15
Cameron, Alan, 57, 266
Cannon, Billy, 253, 269
Carano, Glenn, 272
Carlos, John, 128
Carnera, Primo, 240
Carter, Jimmy, 315
Carter, Rosalynn, 315
Celler, Emanuel, 278
Cherry, Blair, 241
Christensen, Todd, 26
Christiansen, Jack, 170

Clark, Dwight, 121
Clarke, Frank, 300
Collier, Reggie, 299
Collins, Fred, 297
Collins, Mansfeld, 106
Collins, Ted, 177
Collinsworth, Chris, 269
Cook, Jack Kent, 146
Corcoran, Jerry, 165
Corey, Walt, 6
Corley, Paul, 254
Coryell, Don, 306
Cosbie, Doug, 86, 144, 150, 152, 272
Cosell, Howard, 88, 93, 279
Court, Kandy Schramm, 278, 353
Cowboy Cheerleaders, 41-43
Crain, Jack, 223, 227
Cronkite, Walter, 217
Csonka, Larry, 90
Culverhouse, Hugh, 142, 144
Cunningham, Randall, 145, 295
Cunningham, Sam, 158

D

Davis, Al, 19-30, 87-88, 203, 276, 336-37
Davis, Glenn, 15, 177
Dean, Vernon, 269
DeBartolo, Edward Jr., 204
Devlin, Art, 217
Dial, Buddy, 267
Dickerson, Eric, 71, 302
Ditka, Mike, 7, 160, 182, 276, 302
Dodd, Bobby, 207
Donlan, Jack, 145, 154
Donovan, Pat, 8
Dorsett, Tony, 13, 31, 35, 37, 44, 45, 71, 75-76, 82-86, 93, 97-99, 113, 142-43, 146-47, 150, 158, 272, 302, 309
Duper, Mark, 269
Dutton, John, 25, 145, 269
Dwyer, Mick, 146

E

Edwards, Dave, 160
Erdelatz, Eddie, 207
Erkenbeck, John, 7, 8
Ervin, Mike, 272
Eskridge, Jack, 125

Evans, Vince, 304
Evans, Wilbur, 237
Everett, Jim, 145

F

Fears, Tom, 177, 178-79, 190
Fette, Jack, 103-4, 203
Finks, Jim, 336
Finley, Charles O., 337
Flores, Tom, 26
Flutie, Doug, 7, 87
Foss, Joe, 275
Fouts, Dan, 306
Fowler, Todd, 89
Frontiere, Georgia, 71
Fuller, Frank, 206

G

Gabriel, Roman, 162, 276
Gaechter, Mike, 49
Gallagher, Jack, 238, 240
Galloway, Randy, 147
Gansz, Frank, 6
Garrett, Carl, 106
Garrison, Walt, 44, 108
Garvey, Ed, 137, 141-42, 154, 235
Gehrke, Fred, 171-72
Gelhorn, Martha, 328-29
Gent, Pete, 45, 48, 126
George, Phyllis, 4
Gibbs, Joe, 306
Gibson, Charles, 92
Gifford, Frank, 315, 330, 332
Gillman, Sid, 181, 207-8
Gilmer, Harry, 241
Gish, Eilene, 252
Gogolak, Pete, 276
Gowdy, Curt, 315, 330, 332
Grabowski, Jim, 274
Graham, Otto, 189
Grange, Red, 165
Granholm, Bill, 180
Green, Allen, 242
Green, Charley, 238-39
Green, Cornell, 48, 123, 300
Griffin, Connie, 253
Grim, Judge Allan K., 190
Groza, Lou, 189

Grumbles, Ken, 66, 68-69
Gunsel, Austin, 251-52

H

Hackett, Paul, 26, 295, 304-5, 310
Hagen, Halvor, 106
Halas, George, 7, 29, 56, 166, 177, 181,
   183-84, 191, 204, 228, 246, 249,
   250, 251, 314
Halliday, Jack, 195
Hargis, John, 241
Harmon, Tom, 173
Harris, Cliff, 44, 49
Harris, Dick, 241
Harris, James, 258-59, 298
Hart, Leon, 180
Hart, Senator Philip, 278, 279
Hart, Weldon, 238
Haskell, Dave, 67
Hauser, Ed, 206
Hawn, Fritz, 250
Hayes, Bobby, 44, 45, 48-49, 125, 126,
   128-29, 266, 300
Hegman, Mike, 86
Henderson, Thomas, 45, 129-31
Hendricks, Ted, 25
Hickey, Red, 102-3, 182
Hickman, Larry, 206
Hill, Calvin, 89, 102, 105, 268
Hill, Rod, 270
Hill, Tony, 86, 121, 160
Hirsch, Elroy, 177, 178-79, 252
Hobby Law, 259-60
Hoerner, Dick, 177, 192, 195
Hogeboom, Gary, 32, 47, 122, 272, 305
Holtzman, Glenn, 206
Holub, E. J., 258
Hood, Buck, 238
Hope, Bob, 171
Howell, Jim, 254
Howley, Chuck, 117
Hughes, U.S. District Judge Sarah T.,
   293-94
Humphrey, Claude, 119
Hunt, Lamar, 6-7, 23, 148, 177, 189,
   243, 245-60, 266, 275, 276, 279,
   342
Hunt, Norma (Knobel), 277

I

Irsay, Robert, 22, 72

J

Jackson, Honor, 106
January, Don, 303
Jeffcoat, Jim, 272
Jefferson, John, 154
John Madden's Journeys, 90
Johnson, Butch, 25, 95
Johnson, Mathew, 282
Johnson, Peter, 85, 94
Jones, Cleveland (Pussyfoot), 267
Jones, Ed (Too Tall), 25, 97, 110, 144,
   146, 150, 269, 308
Jordan, Billy, 255
Jordan, Lee Roy, 32, 98, 114-18, 299

K

Karl, Larry, 19
Keane, Tom, 195
Kelly, Jim, 94
Kerbel, Joe, 101
Kiick, Jim, 90
Kimbrough, John, 166
Klein, Gene, 109
Klosterman, Don, 73, 280
Knight, Bobby, 49
Knight, Dr. Marvin, 40
Kondziela, Jack, 330, 349-50
Koppel, Ted, 92
Kuharich, Joe, 200-201
Kutner, Malcolm, 223
Kyle, Aaron, 269

L

Landry, Alicia, 75
Landry, Mrs. Jack, 81
Landry, Tom, 7-9, 15, 25-26, 32-33, 42,
   44, 75, 95, 103, 107, 109, 111,
   115, 119, 125, 128-29, 146, 151,
   195, 207, 219, 242, 254, 262-64,
   266, 267, 271, 296, 301, 303,
   304-5, 311-14
Lang, Kay, 255
Lavan, Al, 296
Layden, Pete, 223
Layne, Bobby, 182, 227, 241
Leachman, Lamar, 96
Leahy, Marshall, 276
LeBaron, Eddie, 335, 336-37
Lee, Melvin, 297

Leisure, Peter (federal judge), 86
Levy, Fred, 171, 209
Lewis, D. D., 89, 118
Leyrer, George, 68
Lilly, Ann, 114-15
Lilly, Bob, 114-17, 258, 268, 272
Lipscomb, Gene (Big Daddy), 173
Littlefield, Clyde, 223-24
Lockhart, Eugene, 269
Lomax, Neil, 269
Lombardi, Vince, 276, 336-38
Louis, Joe, 159
Lowery, Nick, 6
Luckman, Sid, 228
Lynn, Mike, 148

M

McAfee, George, 228
McCallum, Napoleon, 95
McCaskey, Mike, 7
McDonald, Paul, 304
McKay, Roy Dale, 223
Mackey, Bill, 81
Mackey, John, 139-40
Mackey, Lois, 81-82
McKissack, Rich, 195
Mackovic, John, 6, 302
McMillan, Ernest, 282
McNally, Art, 202
McPhail, Bill, 213-14, 216, 219
Madden, John, 26
Madsen, Al, 241
Manders, Dave, 104, 116, 203
Mann, Bobby, 289
Manning, Billy, 297
Mann, Jack, 315
Mara, Tim, 183
Mara, Wellington, 74, 79, 96, 210, 275, 276, 278, 343
Marchetti, Gino, 201, 249
Marino, Dan, 269, 272
Marion, Ed, 343
Marshall, George Preston, 165, 184-85, 205, 253
Martin, George, 307
Martin, Harvey, 45, 160
Martin, Slater, 241
Matheson, Jack, 171
Matson, Ollie, 201, 206
Matusak, John, 25

Maule, Tex, 170, 201, 238
Mauzy, State Senator Oscar, 293
Mayes, Rueben, 9
May, Mark, 145
Mazur, John, 107
Mecom, John, 22
Medina, Connie, 3, 6, 9, 143
Meredith, Don, 4-5, 44, 48, 117, 119, 122-24, 251, 258, 291
Miller, Alan, 139, 141
Miller, Giles, 249
Miller, Vance, 323
Mitchell, Bobby, 185
Modell, Art, 77, 80, 264, 276
Montana, Joe, 121, 272, 304, 306
Montgomery, Mike, 89, 109
Montley, Marion, 189, 290
Moon, Warren, 295
Morabito, Vic, 264
Morrall, Earl, 103
Morris, Joe, 145
Morris, Mercury, 101, 131
Morton, Craig, 45, 89, 103, 107, 119-20, 125, 160
Mosher, Curt, 230
Murchison, Clint, 80-81, 219, 254-60, 267-68, 277, 280, 301, 311, 315, 317, 319-22, 324-25
Murchison, Clint Jr., 247-54
Murchison, Clint Sr., 321, 332
Murphy, Mark, 145, 154
Myers, Gary, 79
Myers, Jim, 8, 302
Myerson, Harvey, 86, 88-89, 91

N

Neely, Ralph, 8
Newsome, Timmy, 307, 309
Newton, Nate, 144
Niland, Jim, 274
Niland, John, 8
Nitschke, Ray, 117, 118
Nobis, Tommy, 117, 118
Nolan, Dick, 302
Nolan, Loyd, 180
Noll, Chuck, 23, 29
Noonan, Danny, 269, 272, 311
Norman, Pettis, 300
Nuckols, Bill, 232
Nye, Blaine, 8

O

Oates, Bob, 288, 337
O'Brien, Davey, 247
O'Brien, Jim, 103
Olsen, Merlin, 162
O'Malley, Walter, 337

P

Paige, Rufus (Roughhouse), 267-68
Panfil, Ken, 206
Parker, Buddy, 207
Parker, Jimmy, 8
Parks, Bill, 109-10
Paterno, Joe, 49
Pate, Steve, 311
Paul, Don, 160, 180-81, 192
Pauley, Ed, 171, 209
Payne, Bob, 151
Payton, Walter, 84
Pearson, Drew, 44, 110, 119, 160, 296, 300
Pelluer, Steve, 9, 307, 308-9, 310
Perkins, Don, 102, 117, 251, 291, 300
Perry, Refrigerator, 28
Petrovich, Johnny, 225-26
Phillips, Aubry, 195
Phillips, Red, 206
Pittman, Ralph, 278, 279
Ponder, David, 74-75
Pool, Hamp, 174, 193-97, 252
Porter, Michael, 88
Powell, Marvin, 154
Pozderac, Phil, 307
Preston, George, 253
Pugh, Jethro, 49, 89, 114, 268

Q

Qureishi, Salam, 262

R

Rattemann, George, 339
Rauch, John, 26
Razzano, Tony, 96
Reddick, Dewitt, 237
Reed, Joe, 195
Reeves, Dan, 6, 71, 102, 125, 161-74, 177-78, 185-86, 192-96, 210, 251, 264, 268, 274, 286, 302

Renfro, Mel, 73-74, 117, 160, 266, 293, 300
Renfro, Mike, 25, 95, 144, 146
Renfro, Ray, 109
Rentzel, Lance, 25, 45, 126-27
Reynolds, Jack (Hacksaw), 351-52
Rhome, Jerry, 123
Richard, Howard, 269
Richter, Les, 194-95
Rickey, Branch, 337
Robbie, Joe, 145
Robinson, Eddie, 289, 296
Robinson, Eddie Jr., 297
Robinson, Jackie, 68, 165
Robustelli, Andy, 173, 281
Rogers, Don, 133-35
Rohrer, Jeff, 142, 152
Rooney, Art, 166, 183, 195
Rooney, Dan, 74, 144
Rose, Bert, 174, 187
Rosenbloom, Carroll, 15, 71-73, 276, 298
Rothman, Frank, 89
Roy, Alvin, 126
Rozelle, Carrie, 205-6, 210
Rozelle, Mrs. Pete, 81
Rozelle, Pete, 4, 21, 23, 45, 58, 65, 88, 106-7, 127, 134, 139, 148-49, 179, 185, 196-97, 199-211, 242, 259, 273, 276-78, 324, 330, 340
Ryan, Frank, 206

S

Sansing, Bill, 215, 224-25, 232-33, 250
Schissler, Paul, 165
Schmidt, Joe, 170
Schramm, Elsa Steinwender, 56-57
Schramm, Marty, 6, 65, 73, 75, 206, 215, 219, 231-32, 237, 278
Schramm, Tex
  and 1987 strike, 143-55
  and AFL/NFL merger, 271–78
  on agents, 156–58
  in armed forces, 231–35
  at *Austin American-Statesman*, 236–42
  at CBS television, 210, 213–19
  and awarding of franchise to Dallas, 248–58
  background information, 53–70
  athletics, 65–68

Schramm, Tex (*cont.*)
  background information (*cont.*)
    educational background, 57–59,
      68–69, 221, 222–23, 236–37
    family background, 56–57
    hyperactivity of, 57–58
    interests as youth, 62, 63–64
    journalism and, 63, 68, 167,
      234, 236
    organizational skills, 65–66
  and Bailey, Joe, 313–15
  and Competition Committee,
    333–45
  and computers, use for scouting,
    218, 260–70
  and Dorsett, Tony, 75, 82–84,
    85–86, 97–98, 113–14
  on drug abuse by professionals,
    135–37
  fishing/marina at Key West,
    328–32, 347–50, 352
  on fixing games, 344–45
  future view of Cowboys, 352–53
  hired by Murchison, 248–49
  and Hunt, Lamar, 243–46
  and Landry, Tom, 299–313
  media involvement, 35, 39–40,
    45–46
  Nightline interview, 92–93
  personality profile, 4
  on racism in football, 285, 293–95,
    296–97
  and Rams, 168–198
  and Reeves, Dan, 161–74, 185–86
  and Rozelle, Pete, 200–211
  and selling of Cowboys, 317–23
  and Walker, Herschel, 85, 93–98
Schramm, Texas E. Sr., 56
Scott, Herb, 8
Scott, Victor, 143
Scovell, Field, 285
Seitz, Peter, 77
Seley, Hal, 171, 209
Sepo combines, 265
Septien, Rafael, 25, 45, 307
Shanahan, Mike, 26
Shaughnessy, Clark, 191–92
Shaw, Robert, 269
Sherertz, Greg, 349
Sherrard, Mike, 93, 272, 311
Sherrod, Blackie, 46
Shofner, Del, 206
Shofner, Jim, 303, 305

Shula, Don, 26, 29, 65, 130, 302, 306,
  314, 335, 338
Simmons, Marshall, 90
Sims, George, 195
Singletary, Mike, 269
Sipe, Brian, 304
Slusher, Howard, 13, 34, 84, 156, 158
Smerek, Don, 144, 146
Smith, Billy Ray, 104
Smith, Jamie Anne, 353
Smith, Jim Bob, 75
Smith, Mardee Schramm, 215, 233, 353
Smith, Rankin, 82
Smith, Todd, 353
Smith, Tommy, 128
Smith, Vitamin T., 177
Snowden, Martha Anne, 64
Snyder, Bob, 191
Snyder, Jimmy (The Greek), 93
Spadia, Lou, 264, 275, 276
Speedy, Mac, 189
Springs, Ron, 31–33
Stallings, Gene, 74, 270, 302-3, 305
Starr, Bart, 337
Staubach, Roger, 5, 44, 49, 75, 95, 103,
  107, 108, 115–17, 119–21, 125,
  141, 183, 266, 268, 272, 299,
  310
Stautner, Ernie, 302
Steadman, Jack, 6-7
Steinbrenner, George, 76
Sterling, Ernest, 297
Stevens, Ed, 297
Stewart, Jimmy, 285
Stewart, Witt, 13, 35, 82, 84, 98, 156
Stiles, Maxwell, 191
Stoltz, Dr. Robert, 263
Stowe, Otto, 89, 110
Stowers, Carlton, 37
Stram, Hank, 280
St. Clair, Bob, 201
Stydahar, Joe, 192-94, 288, 298
Sullivan, Billy, 279
Sullivan, Charles, 145
Sweeney, Kevin, 146

T

Tanguay, Raymond, 72
Tarkenton, Fran, 278
Tatum, Jack, 23, 25
Taylor, Lawrence, 133

Taylor, Otis, 258
Taylor, Ron, 297
Thomas, Duane, 98, 101-11, 130, 203, 256, 268
Thomsen, Judge R. C., 246
Thornton, Mayor Robert, 256
Titensor, Glenn, 308
Tobin, Bill, 96
Todd, Doug, 316
Toler, Burt, 201
Toomay, Pat, 89
Tose, Leonard, 22
Towler, Dan, 173, 177, 286, 288
Townes, Willie, 16
Tracey, John, 206
Trafton, George, 171, 289
Triplett, Mel, 289
Troika scouting combine, 264-65
Trope, Mike, 158
Trump, Donald, 87, 93-95
Tubbs, Jerry, 242, 302
Tunnell, Emlen, 289
Turner, Clyde (Bulldog), 228

U

Ueberroth,, 75-76
Unitas, Johnny, 103, 160, 177
Upshaw, Gene, 134, 137, 144, 154
Usher, Harry, 88, 92

V

Vainisi, Jerry, 7
Valley, Wayne, 280
Van Brocklin, Norm, 174, 177, 179, 182, 190, 206, 208
Vasicek, Vic, 195

W

Wade, Billy, 206, 208
Walker, Doak, 182, 241-42, 257
Walker, Herschel, 44, 45, 85-86, 93-97, 143, 151, 266, 272, 307, 309-10, 311, 324-25
Walls, Everson, 32, 145, 151, 308
Walsh, Adam, 191
Walsh, Bill, 130, 304, 306, 337
Walsh, Chilie, 167, 191
Walter, Mike, 270

Wansley, Larry, 296
Ward, Al, 22, 255
Warfield, Paul, 90, 267
Washington, Kenny, 165, 283
Washton, Dr. Arnold, 133
Waterfield, Bob, 164, 174, 178-79, 189, 191-92, 241, 283
Webb, Tom, 253
Weiss, Don, 202
Weiss, George, 337
Werblin, Sonny, 278, 279
White, Danny, 9, 32, 40, 47, 86, 121, 144, 146-47, 150, 272, 307, 310-11
Whitehead, Marv, 172
White, Randy, 13-14, 34-35, 44, 76, 82, 97, 130, 144, 146, 152, 156, 268, 269, 272
Wilder, James, 269
Wilkinson, Bill, 352-53
Wilkinson, Christi Schramm, 353
Wilkinson, Shane, 353
Wilkins, Richard, 195
Wilkins, Roy, 284
Williams, Dokie, 308, 341
Williams, Doug, 295
Williams, Gus, 158
Wilson, Ralph, 279
Wilson, Tommy, 173
Winter, Max, 247
Wise, Wes, 284
Wolfner, Violet, 246
Wolfner, Walter, 246
Wood, Norman, 328, 330
Wooton, John, 294
Wright, Nate, 119
Wright, Rayfield, 8, 89, 160
Wynne, Bedford, 81, 250
Wynn, Todde Lee, 250

Y

Young, Andrew, 281
Young, Buddy, 249
Younger, Paul, 286-90
Younger, Tank, 173, 177
Young, George, 79, 96, 148

Z

Zimmerman, Paul, 111, 167-70